Man, Economy, and Liberty

Essays in Honor of Murray N. Rothbard

D0877760

The Ludwig von Mises Institute and
the editors of this Festschrift wish to
thank the following contributors whose
generosity made this volume possible:

O. P. Alford, III
Burton S. Blumert
Dr. William A. Dunn
George Edward Durell Foundation
Robert D. Kephart
Matthew T. Monroe
Victor Niederhoffer
William O. Sumner
Mr. and Mrs. Donald F. Warmbier

Man, Economy, and Liberty

Essays in Honor of
Murray N. Rothbard

Edited with an Introduction by

Walter Block
The Fraser Institute

and

Llewellyn H. Rockwell, Jr.
The Ludwig von Mises Institute

The Ludwig von Mises Institute
Auburn University
Auburn, Alabama 36849

Published by The Ludwig von Mises Institute, Auburn University, Auburn, Alabama 36849.

Printed in the United States of America.

Typesetting by Thoburn Press, Tyler, Texas.

Library of Congress Catalog Card Number: 88-060980

ISBN 0-945466-02-1

TP

Table of Contents

Introduction ix

Part I: Economics

1. Rothbardian Monopoly Theory and Antitrust Policy
   Dominick T. Armentano 3

2. Prisoner's Dilemma, Transaction Costs, and Rothbard
   Roger A. Arnold 12

3. Fractional Reserve Banking:
   An Interdisciplinary Perspective
   Walter Block 24

4. Gold and the Constitution: Retrospect and Prospect
   Gregory Christainsen 32

5. Professor Rothbard and the Theory of Interest
   Roger W. Garrison 44

6. From the Economics of Laissez Faire to
   the Ethics of Libertarianism
   Hans-Hermann Hoppe 56

✓ 7. Welfare Economics: A Modern Austrian Perspective
   Israel M. Kirzner 77

8. Why Rothbard Will Never Win the Nobel Prize!
   Gary North 89

✓ 9. Economic Efficiency and Public Policy
   E. C. Pasour, Jr. 110

10. Comparable Worth: Theoretical Foundations
    Ellen Frankel Paul 125

v

11. Three National Treasures: Hazlitt, Hutt, and Rothbard
    Llewellyn H. Rockwell, Jr. 139

12. Murray Rothbard as Investment Advisor
    Mark Skousen 151

13. Utility and the Social Welfare Function
    Leland B. Yeager 175

Part II: Philosophy

14. Freedom and Virtue Revisited
    Douglas J. Den Uyl 195

15. Particular Liberties Against the General Will
    Antony Flew 214

16. In Defense of Rights
    David Gordon 229

17. Ethics vs. Coercion: Morality or Just Values?
    Tibor R. Machan 236

18. Historical Entitlement and the Right to
    National Resources
    Jeffrey Paul 247

Part III: Political Science

✓19. The Role of Government
    Randall G. Holcombe 269

20. Caste and Class: The Rothbardian
    View of Governments and Markets
    David Osterfeld 283

21. The Political Importance of Murray N. Rothbard
    Ron Paul 329

Part IV: History

22. A Utopia for Liberty: Individual Freedom in
    Austin Tappan Wright's *Islandia*
    Arthur A. Ekirch, Jr. 335

23. John Prince Smith and the German
    Free-Trade Movement
    Ralph Raico 341

24. Commentator on Our Times: A Quest for the
    Historical Rothbard
    Sheldon Richman 352

Part V: Personal

25. A Funny Thing Happened on the Way to the
    Forum or the Reviews of "Mr. First Nighter"
    Justus D. Doenecke 383

26. Himself, at Sixty—With Apologies to Ogen Nash
    Robert Kephart and Dyanne Petersen 392

27. Rothbard as Cultural Conservative
    Neil McCaffrey 395

28. My View of Murray Rothbard
    JoAnn Rothbard 398

29. Testimonial
    Margit von Mises 400

Rothbard Bibliography 403

Name Index 411

Subject Index 415

Editors and Contributors 421

Murray N. Rothbard

BKT

0329

Introduction

Murray N. Rothbard is a scholar of unique, indeed monumental achievements: the founder of the first fully-integrated science of liberty.

Consider, first, his accomplishments in economics. His Ph.D. dissertation from Columbia University—*The Panic of 1819*—showed how the Bank of the United States, the Federal Reserve's ancestor, caused the first American depression. It remains the only in-depth historical account of that particular monetary debacle.

In *America's Great Depression*, still the most definitive work on the subject, Rothbard used Austrian trade cycle theory to show that the Federal Reserve caused that economic calamity, and that other government interventions prolonged and even deepened the Depression. In addition, the first two chapters present the most clear and convincing explanation of the Austrian theory of the trade cycle in existence.

Both books utilized tools drawn from the great tradition of Austrian economics—Carl Menger's theory of the development of monetary institutions, Eugen von Böhm-Bawerk's theory of capital and the time-preference theory of interest, and Mises's trade cycle theory and method —perfected each, and wove them together into a systematic praxeological model. He succeeded not only in explaining cyclical fluctuations caused by central bank intervention, but also proved the case for the gold coin standard, no central bank, 100% reserves, and laissez-faire.

After Rothbard's masterful integration, economists can no longer dismiss recessions and depressions as an "inevitable" part of the market process. Instead, he showed, they are caused by central bank inflation and the corresponding distortion of interest rates, malinvestment of capital, theft of savings, and price increases that go with it. Government, of which the central bank is only one arm, is the real source of business cycles.

Rothbard was also the first to explode the fallacy of distinguishing between monopoly prices and competitive prices. This distinction makes sense only in neoclassical pricing models, where businessmen charge higher and higher prices in the inelastic portion of consumers' demand curve. But these static models have nothing to do with the dynamic market process. In the real world, we can only distinguish between free market prices and those controlled by the government.

This discovery has momentous policy implications: in a free market, where we never see "monopoly (non-competitive) prices," there can be no unjust monopoly profits. This destroys the entire neoclassical justification of anti-trust policy. Monopolies do exist, Rothbard shows, but only when government erects a barrier to entry into the market by granting some firm or industry a special privilege.

Rothbard also revolutionized the entire field of utility and welfare economics—and laid a foundation for other Austrian scholars to build upon—by showing that utility is something that we can know only by observing individual preferences revealed through human action. Utility, a strictly ordinal and subjective concept, cannot be aggregated among individuals, and thus there can be no social utility.

Because of Rothbard's irrefutable theory of utility and demonstrated preference, neo-classical welfare economics can no longer be used to justify State planning. When individuals are free to trade without interference from government, we know that each party expects to benefit from the exchange, i.e. to maximize his own subjective utility, or the parties would not exchange in the first place. Rothbard's conclusion: free markets maximize utility and welfare, whereas government intervention, by the very fact that it forces people to behave in ways in which they otherwise would not, only diminishes utility and welfare.

It was this foundation that allowed Rothbard to integrate a rigorous theory of property rights with a scientific theory of economics. Today, others within the profession are trying to do the same, but they will not succeed so long as they cling to theories of efficiency built around faulty utility and welfare concepts.

In his great work *Man, Economy, and State*, Rothbard provides a rigorous defense of economic science and the pure logic of action. In the bygone days of "real economics," every scholar aspired to write a treatise covering the whole subject. Since the Keynesian and neo-classical warping of the profession, however, this has gone out of fashion, and *Man, Economy, and State* is the last such great work. In it, clearly and logically, Rothbard deduces the whole of economics from its first principles. It is a tour-de-force unmatched in modern economics.

If only his contribution to economics in general were considered, his refutations of neo-classical, socialist, interventionist, and Keynesian fallacies would put him head and shoulders above all other living economists. If only his accomplishments in the field of Austrian economics were taken into account, his place in the firmament would be secure. For it is an understatement to say that he is the most productive of the students and followers of Ludwig von Mises.

But his attainments in economics are only the tip of the iceberg. His productivity as a historian is more than sufficient to establish him as a leader in that field as well. In addition to many scholarly articles, his four-volume colonial history of the United States, *Conceived in Liberty*, shows that libertarian ideas have been an American staple since almost the earliest days, and that the American Revolution was very much a libertarian affair. He shows that the received wisdom in history is almost always wrong, since it usually reflects the State's bias.

Permeating all of Rothbard's historical writing is a brilliant and original revisionism, a unique and rigorous refusal to accept uncritically the official version. (He is also one of the few historians ever to place his presuppositions, his theory of history itself, on record. He does so properly in the introduction where it belongs, and not all throughout the book in the form of implicit presuppositions.) Whether discussing monetary history, the history of economic thought, the Progressive Era, the New Deal, World War I, or any of his other areas of expertise, Rothbard eruditely and unerringly turns the Statist worldview upside down, in search of a commodity unusual among modern historians—truth.

But his exploits in economics and history, extraordinary as they are, are matched by what he has done for the cause of liberty. If he is an eminent historian, and the world's leading Austrian economist, he is no less than the father of libertarianism. He is, as even *National Review* has acknowledged, "Mr. Libertarian."

In his *Power and Market*, Rothbard develops a comprehensive critique of government coercion. He vastly expanded the scope of the theory of intervention, and developed three useful categories: autistic, binary, and triangular. Autistic intervention prevents a person from exercising control over his own person or property, as with homicide or infringements on free speech. Binary intervention forces an exchange between two parties, as in highway robbery or income taxes. Finally there is the triangular mode, in which the government "compels a pair of people to make an exchange or prohibits them from doing so," as in rent control or minimum wages. He carefully outlines the deleterious effects of every possible intervention in the economy, and is especially insightful in analyzing the harmful effects of taxation.

In *For a New Liberty*, Rothbard leaves the world of theory and gets down to brass tacks. How would a totally free society actually function? While it is always impossible to predict the future exactly, he shows how the challenges of education, poverty, private roads, courts, police, and pollution might be dealt with under a complete laissez-faire system. In his masterful *The Ethics of Liberty*, Rothbard deals with the hard questions: the criminal system, land redistribution, the vexing problem of children's rights, bribery, boycotts, lifeboat situations; his critiques of other, less-pure advocates of the freedom philosophy such as Hayek, Nozick, and Berlin are alone worth the price of admission.

Nor must we lose sight of yet another of Rothbard's particular excellences: his masterful ability to integrate intellectual thought, to see connections where others see only a bewildering complexity, to weave the threads from all of knowledge into a shield which can preserve human rights. He has long called for, and has indeed been the leading exponent of, what he calls the "interdisciplinary study of liberty." From this perspective, the disciplines of economics, history, law, philosophy, sociology, etc., must all be harnessed together to comprise a "seamless web" of liberty. All must be utilized in the glorious struggle to promote the free society, with the teachings of none remaining inconsistent with any other.

Were Rothbard's accomplishments limited merely to any one of the many disciplines he has so eloquently mastered, we could be very laudatory. But when we reflect on the fact that he has already made significant contributions to each of them, of the sort that any person would be justly proud to call an entire life's work, we must simply stand in awe.

And when we realize that Rothbard has not only spread himself over practically every social science, but also has integrated them into a moral and intellectual product never before known, that he has, in effect, created an entirely new academic discipline of liberty, then all we can say is that we are delighted, proud, and honored to be the editors of *Man, Economy and Liberty: Essays in Honor of Murray N. Rothbard.*

As to the content of this volume, the essays reflect Rothbard's scholarly achievements in economics, ethics, libertarianism, philosophy, history, public policy, and methodology. They also reflect Rothbard's success at integrating these disciplines while still maintaining the distinctions among them.

While Misesian-Rothbardian economics claims to be objectively true, neither Mises nor Rothbard made any secret of his belief in laissez-faire and the "free and prosperous commonwealth." By coming to their conclusions, do Mises and Rothbard sacrifice scholarly objectivity? Can Rothbard be a scholar and, at the same time, the "State's greatest living enemy"? "Given his strong commitment to the value of liberty," asks Dr. David Gordon, "can the claim to objectivity be made good?"

Rothbard has defended Mises against similar charges. In his contribution to this volume, Gordon defends Rothbard against his opponents. The answer, as he shows, lies in Misesian methodological individualism and deductivist *a priorism*. Gordon also demonstrates the impressive range, and significance, of the polymathematic scholarship of Rothbard.

The charge of bias is seldom laid against Keynes and the Keynesians, despite their constant calls for state intervention. Mainstream economists object to Mises and Rothbard because liberty and logic are unpopular in the profession, says Dr. Gary North. And that's "Why Rothbard Will Never Win the Nobel Prize."

In support of this contention, North points to Rothbard's unusual clarity, historical curiosity, opposition to strict mathematical economics, adherence to Misesian ideals, and commitment to liberty, as well as the nature of the "academic priesthood." He then lists Rothbard's fourteen "Nobel Prize-Losing Insights."

In this era of growing government, Rothbard's critique of statism is the most comprehensive. Professor Randall G. Holcombe's essay argues in favor of the Rothbardian position that preemptive coercion exercised through taxation is unjust and immoral. Further, he agrees with Rothbard that the case against the State can also be made on grounds of economic efficiency.

Professor David Osterfeld analyzes Rothbard's entire theoretical framework. He points out that Rothbard is not opposed to coercion as such, but only wants to limit it to defense and retaliation. Osterfeld also deals with the notion of markets and government, and the concept of ordinal vs. cardinal utility, and its implications (also examined in Yeager and Kirzner). He then explores the libertarian caste and class analysis of history and government, supports it with empirical studies, and shows how Rothbard unstintingly follows the implications of his analysis.

Professor Roger Arnold's essays on the prisoner's dilemma and transactions costs is relevant to Nobel Laureate James Buchanan's work. As Arnold notes, these arguments are used by Buchananites to justify the government's existence, and as a test of its proper role. Arnold analyzes the weaknesses of these arguments, and uses Rothbard's analysis of intervention to show that government by its very nature lowers social welfare.

Utility and welfare are considered again in articles by Professor Leland Yeager and Professor Israel Kirzner. Both deal with the legitimacy and proper use of concepts such as welfare and social utility, but from very different angles. Yeager uses the writings of John Harsanyi as a springboard, and includes some of the works of David Gauthier (who shares with Rothbard an interest in anarchism).

Kirzner notes that "Utility is, for Austrians, not a quantity of psychological experience, it is merely an index of preferability as expressed in acts of choice. To attempt to aggregate utility is not merely to violate the tenets of methodological individualism and subjectivism . . . it is to engage in an entirely meaningless exercise."

Though never explicitly arguing for one definition of utility over another, Yeager implies that utility is "human well-being." He appeals for the reader to "be patient . . . with language . . . seeming to suggest that utilities are measurable and interpersonally comparable and that social welfare is a maximizable function of them," which Kirzner calls a "meaningless exercise." Rothbard, like Mises, would claim that there can be no such thing as "average" utility. Yeager disagrees.

From Menger to Rothbard, all Austrian economists have held that subjectivism is a cornerstone of good economic analysis. Professor E. C. Pasour elaborates on Rothbard's application of subjectivism to the determination of efficiency. Because costs are subjective, as Rothbard shows, economists cannot pretend to know whether one particular course of action is more or less efficient than another. So "proper" resource allocation by the State is not an appropriate field of study for the economist to begin with.

Pasour also considers the role of public policy and finds common ground between the views of Buchanan and Rothbard in the notion that the "logical goal of public policy is to develop an institutional framework that maximizes the scope for mutually beneficial behavior."

Consistent subjectivism is no hallmark of the profession, however, and to the extent it is, the implications of this doctrine for public policy are overlooked. In the field of anti-trust, Professor Dominick Armentano contrasts three groups: the traditionalists, the reformers, and the radicals. The traditionalists still adhere to perfect competition models, long ago shown to be fallacious and useless, and talk of "market failure." The radicals, whose analysis emphasizes the market process and rivalry, want total repeal. (These are the Austrians, and Armentano discusses Rothbard's improvements on the earlier representatives of this school of thought.) The reformers (Bork, Posner, Brozen) appear to differ strongly with the traditionalists in policy, but their analysis is still caught up in the "social welfare" implications of perfectly competitive models. Only Rothbardian Austrians, Armentano shows, demonstrate that all monopolies are based on grants of government privilege.

Professor Antony Flew dedicates his criticism of Jean-Jacques Rousseau to Rothbard for developing and expanding the individualist tradition of John Locke. Rousseau, in contrast to Locke and Rothbard, promoted a "peculiar, distinctive, and catastrophically collectivist concept of the general will," which promoted statism.

Rothbard has been a persistent critic of fractional-reserve banking as inflationary and fraudulent. He argues for the 100% reserve gold standard as the only free-market, non-inflationary alternative to government fiat money. Not surprisingly, he has been attacked by Keynesians. However, some libertarians take the same position, arguing that in a free society, banks should be allowed to loan out their customers' demand deposits at interest.

Dr. Walter Block discusses note issuance in the free market and shows that permitting banks to inflate past their reserves is not consistent with Austrian economics, the free market, sound monetary policy, or libertarianism.

Another source of confusion among economists is the theory of interest, which often serves as a defining characteristic of a broader world-view. In fact, Professor Roger W. Garrison believes that "You tell me your theory of interest, and I'll have a good guess about the rest of your economics." The Austrian economists teach that interest rates exist only as a pure reflection of individuals' preference for present goods over future goods. Garrison defends the pure time-preference theory of interest, expounded by Böhm-Bawerk, advanced by Mises, and perfected by Rothbard.

He also compares Austrian time-preference with the theory of "waiting" advanced by Knight, Cassel, and Yeager. While there are similarities, which Garrison details, and often complementary conclusions, Austrians "cannot fully embrace this alternative mode of analysis."

W. H. Hutt introduced the concept of consumer sovereignty in the 1930s, and controversy has surrounded the idea ever since. Mises appreciated it as a positive description of economic arrangements in the free market, but Rothbard questioned the concept's ultimate usefulness as a guide for policy, preferring instead the term "individual sovereignty."

Professor Jeffrey Paul asks how we determine rights to natural resource ownership. He first criticizes the views of Robert Nozick and
Hillel Steiner, and the application of the principle of distributive justice. Paul's own view seeks to reconcile the problem of treating unowned vs. owned resources inconsistently.

Professor Ralph Raico discusses the late nineteenth-century champion
of laissez-faire, John Prince Smith. Prince Smith, the leader of the German free trade movement and an activist for freedom, was attacked
by his contemporaries for adherence to principle and opposition to
statism.

Professor Douglas J. Den Uyl joins the long-running debate between libertarians and conservatives over which is more important,
freedom or virtue. Rothbard agrees that "Virtue is the daughter, not
the mother, of liberty." Many conservatives disagree, saying it is government's responsibility to foster virtue in "its" citizens. Order and virtue must take precedence over liberty. Recasting the debate in terms of
liberty vs. violence, Den Uyl sides with Rothbard, and examines the
meaning of virtue in a free society.

Professor Tibor Machan first attacks Rothbard's views on the
nature of government, and then defends his position on the necessity
of freedom for real morality and virtue.

Professor Hans-Hermann Hoppe sets out to construct an irrefutable
defense of property rights and liberty without reference to natural
rights or natural law. The "libertarian ethic," he says, "not only can be
justified, and justified by means of aprioristic reasoning, but . . . no alternative ethic can be defended argumentatively." He also criticizes the
public goods justification of government intervention, clarifying
Mises's position on the role of government.

Much of the modern feminist movement views the State as the
means to economic liberation, forgetting the secondary consequences
of such programs as comparable worth. Professor Ellen Frankel Paul
criticizes this interventionist program and shows how truly statist it is.
She emphasizes the subjective valuations that ultimately determine
wages in the free market, and how an exogenous government can
never have the information necessary to set wage scales according to a
laborer's "worth."

Rothbard, like Mises, Menger, and Böhm-Bawerk, is an advocate of
the gold standard as the monetary system best able to preserve liberty
and promote prosperity. Professor Gregory Christainsen argues that
the U.S. Constitution explicitly mandates gold coinage, and surveys
America's experience with gold over two centuries.

Rothbard's advocacy of gold has had many followers among Austrian economics-oriented investment letters, often called the "hard-money movement." Professor Mark Skousen has traced the history of this hard-money movement, showing Rothbard's link with it since the early 1960s.

All economists outside the Austrian school hold that "Science is Prediction," but praxeologists recognize that economies are made up of human actions and changing subjective valuations, and therefore cannot be made to fit into mechanistic computer models. In fact the attempt to make economics a predictive science has been an embarrassing failure.

Rothbard's role in the hard-money movement has been to teach solid economic theory, illuminate historical examples like the Great Depression, and inspire with a vision of the free society.

Rothbard's comprehensive vision of the free society is not the first, of course, and Professor Arthur Ekirch, Jr., discusses Austin Tappan Wright's now-forgotten *Islandia*. This novel, written in 1942, describes an imaginary South Pacific isle with an isolationist foreign policy and high regard for individual liberty.

Continuity and consistency of thought have distinguished the great thinkers of every age. "Looking back through the telescope of 34 years," Sheldon Richman concludes after surveying dozens of early book reviews by Rothbard, "one is impressed at how steady he is in so many ways, a Rock of Gibraltar—intellectually, philosophically, even stylistically. . . . On matters of bedrock principle, methodology, scholarly commitment, and above all human liberty, he is admirably—refreshingly—steady and uncompromising."

Llewellyn H. Rockwell, Jr., writes about three "living national treasures" in economics: W. H. Hutt, Henry Hazlitt, and Murray N. Rothbard.

Former Congressman Ron Paul explains how he has been influenced by Rothbard's works on money and banking, business cycles, and many other areas, and gives us an insight into his Rothbardian view of politics and strategy. Paul shows how Rothbard has affected public policy, not through compromise with the State, but through principled confrontation with the enemies of liberty.

The Appendix contains five personal tributes. Professor Justus Doenecke writes about "Mr. First Nighter," Rothbard's movie review column in the *Libertarian Forum*. Not surprisingly, Rothbard plugs movies that champion justice, natural rights, libertarian themes, and Old World orthodoxy. He disdains the psychologizing and relativistic ethics characteristic of many modern films, praising John Wayne and Clint Eastwood.

Neil McCaffrey, president and founder of the Conservative Book Club (and much else), discusses the cultural conservatism and love of jazz that he shares with Rothbard. (Note: McCaffrey and Rothbard are both scholars of the popular music of the 20s, 30s, and 40s.)

In the editors' favorite essay, Rothbard as husband gets a warm and funny tribute from his wife and partner, Joey, whom he has called "the indispensable framework." Robert Kephart, whose birthday dinner inspired this volume, and Dyanne Petersen present a charming poem for Rothbard's 60th birthday, and Margit von Mises talks of the close personal and scholarly relationship that Mises and Rothbard enjoyed.

The essays in this *Festschrift*, which is proudly sponsored by the Ludwig von Mises Institute, show just some of the effects of Rothbard's writing and teaching. His passionate commitment to individual liberty, Austrian economics, the free market, and the gold standard—his massive and original contributions to economics, history, political science, law, ethics, libertarianism, and philosophy—have made him a giant of liberty.

Rothbard is a writer of singular style, humor, and power. Like Mises, he has inspired millions with his vision of the free society. In the academic world, where devotion to principle is as popular as it is in Washington, D.C., he has carried the torch of Misesianism.

And also like Mises, he exhibits extraordinary personal gentleness along with his unbending adherence to principle. In an age when selling-out is the norm among politicians—governmental and academic—Rothbard has held high the banner of truth and freedom. He has faced immense pressure to retreat, but never wavered. Today he is still at work extending the scholarship of freedom.

On Murray N. Rothbard's 60th birthday, the Mises Institute sponsored a conference on his work. Out of that conference came this book.

The Institute, and the editors of this volume, are grateful to be associated with the joyous libertarian; this magnificent teacher, writer, scholar, activist; this great champion of liberty—whose achievements, integrity, courage, optimism, and humor, have made him the leader in the battle for freedom.

Llewellyn H. Rockwell, Jr. and Walter Block
The Ludwig von Mises Institute
Auburn University
July 1988

Part 1

Economics

1

Rothbardian Monopoly Theory and Antitrust Policy

Dominick T. Armentano

This essay will discuss some of Murray N. Rothbard's contributions to monopoly theory in light of the current reforms in the administration of the antitrust laws of the United States.

Theory and Policy

Public policy is usually grounded on some theory of how the world works or should work. If the theory supporting the public policy is flawed, the policy will produce unintended consequences. The consequences in turn will often lead to a debate over alternative theoretical models and eventually, perhaps, to different public policies.

In the 1960s and 1970s, many microeconomic policies, including antitrust, generated consequences that many economists judged to be inappropriate. Energy regulation produced oil and natural gas shortages, air carrier regulation kept air travel costs and prices high, and many important antitrust cases were initiated against efficient business organizations seemingly *because* they were efficient. Such a thoroughly perverse state of affairs created a strong constituency for a substantial deregulation in some industries, and for important changes in the administration of the antitrust laws.

Antitrust policy *has* certainly changed markedly over the last ten years.[1] Despite some glaring exceptions such as the unwarranted divestiture of the American Telephone and Telegraph Company, the antitrust authorities are far less likely to intervene in traditional antitrust areas such as price discrimination, tying agreements, increased firm market share and merger. Yet despite these important changes, it is not at all clear that the shift in antitrust policy represents any fundamental change in *theoretical* perspective. Indeed, we will argue that those who advocate antitrust reform have tended to rely upon the very same theoretical model as did the previous antitrust "traditionalists," and that, as a consequence, the current antitrust administrative changes are neither as radical nor as permanent as they appear. Further, we will argue that really fundamental antitrust reform or repeal would depend upon a radically different theoretical perspective, and that the monopoly theories of Murray Rothbard may provide that radical perspective.

The Competitive Model

To understand traditional antitrust policy, and the fundamental conservatism of the current reform movement, we must first review the formalistic theory of competition and monopoly power that has dominated micropolicy discussions for 100 years: the perfectly competitive equilibrium model. This model assumes that products sold in markets are homogeneous and that consumers and producers are "fully informed" concerning their conditions of sale. If sellers have no "control" over market price, each seller is induced to generate an output where marginal cost and market price are equal. Such behavior, economists hold, will produce an equilibrium condition that is socially "efficient" and tends to maximize social "welfare." If real-world markets are perfectly competitive, presumably, there would be no legitimate reason to regulate microeconomic activity.

Except for some very special market situations, however, it has always been apparent that real markets are neither competitively structured nor in equilibrium. Sellers in most markets attempt to differentiate and advertise their product, and competition in such situations is interdependent and rivalrous rather than a static state of affairs. But since little behavior in the actual business world appears consistent with the equilibrium conditions of the "competitive" model, how is such behavior to be understood and evaluated in terms of public policy?

Market Failure and the Traditionalists

The older, more traditional perspective among industrial organization specialists was to treat each deviation from the competitive equilibrium condition as some regrettable "market failure" that might be remedied with appropriate antitrust regulation.[2] And since the real-world behavior of firms can differ sharply from the competitive equilibrium assumptions, this approach opened up a vast array of regulatory opportunities. For example, business firms that were profitable—especially over long periods of time—were always suspected of monopolizing since all economic profits should be "competed away" in the competitive equilibrium. Firms that differentiated their products were always suspect since products should be homogeneous in competition. Firms that advertised and employed expensive selling and marketing techniques were always suspect since, in competition, market information was simply assumed to be perfect. Even technological change, innovation, and lower product prices could be exclusionary, a barrier to entry, and evidence of monopoly power. This sort of analysis, of course, was and is totally perverse, yet it dominated the traditionalist period of antitrust enforcement and intellectually rationalized some of its most absurd legal actions.

Antitrust Reform

Eventually this combination of poor theorizing and silly antitrust cases produced a crisis in antitrust enforcement. An increasing number of economists and lawyers (led by Robert Bork, Richard Posner, Harold Demsetz, Yale Brozen, and others) became severely critical of the traditionalist analysis, and called for specific reforms in the administration of antitrust policy.[3] Many of these reforms stemmed directly from increasing empirical evidence that demonstrated (to the reformers, at least) that concentrated markets did not perform poorly and need not be tightly regulated by the antitrust authorities. The reformers were also critical of the barriers to entry doctrine and argued that firms tended to gain and hold market share by being continuously more efficient than their rivals. In addition, the reformers tended to accept price discrimination, advertising, product differentiation, and most tying arrangements as part and parcel of an efficient market process— not as the evidence of market failure or resource misallocation. Finally, many more business consolidations could be permitted without specific antitrust scrutiny since few mergers harbored any real probability of restraining trade.

Based on these policy changes it would appear that the current antitrust reform movement holds a sharply different theory of monopoly power and market failure than that held by the antitrust traditionalists. But this is *not* really the case. The reformers, to be sure, are far more willing than the traditionalist to admit the existence of market disequilibria, and they are far more willing to acknowledge the beneficial nature of *most* voluntary business agreements. Despite these differences, however, the reformers and the traditionalists share a basic theoretical commonality: the welfare analysis implicit in the perfectly competitive model. When push comes to shove—and it always does in any evaluation of price-fixing or so-called "predatory practices"—the reformers admit that certain business action can be socially inefficient and can lower social welfare, and that such action ought to remain illegal.

Market Failure and Antitrust Reform

This reliance by the reformers on the perfectly competitive perspective can be easily observed in their general unwillingness to oppose antitrust in principle, and in their enthusiasm for vigorous enforcement of antitrust law in the area of horizontal agreements and price-fixing.[4] Business agreements that can reduce market output or raise (or stabilize) market price are seen by the reformers (and, of course, by the traditionalists) as socially harmful and inefficient; such practices ought to remain illegal *per se*. Firms that can restrict market output have market power, and such power can impose a "dead-weight" welfare loss or allocative inefficiency on society. Business agreements that harbor both social benefits as well as social costs are more complicated and ought to be judged by a "rule of reason."[5] Here the reformers would have the antitrust regulatory establishment sit in economic judgment of those agreements, and permit only those whose social benefits exceeded their social costs. Thus the reformers still see a significant role for antitrust regulation—especially with respect to mergers, joint ventures, and other cooperative agreements—and this regulatory responsibility can be derived directly from orthodox competition theory and welfare analysis.

The antitrust reform movement, and the debate between the reformers and the traditionalists, can now be put in a clearer perspective. The traditionalists see market failure and monopoly power almost everywhere and want additional antitrust regulation to deal with such failures. The reformers, on the other hand, see market failure only with respect to business behavior that might reduce market output or raise (or stabilize) market price; only that manifestation of monopoly power would be regulated. *Both* claim that free markets can fail, and both agree that it is a legitimate responsibility of government to prevent such failures. *Both* agree that social welfare and efficiency can be lessened by "monopoly power." *Neither* would grant that a free market ought to be totally unregulated, and *both* would agree that some economic liberty—say the liberty to collude—must be sacrificed in order to promote economic efficiency.

The Case Against Antitrust

There are several ways to object to the limited nature of this antitrust debate and to argue, instead, that *all* of the antitrust laws should be repealed. The first approach would be to assert (or demonstrate) that liberty, including the right to make *any* business agreement, is a higher value than any alleged increase in welfare or efficiency, and that a higher value ought never to be sacrificed to any lesser value. A second approach would be to argue that social efficiency, correctly understood, must incorporate the notion of complete buyer and seller liberty.[6] A third approach would be to hold that any truly inefficient business agreement will be short-lived and dissolve naturally, and that open markets always *tend* toward an equilibrium outcome; any antitrust enforcement would either be premature or redundant. A fourth approach would be to argue that even though free markets might contain single sellers and cartels, no theory of monopoly price is tenable or could justify any antitrust enforcement. Although Murray Rothbard has argued on behalf of all these points, this last position is his unique contribution to the literature on monopoly theory and policy.

Rothbardian Monopoly Theory

Since Rothbard's economic theories are generally within the Austrian economic tradition, it might be useful to compare his position on monopoly with those of Ludwig von Mises and Israel M. Kirzner. Mises held that monopoly could exist in a free market whenever the entire supply of a commodity was controlled by one seller or a group of sellers acting in concert. Such a situation was not necessarily harmful unless the demand curve for the commodity was inelastic. Then, according to Mises, the monopolist would have a perverse incentive to restrict production and create a monopoly price, and that price would be "an infringement of the supremacy of the consumers and the democracy of the market."[7] Kirzner has suggested that the monopoly ownership of some resource could have "harmful effects" since it would create an incentive on the part of the resource owner to *not* employ the resource to "the fullest extent compatible with the pattern of consumer tastes" in the market.[8]

Rothbard's position on monopoly price and consumer welfare is distinctly different. He argues initially that it may be confusing (and even absurd) to define monopoly as the control over the entire supply of some commodity or resource. This definition may be inappropriate since the slightest consumer perceived difference between different units of some commodity or resource (with respect to location for example), would then mean that each seller of anything is a "monopolist."[9] But even *if* this were an appropriate definitional approach, the entire notion of "monopoly price" in a free market is simply untenable according to Rothbard. Any acceptable theory of "monopoly price" is itself conditional on an independent determination of a "competitive" price against which the monopoly price might be compared. For Rothbard, however, any independent determination of a competitive price in a free market is impossible. Free markets contain *only* free-market prices.[10]

Competitive prices in the orthodox literature have usually been associated with marginal cost pricing, particularly under conditions of long-run equilibrium. For Rothbard, however, such prices are meaningless and irrelevant since they are associated with a static equilibrium condition that could never actually exist, and would not necessarily be optimal even if it did exist. In any actual market situation all sellers have some influence over price and market information is never perfect. In all real markets sellers face a sloped demand curve, not the perfectly elastic demand curve associated with the competitive equilibrium. Thus, all market pricing is free-market pricing whether it is accomplished by atomistic sellers or by firms with significant market share. Competitive prices are as fictitious as the medieval notion of the "just" price.

Mises, it will be recalled, defined a monopoly price as that price accomplished when output is restricted under conditions of inelastic demand, thus increasing the net income of the supplier. Rothbard argues, however, that there is no objective way to determine that such a price is a monopoly price or that such a "restriction" is antisocial. All we can know is that *all* firms attempt to produce a stock of goods that maximizes their net income given their estimation of demand. They attempt to set the price (other things being equal) such that the range of demand above their asking price is elastic. If they discover that they can increase their monetary income by producing less in the next selling period, then they do so.

Rothbard maintains that to speak of the initial price as the "competitive" price, and the second-period price as the "monopoly" price makes no objective sense. How, he asks, is it to be objectively determined that the first price is actually a "competitive" price? Could it, in fact, have been a "subcompetitive price"? Presumably even competitive firms can make mistakes and produce "too much."[11] If they do they must "restrict production" and increase market price; but this does not mean that the second price is a monopoly price. Indeed, the entire discussion is absurd since there are no *independent* criteria that would allow such determinations. All that can be known for sure, Rothbard argues, is that the prices both before and after any supply change are free-market prices.

In addition, the negative welfare implications concerning alleged monopoly prices would not follow even if such prices could exist. Since the inelasticity of demand for Rothbard is "purely the result of the voluntary demands" of the consumers, and since the exchange (at the higher prices) is completely "voluntary" anyway, there is no ambiguous way to conclude that societal "welfare" has been injured.

Rothbard has been severely critical of orthodox utility and welfare analysis.[12] The conventional wisdom in antitrust, among both reformers and traditionalists, has been to assert that business agreements such as price-fixing ought to be prohibited since they tend to reduce consumer welfare and lower social efficiency. For Rothbard, however, the costs and benefits associated with exchange are personal and subjective, and do not lend themselves to any cardinal measurement or aggregation. He holds that there is no unambiguous manner by which the costs for consumers and the benefits for producers (or vice versa) might be totalled up across various markets, and then compared to make a determination as to whether a business agreement is *socially* efficient or not. Indeed, the entire notion of *social* efficiency is a myth for Rothbard.[13] Individual consumer and producer utility and "surplus" may exist, but these notions cannot be mathematically manipulated to allow any regulatory "rule of reason" judgments.

Indeed, the only unambiguous conclusion that can be derived from the existence of a voluntary agreement—price fixing or otherwise—is that the parties to the agreement were attempting, *ex ante*, to maximize their respective utilities. Any additional welfare conclusions beyond that, i.e., that other parties are worse off or better off, are mere speculations and cannot be scientifically rationalized. From this it would follow, presumably, that no antitrust regulation can be scientifically rationalized against any voluntary business exchange since no intervention could be shown to increase social welfare.

Rothbard's criticism of conventional and Austrian monopoly theory allows him to conclude that "monopoly" can be best defined as a grant of special privilege from government that legally reserves "a certain area of production to one particular individual or group."[14] This definition of monopoly is both historically relevant and unambiguous in Rothbard's judgment. It is historically relevant since it is the original meaning of the term in English common law, and much of this sort of monopoly still survives today. It is unambiguous since such an approach allows a clear distinction to be made between free-market prices and monopoly prices. Free markets—that are either rivalrous or cooperative in varying degrees—can only give rise to free-market prices. On the other hand, monopoly prices can arise whenever government legally restrains trade. Presumably an unambiguous anti-monopoly policy would conclude that all such privileges, including orthodox antitrust policy itself which restrains free trade, be abolished.

Some commentators who are sympathetic to Rothbard's theories have suggested that antitrust policy could be used exclusively to attack *legal* monopoly. There are some very practical difficulties with this proposition, however. In the first place, most, if not all, legal monopolies at the state level are immune from antitrust jurisdiction under the so-called *Parker* doctrine.[15] In addition Congress has recently gone further and immunized municipal officials from any antitrust liability should such cases ever prove successful.[16] Finally, the retention of any part of the antitrust system—the antitrust bureaucracy and judicial review—would invite its use and abuse in other areas; such is the very nature of governmental regulatory policy. It is politically naive, therefore, to believe that antitrust could be salvaged to deal exclusively with government-created monopolies. The practical and principled position from a Rothbardian perspective would appear to be the total and immediate repeal of all antitrust regulations.

Notes

1. James C. Miller, "Report from Official Washington," *Antitrust Law Journal* 53 (1984): 5-13.
2. For the more traditional antitrust perspective see, William G. Shepherd, *The Economics of Industrial Organization*, 2nd ed. (Englewood Cliffs, N.J.: Prentice-Hall, 1985). This traditional perspective is reflected in articles and editorials in almost any issue of the *Antitrust Law and Economics Review*.
3. Robert Bork, *The Antitrust Paradox: A Policy at War with Itself* (New York: Basic Books, 1978); Richard A. Posner, *Antitrust Law: An Economics Perspective* (Chicago: University of Chicago Press, 1976); Yale Brozen, *Concentration, Mergers, and Public Policy* (New York: Macmillan, 1983); D. T. Armentano, *Antitrust and Monopoly: Anatomy of a Policy Failure* (New York: John Wiley and Sons, 1982).
4. Bork, *The Antitrust Paradox*, Chapter 13.
5. Wesley J. Liebeler, "Intrabrand Cartels under GTE Sylvania," *UCLA Law Review* 30 (1982).
6. D. T. Armentano, "Efficiency, Liberty, and Antitrust Policy," *Cato Journal* 4, no. 3 (Winter 1985): 925-32.
7. Ludwig von Mises, *Human Action: A Treatise on Economics* (New Haven: Yale University Press, 1963), p. 358.

8. Israel M. Kirzner, *Competition and Entrepreneurship* (Chicago: University of Chicago Press, 1973), p. 111.

9. Murray N. Rothbard, *Man, Economy, and State* (New York: Van Nostrand, 1962), p. 591.

10. Ibid., pp. 604-15.

11. Ibid., p. 607.

12. Murray N. Rothbard, *Toward a Reconstruction of Utility and Welfare Economics* (New York: Center for Libertarian Studies, 1977).

13. Murray N. Rothbard, "The Myth of Efficiency," in Mario Rizzo, ed., *Time, Uncertainty, and Disequilibrium* (Boston: D. C. Heath, 1979), pp. 90-95.

14. Rothbard, *Man, Economy, and State*, p. 591.

15. *Parker v. Brown.* 317 U.S. 341, 1943.

16. The recently enacted "Local Government Antitrust Act of 1984" eliminates personal liability for municipal officials. See *Antitrust and Trade Regulation Reporter*, Bureau of National Affairs, 47, no. 1178 (August 16, 1984).

2

Prisoner's Dilemma, Transaction Costs, and Rothbard

Roger A. Arnold

There is today no better known, more articulate, or more persuasive expositor of the case against government than Murray Rothbard. In a world where surely 999 out of every 1000 persons readily accept the need for government—in much the same way that they accept the need for the absolute essentials of life: food, water, and air—Murray Rothbard has the uncanny knack of shaking their (heretofore unexamined) acceptance of government. He does so by combining refreshingly clear writing, finely crafted logically-deduced conclusions, intermittent thought-provoking questions ("Why is it ethically better to follow the wishes of the greater as against the lesser number? What's so good about the greatest number?"), an ability to find the usually hidden weak point in an opponent's argument and draw it out in the open where it is thoroughly thrashed, and an uncompromising dedication to the cause of liberty that can be felt and is appreciated, at an intellectual level by some and at a subconscious level by others.

Part of Rothbard's continuing, long, impressive, and interdisciplinary career may be seen in terms of his replying to, and disposing of, the dozen or so major reasons and arguments put forth to support the notion that the State is necessary. In retrospect, we would have to conclude that some of these reasons and arguments have been more difficult to dispose of than others. One that has been particularly difficult purports that government is necessary in situations where game-playing is present (of the iterated prisoner's dilemma variety), or where high transaction costs exist, or where game-playing and high transaction costs exist together. In fact, we may note that the arguments for the State fall into one of two broadly-based categories. There are those arguments which, on the surface, stress the need for the State on grounds that it will do good, prevent bad: but below the surface they appear to be motivated by the desire for pure redistribution or by paternalism. Simply put, the arguments are based on a desire to "take from others," or to have others "do what they *should* be doing." In the former, one person is the pawn of another: in the latter, one person is the "adopted adult-child" of another. In both cases, one person's will is subject to that of another's. Once this is pointed out, as Rothbard so often does, the argument loses much of its moral force; individuals who continue to advance it are finally seen for what they are.

There is another argument for the State that is not so easily disposed of. This argument emphasizes that there are times when large majorities, if not everyone, would prefer certain goods and services, but because of free-rider problems, high transaction costs, strategic game-playing, etc., such goods and services can only be brought about through the imposition of taxes, thus implying the need for the State. When the argument is constructed in terms of "everyone" wanting X but no one being able to obtain it (because of the problems cited above), the State is thus seen as an agent that helps individuals obtain what they want, and not as an agent aiding one group of persons at the expense of another group. As noted above, this construction of the argument is harder to dispose of than the former argument for the State. Murray Rothbard has directed his attention to this argument, but not usually within the same framework of analysis used by the proponents of the argument. This turns out to mean that there is scant mention of "prisoner's dilemma" and "high transaction costs" within the works of Rothbard. Some critics have noted this and then continued on to argue that prisoner's dilemma and high transaction costs present a problem for Rothbard's no-government position. A major objective of this paper will be to show that the overall Rothbardian economic and political philosophical framework provides a strong reply to these critics.

The plan of the paper is as follows: First, to outline and discuss in greater detail (than above) the argument that purports the State as necessary on PD (prisoner's dilemma) and TC (transaction costs) grounds. Second, some general criticisms of this argument will be made. Third, Rothbard's position on PD and TC problems will be noted and amplified.

The State as "Market Mechanism"

The point in the argument we wish to discuss in detail is commonly made through a story-example. It goes something like this: Consider a community of 1000 persons. Every individual in the community wishes to have good X, but unfortunately the ordinary market mechanism has not provided it. The reason might be that individuals are engaged in strategic game playing, behavior they can realize reduces the probability of achieving their ends, yet behavior they do not seem capable of freeing themselves from. Or it might be that the costs (usually called "transaction costs") to realizing an exchange are so high that the exchange will not be realized. Lastly, it might be a combination of both: game-playing and high transaction costs. In any case, since it appears that individuals can not obtain good X through the ordinary forces of (voluntary) supply and demand, something beyond this is needed. Often that "something" is government; government, through its levying of taxes, collects the necessary funds to provide good X, and in the process overcomes any game-playing behavior and/or high transaction costs. We conclude that when the market fails, government must rise to the occasion. And in that government aids individuals in obtaining what they want (but do not seem to be able to get), government is seen as something of a "market." Simple market exchanges ($1 for one apple) allow individuals to move to higher utility levels; complex "market exchanges" through government (taxes for roads), so the argument goes, do the same. On the surface, government coerces ("pay those taxes, or else!"); further below, it is seen as the visible manifestation of voluntary agreement.

On one level, it is an appealing argument. First, it paints government as a market mechanism of sorts, and therefore not much of a different animal than we are used to. Second, its policy conclusion appears reasonable: government should only do what the simple market mechanism cannot. Third, it is built on identifiable phenomena, that is, most individuals realize that game-playing is evident in real life, and that transaction costs sometimes do exist. For these reasons in particular, the argument has become widely accepted, even amongst those whose work is noted for pointing out the "costs" associated with government and who have taught us much about "government failure." For one, the two major roles of the State—usually noted as "protective" and "productive"—both may be seen as tied to the solution to the prisoner's dilemma problem. With respect to the protective State, consider the discussion of two (generally considered) free-market economists, Richard McKenzie and Gordon Tullock, in their text, *Modern Political Economy*.

They speak of two individuals, Fred and Harry, who live alone on an island. At first Fred and Harry have no behavioral rules to naturally divide their spheres of interest. Soon each learns that he has two options he can follow: one, he can steal from the other, or two, he can choose not to steal. If both find it advantageous to steal, and do not feel a conscience cost high enough to outweigh the benefits, then both will become involved in theft. Soon after they realize that theft, and the protection from theft, is expensive: it diverts resources away from production. Realizing this, they agree on certain rights, on a social contract. But once this is done, Fred and Harry find themselves with an incentive to cheat on the agreement. Each has two options: either to respect the other's rights, or to violate the other's rights. Here, then, is a prisoner's dilemma setting. It so turns out that each alone is better off if the other respects his rights while he violates the other's rights. Attempting to minimize the maximum loss in utility that can occur, each violates the other's rights. The result is that they are once again back to where they started, where each is stealing from the other. McKenzie and Tullock then go on to generalize this situation to a large numbers setting, and state: "To prevent violations, both of offensive and of defensive nature, a community may agree to the establishment of a police, court, and penal system to protect the rights specified in the social contract."[1] While McKenzie and Tullock do not explicitly state that the police, court, and penal system should be provided through the State, as opposed to privately, it is clear that this is their intent. We see that here the protective role of the State is justified on prisoner's dilemma grounds.

This is also the case with respect to the justification of the productive role of the State. It is argued that the State is necessary to impose the taxes that are necessary for the provision of goods that exhibit "publicness." The reasoning is as follows: first, a public good is identified: call it X. Second, the point is made that if X is consumed by one it is available for consumption by all. Third, because of the second point, consumers will become free riders. There is here a prisoner's setting in that each person who benefits from X has the option to pay or not pay for it, the best outcome for each individual being where he does not pay and all others pay. However, behaving in a manner to bring this outcome about is said to end with no one paying for the good. The way out is to opt for state-imposed taxation. Assuming everyone benefits from good X, and would end up paying a dollar tax equal to or less than the marginal benefit of the good, then it is better to have state-imposed taxation and X than to be without taxation and not have X. Notice again that the State is here justified on grounds that it does what simple supply and demand cannot. Also, in that individuals are getting through government what it is they want, the government is seen as a "market mechanism" of sorts.

The same theme often exists in the transaction-costs argument for the State. With respect to the productive role of the State, it is often argued that a good, such as X again, will not be produced because of the high transaction costs involved. It is often argued the following way: One thousand persons want X, but a potential supplier finds it too costly to obtain the agreement of, and payment from, all 1000 persons; consequently he does not provide X to these persons. The solution? The State should detour around the high transaction costs. It should provide X, tax people into paying for it, and that is that. We see then that the productive role of the State is often justified in terms of game-playing (prisoner's dilemma) and high transaction costs.

Besides being used to justify the productive role of the State, the transaction-costs argument is also used to justify the wealth-maximizing role of the State. This is perhaps most clearly seen in the work of Richard Posner. Posner, drawing on the highly-idealized Coasian setting—where there are zero transaction costs and no income effects—argues that government, through the courts, ought to assign property rights to the party who would buy them, and place liability (in liability cases) on the party who could have averted the accident at lower cost.[2] According to Posner, such arrangements are consistent with what individuals would voluntarily agree to amongst themselves if high transaction costs did not get into their way.[3] Once again, the subtle message is that government, through its court system, is justified on the grounds that it does what the market wants do to (but somehow can not).

Criticisms of the PD and TC Justifications of the State

Can the State in its protective, productive, and wealth-maximizing roles be justified on PD (prisoner's dilemma) or TC (transaction costs) grounds? The answer is "yes," if and only if those who advance the argument for the State and certain State actions based on PD and TC grounds can prove that the state is what they say it is: a "market mechanism" through which individuals increase their utility levels. James Buchanan defines the condition that must be met before the State can be justified. He notes: "The justification for all collective action, for government, lies in its ability to make men better off."[4] It needs to be proved that the State makes men better off. So far, it has only been asserted that it does. To their credit, the proponents of the PD and TC justifications have pointed out that game-playing and transaction costs exist, but this is not enough to justify the State. Additionally, they implicitly argue that the coercion the State imposes is voluntarily agreed to, that is, individuals agree to it, seeing it as the only way to obtain what they (all) want, and that the benefits of the byproducts of the coercion—e.g., protection (of rights), production (of public goods), and wealth maximization—are greater than the costs of coercion. First, the agreement spoken of has never been witnessed. Second, telling a story where the benefits of the byproducts of coercion appear to be greater than the costs of coercion is not the same as *proving* that they are. The justification of the State based on PD and TC grounds is weak.

Contrast the unproved PD and TC justification of the State and of the coercion implicit in the State with Murray Rothbard's attempts to prove that the State cannot be justified. Stated differently, contrast the unproved PD and TC justification of the State that makes men better off with Rothbard's attempts to prove that the State makes men worse off. In *Power and Market*, Rothbard provides a framework in which a long list of activities of the State are categorized and analyzed. A major conclusion of the analysis is that the State decreases social welfare. The reasoning is as follows: One, the State uses coercion. Two, if individuals are coerced it follows that they are doing something they wouldn't be doing.[5] Three, one can not get more utility from doing something he wouldn't be doing than doing something he would want to do. We conclude that the State decreases utility levels—if not of all persons, of at least some. And as long as we can not measure whether the "winners" gain more in terms of utility than the "losers" lose, we cannot guarantee that there is even, at minimum, a net gain to having the State.

The often-cited retort by the persons who put forth either the PD or TC justification of the State, is that Rothbard does not see that individuals may voluntarily agree to the State in their attempt to make themselves better off.[6] Whether this is or is not the case is not relevant to the discussion. As we noted above, the point is that this agreement has not been witnessed, nor has it been proved that the benefits of the byproducts of coercion are greater than the costs of coercion. In short, if we accept Buchanan's criterion for the justification of the State— "The justification . . . for government, lies in its ability to make men better off"—then we would have to admit that since those who advance the State on PD and TC grounds have not proved that "men are made better off" through the State, it follows that they have not justified the State. In contrast, Rothbard does seem to have proved that the State is capable of making persons worse off. The PD and TC justification of the State, attempting to get at the idea that through the State persons are made better off, is not as strong an argument for the

State as Rothbard's argument that coercion decreases social welfare is against the State. This does not mean to suggest that there is no justification of the State, only that the attempt to justify the State based on PD and TC grounds, with the underlying theme that individuals are made better off through the State, has not been proved conclusively, or even to the degree that Rothbard has proved that individuals are made worse off through the State, and therefore presently must be judged a failed attempt.

Eliminating PD and TC Problems at any Cost?

Where PD and TC problems exist, the State has been proposed as the solution to the problems. Little thought has been given to other possible ways of dealing with them. It is analogous to a person having a high fever and only a medical doctor being considered as capable of bringing the fever down. No one and nothing else is considered.

We put forth the question to focus our attention on the alternatives: Are there ways other than a State's dealing successfully with prisoner's dilemma and transaction costs? We hold that there are. Furthermore, we hold that these ways are implicit within the Rothbardian framework of analysis although they have not been (to my knowledge) directed or proposed as a possible solution to the PD and TC problems at hand. We shall return to this main point after a short detour.

Consider a potential exchange in which high transaction costs are identified. Next, we ask ourselves, is the existence of high transaction costs reason enough to do anything in order to reduce them? If the answer is yes, then we must conclude that nothing is as bad as living in a world where high transaction costs exist. This implies that all else is secondary to a world of zero transaction costs. Put this way, it is perhaps easier to put the whole discussion of high transaction costs in perspective. If the answer to our question is no, then it follows that some things are more important to us than ridding the world of high transaction costs.[7]

We can say the same about prisoner's dilemma settings. Once the PD problem has been identified, is this reason enough to do anything to successfully eliminate it? If the answer is no, then it follows that some things are more important to us than ridding the world of PD settings. One point and one question naturally emerge from our questions and answers: We are not only concerned with reducing high transaction costs and eliminating prisoner's dilemma settings, but in how each objective is met. Besides, if there are some things more important to us than ridding the world of high TC and PD settings, then what are they? Recognition of our point and an attempt to answer our question comprise a direction that a close reading of Rothbard would cause us to push the discussion of PD and TC in. But it is also a direction that those persons who justify the State on PD and TC grounds choose not to be pushed in. For example, where in the literature on PD and TC is there anything but the sketchiest discussion of the importance of the way in which PD and TC problems are solved? Where is there any discussion of the trade-offs involved in reducing transaction costs or eliminating prisoner's dilemma settings?

Non-Governmental Solutions to PD and TC Problems

In order to make the world a better place in which to live, Rothbard puts emphasis on two important factors: reason and persuasion. Reason is necessary in order to discover what the good life is comprised of. In Rothbard's words, ". . . what ends man should pursue that are most harmonious with, and best tend to fulfill, his nature."[8] Once this is known, persuasion is then necessary to convince others, to educate others, as to the ingredients of the good life for themselves and others. One wonders if there is a solution to PD and TC problems that is characterized by reason and persuasion, as opposed, say, to the activities of the State. We hold that there is.

Consider PD problems first. By now it is well-known that under certain conditions, the strategy of "tit-for-tat" solves the prisoner's dilemma problem.[9] Stated differently, tit-for-tat is a strategy which can under certain conditions bring forth cooperation without any central authority, without a State. We shall first speak of the characteristics of tit-for-tat, and of its role in bringing forth ethical behavior, and then compare it to the state as a solution to PD problems.

Robert Axelrod has described tit-for-tat as "nice, retaliatory, forgiving, and clear. Its niceness prevents it from getting into unnecessary trouble. Its retaliation discourages the other side from persisting whenever defection is tried. Its forgiveness helps restore mutual cooperation. And its clarity makes it intelligible to the other player, thereby eliciting long-term cooperation."[10] Contrast the essence of tit-for-tat with golden-rule behavior. A person exhibiting tit-for-tat behavior responds "in kind." If someone does X to him, he does X back; if someone does Y to him, he does Y back.

A person who exhibits golden-rule behavior does to others what he wishes others to do to him. He does not, in contrast to tit-for-tat behavior, respond "in kind." If X is done to him, and he does not want others to do X to him but would prefer Y, then he will do Y.

The question emerges: Which type of behavior, tit-for-tat or golden-rule, is more likely to bring on the golden-rule world: where individuals behave to others as they would have others behave to them? It may appear paradoxical, but nevertheless it is true: golden-rule behavior does not bring on a golden-rule world, because it is consistently exploitable. Individuals who exhibit golden-rule behavior are easily taken advantage by others who do not. Furthermore, the latter group is not retaliated against by the former group (and therefore feels no cost to its actions) because the former group would not act in a way that it wouldn't want others to act towards it. Tit-for-tat behavior is more likely to bring on a golden-rule world. The reason is simple: It signals that to get good, one must give good. There is a boomerang effect: what one gives, one gets back. The golden-rule world is brought about through pure self-interest. We need to note two points before we continue: First, under certain conditions, tit-for-tat has been shown to solve the PD problem. Second, tit-for-tat behavior is capable of bringing on an outcome—a golden rule world—that one might have thought could only have been brought about by golden-rule behavior.

Turn now to the State as the solution to the PD problem. With the State, not only is the PD problem solved in a non-voluntary or less voluntary way (depending on whether or not one believes the State is agreed to), but there is no desirable byproduct: such as the golden rule world. It may be that the time that elapses between when a PD problem is identified and it is solved is shorter when the State is the solution than when tit-for-tat is, but surely consideration should also be paid to the way in which the PD problem is solved, as well as to the intended and unintended consequences of the particular solution.

We need now ask: Suppose there are instances where tit-for-tat cannot solve a particular PD problem, what then? Do we turn to the State, or do we simply allow the problem to exist? In such instances, the State would appear to be the only solution to the problem. Even if we accept this as fact it does not, *per se*, justify the State, for not all problems are worth solving. When all is said and done, the cure might turn out to be worse than the sickness. As Rothbard has pointed out numerous times, it is not likely that the State will do only what it is told to do, much like a disobedient servant. With time, it will expand. As Rothbard notes, ". . . it is in the economic interest of the State rulers to work actively for such expansion."[11] Casual empiricism confirms this.

The Rothbardian approach to solving PD problems—discernible from a close reading of his works—is that truly voluntary solutions such as tit-for-tat need to be emphasized, not only because of their desirable quality of voluntariness but because they often generate desirable unintended consequences. And if, by chance, they do not work, this is not reason enough to justify the State, for there are strong logically-deduced reasons and empirical evidence to support the hypothesis that the State will not solve one problem without creating another.

Transaction Costs and Subjectivism

While most economists today will admit that cost is subjective, few will raise the red flag when cost is spoken of as if it were not. One of the few, and perhaps the most vocal, is Murray Rothbard. Without Rothbard to continually remind us that cost is subjective, and to point out when and where policy proposals are based (sometimes even unbeknownst to the framers of the proposals) on the assumptions that costs are not subjective, many of us would fall into numerous traps. The lesson we should learn, once and for all, is: Proposals, conclusions, and advice that either assert or assume that cost is not subjective ought to be discarded. With respect to our discussion of the State, any transaction cost-justification of the State directed to either the issue of its existence, or to the issue of what the State ought to do (once it exists), is immediately invalidated if it asserts or assumes that transaction costs are not subjective. But, of course, this is precisely what all those who justify the State on transaction costs grounds do. How else could they propose the State to do this or that when transaction costs are "high"?

Our points are simple. All costs, no matter what names we attach to them, are subjective; therefore they are unmeasurable. Given this, it does not make sense to say that transaction costs are high, or low, or somewhere in between. We conclude that the argument that purports to justify the State's existence, or State interventions, on the grounds that transaction costs are high makes as much sense as an argument that purports to justify the State on the grounds that Tuesday follows Monday.

Of course, even if we assumed that it made sense to speak of high transaction costs there could still be no reasonable transaction cost-justification of the State or its actions without a way of our telling how high transaction costs need to be before the State is warranted. If one person states that potential exchange X is not being actualized because of high transaction costs, would we conclude that transaction costs are high enough for the State to step in? Of course, no matter who, or what group, were to decide such matters, the potential for abuse would exist and is likely to be acted upon.

Concluding Remarks

The Rothbardian framework, in which the need to prove the assertions made is stressed, the unintended consequences of natural market forces are noted, and the subjectiveness of cost is realized, provides a solid response to those persons who see the State as a "market mechanism." It is farfetched to believe that simply because prisoner's dilemma settings and transaction costs exist that individuals will voluntarily agree to the State, and that there are no other ways besides the State to deal with these problems—assuming, of course, that dealing with them is considered worthwhile.

When it comes to prisoner's dilemma settings and transaction costs, Rothbard is satisfied to admit that both may exist, but he is not so quick to jump on the bandwagon of persons calling for the State to deal with them. Instead, he asks if PD problems might not be solved in a voluntary way, realizing that not only is the voluntary way the way of liberty, but that it is also often the way of desirable unintended consequences. As to high transaction costs, he notes that cost is subjective, unmeasurable, and that there really is no way of our deciding when transaction costs are high enough to warrant anything other than a "hands off" policy. Rothbard's prescription is to let entrepreneurs deal with transaction costs much as they deal with production costs, or any other kind of costs.

In a world where the State plays a big part in our lives, and where individuals unthinkingly accept that there exist good reasons for its being, and where arguments are easily swallowed if they simply appear to be relevant, Murray Rothbard is there urging us to stop, to check around, to ask a few hard questions, and then, proceed with caution. When it comes to something as important as whether or not the State is legitimate, and how much personal liberty we shall have, this is extremely good advice. Thankfully, Murray Rothbard has been there for us leading the way: asking the hard questions, picking apart the weak arguments, making the strong points, and raising the red flags. The cause of liberty cannot say it has no champions.

Notes

1. Richard McKenzie and Gordon Tullock, *Modern Political Economy: An Introduction to Economics* (New York: McGraw-Hill, 1978), p. 82.
2. For a thorough discussion of the Posner position, see his *Economic Analysis of the Law* (Boston: Brown and Company, 1972).
3. Consider the following statement as illustrative of this position. Posner states, "Suppose the rule were that a magazine could not sell the list of its subscribers to

another company for purposes of soliciting unless the subscribers consented. It would be costly to obtain such consent, so if we are reasonably confident that the value of the list to the purchaser ordinarily is greater than the cost to the subscribers of the slight impairment of their interest in being let alone by direct-mail advertisers, we would want to assign the property right to the magazine," ibid., p. 33.

4. James M. Buchanan, *The Bases of Collective Action* (Morristown, N.J.: General Learning Corporation, 1971), p. 2.

5. Rothbard puts it this way: "Coercive intervention . . . signifies *per se* that the individual or individuals coerced would not have done what they are now doing were it not for the intervention," *Power and Market* (Kansas City, Kans.: Sheed Andrews and McMeel, 1977), p. 70.

6. The statement by H. E. Frech, III is representative of the sentiments of the group that advances this position. It is: ". . . individuals may all be better off by agreeing to be coerced," "The Public Choice Theory of Murray N. Rothbard: A Modern Anarchist," *Public Choice* 14 (September 1973): 150.

7. Consider a specific example to make the points clearer. Ten thousand individuals live in a particular area. Someone believes that the 10,000 individuals all want good X, but because of the "publicness" of X, and because of high transaction costs, there is no agreement as to how X will be paid for. In order to reduce the transaction costs, someone proposes that 6,000 of the 10,000 individuals should be killed. This act will reduce transaction costs but it is unlikely that individuals who value human life will find it an acceptable means of reducing transaction costs. The point being that we are not simply concerned with reducing high transaction costs, but in how they are reduced, too.

8. Murray Rothbard, *The Ethics of Liberty* (Atlantic Highlands, N.J.: Humanities Press, 1982), p. 10.

9. For a complete discussion of the tit-for-tat strategy, see Robert Axelrod, *The Evolution of Cooperation* (New York: Basic Books, 1984).

10. Ibid., p. 54.

11. Rothbard, *The Ethics of Liberty*, p. 176.

3

Fractional Reserve Banking:
An Interdisciplinary Perspective

Walter Block

Freshman economics students are taught to understand the miracle of fractional reserve banking: it can create money out of thin air! Kindergartners are encouraged to save their pennies at institutions based on this system. Fractional reserve banking (FRB) is a pillar of our community, the underpinning of our entire banking system. There are even many libertarians who favor the arrangement. Professor Murray N. Rothbard, a staunch critic of FRB,[1] has been widely attacked on his stance, even by libertarians.[2] I think it is no exaggeration to characterize FRB as almost universally beloved, defended by people from virtually all shades of political opinion. Yet, as will be shown in this paper, FRB is a fraud and a sham, whose intellectual pretensions of honesty deserve to be exposed once and for all.

What, exactly, is fractional reserve banking? Since we are dealing here with a classical case of "The Emperor Having No Clothes," FRB can perhaps best be explained by the use of a fairy tale:

> Once upon a time, in a land far, far away, at a time long, long ago (when the gold standard was in its infancy) there lived a goldsmith, humble, meek and pure.
>
> Since the goldsmith had the strongest safe in town, the people were accustomed to leaving their jewelry, gold, and other valuables with him. The goldsmith, for a small fee, would give the townsfolk a receipt for leaving their deposits with him. The receipt would say that: "Jones has deposited ten (10) ounces of gold with Humble, Meek, and Pure Goldsmith to the trade; Humble, Meek, and Pure Goldsmith will, therefore, pay to the bearer of this note, ten (10) ounces of gold, on demand."

24

ᵔThe citizens of the town, lazy by disposition, though highly aware of the cost of goods like shoe leather, food, hay for their horses, etc., would rarely go to the goldsmith to withdraw their gold before making a purchase. Rather, they would merely hand over the receipt for gold to the tanner, the food supplier, or the merchant at the stable. The merchant would accept this note for his goods knowing that he, too, could trade it for something else, or return it to Humble, Meek, and Pure Goldsmiths, and receive his 10 ounces of gold, on demand.

All was well with this tranquil tale until the Wicked Witch of the West cast a spell over the goldsmith's wife and made her covetous, dissatisfied, and consumed with a passion for expensive living. She, in turn, "leaned" on her husband. She gave the goldsmith not a moment's peace until he concocted a "brilliant" scheme for "earning" more money. The goldsmith realized that most of the villagers were content to leave their gold permanently on deposit, and that those few who withdrew gold spent it in such a way (on local merchandise) that it would eventually reach him again. So the goldsmith took some of the hard earned gold that had been entrusted to him and *gave it to his wife to spend on fripperies.* Other funds that did not belong to the goldsmith were, nevertheless, lent out by him, the proceeds going to his good lady.

Noticing that his previous financial manipulations went undiscovered, the goldsmith escalated. Now, not content with seizing the gold belonging to others, he manufactured receipts *for gold that had never been given* to him; he thereupon turned these notes over to his favorite charitable cause, and she went out and spent them.

This particular fairy tale ends happily—for the goldsmith and his wife, that is. Their financial irregularities are never discovered, and the townspeople remain content to leave their valuables with the goldsmith and to use his ever increasing bank notes to transact business.

The question we are faced with is: How is fractional reserve banking to be evaluated? (We formally define FRB as a system where some fraction less than 100% of the assets is kept on reserve against the deposits outstanding).

The goldsmith's first method, giving his wife gold that had been entrusted to his care, is a rather straightforward case of embezzlement.

(Webster defines embezzlement as "to appropriate property entrusted to one's care fraudulently, to one's own use.") It may well be true that such a great amount of trust and goodwill had been built up in the business that none of the townspeople would be suspicious of the mal-appropriation. If this is so, then there will be no ruinous run on the bank. But this means only that the embezzlement will not be *discovered*, not that it did not take place.

The second method, giving his wife warehouse receipts for nonexistent gold, is likewise a clear example of counterfeiting. (Defined by Webster's as "copying, imitating, with intent to deceive.") As in the easily recognized case of counterfeiting, the goldsmith passes off his unbacked gold receipts (fake money) for those that are fully backed by gold (legitimate money). This is logically equivalent to forgery (defined as, imitating falsely, with intent to deceive), or passing bad checks.

But whatever the name, the results are clear. The dishonest goldsmith diverts sizeable amounts of real resources belonging to other people to his own use. The economic effects of such a procedure are morally indistinguishable from the highwayman's[3] case; there is a bit more openhandedness, since everyone knows him as the thief he is, while the goldsmith is widely thought to be an honest merchant.

Nor will the case change when modern banking methods are introduced, with demand deposits and checkbook money largely taking the place of bank notes. The principle is still the same: with the advent of FRB, real wealth is shifted from the non-bank public to the banking industry, exactly in the same way as in the operation of the goldsmith's counterfeiting ring.

Any institution engaging in FRB, moreover is bankrupt as soon as it begins. For as soon as it has more obligations outstanding against it than it has assets with which to pay, it is unable to meet its debts. And once an institution is unable to pay the debts which fall due, it is in a state of *bankruptcy*, the "moratorium" and other fancy obfuscations in the New York City financial crises of 1976 notwithstanding. Again, as in the case of embezzlement, the bankruptcy may not be discovered until a run on the bank occurs,[4] but a bank is technically in a state of bankruptcy as soon as it embarks upon a policy of fractional reserve banking.

One common objection to our FRB analysis is as follows: If a FRB system is bankrupt because it cannot pay off all its debts, then virtually *all* businesses are bankrupt, because most of them would not be able to pay off all their debts at any given moment. It is true that most business firms have heavy mortgages, that they cannot retire for years. But any view that implies that almost our entire business community is now and always in a state of bankruptcy, must be seriously deficient.

The problem with this objection is that it misunderstands the time element. In the ordinary business case, it may be true that total liabilities often far exceed total assets on hand. Assets on hand may be virtually zero, right after a company has made a heavy investment and right before it recoups the returns. But in the usual case, not all the liabilities are *instantaneous*. Most are not. In the case of mortgages, there are payments which are not *due* for 20 to 30 years. We may then safely ignore the case where assets on hand are not sufficient to make payments that are not due for 30 years! The business is not thereby bankrupt. True, if the company cannot come up with the money in 30 years (or whenever it is due), *then* it will be bankrupt.

But the case of FRB is altogether different. Like other businesses, many of its assets are illiquid. Unlike them, however, its liabilities, at least as far as notes and demand deposits are concerned, are *instantaneous*. A demand deposit is just that: an amount of money placed with the bank which, according to the contract, the bank has agreed to pay back on *demand, forthwith, immediately*. Only in rare case are the instantaneous liabilities of an ordinary business greater than its instantaneous (liquid) assets. When this occurs, the business is truly bankrupt. But in the FRB system, instantaneous liabilities are *always* greater than instantaneous (liquid) assets. This is because the fractional reserve banking system is *defined* as one in which only a *fraction* of the demand deposits are held in reserve; the remainder is in the form of long term loans, or illiquid assets.

The same distinction holds with regard to insurance companies. Critics of our FRB analysis are often wont to point to insurance companies as examples of bankruptcy, according to our criteria, on the grounds that, if a large scale calamity occurs, the insurance industry, based on the principle of dividing risk, could not possibly pay off all the legitimate claims made against it.

Now it is certainly true that insurance is a method of pooling risks, and can only remain profitable on the assumption that a disaster does not strike *all* customers of any one company. That is why, other things equal, the larger company will be better able to pool risks. It therefore follows that *if* a nation-wide catastrophe were to strike, many, if not all of our insurance companies, would be rendered bankrupt.

But this is a far cry from allowing that they are *now* bankrupt, in the *absence* of such a calamity. The analogy fails, for banks under FRB are *presently* bankrupt, even assuming no out-of-the-ordinary circumstances. Just because a company *could* become bankrupt, in certain very extraordinary situations, does not mean that it is bankrupt at present.

A second objection concerns not so much a supposed flaw in the present critique of FRB, but rather a charge of inconsistency against the present author who, in the present paper attacks counterfeiting "as a fraud and a sham" while in a book,[5] *Defending the Undefendable*, explicitly singles out the counterfeiter as "heroic."

I plead "not guilty" to this charge of inconsistency. In the book I went out of my way to point out that I was *opposed* to counterfeiting, on moral grounds, but that the people who were commonly blamed for this activity, private, non-governmental agents, were not really counterfeiters at all. As I stated:

> The justification for calling the common, private counterfeiter heroic is that there is a prior counterfeiter in action and that the money falsified by the private counterfeiter is not really legitimate money; instead, it is itself counterfeit. It is one thing to say that counterfeiting *genuine* money amounts to theft; it is quite another thing to say that counterfeiting *counterfeit* money amounts to theft.[6]

The case we are dealing with in the present paper is one of counterfeiting *genuine* money. There was nothing in *Defending the Undefendable* that would compel defense of *this* kind of activity. The goldsmith, in creating "extra" notes, for which no gold exists, and the modern banker, in lending out money in the form of demand deposits unbacked by any money, are both guilty of no more and no less than counterfeiting genuine money—and both are therefore guilty of theft.

Let us now consider a defense of FRB, not as presently constituted, but as it *might* be. There is a singular group of economists who concede that all FRB systems that have ever existed may have been equivalent to theft, but who nevertheless contend that *voluntary* fractional reserve banking (VFRB) is plausible, would be workable, and need not be fraudulent.

In the view of voluntary fractional reserve banking advocates, the chief evil of the present system is the cumulative statement on the face of the notes (or on the contract upon which the demand deposits are based) to the effect that there is more money on deposit than is actually the case. If there are 100,000 notes in existence, each with a face value of 10 gold ounces, then according to all the warehouse receipts for gold outstanding, there are 1,000,000 golds ounces. But assuming that the fraction on reserve is only 20%, this is a blatant falsehood. Actually, under this type of FRB, there would only be 200,000 gold ounces in existence.

The VFRB advocates, seeing the truth of this claim, act so as to obviate it. Given the preceding set of assumptions, they advocate something like the following statement appear on each and every 10-ounce note:

> By the way folks, our policy is to keep only one-fifth of an ounce of gold on hand for each of the ounce value notes that we put into circulation. Since this here is a 10-ounce note, we've got only two ounces in reserve backing it. Thus, if all you people, the holders of our notes (or demand depositors, as the case may be) come into the bank at the same time, demanding your money back, only 20% of you will get your money back. We'll pay off the people presenting the first 20% of our notes outstanding in the order that they demand their money. The rest of you suckers (depositors! a thousand pardons!) will just be out of luck. We'll have to hold a forced sale of our assets. You'll have to wait until our loans fall due. In the meantime, there will be a "moratorium" on payments. In other words, our bankruptcy will be evident.

Whatever else may be said, it must be admitted that at least this VFRB scheme cannot be called purposefully deceptive. It goes out of the way, to a degree probably never seen before, to make clear just what is involved in FRB. If the preceding statement appears in bold lettering, and not in "small (invisible) print" the claim to voluntariness is strong indeed.

The VFRB argument is also buttressed by the phenomena of "fractional reserve parking lots" which flourish on several college campuses. The patrons of such parking facilities are told, quite clearly and forcefully, that if they purchase a "permission" to park, it is a conditional one. The parking lot makes it clear that more "permissions" to park are sold than there are parking places on the lot. Therefore, if the demand is low (within the limits set by the number of spaces on the lot), the permission functions much the same as the more traditional parking permit: It "guarantees" a parking space. But if the demand on any one day exceeds the number of spaces, "first-come-first-served" is the order of the day. (Because of the risk, such "permissions" usually sell at a discount compared to the more traditional permits.) This, contends the VFRB advocates, is truly a *voluntary* fractional reserve parking lot, not in violation of any libertarian principles prohibiting fraud and theft. Why, they ask, cannot the same principles be applied to banking?

Plausible as the argument sounds, it does not succeed. We must question the claim that the 10-ounce bank note, even with the statement clearly visible, is really a 10-ounce note (or a demand deposit for 10-ounces of gold). What right, it may be asked, do the VFRB advocates have to the claim that 10 ounces of gold are really payable, to the bearer, *on demand*. All of economic reality rebels against such a claim. By the admission of the VFRB people, there is no such guarantee. On the contrary, the VFRB people *admit* that all the notes may *not* be paid on demand (if too many people make this request).

Suppose the statement were to be altered to the following, in an attempt to get around this criticism:

> Ok you guys, now hear this. This is your friendly local neighborhood banker speaking. If you turn in this piece of paper which purports to be a 10-ounce gold bank note (or warehouse receipt for gold, or demand deposit for 10 ounces of gold) you have a 1 to 5 chance of getting your money back. However, if no one claims his money before you do, (or if fewer people claim their money than we have money available), then you are guaranteed to receive your money back—for sure. Cross our hearts and hope to die.

The second statement is clearly free of the claim that there is no legitimacy to calling the relevant piece of paper a 10-ounce bank note. Moreover, it places the bank note clearly in the tradition of the "fractional reserve" parking lot, certainly a legitimate institution. But note now that the VFRB position is free of the claim, at long last, that it is in *any* way fraudulent, or misleading, it is open to another criticism: this piece of paper is a bank note no longer; rather, it is a *lottery* ticket.

What, indeed, can be the justification for calling a piece of paper (or a contract, in the case of checkbook money) a *bank note*, when it is only offering (under certain conditions) a 1 to 5 *chance* of receiving money. How is such a supposedly voluntary fractional reserve *banking* system to be distinguished from a voluntary *lottery*?[7] It cannot be so distinguished, and therefore VFRB if it adheres scrupulously to the dictates of honesty, must of necessity reduce itself to a lottery, and not a system of banking at all.

Let us conclude by disposing of the claim that on the market, the value of a fractional reserve banking note will tend to trade at its par value multiplied by the reserve fraction. Thus, a 10-ounce gold note, with a 20% reserve behind it, will, it is claimed, tend to trade at two gold ounces; a 30-ounce gold note backed by a 40% reserve, at 12 gold ounces.

This would be equivalent, in our lottery analogy, to the claim that lottery tickets will sell at mathematically "fair" prices. In other words, a lottery with a first and only prize of 1,000,000 gold ounces will sell no more than 100,000 chances, for 10 gold ounces each. But this would mean that the lottery entrepreneur would undertake to give out *all* his income from the sale of tickets to the prize winner, leaving zero profit for himself. Such a businessman could not thrive for long.

In the banking case, the 10-ounce gold "note" need not trade at two gold ounces (assuming a 20% reserve). It might sell at far less, if people do not trust the bank, and it might be worth more, if people do not fully digest the import of the second statement printed on it.[7]

Notes

1. See Murray N. Rothbard, *Man, Economy, and State*, (New York: Van Nostrand), pp. 701-03. See also his *What Has Government Done to our Money?* (Santa Ana, Calif.: Rampart College, 1974).
2. Exhaustive research, however, fails to uncover any published critiques in this regard.
3. Lysander Spooner, *No Treason* (Larkspur, Colo.: Pine Tree Press, 1966).
4. It is presently unlawful to encourage runs on banks, or to cast aspersions on their financial probity. Presumably, the better to "protect" the public.
5. Walter Block, *Defending the Undefendable* (New York: Fleet Press, 1976), pp. 109-20.
6. Ibid., p. 113.
7. Ludwig von Mises, *Human Action* (Chicago: Henry Regnery, 1949), pp. 106-16.

4

Gold and the Constitution: Retrospect and Prospect

Gregory B. Christainsen

A narchists such as Murray Rothbard have long maintained that no constitution can ultimately be effective in limiting the powers of government. The political pressures to engage in this or that prohibited activity are always present, and when a prohibited activity can be rationalized in terms of plausible views which are opposed to those of the constitution's founders, the founders' intentions may have little force.

A striking example in support of the above contention concerns the desire of the authors of the American constitution to limit the power of government with respect to money. This paper documents the role the Founding Fathers intended for gold in a monetary system which was supposed to be devoid of fiat money. It then discusses the actions of the U.S. Supreme Court in two key episodes during which gold was effectively removed as an important factor in the U.S. monetary system. The two episodes concern the so-called "legal tender cases" of the post-Civil War period and the "gold clause cases" of the 1930s. If one interprets the Constitution in accordance with the intentions of the Founding Fathers, it is argued that there was no legal basis for the Court's behavior during these episodes. The Court's behavior in the gold clause cases appears to have been especially sinister. The paper concludes by discussing the future of gold.

The Flow and Ebb of Gold: 1787-1834

The Founding Fathers intended for gold to have a central, if not preeminent, role in the U.S. monetary system. Article 1, Section 8 of the Constitution gives Congress the power to "coin" money, by which it was meant simply that Congress was authorized to operate mints.

Article 1, Section 8 also gives Congress the power to borrow money "on the credit of the United States." What is noteworthy about that particular provision is that the corresponding phrase in the Articles of Confederation, the document which the Constitutional Convention of 1787 had the purpose of revising, also gave Congress the power to "emit bills of credit." The initial draft of the Constitution also gave Congress the power to "emit bills." In the parlance of the time, "bills" referred (with few exceptions) to non-interest-bearing assets, payable on demand, i.e., paper currency. On August 16, 1787, however, eleven state representatives debated and voted on whether Congress should retain the power to issue paper currency in the new constitution, and by a 9-2 margin[1] they moved to *strike out* the words "emit bills." In the account of James Madison, "[s]triking out the words . . . cut off the pretext for a paper currency, and particularly for making the bills a tender either for public or private debts."[2]

The Tenth Amendment to the Constitution reserved to the states those powers not expressly given to the federal government, so it was important for Article 1 to be supplemented by Section 10: "No state shall coin money, emit bills of credit; make anything but gold or silver coin a tender in payment of debts." In the context of the then-dominant Anglo-Saxon common law, which gave legal tender status only to gold and silver, it is thus clear that the Founding Fathers were laying down a policy of "hard" money. Article 1, Section 10, it appears, was written in order to deny the states powers which had already been denied to the federal government.

After the Constitution was ratified the Congress acted on its minting authority and passed the Coinage Act of 1792. A "dollar," which was understood to refer to the silver Spanish milled dollar, was fixed at 371.25 grains of fine silver. Given the then-prevailing free-market exchange rate between gold and silver of (roughly) 15 to 1, a dollar was also set equal to 24.75 grains of fine gold (24.75 = 371.25/15). So it appeared that a sound monetary system was in place, with gold—"the universal prize in all countries, in all cultures, in all ages"[3]—playing a central role.

But it was not to be. The Coinage Act of 1792 established a fixed rate of exchange between gold and silver—15 to 1—but not long after the passage of the act, the market value of gold relative to silver rose above the 15-to-1 level. Given the legal tender status of silver, Gresham's Law was set in motion: "Bad" money drove out "good" money. In payment of debts, creditors were forced to accept silver which had less value than the official exchange rate indicated, and since gold had *more* value than the official exchange rate indicated, people turned their gold holdings to *nonmonetary* uses. Many gold coins were thereby led to disappear from circulation until the Coinage Act of 1834, which made an upward adjustment in the exchange rate.

Moreover, bills of credit were emitted under government auspices early in the life of the new republic. The First and Second Banks of the United States, incorporated in 1791 and 1816, respectively, helped to manage the finances of the federal government, which, in turn, owned about one-fifth of the banks' stock. The banks issued bills of credit, but these bills did not claim to be legal tender.

It was left to the War Between the States for bills of credit to lose their virginity as an untendered medium. To help finance this period of fratricide, creditors were forced to accept in undiscounted form the so-called greenbacks which were issued, but it was not long before the constitutionality of this move was challenged. A key player in the drama was Salmon Chase, the secretary of the Treasury when the bills were first emitted, and later the chief justice of the Supreme Court. In *Veazie Bank v. Fenno* (1869), which upheld the legality of the federal government's enactment of a tax on state banknotes, Chase offered the view that the constitutionality of the issuance of paper currency had been "settled by the uniform practice of government and by repeated decisions,"[4] but he cited no such decisions. In *Hepburn v. Griswold* (1870), on the other hand, Chase, writing for the court, argued that Congress could *not* make the greenbacks legal tender for debts incurred before the legislation that provided for their issuance.[5]

Knox v. Lee (1871) marked a turning point in the ultimate transition from precious metals to paper money. During the fifteen months between the *Hepburn* and *Knox* decisions, the Court's composition changed, with critics charging that President Grant had appointed at least one of two new justices on the understanding that he (Justice Bradley) would sustain the legal tender legislation. This claim has never really been proved, but the two new justices were responsible for a 5-4 vote to uphold the constitutionality of the greenbacks' legal tender status for debts incurred *either* before or after the legislation was enacted. In concurring with the majority, Justice Bradley alluded to the (false) view that Congress's borrowing power extended to bills of credit, saying that the greenback legislation "is a promise by the government to pay dollars; it is not an attempt to make dollars."[6] The majority opinion authored by Justice Strong, the other new justice appointed by Grant, made a vague and unfounded argument for the constitutionality of the greenback legislation by claiming that it was necessary for "government self-preservation."[7]

Juilliard v. Greenman, decided in 1884, however, bolstered the rationale for the groundless "national necessity" argument by citing the Constitution's clause which states that, within the powers granted by the Constitution, the U.S. government can do what is "necessary and proper" for the achievement of its ends, and while no less an authority than Justice Marshall had argued forcefully that this clause in no way enlarged the powers of the U.S. government beyond those provided for by the other parts of the Constitution,[8] the Juilliard court argued that *Congress itself*, not the Supreme Court, was the appropriate judge of what was necessary and proper, whether in wartime or peacetime. Other parts of the decision wrongly asserted that the emission of bills of credit was part of Congress's borrowing power, and it was also claimed that their emission was *inherently* constitutional—"one of the powers of sovereignty in other civilized nations."[9]

Even the Juilliard decision, however, did not alleviate Congress of its obligation to maintain the ultimate redeemability of the greenbacks into specie. It was not until the 1930s, with the gold clause decisions, that redeemability into gold was officially ended, and incredibly, from 1934 to 1974, the federal government was able to largely outlaw gold from the private possession of the citizens of the United States.

The debate over the great gold confiscation[10] of the 1930s is a classic example of an ideological struggle. As with other such struggles, the parties to the controversy were caught up in momentous times that few really comprehended, but about which people nevertheless held strong opinions. In pursuing their objectives, there was one sense in which many of the people involved could be said to have been idealists; they believed in the ultimate objectives they were pursuing. In trying to surmount the barriers to either their ideological goals or their narrower self-interest, however, people were led to undertake actions which they would never have otherwise condoned.

The Rationale

The Great Confiscation occurred, of course, against the backdrop of the Great Depression. The role of the Federal Reserve in causing the Great Depression remains in dispute, but it is now widely agreed that the Fed at the very least exacerbated the Depression by failing to prevent or offset bank runs of the very sort it had been created to avert. Since each dollar of deposits backs several dollars-worth of money supply, the fact that large numbers of people wanted to convert deposits into currency resulted, absent any Fed counter-measures, in a multiple contraction of the nation's stock of money (currency plus bank deposits). From 1929-1933, the money supply declined by about a third. Whether the inaction of the Fed in the face of bank runs was the primary cause or just a notable accompaniment of the economic events of those years, the demand for goods and services generally collapsed, and by 1933 a quarter of the labor force was unemployed.

Banks' efforts to protect themselves from depositor runs only made matters worse. Each dollar of deposits normally backs several dollars-worth of money supply because banks need keep only a fraction of each dollar of deposits on reserve. This enables banks to lend out the remainder, and as loaned funds are spent and, in turn, deposited at other banks, the money supply swells. If banks hold added reserves in-stead of making loans, however, the multiple by which the money supply can expand is reduced. Faced with low demand for credit and the risk of bank runs, banks greatly increased the ratio of reserves to deposits, causing the money supply to shrink drastically. This factor became very important beginning in 1931.

Many states were led by these events to declare "bank holidays" and ordered banks to close their doors. These moves culminated in the New York holiday which began on March 4, 1933, and finally, the na-tional banking holiday ordered by President Roosevelt on March 6, 1933. Banks were permitted to open one week later provided that they obtained a license from the secretary of the Treasury certifying that they were sound.[11] This certification was intended to restore some con-fidence to the banking system, and by March 15 more than two-thirds of the banks with about seven-eighths of the nation's deposits were licensed and open. By the end of 1933 about half of the unlicensed banks with about a quarter of the unlicensed deposits had reopened.

Under the terms of the banking holiday, banks were prohibited from paying out gold or dealing in foreign exchange. On March 10, be-fore the expiration of the banking holiday, Roosevelt issued an ex-ecutive order extending the restrictions on gold and foreign exchange dealings beyond the duration of the holiday, unless a bank obtained a special license. March 10 also saw the proposed Thomas amendment to the Agricultural Adjustment Act, which was enacted into law on May 12. This contained a provision authorizing the President to re-duce the gold value of a dollar by as much as 50 percent.

It was now clear what government policymakers were up to. Aside from trying in their own way to restore confidence in the banking sys-tem, they were deliberately seeking to debase the nation's currency in the hopes of stimulating economic activity. But much more was done besides setting new terms for the relationship between gold and the supply of dollars. On April 5 the President issued another executive order forbidding the "hoarding" of gold and commanded that all gold coins, bullion, and certificates be turned into Federal Reserve banks by May 1 at the legal price of $20.67 per fine ounce of gold. Each individual was allowed, however, to keep a maximum of $100 in gold coin or certificates, plus any coins considered rare. Industry and the arts were allowed to keep minimal amounts of gold as well.

At a news conference on April 19, the President indicated that he wanted the dollar to depreciate relative to other currencies in order to bring about an increase in domestic prices. And so it happened. The restrictions on gold ownership greatly limited U.S. exports of gold, and purchases of foreign gold by the U.S. government increased total imports. American exporters ultimately want dollars; exports generate a *demand* for converting foreign currencies into dollars. Imports on the other hand generate a *supply* of dollars to be converted into foreign currencies. Thus, government policy caused the supply of dollars in foreign exchange trading to *increase* and the demand to *decrease*, leading to a fall in the value of the dollar.[12] With prices of key commodities being set, not unilaterally by U.S. sellers, but in a competitive world market, the fall in the value of the dollar meant that the dollar prices of those commodities had to rise in order for dollar prices to equal the real world levels prevailing at that time. That is, if a foreign seller were being paid in dollars that had depreciated relative to his own currency by 10 percent, his dollar prices would have to increase by 10 percent if each unit sold were to generate the same amount of real revenue as before.

The effect of U.S. policies on other countries, however, was in precisely the opposite direction. The value of foreign currencies rose relative to the dollar and there were net outflows of gold from those countries to the United States. So while the dollar prices of traded commodities *rose* in the United States, other countries experienced additional *deflationary* pressures.

Of course, for these policies to be effective in stimulating economic activity in the United States, supplementary policies were required. First, it was important that the Federal Reserve not "sterilize" the inflows of gold from abroad by engineering an offsetting decrease in the money supply. And second, there had to be some assurance that any increases in the money supply would lead to increases in *real* output and employment, and not be purely inflationary.

The first concern was addressed with the help of the Gold Reserve Act, passed on January 30, 1934. Under this Act, title to all gold coin and bullion was vested in the United States, and the President was authorized to fix the gold value of a dollar at between 50 and 60 percent of its prior legal level. The next day Roosevelt changed the legal price of an ounce of gold from $20.67 to $35.00. At this higher dollar price, many people were indeed led to turn in their gold holdings, and the Federal Reserve purchased sizable amounts of the metal with newly-created fiat money. So despite an increasing problem with banks holding excess reserves—a problem which did not even begin to subside until June 1935—the quantity of money accelerated tremendously, with the M2 measure of the money supply (which includes savings deposits as well as checking deposits) growing almost 25 percent from the spring of 1934 to the spring of 1936.

If they had been permitted to do so, people might have been able to protect themselves from the resulting inflation[13] through the use of "gold clauses" in contracts, as they had done to some extent during the greenback era. But a joint resolution of Congress had been introduced as early as May 6, 1933, and passed on June 5, 1933, which abrogated all gold clauses in contracts, both public and private.

Under "gold clauses," an individual who was owed payment could stipulate that any debasement of the dollar relative to gold had to be matched by the payment of additional dollars so that the real payment, in terms of gold, would be the same as if the debasement had not occurred. Contracts could thus effectively provide for a gold standard, and dollar inflation would not, in principle, have any real effects. In other words, if such contracts could be negotiated frictionlessly and universally, inflation would have *no effect* on real output, employment, and economic activity generally! But generating inflation which would provide a short-run stimulus to economic activity was precisely one of the Roosevelt Administration's objectives.

There was yet another motive for abrogating the gold clauses. In light of the fact that the clauses were annulled before people could effectively make alternative arrangements, the annulment produced an immediate transfer of wealth from creditors to debtors, one of whom was the U.S. government. If individuals could have enforced gold clauses for their loans to the U.S. government, the fact that the value of the dollar declined relative to gold would have entitled them to additional dollar payments as compensation when their loans were settled. Instead, the U.S. government was enriched by an estimated $3 billion in terms of payments it no longer had to make.[14]

So at least in a short-run, pragmatic, utilitarian sense, government policymakers achieved their objectives. As a result of government policies, the average level of real income expanded at a 9 percent annual rate from 1933 to 1937 and reattained its 1929 level. In addition, the unemployment rate, properly measured,[15] fell back below 10 percent. For better or for worse, the nation's monetary system and its implied respect for individual sovereignty, were, however, never quite the same.

The Supporting Court Decisions

The key Supreme Court decisions pertaining to the constitutionality of the U.S. Government's confiscation of the gold stock, and its abrogation of gold clauses in contracts, comprise one of the most curious episodes in the curious history of that distinguished body. There were three crucial cases which the Court elected to hear in 1935: *Norman v. Baltimore & Ohio Railroad Co.*, *Nortz v. United States*, and *Perry v. United States.*

In the *Norman* case, the plaintiff noted that he had bought a railroad bond valued at $22.50 "in gold coin of the United States . . . of or equal to the standard of weight and fineness existing on February 1, 1930." He then argued that since the President and the Congress had deliberately devalued the dollar in terms of gold, he should receive considerably more than the nominal value of $22.50 as payment. The Court argued, however, that the contract in question did *not* specifically call for payment in gold coin; it called for payment of 22.5 "dollars," *deliverable* in gold coin of a certain weight and fineness. In addition, the plaintiff conceded that the gold clause implied payment in the "equivalent" of gold if payment in gold became impossible. The plaintiff in fact received silver worth 22.5 dollars and was thus ruled to have suffered no damages. Case dismissed.

What is all the more remarkable about this case is that the plaintiff did not protest the fact that the silver he was paid was worth much less in terms of gold than the amount of silver that $22.50-worth of gold could fetch on February 1, 1930. It should also be noted that the majority decision, authored by Chief Justice Charles Evans Hughes, opined that Congress itself, not the Supreme Court, was the proper judge as to whether gold clauses represented an unwarranted interference with Congress's monetary powers![16]

In the *Nortz* case, the plaintiff argued that the true value of gold certificates in his possession exceeded their face value in dollars. He thus claimed that a requirement that he redeem his certificates for dollars was an expropriation of property in violation of the Fifth Amendment, which allows takings only if "just" compensation is paid. In a truly remarkable opinion, Chief Justice Hughes replied that, because gold had been seized nationwide, "a free market for gold in the United States, or any market available to [Nortz] for the gold coin to which he claims to have been entitled" no longer existed, and Nortz "had no right to resort to such markets."[17] In other words, in upholding the abrogation of Nortz's gold clause, Justice Hughes presupposed the constitutionality of the nationwide gold seizure! Ergo, gold didn't have the value Nortz claimed it had! Justice Hughes also noted, correctly, that Nortz never questioned the constitutionality of the nationwide gold seizure *per se*.

Finally, in *Perry v. United States*, the Court considered a gold clause in one of the U.S. Government's own bonds, and despite the fact that the clause was similar to many gold clauses in private contracts, the Court reached what by now must be regarded as the surprising conclusion that the abrogation of the clause *was* unconstitutional. Here, Hughes, citing Article I, Section 8 of the Constitution, argued that Congress, of course, had the power to borrow, but only "on the credit" of the United States. Thus, according to Hughes, "the Congress has not been vested with authority to alter or destroy those obligations."[18]

But the Court was not done. Whether Perry could recover damages, Hughes continued, "is a distinct question."[19] Hughes argued that the change in the amount of gold considered equivalent to a dollar could not be said to have caused losses to the extent that Perry claimed because, before the change in the gold content of the dollar, gold coin had been withdrawn from circulation! Hence, gold was not as valuable as Perry claimed! In other words, even in declaring *some* of Congress's actions unconstitutional, the Court effectively sustained those actions by *assuming* that the seizure of gold was constitutional. Furthermore, the court held that, irrespective of the changed nature of the gold-dollar relationship, Perry had not shown that he had suffered a loss of "buying power." But, of course, the bond which Perry possessed did not promise payment of a number of dollars which was tied somehow to, say, the Consumer Price Index. Instead, he was promised payment in a number of dollars equivalent to a certain amount of gold. Legally speaking, the dollar was still redeemable in silver, so if Perry could have shown that he was losing the equivalent of X amount of silver because of the abrogation of the gold clause, he might have been able to recover damages.[20] He did not try to do this.

In summary, nowhere in the gold clause cases was the constitutionality of the gold seizure itself a formal issue before the Court. Yet, in arriving at its decisions the Court assumed the seizure's constitutionality.

Also curious is the fact that the Court never heard a case in which the plaintiff's contract specifically insisted on payment in gold. Finally, the plaintiffs in all of the gold clause cases were noticeably incompetent in pleading their cases. In the *Norman* case, Norman did not protest the fact that the change in the relationship between gold and silver during the term of his contract meant that he ultimately received less silver than his contract legally called for. In the *Nortz* case, Nortz never questioned the constitutionality of the gold seizure; the seizure was the reason why the Court argued that gold was no longer worth what Nortz claimed. And in the *Perry* case, Perry made no use of the fact that dollars were still legally redeemable in silver in his attempt to show that he had suffered harm from the abrogation of his contract's gold clause.

Note, too, that the Supreme Court *elected* to hear these cases. It did not have to hear these cases. It could have heard cases presented by other plaintiffs. In his 1982 report to the U.S. Gold Commission Edwin Vieira argued:

> To conclude that all of these circumstances were purely accidental strains credibility to the breaking-point. That the only cases the Court selected for review simply *happened* to involve litigants so devoid of any coherent conception of their own interests that they willingly conceded the key constitutional issue is not merely implausible, but unbelievable. . . . [t]hat someone may have planned the aberrant decisions in the *Gold Clause Cases* . . . strong circumstantial evidence tends to prove.[21]

Officially speaking, precious metals were not completely removed from the nation's monetary system until 1971. In 1968, Congress declared it would no longer redeem silver certificates in silver. In 1971, the U.S. Government ended its pledge to deal in gold with foreign governments. Since 1971, gold has staged a mild comeback. In 1974, gold ownership by private citizens was relegalized, and in 1977, gold clauses in contracts became legally enforceable again. The 1980s saw the creation of the U.S. Gold Commission, which ultimately recommended against a return to any form of gold standard, but which did provide the impetus for the government's minting of new gold coins.

The Future of Gold

Suggestions that gold could, if given the chance, play a useful role in today's complex world have become more frequent in the last few years, but, at least in most intellectual circles, the metal is still taboo.

The taboo persists despite the fact that gold more than any other agent was responsible for the remarkable secular price stability prevailing from the founding of the Constitution until the early twentieth century. Revisionist historical work has also indicated that any short-term instabilities during that time can be traced to government injections of bills and notes and to ill-advised bank regulations. Instabilities are not properly attributed to so-called "free banking."[22]

If the money market were today to be restored to one consistent with the intentions of the Constitution's founders, the creation of fiat money would have to cease. In order for gold or other candidates to then be able to freely compete for money-holders' affections, sales and capital gains taxes on commodities would have to be ended, and legal tender laws would have to be repealed. In a truly free money market, gold has, historically, emerged again and again as a dominant money ("the universal prize in all countries, in all cultures, in all ages"), but no individual can predict with absolute confidence whether it would prevail today because a free market utilizes more information than any single individual can ever possess. It may also be the case that a truly free money market would not be perfectly efficient, as judged from the standpoint of neoclassical economic theory.[23] But except for a few relatively isolated instances,[24] recent theoretical and historical work makes clear that the incentives faced by fiat money suppliers are likely to be positively perverse by comparison. The person to whom this volume is dedicated reached that conclusion a long time ago.

Notes

1. Voting with the majority were George Mason, James Madison, Gouverneur Morris, Pierce Butler, Nathaniel Gorham, Oliver Ellsworth, James Wilson, George Reed, and John Langdon. Dissenters: John Mercer and Edmund Randolph.
2. Max Farrand, ed., *Records of the Federal Convention*, vol. 2 (New Haven: Yale University Press, 1937), p. 310.
3. This quotation is attributable to Jacob Bronowski.
4. *Veazie Bank v. Fenno*, 75 U.S. 548 (1869).
5. *Hepburn v. Griswold*, 75 U.S. 603 (1870).
6. *Knox v. Lee*, 79 U.S. 560.
7. Ibid., 529.
8. *McCulloch v. Maryland*, 17 U.S. 316, 421 (1819).
9. *Julliard v. Greenman*, 110 U.S. 450 (1884).
10. For a more detailed discussion of the material in this section, see Milton Friedman and Anna J. Schwartz, *A Monetary History of the United States, 1867-1960* (Princeton: Princeton University Press, 1963), pp. 462-74.
11. Licenses were issued by state banking officials for banks which were not members of the Federal Reserve System.

12. As noted by Friedman and Schwartz, *A Monetary History*, p. 466, the same effects would have followed from government purchases of foreign wheat, perfume, or art masterpieces. It was not necessary to purchase gold.

13. Wholesale prices rose an average of 31% from 1933 to 1937. (Data obtained from U.S. Department of Labor, Bureau of Labor Statistics.)

14. See Friedman and Schwartz, *A Monetary History*, p. 470.

15. See Michael R. Darby, "Three-and-a-Half Million U.S. Employees Have Been Mislaid: Or, An Explanation of Unemployment, 1934-1941," *Journal of Political Economy* 84 (February 1976): 1-16.

16. *Norman v Baltimore & Ohio Railroad Co.*, 294 U.S. 311. Hughes also argued that "contracts . . . cannot fetter the constitutional authority of Congress," ibid., p. 307.

17. *Nortz v. United States*, 294 U.S. 329-30 (1935).

18. *Perry v. United States*, 294 U.S. 354 (1935).

19. Ibid.

20. This point was made by Edwin Vieira, *Pieces of Eight: The Monetary Powers and Disabilities of the United States Constitution* (Atlanta, Ga.: Darby Printing Co., 1983), pp. 276-77.

21. Ibid., p. 282.

22. See the contributions by Lawrence White in Thomas D. Willett, ed., *Political Business Cycles* (San Francisco: Pacific Research Institute for Public Policy, forthcoming).

23. See Leland B. Yeager, "Stable Money and Free-Market Currencies," *Cato Journal* 3 (Spring 1983): 305-26.

24. One might note the case of West Germany from 1948-1966 or Switzerland and Japan in most recent years.

5

Professor Rothbard and the Theory of Interest

Roger W. Garrison

The Theory of Interest in Perspective

It has become increasingly true that individual economists are categorized in accordance with their chosen fields of specialization—regulation, for instance, or theory of finance, or monetary theory. Economists become known for some special insight or assumption that sets their analysis apart from the analyses of others—rent-seeking behavior, the efficient-market hypothesis, or so-called rational expectations. Name recognition and professional stature are directly proportional to the single-mindedness of the approach and to the extremes to which the economist is willing to push the analysis.

Students of economics have little difficulty grasping these special insights—unless the doggedness with which their expositors flush out implausible implications lead to a questioning of the underlying kernels of truth. The difficulties come in understanding how all these separate insights fit together into a coherent view of the economy. Rational expectations and the political business cycle, for example, are difficult to reconcile. The easy way out, students soon discover, is to pick a field, focus on an idea within the field, and leave the rest to others. Increased specialization, though, comes at the cost of a comprehension of and appreciation for economics more broadly conceived.

Professor Rothbard has provided for students a more rewarding, but more demanding, alternative—a coherent and comprehensive treatment of man, economy, and state. His treatise on economics offers a well integrated view of economic relationships, one that ignores artificial boundaries that confine the specialists to their own sub-disciplines. His writings taken as a whole advance the level of integration still further. The economics of liberty meshes with the ethics of liberty, and

44

together they help us to understand the history of a country that was conceived in liberty. Although economics, ethics, and history are distinct disciplines in academe, Professor Rothbard has regarded them as different perspectives within a single discipline. By repackaging his ideas as libertarian studies, he has provided a coherent and comprehensive world view.

Thus, a full appreciation of Professor Rothbard's achievement requires that we recognize the breadth of his contribution. It is with some reluctance, then, that I narrow the focus of attention in order to consider the Austrian theory of interest and Professor Rothbard's treatment of it. It is as if we were to try to appreciate the handiwork of a highly skilled stonemason by focusing upon a particular stone. But at least we have picked an interesting and revealing stone. You tell me your theory of interest, and I'll have a good guess about the rest of your economics. Interest is just another word for profit? You're a Ricardian. To collect interest is to exploit labor? You're a Marxian. The interest rate is wholly determined by the growth rate of capital? You're a Knightian. Interest is fundamentally a monetary phenomenon? You're a Keynesian.

Professor Rothbard is none of these. This much is not in dispute. The controversy comes when we begin to distinguish Rothbardians from Fisherians. Are time preferences of market participants and capital productivity independent co-determinants of the rate of interest, as Irving Fisher would have it? Or does time preference alone—the systematic discounting of the future—account for the payment that we call interest?

This latter view, which is properly attributed to Ludwig von Mises, is adopted by Professor Rothbard. Borrowing phraseology from Milton Friedman, it might be claimed that interest is always and everywhere a time-preference phenomenon in the same sense that inflation is always and everywhere a monetary phenomenon. Rothbard's defense of the time-preference theory of interest and his use of the theory as a building block in his treatise on economics inspires the remainder of this essay.

Productivity of the Factors

Those who have learned their interest theory from Professor Rothbard have learned to be suspicious about the use—the many uses—of the word "productive" in the literature on distributive shares, or factor imputation. The factors of production (land, labor, and capital) are employed in some combination to produce output. The idea that the factors are considered to be "productive" is indissociable from our understanding of what the factors are and what they can do. But using the term in this sense has no specific implications about the value of the separate factors or about the phenomenon of interest.

An additional dose of one of the factors of production, the other factors being employed in unchanged quantities, will allow for an increase in output. Each factor is productive at the margin. This marginal productivity, measured in value terms, has important implications about the prices of the factors—the price of an acre of land, of an hour's labor, or of the services of a capital good. Through the pricing mechanism, the value of the output is imputed to the individual factors in accordance with the values of their marginal products. The process of imputation, however, has no simple or direct bearing on questions concerning the rate of interest. The relationship between factor prices and the interest rate will be discussed at greater length in subsequent sections.

Does one of the factors of production allow for an output whose value exceeds the combined values of the factors of production? If such a factor exists, it would be productive in a very special sense. This factor would produce *surplus* value. If the search for the source of a supposed surplus value is confined to questions concerning the nature of the individual factors of production, the possible answers are few in number. A survey of the different positions taken, however, is revealing. Without digging very deep into the history of economic thought, we can find four points of view that, collectively, exhaust the possibilities.

Francois Quesnay believed that only land was capable of producing a surplus. The inherent productive powers of the soil allow for a given quantity of corn—employed as seed and worker sustenance—to be parlayed into a greater quantity of corn. The notion of land's natural fecundity lies at the root of Physiocratic thought.

Karl Marx believed that only labor can produce surplus value. Without labor, nothing at all can be produced. This one factor, then, is the ultimate source of all value. Income received by other factors represents not the productivity of those factors but the exploitation of labor.

Frank Knight believed that there is only one factor of production and that it should be called capital. Rather than argue in terms of a factor that yields a surplus, he argued in terms of a stock that yields a flow. Capital consists of all inputs that have the dimensions of a stock (land, machines, human capital); the corresponding flow is the annual output net of maintenance costs. This net yield is a consequence of capital productivity. The net yield divided by the capital stock is the rate of interest.

Joseph Schumpeter, following Leon Walras, denied that there was any surplus to be explained. In long-run general equilibrium, the sum of the values imputed to the several factors of production must fully exhaust the value of the economy's output. Schumpeter insisted that in the long run, the interest rate must be zero; the positive rate of interest that we actually observe is to be understood as a disequilibrium phenomenon.

We can pause at this point for a midterm exam: Which of the factors of production is *truly* productive? (a) Land; (b) Labor; (c) Capital; (d) None of the above. Quesnay, Marx, Knight, and Schumpeter would answer (a), (b), (c), and (d), respectively. Professor Rothbard would reject the question. The notion of productivity in this sense—and hence the issue of the source of such productivity—vanishes once we take adequate account of the temporal pattern of inputs and outputs and of the effects of time preference on their relative values.

Analogies, Time Preference, and the *Pons Asinorum*

Analytical constructions that pass as theories of capital and interest are, in many instances, question-begging analogies. Hardtack is nonperishable; sheep multiply; a Crusonia plant grows. The rates of growth of these things—zero for hardtack—are dimensionally similar to the rate of interest. The interest rate is based on the comparison of the value of output net of inputs to the value of the inputs. It is tempting to think of the implied growth in *value* as being analogous to the *physical* growth rates of sheep or of Crusonia plants. But does the analogy hold? If not, then the economics of an all-sheep economy or of a Crusonia plant will result in a hopeless conflation of interest rates and growth rates.

Such analogies serve to obscure what the phenomenon of time preference can illuminate. According to Menger's Law, the value of ends is imputed to the means that make those ends possible. But if the end, the final output of a production process, lies in the future, its current value will be discounted in the minds of market participants. The general preference in the market for output sooner over output later has—or should have—the same status as the general preference for more output over less output. Market participants discount the future. The extent to which a particular individual discounts it depends upon his own time preferences, which in turn depend upon his particular circumstances.

Currently existing means are valued in the marketplace in accordance with the *discounted* value of the corresponding (future) ends.

Because of this discounting, the total value of the currently existing factors of production falls short of the value of the future output that these factors make possible. It would be misleading to claim that there is a "growth" in value between the employment of inputs and the emergence of output. And the value difference (between output and inputs) does not constitute a "surplus" in any meaningful sense.

The existence of (positive) time-preferences—the general preference for achieving ends sooner over achieving them later—is both necessary and sufficient for the emergence of the market phenomenon called interest. If market participants were characterized by a general indifference about when their ends are achieved, about the remoteness in time of output, then the value of the means, of inputs, would reflect the full, undiscounted value of their contribution to the production of output. There would be no value difference, no interest return to account for. If market participants do discount the future, then the value of present inputs will be systematically less than the value of future output. The value difference is interest.

These propositions hold for all production processes. The inputs may grow in some literal, biological sense into outputs, or the inputs may be converted into outputs by means of some technologically advanced—or technologically backward—production process. Indeed, with appropriate changes in wording, these propositions that establish (positive) time preference as a necessary and sufficient condition for the emergence of interest in a production economy can be applied to a pure-exchange economy as well: Goods promised for future delivery will exchange at a discount for goods presently available.

The time-preference theory of interest provides us not only with a firm understanding of the phenomenon of interest but also with a *pons asinorum*, or acid test, for productivity theories of whatever variety. A particular input, or factor, may be productive, maybe even especially productive, in some sense. There is no simple relationship, however, between this productivity and the phenomenon of interest. The critical question is tirelessly posed by Professor Rothbard: Why is the ability of this factor to produce not fully reflected in its market price?

The answer, of course, is that the discounting is a direct implication of the existence of time preferences. The output which this productive factor helps to produce lies in the future. The market value of the factor itself, then, is discounted accordingly. An argument that a particular factor is highly productive may explain why its price is as high as it is, but it does not and cannot explain why its price is not higher still. That is, productivity does not and cannot explain why the factor's price fails to exhaust the undiscounted contribution to the production of output.

Is the Interest Rate the Price of a Factor Called "Waiting"?

Somewhere between the time-preference theory of interest and the alternative theories already mentioned lies the view that the interest rate is the price of a factor of production called "waiting." The notion of waiting or abstinence as the basis for interest payments has a rich history and predates the Austrian school and its time-preference theory. Abstinence was treated as a "real cost" in Nassau Senior's nineteenth-century analysis. Waiting or abstinence in a more abstract sense figured heavily in the turn-of-the-century writings of Gustav Cassel and of John B. Clark and in the subsequent writings of Frank Knight. In recent years Leland Yeager, following Cassel, has directed our attention once again to the centrality of the concept of waiting in theories of interest-rate determination.

Although theorizing in terms of time preferences and theorizing in terms of the factor of production called waiting can yield the same conclusions, the Austrians have not fully embraced this alternative mode of analysis. Eugen von Böhm-Bawerk was critical of Cassel's formulation; Friedrich Hayek considered Knight's productivity theory to be counterproductive; and Israel Kirzner has taken issue with modern reformulations. Neither Mises nor Rothbard has specifically addressed the question of waiting as a factor of production, but passages can be found in the writings of each suggesting that the time-preference view and the waiting-as-a-factor view are to some extent compatible. It may be worthwhile, then, to consider the kinship between the two views.

Cassel was careful to point out that the word 'waiting' is not being used with its ordinary dictionary meaning. Waiting as a factor of production and waiting for a bus are two different things. In fact, they are even *dimensionally* different. The latter is measured strictly in units of time; the former is measured in compound units that account for both value and time. More specifically, Casselian waiting is the product of value and time and is measured in dollar-years (or $-years). Thus, an individual who forgoes the spending of $100 for a period of two years supplies (neglecting the effects of compounding) 200 $-years of waiting. This constitutes more waiting than a second individual who forgoes the spending of only $75 for the same two years, and more waiting than a third individual who forgoes the spending of $50 for three years.

The issue of units is a critical one not only for understanding what waiting means and how it is measured but also for checking the dimensional conformability between waiting as a factor and the interest rate as its price. The price of any factor is measured in terms of dollars per unit of the factor. Land rent is measured in $/(acre-year); the wage rate in $/(worker-hour); the service price of a capital good, say a machine, in $/(machine-hour). The interest rate is measured in frequency units, in inverse time. That is, the dimensions of the interest rate are 1/year— e.g. 10% *per year*. Any attempt to recast the interest rate as the price of a factor must be squared with this dimensional characteristic.

It can be seen immediately that the interest rate cannot be the price—or even the service price—of capital goods. The dimensions of $/machine—or of $/(machine-hour)—are not the same as the units of the interest rate. Nor can waiting in the ordinary dictionary sense be the thing whose price is the interest rate. The price of waiting in this sense would be measured in $/year.

But the concept of waiting introduced by Cassel and adopted by Yeager is measured in $-years. The price of Casselian waiting, then, is measured in units of $/($-year), or, simplifying, in units of 1/year. Thus, the claim that waiting is a factor of production whose price is the rate of interest squares with the fact that the interest rate is measured in units of inverse time. It should be argued, though, that the interest rate is determined by the supply and demand for waiting whether or not the waiting is employed as a factor of production. In fact, this argument can be seen as no more than a generalization of the fact that the more narrowly conceived loan rate of interest is determined by the supply and demand for loans. Loans, whether to producers or consumers, have both a value and a time dimension, are measured in units of $-years, and constitute one form of waiting. Theorizing in terms of waiting—whatever particular form it may take —serves to emphasize the pervasiveness of the phenomenon of interest. And this emphasis is characteristic of the writings of both Yeager and Rothbard.

The generalizing from loans to waiting, however, introduces some analytical difficulties. Marshallian partial-equilibrium analysis applies in its conventional way to the market for loans. Shifts in the supply or in the demand for loans can be analyzed on the basis of the familiar *ceteris paribus* assumption: Prices in other markets, such as factor markets, are assumed not to change. The *ceteris paribus* assumption breaks down, though, when the analysis is extended from the market for loans to the general phenomenon of waiting. This is only to say that partial-equilibrium analysis cannot be applied in any straightforward way to an all-pervasive economy-wide phenomenon. The particular difficulties introduced can be illustrated with a simple example.

Suppose the current rate of interest (the price of waiting) is 5 percent and that the equilibrium quantity of waiting supplied and demanded is 1000 $-years, which consists of owning durable machines, whose current value is $1000, for one year. Now suppose that the demand for waiting increases. Simple supply-and-demand analysis would allow us to predict that the interest rate will rise, say from 5 to 10 percent, and that the quantity of waiting supplied and demanded will increase.

If the value of the machines could be assumed not to change, this prediction would be valid. But a rise in the interest rate will cause the value of the machines, which is simply the discounted value of the machines' future output, to fall. More specifically, the doubling of the rate of interest, which serves as the basis for the discounting, will cause the value of the machines to decrease from $1000 to $500. Owning those same machines for a year now constitutes only half the waiting. It is possible, then, that in the subsequent equilibrium, more machines will be owned for a longer period of time yet the amount of waiting, which is now based on a lower machine price, may be less than in the initial equilibrium.

The ambiguity identified in the example is unavoidable. The amount of waiting increases as we move up the supply schedule because of the nature of the supply relationship, but it decreases as the interest rate rises because of the way waiting is linked computationally to factor prices, which in turn are affected by changes in the rate of interest. There is no ambiguity, however, about the direction of change in the rate of interest given a particular shift in supply or in demand. An increase in the demand for waiting, which is the same thing as a rise in time preferences, will cause the rate of interest to rise.

Thus, the view that the interest rate is determined by the supply and demand for waiting is compatible with the view that it is determined by time preferences. But the waiting-as-a-factor theory strains our intuition about the meaning of waiting, involves unavoidable ambiguities about the direction of changes in the "amount" of waiting, and adds little to our understanding of the phenomenon of interest. Occam's Razor provides a clear basis for favoring the time-preference theory embraced by Professor Rothbard.

The Eclectic View: Time
Preference and Capital Productivity

The comparison of the waiting-as-a-factor view and the time-preference view paves the way for a summary assessment of the more conventional treatment of interest-rate determination. Following Irving Fisher, modern textbooks make use of a two-period model which includes a convex intertemporal opportunity curve and a family of concave intertemporal indifference curves. The slope of the opportunity curve is intended to represent the marginal productivity of capital; the slope of the indifference curves represents the marginal rate of time preference. Self interest and unhampered markets are enough to assure that the actual intertemporal pattern of consumption is the one represented by the point at which an indifference curve is tangent to the opportunity curve. The slope at the point of tangency reflects the equilibrium rate of interest.

Time preferences and the productivity of capital, then, are depicted as independent co-determinants of the market rate of interest. Neither co-determinant, by itself, is capable of determining anything. And the question of which determinant is the more decisive, is at best, a question of the relative degrees of curvature. To illustrate the polar cases, if either the indifference cures or the opportunity curve is a straight line, then the slope of the straight line will determine the rate of interest no matter where on that line the point of tangency occurs.

The Fisherian analytics are simple enough, but the basic construction is conceptually flawed. Again, the issue of dimensions comes into play. The slope of the indifference curves has the dimensions of the interest rate (1/year). The slope of the opportunity curve must be dimensionally the same if the point of tangency is to have any intelligible meaning at all. If the slope is a marginal value product, then it must be the marginal value product of *waiting*, not of *capital*. But as demonstrated in the previous section, the quantity of waiting is itself dependent upon factor prices, which in turn are dependent upon the interest rate. It cannot legitimately be argued, then, that the rate of interest has two independent co-determinants; one of those co-determinants is dependent upon the magnitude it supposedly helps to determine.

Modern textbook writers have attempted to skirt this problem by using a one-good model. In all such models, questions of value, which may be affected by changes in the rate of interest, simply do not arise. Value productivity and physical productivity are indistinct; productivity is modelled as the rate of increase in the quantity of the good. The phenomenon of interest is being analogized once again to sheep that reproduce or to plants that grow. But, as Professor Rothbard often reminds us, the rate of interest is a ratio of values, not of quantities. This modelling technique unavoidably conflates growth rates with interest rates and fails thereby to shed any light on the phenomenon of interest.

It is interesting to note that Fisher himself clearly acknowledged the actual interdependency of the two co-determinants, but he seemed not to realize the problem that this poses for the eclectic view. Once it is understood that the opportunity curve incorporates interest-rate considerations, the time-preference view comes into its own. The formal demonstration that the equilibrium rate of interest is given by the slope of the tangency in a Fisher diagram can be easily reconciled with the Mises-Rothbard view. The equilibrium rate, which on grounds of logical consistency must reflect both time preferences and the rate of discount on which the opportunity curve is based, is to be attributed to the interaction of market participants who systematically discount the future. That is, the rate of interest is simply the market's reflection of time preferences.

The rejection of the idea that the Fisher diagram identifies two independent co-determinants does not mean that the diagram is totally without meaning. And the recognition that time preferences are represented on both sides of the tangent suggests a particular reinterpretation. The family of indifference curves can retain their conventional interpretation. At the point of tangency, the opportunity curve depicts the time preferences of market participants as currently embodied in the economy's capital structure. Points on the opportunity curve to either side of the point of tangency depict the extent to which the capital structure can be modified so as to alter the time pattern of output in each direction.

This reinterpretation is consistent with that of Hayek, who went on to argue that the slope of the opportunity curve at a given point may depend upon which direction market forces are pushing. More specifically, he argued that once the construction of a particular capital structure is underway, the opportunities for producing output sooner than initially planned may be severely limited. But employing Fisherian analytics to illustrate the limited modifiability of the economy's capital structure is not at all at odds with the time-preference theory of interest.

A Summary Assessment

Theories of capital and interest are considered by many to be the most difficult theories in the discipline of economics. The difficulties stem in large part from the multiple meanings of productivity and from the issue of units—the fact that the quantity of capital or the quantity of waiting is reckoned in terms of its own price. Biological and botanical analogies have added confusion. Their deceptively simple answers come at the cost of losing sight of the question. Propositions about growth rates cannot be translated in any direct way into propositions about interest rates.

The Fisher diagram has its uses. This is not to be denied. And the payment of interest can be accounted for in terms of the supply and demand for waiting. But these conceptual contrivances mask more than they reveal. Those who have learned their capital and interest theory from *Man, Economy, and State* should be able to strip the mask away and pass the final exam: What economist has tirelessly and eloquently reminded us that (positive) time preference is a necessary and sufficient condition for the emergence of the phenomenon we call interest and that the productivity of capital (or of waiting) is neither necessary nor sufficient for interest payments to occur? (a) Gustav Cassel, (b) Irving Fisher, (c) Frank Knight, (d) Murray Rothbard.

Professor Rothbard has taught us a theory of interest that allows us to sort out some of the thorniest issues in economic theory and in the history of economic thought. And he has used this theory as an important building block in his system of economics, which he in turn has integrated into a coherent view of social relationships. For all this we owe him our deepest gratitude.

Over a period of more than a decade, I have participated in a number of seminars and symposiums where I have had the opportunity to hear Professor Rothbard lecture and to discuss economic issues with him on an informal basis. This essay draws heavily from those experiences. It also draws from similar interactions with Israel M. Kirzner, Gerald P. O'Driscoll, Jr., and Leland B. Yeager. Although specific references to the published work of these or other theorists is not provided in the essay, a selected bibliography has been appended.

References

Böhm-Bawerk, Eugen von. *Capital and Interest.* Translated by George D. Huncke and Hans F. Sennholz. 3 vols. South Holland, Ill.: Libertarian Press, 1959.

Cassel, Gustav. *The Nature and Necessity of Interest.* London: Macmillan, 1903.

Clark, John B. *The Distribution of Wealth.* New York: Macmillan, 1899.

Dewey, Donald. *Modern Capital Theory.* New York: Columbia University Press, 1965.

Fetter, Frank A. *Capital, Interest, and Rent: Essays in the Theory of Distribution,* edited with an introduction by Murray N. Rothbard. Kansas City. Kans.: Sheed Andrews and McMeel, 1977.

Fisher, Irving. *The Theory of Interest*. New York: Macmillan, 1930.

Garrison, Roger W. "In Defense of the Misesian Theory of Interest," *Journal of Libertarian Studies* 3, no. 2 (Summer 1979): 141-49.

_____. "Comment: Waiting in Vienna." In *Time, Uncertainty, and Disequilibrium*, edited by Mario J. Rizzo, 215-26. Lexington, MA: D. C. Heath, 1979.

Hayek, Friedrich A. "The Mythology of Capital," *Quarterly Journal of Economics* 50 (February, 1936): 199-228.

_____. "Time-Preference and Productivity: A Reconsideration," *Economica* (n.s.) 1, no. 45 (February, 1945): 22-25.

Hicks, John R. "Is Interest the Price of a Factor of Production?" In *Time, Uncertainty, and Disequilibrium*, edited by Mario J. Rizzo, 51-63. Lexington, Mass.: D. C. Heath, 1979.

Kirzner, Israel M. "Pure Time Preference Theory: A Postscript to the 'Grand Debate,'" manuscript, circa 1983.

Knight, Frank H. "Capital, Time, and the Interest Rate," *Economica* (n.s.) 1, no. 3 (August 1934): 257-86.

_____. "Diminishing Returns from Investment," *Journal of Political Economy* 52, no. 2 (March, 1944): 26-47.

Lutz, Friedrich A. *The Theory of Interest*. Chicago: Aldine Publishing, 1968.

Menger, Carl. *Principles of Economics*. Translated by James Dingwall and Bert F. Hoselitz, with an introduction by F. A. Hayek. New York: New York University Press, 1981.

Mises, Ludwig von. *Human Action: A Treatise on Economics*. 3rd rev. ed. Chicago: Henry Regnery, 1966.

O'Driscoll, Jr., Gerald P. "The Time Preference Theory of Interest Rate Determination." Paper presented at the meetings of the History of Economics Society, Toronto, 1978.

Rothbard, Murray N. *Man, Economy, and State: A Treatise of Economic Principles*. 2 vols. Los Angeles: Nash Publishing, 1970.

Schumpeter, Joseph A. *The Theory of Economic Development*. Oxford: Oxford University Press, 1961.

Yeager, Leland B. "Capital Paradoxes and the Concept of Waiting." In *Time, Uncertainty, and Disequilibrium*, edited by Mario J. Rizzo, 187-214. Lexington, Mass.: D. C. Heath, 1979.

6

From the Economics of Laissez Faire to The Ethics of Libertarianism

Hans-Hermann Hoppe

I

Ludwig von Mises, without a doubt one of the most rigorous defenders in the history of economic thought of a social system of laissez faire unhampered by any governmental intervention, admits to two and only two deficiencies of a pure market system. While according to Mises it is generally true that a market economy produces the highest possible standard of living, this will not happen if any firm succeeds in securing monopoly prices for its goods. And the market cannot itself produce the goods of law and order. Law and order, or the protection of the legal framework underlying the market order, are rather considered by Mises, in current terminology, as "public goods," whose production must be undertaken by the state, which is not itself subject to the discipline of the market, but instead relies on coercion, in particular on compulsory taxation.

When Murray N. Rothbard entered the scene in 1962 with his *Man, Economy, and State* he not only immediately became the foremost student of his revered teacher Ludwig von Mises, but also, standing on the shoulders of this giant, established himself at the age of 36 as an intellectual giant in his own right, going, in truly Misesian spirit, beyond Mises himself. He recognized Mises's position regarding the exceptional character of monopoly prices and public goods as incompatible with the very edifice of subjectivist economic theory as laid down in *Human Action*, and presented, for the first time, a complete and fully consistent economic defense for a pure market system.

Regarding the problem of monopoly prices, Rothbard demonstrated that on the free market no price whatever can be identified as monopolistic or competitive, either by the "monopolist" himself or by any "neutral" outside observer. Economic orthodoxy, which includes Misesian Austrian economics, teaches that monopolistic prices are higher prices attained by restricting production, at which prices sales then bring higher returns than those to be gained by selling an unrestricted output at lower, competitive prices. And, so the story continues, since such restrictive measures which the profit motive impels the monopolist to use would imply that the consumers would have to pay more for less, then existence of monopoly prices provides for the possibility of market failures.[1] As Rothbard points out, there are two related fallacies involved in this reasoning.[2]

First, it must be noted that every restrictive action must, by definition, have a complementary expansionary aspect. The factors of production which the monopolist releases from employment in some production line A do not simply disappear. Rather, they must be used otherwise: either for the production of other exchange goods or for an expansion in the production of the good of leisure for some owner of a labor factor. Now suppose the monopolist restricts production in line A at time t_2 as compared with t_1 and prices and returns indeed go up. Following orthodoxy this would make the higher price at t_2 a monopoly price and the consumers worse off. But is this really the case? Can this situation be distinguished from a situation in which the demand for the product in question changed from t_1 to t_2 (the demand curve shifted to the right)? The answer, of course, is no, since demand curves are never simply "given" for any good. Because of the change in demand for the good in question the competitive price at t_1 has become subcompetitive at t_2, and the higher price at t_2 is simply a move from this subcompetitive to the new competitive price. And the restrictive move of the monopolist also does not imply a worsening of the situation of the consumers, since, by necessity, it must be coupled with a complementary expansionary move in other production lines. The monopolist's restrictive action could not be distinguished from any "normal" change in the production structure that was caused by relative changes in the consumer demand for various goods, including leisure. "There is no way whatever" writes Rothbard, "to distinguish such a 'restriction' and corollary expansion from the alleged 'monopoly price' situation."[3] "But if a concept has no possible grounding in reality, then it is an empty and illusory, and not a meaningful, concept. On the free market there is no way of distinguishing a 'monopoly price' from a 'competitive price' or a 'subcompetitive price,' or of establishing any changes as movements from one to the other. No criteria can be found for making such distinctions. The concept is therefore untenable. We can speak only of the free market price."[4]

Regarding the second alleged imperfection of markets, the problem of public goods, and in particular of the good of law and order, Rothbard demonstrates that the advocates of this position do not succeed in establishing their claim that there are two categorically different types of goods—public and private—for which categorically different types of economic analysis would have to apply; nor, even if this distinction were assumed to hold water, can they furnish any economic reason why such public goods have to be supplied by the state.[5] Orthodoxy holds that certain goods and services, of which law and order are usually considered to be the prototypes, have the special characteristic that their enjoyment cannot be restricted to those persons who actually finance their provision. Such goods are called public goods. And as they cannot, because of this "free rider" problem connected with them, be provided by markets, at least not in sufficient quantity or quality, but are nonetheless without a doubt valued goods, so the argument goes, the state has to jump in to secure their production.[6] In his refutation of this reasoning Rothbard first makes us aware of the following: for something to be an economic good at all it must be scarce and must be realized as scarce by someone. Something is not a good-as-such, that is to say, but goods are goods only in the eyes of some beholder. But then, when goods are never goods-as-such, when no physico-chemical analysis can establish something as an economic good—then there is also no fixed, objective criterion for classifying goods as public or private. They can never be private or public goods as such, but their private or public character depends on how few or how many people consider them goods (or for that matter, bads) with the degree to which they are private or public changing as these evaluations change, and ranging from 1 to infinity. Even seemingly completely private things like the interior of my apartment or the color of my underwear thus can become public goods as soon as somebody starts caring about them. And seemingly public goods like the exterior of my house or the color of my overalls can become extremely private goods as soon as other people stop caring about them. Moreover, every good can change its characteristics again and again; it can even turn from a public or private good to a public or private bad and vice versa, depending solely on the changes in this caring and uncaring. However, if this is so, no decision whatever can be based on the classification of goods as private or public: in fact, if this were done, it would not only become necessary to ask virtually each individual person, with respect to every single good, whether or not one happened to care about it, and if so, to what extent, in order to find out who might profit from what and should hence participate in its financing. It would also become necessary to monitor all changes in such evaluation continually, with the result that no definite decision could ever be made regarding the production of anything, and all of us would be long dead as a consequence of such a nonsensical theory.

Secondly, even if all these difficulties were set aside, the conclusion reached by the public goods theorists is a glaring non sequitur, as Rothbard shows. For one thing, to come to the conclusion that the state has to provide public goods that otherwise would not be produced, one must smuggle a norm into one's chain of reasoning. Otherwise, from the statement that because of some special characteristics certain goods would not be produced, one could never reach the conclusion that these goods *should* be produced. But with a norm being required to justify their conclusion, the public goods theorists clearly have left the bounds of economics as a positive science and transgressed into the field of ethics. None of them, however, offers anything faintly resembling a clear system of ethics. Moreover, even the utilitarian reasoning employed by them is blatantly wrong. It might well be that it would be better to have these public goods than not to have them, though it should not be ignored that there is no *a priori* reason that even this must be so, as it is clearly possible, and indeed known to be a fact, that an anarchist exists who abhors any state action and would rather prefer not having the so-called public goods at all if the alternative is having them provided by the state. But even if the argument thus far is conceded, the conclusion drawn is still invalid. Since in order to finance the supposedly desirable goods resources must be withdrawn from possible alternative uses, the only relevant question is whether or not these alternative uses to which the resources could have been put are more valuable than the value that is attached to the public goods. And the answer to this question is perfectly clear: in terms of consumer evaluations the value of the public goods is relatively lower than that of the competing private goods, because if one leaves the choice to the consumers, they evidently will prefer different ways of spending their money (otherwise no coercion would have been necessary in the first place). This proves that the resources used up for the provision of public goods are wasted in providing consumers with goods and services which are at best only of secondary importance. In short, even if one assumes that public goods exist, they will stand in competition to private ones. To find out if they are more urgently desired or not, and to what extent, there is only one method: analyzing the profit and loss accounts of freely competing private enterprises.

Hence, regarding the provision of law and order, the conclusion is reached that, even if it *is* a public good, the only way to make sure that its production does not take place at the expense of more highly valued private goods and that the kind of law and order that is supplied is indeed the most highly valued one, law and order, like any other good, must be provided by a market of freely competing firms.[7] Rothbard sums it up as follows: the "view (that free-market action must be brought back into optimality by corrective State action) completely misconceives the way in which economic science asserts that free-market action is *ever* optimal. It is optimal, not from the standpoint of the personal ethical views of an economist, but from the standpoint of the free, voluntary actions of all participants and in satisfying the freely expressed needs of the consumers. Government interference, therefore, will necessarily and always move *away* from such an optimum."[8]

II

Yet Rothbard is not content with having developed a full-fledged *economic* defense of a pure market system. He proceeds—culminating in 1982 with his second magnum opus, *The Ethics of Liberty*—to provide us with a comprehensive system of ethics to complement and complete the task of justifying laissez faire.

Mises, along with most social scientists, accepts the Humean verdict that reason is and can be no more than the slave of the passions. That is to say, reason, or science can do no more than inform us whether or not certain means are appropriate for bringing about certain results or ends. It is beyond the powers of reason, though, to teach us what ends we should choose or what ends can or cannot be justified. Ultimately, what ends are chosen is arbitrary from a scientific point of view; a matter of emotional whim. To be sure, Mises then, like most other economists, is in fact committed to some sort of utilitarianism. He favors life over death, health over sickness, abundance over poverty. And insofar as such ends, in particular the goal of achieving the highest possible standard of living for everyone, are indeed shared by other people, as he assumes they generally are, as an economic scientist he then recommends that the correct course of action to choose is a policy of laissez faire.[9] And doubtlessly, insofar as economics can say this much, its case for laissez faire is a highly important one. However, what if people do *not* consider prosperity to be their ultimate goal? As Rothbard points out, economic analysis only establishes that laissez faire will lead to higher standards of living in the long run. In the long run, however, one might be dead. Why then would it not be quite reasonable for a person to argue that while one perfectly agreed with everything economics had to say, one was still more concerned about one's welfare in the short run and there, clearly for no economist to deny, a privilege or a subsidy given to a person would be the nicest thing? Moreover, why should social welfare in the long run be one's first concern at all? Couldn't people advocate poverty, either as an ultimate value in itself or as a means of bringing about some other ultimate value such as equality? The answer, of course, is that things like that could and indeed do happen all the time. But whenever they happen, not only has economics nothing to say, but according to Mises and other utilitarians there is nothing more to be said at all, since there exists no reasonable, scientific way of choosing between conflicting values, as ultimately they are all arbitrary.[10]

Against this position Rothbard takes sides with the philosophical tradition of rational ethics claiming that reason *is* capable of yielding cognitive value statements regarding man's proper ends.[11] More specifically, he aligns himself with the natural law or natural rights tradition of philosophic thought, which holds that universally valid norms can be discerned by means of reason as grounded in the very nature of man.[12] *The Ethics of Liberty* presents the full case for the libertarian property norms being precisely such rules.

Agreeing with Rothbard on the possibility of a rational ethic and, more specifically, on the fact that only a libertarian ethic can indeed be morally justified, I want to propose here a different, non-natural-rights approach to establishing these two related claims. It has been a common quarrel with the natural rights position, even on the part of sympathetic readers, that the concept of human nature is far "too diffuse and varied to provide a determinate set of contents of natural law."[13] Furthermore, its description of rationality is equally ambiguous in that it does not seem to distinguish between the role of reason in establishing empirical laws of nature on the one hand and normative laws of human conduct on the other.[14] Avoiding such difficulties from the outset, I claim the following approach to be at once more straightforward and more rigorous as regards its starting point as well as its methods of deriving its conclusions. Moreover, as I will indicate later, my approach also seems to be more in line with what Rothbard actually does when it comes to justifying the specific norms of libertarianism than the rather vague methodological prescriptions of the natural rights theorists.[15]

Let me start with the question: what is wrong with the position taken by Mises and so many others that the choice between values is ultimately arbitrary? First, it should be noted that such a position assumes that at least the question of whether or not value judgments or normative statements can be justified is itself a cognitive problem. If this were not assumed, Mises could not even say what he evidently says and claims to be the case. His position simply could not exist as an arguable intellectual position.

At first glance this does not seem to take one very far. It still seems to be a far cry from this insight to the actual proof that normative statements can be justified and, moreover that it is only the libertarian ethic which can be defended. This impression is wrong, however, and there is already much more won here than might be suspected. The argument shows us that any truth claim, the claim connected with any proposition that it is true, objective or valid (all terms used synonymously here), is and must be raised and decided upon in the course of an argumentation. And since it cannot be disputed that this is so (one cannot communicate and argue that one cannot communicate and argue), and it must be assumed that everyone knows what it means to claim something to be true (one cannot deny this statement without claiming its negation to be true), this very fact has been aptly called "the a priori of communication and argumentation."[16]

Now arguing never consists of just free-floating propositions claiming to be true. Rather, argumentation is always an activity, too. But then, given that truth claims are raised and decided upon in argumentation and that argumentation, aside from whatever it is that is said in its course, is a practical affair, then it follows that intersubjectively meaningful norms must exist—precisely those which make some action an argumentation—which have a special cognitive status in that they are the practical preconditions of objectivity and truth.

Hence, one reaches the conclusion that norms must indeed be assumed to be justifiable as valid. It is simply impossible to argue otherwise, because the ability to argue so would in fact already presuppose the validity of those norms which underlie any argumentation whatever. In contradistinction to the natural rights theorists, though, one sees that the answer to the question of which ends can or cannot be justified is not to be read off from the wider concept of human nature but from the narrower one of argumentation.[17] And with this, then, the peculiar role of reason in determining the contents of ethics can be given a precise description; in clear contrast to the role of reason in establishing empirical laws of nature, in determining moral laws reason can claim to yield results which can be shown to be valid *a priori*. It only makes explicit what is already implied in the concept of argumentation itself; and in analyzing any actual norm proposal its task is merely confined to analyzing whether or not it is logically consistent with the very ethics which the proponent must presuppose as valid insofar as he is able to make his proposal at all.[18]

But what is the ethics implied in argumentation whose validity cannot be disputed, as disputing it would implicitly have to presuppose it? Quite normally it has been observed that argumentation implies that a proposition claims universal acceptability or, should it be a norm proposal, that it be "universalizable." Applied to norm proposals, this is the idea, as formulated in the Golden Rule of ethics or in the Kantian Categorical Imperative, that only those norms can be justified that can be formulated as general principles which without exception are valid for everyone.[19] Indeed, as it is implied in argumentation that everyone who can understand an argument must in principle be able to be convinced by it simply because of its argumentative force, the universalization principle of ethics can now be understood and explained as implied in the wider *a priori* of communication and argumentation.[20] Yet the universalization principle only provides one with a purely formal criterion for morality. To be sure, checked against this criterion all proposals for valid norms which would specify different rules for different classes of people could be shown to have no legitimate claim of being universally acceptable as fair norms, unless the distinction between different classes of people were such that it implied no discrimination but could rather be accepted as founded in the nature of things again by everybody. But while some norms might not pass the test of universalization, if enough attention were paid to their formulation the most ridiculous norms, and what is more relevant, even openly incompatible norms could easily and equally well pass it. For example, "everybody must get drunk on Sundays or else he will be fined" or "anyone who drinks any alcohol will be punished" are both rules that do not allow discrimination among groups of people and thus could both claim to satisfy the condition of universalization.

Clearly then, the universalization principle alone would not provide one with any positive set of norms that could be demonstrated to be justified. However, there are other positive norms implied in argumentation apart from the universalization principle. In order to recognize them, it is only necessary to call to attention three interrelated facts. First, that argumentation is not only a cognitive but also a practical affair. Second, that argumentation, as a form of action, implies the use of the scarce resource of one's body. And third, that argumentation is a conflict-free way of interacting. Not in the sense that there is always agreement on the things said, but rather in the sense that as long as argumentation is in progress it is always possible to agree at least on the fact that there is disagreement about the validity of what has been said. And this is to say nothing else than that a mutual recognition of each person's exclusive control over his own body must be assumed to exist as long as there is argumentation (note again, that it is impossible to deny this and claim this denial to be true without implicitly having to admit its truth).

Hence, one would have to conclude that the norm implied in argumentation is that everybody has the right to exclusively control his own body as his instrument of action and cognition. It is only as long as there is at least an implicit recognition of each individual's property right in his or her own body that argumentation can take place.[21] Only as long as this right is recognized is it possible for someone to agree to what has been said in an argument and hence what has been said can be validated, or is it possible to say "no" and to agree only on the fact that there is disagreement. Indeed, anyone who would try to justify any norm would already have to presuppose the property right in one's body as a valid norm, simply in order to say "this is what I claim to be true and objective." Any person who would try to dispute the property right in one's own body would become caught up in a contradiction.

Thus it can be stated that whenever a person claims that some statement can be justified, he at least implicitly assumes the following norm to be justified: "nobody has the right to uninvitedly aggress against the body of any other person and thus delimit or restrict anyone's control over his own body." This rule is implied in the concept of argumentative justification. Justifying means justifying without having to rely on coercion. In fact, if one would formulate the opposite of this rule, i.e., everybody has the right to uninvitedly aggress against other people (a rule, by the way, that would formally pass the universalization test!), then it is easy to see that this rule is not, and never could be defended in argumentation. To do so would in fact have to presuppose the validity of precisely its opposite, i.e., the aforementioned principle of non-aggression.

It may seem that with this justification of a property norm regarding a person's body not much is won, as conflicts over bodies, for whose possible avoidance the non-aggression principle formulates a universally justifiable solution, make up only a small portion of all possible conflicts. However, this impression is not correct. To be sure, people do not live on air and love alone. They need a smaller or greater number of other things as well simply to survive—and only he who survives can sustain an argumentation—let alone lead a comfortable life. With respect to all of these other things norms are needed too, as it could come to conflicting evaluations regarding their use. But in fact, any other norm now must be logically compatible with the non-aggression principle in order to be justified itself and, *mutatis mutandis*, every norm that could be shown to be incompatible with this principle would have to be considered invalid. In addition, as the things for which norms have to be formulated are scarce goods—just as a person's body is a scarce good—and as it is only necessary to formulate norms at all because goods are scarce and not because they are particular kinds of scarce goods, the specifications of the non-aggression principle, conceived of as a special property norm referring to a specific kind of good, must already contain those of a general theory of property.

I will first state this general theory of property as a set of rulings applicable to all goods, with the purpose of helping to avoid all possible conflicts by means of uniform principles, and will then demonstrate how this general theory is implied in the non-aggression principle. As according to the non-aggression principle a person can do with his body whatever he wants as long as he does not thereby aggress against another person's body, that person could also make use of other scarce means, just as one makes use of one's own body, provided these other things have not already been appropriated by someone else but are still in a natural unowned state. As soon as scarce resources are visibly appropriated—as soon as somebody "mixes his labor," as John Locke phrased it,[22] with them and there are objective traces of this—then property, i.e., the right of exclusive control, can only be acquired by a contractual transfer of property titles from a previous to a later owner, and any attempt to unilaterally delimit this exclusive control of previous owners or any unsolicited transformation of the physical characteristics of the scarce means in question is, in strict analogy with aggressions against other people's bodies, an unjustifiable action.[23]

The compatibility of this principle with that of non-aggression can be demonstrated by means of an *argumentum a contrario*. First, it should be noted that if no one had the right to acquire and control anything except his own body (a rule that would pass the formal universalization test), then we would all cease to exist and the problem of the justification or normative statements simply would not exist. The existence of this problem is only possible because we are alive, and our existence is due to the fact that we do not, indeed cannot accept a norm outlawing property in other scarce goods next to and in addition to that of one's physical body. Hence, the right to acquire such goods must be assumed to exist. Now if this were so, and if one did *not* have the right to acquire such rights of exclusive control over unused, nature-given things through one's own work, i.e., by doing something with things with which no one else had ever done anything before, and if other people *had* the right to disregard one's ownership claim to things which they did not work on or put to some particular use before, then this would only be possible if one could acquire property titles not through labor, i.e., by establishing some objective, intersubjectively controllable link between a particular person and a particular scarce resource, but simply by verbal declaration, by decree.[24] However, the position of property titles being acquired through declaration is incompatible with the above justified non-aggression principle regarding bodies. For one thing, if one could indeed appropriate property by decree, then this would imply that it also would be possible for one to simply declare another person's body to be one's own. Yet this, clearly enough, would conflict with the ruling of the non-aggression principle which makes a sharp distinction between one's own body and the body of another person. And this distinction can only be made in such a clear-cut and unambiguous way because for bodies, as for anything else, the separation between "mine" and "yours" is not based on verbal declarations, but on action. The observation is based on some particular scarce resource that had in fact—for everyone to see and verify, as objective indicators for this existed—been made an expression or materialization of one's own will or, as the case may be, of somebody else's will. Moreover, and more importantly, to say that property is acquired not through action but through a declaration involves an open practical contradiction, because nobody could say and declare so unless his right of exclusive control over his body as his own instrument of saying anything was in fact already presupposed, in spite of what was actually said.

And as I intimated earlier, this defense of private property is essentially also Rothbard's. In spite of his formal allegiance to the natural rights tradition Rothbard, in what I consider his most crucial argument in defense of a private property ethic, not only chooses essentially the same starting point—argumentation—but also gives a justification by means of *a priori* reasoning almost identical to the one just developed. To prove the point I can do no better than simply quote: "Now, *any* person participating in any sort of discussion, including one on values, is, by virtue of so participating, alive and affirming life. For if he were *really* opposed to life he would have no business continuing to be alive. Hence, the *supposed* opponent of life is really affirming it in the very process of discussion, and hence the preservation and furtherance of one's life takes on the stature of an incontestable axiom."[25]

III

So far it has been demonstrated that the right of original appropriation through actions is compatible with and implied in the non-aggression principle as the logically necessary presupposition of argumentation. Indirectly, of course, it has also been demonstrated that any rule specifying different rights cannot be justified. Before entering a more detailed analysis, though, of *why* it is that any alternative ethic is indefensible, a discussion which should throw some additional light on the importance of some of the stipulations of the libertarian theory of property, a few remarks about what is and what is not implied by classifying these latter norms as justified seems to be in order.

In making this argument, one would not have to claim to have derived an "ought" from an "is." In fact, one can readily subscribe to the almost generally accepted view that the gulf between "ought" and "is" is logically unbridgeable.[26] Rather, classifying the rulings of the libertarian theory of property in this way is a purely cognitive matter. It no more follows from the classification of the libertarian ethic as "fair," "just," etc., that one ought to act according to it, than it follows from the concept of validity, truth, etc., that one should always strive for it. To say that it is just also does not preclude the possibility of people proposing or even enforcing rules that are incompatible with this principle. As a matter of fact, the situation with respect to norms is very similar to that in other disciplines of scientific inquiry. The fact, for instance, that certain empirical statements are justified or justifiable and others are not does not imply that everybody only defends objective, valid statements. Rather, people can be wrong, even intentionally. But the distinction between objective and subjective, between true and false, does not lose any of its significance because of this. Rather, people who do so would have to be classified as either uninformed or intentionally lying. The case is similar with respect to norms. Of course there are people, lots of them, who do not propagate or enforce norms which can be classified as valid according to the meaning of justification which I have given above. But the distinction between justifiable and nonjustifiable norms does not dissolve because of this, just as that between objective and subjective statement does not crumble because of the existence of uninformed or lying people. Rather, and accordingly, those people who would propagate and enforce such different, invalid norms would again have to be classified as uninformed or dishonest, insofar as one had made it clear to them that their alternative norm proposals or enforcements cannot and never will be justifiable in argumentation. And there would be even more justification for doing so in the moral case than in the empirical, since the validity of the non-aggression principle, and that of the principle of original appropriation through action as its logically necessary corollary, must be considered to be even more basic than any kind of valid or true statements. For what is valid or true has to be defined as that upon which everyone— acting according to this principle—can possibly agree. As I have just shown, at least the implicit acceptance of these rules is the necessary prerequisite to being able to be alive and argue at all.

Why is it then, precisely, that other non-libertarian property theories fail to be justifiable? First, it should be noted, as will become clear shortly, that all of the actually *practiced* alternatives to libertarianism and most of the theoretically proposed non-libertarian ethics would not even pass the first formal universalization test, and would fail for this fact alone! All these versions contain norms within their framework of legal rules which have the form "some people do, and some people do not." However, such rules, which specify different rights or obligations for different classes of people have no chance of being accepted as fair by every potential participant in an argument for simply formal reasons. Unless the distinction made between different classes of people happens to be such that it is acceptable to both sides as grounded in the nature of things, such rules would not be acceptable because they would imply that one group is awarded legal privileges at the expense of complementary discriminations against another group. Some people, either those who are allowed to do something or those who are not, therefore could not agree that these were fair rules.[27] Since most alternative ethical proposals, as practiced or preached, have to rely on the enforcement of rules such as "some people have the obligation to pay taxes, and others have the right to consume them," or "some people know what is good for you and are allowed to help you get these alleged blessings even if you do not want them, but you are not allowed to know what is good for them and help them accordingly," or "some people have the right to determine who has too much of something and who too little, and others have the obligation to follow suit," or even more plainly, "the computer industry must pay to subsidize the farmers," "the employed for the unemployed," "the ones without kids for those with kids," etc., or vice versa. They all can be discarded easily as serious contenders to the claim of being a valid theory of norms *qua* property norms, because they all indicate by their very formulation that they are not universalizable.

But what is wrong with a non-libertarian ethic if this is taken care of and there is indeed a theory formulated that contains exclusively universalizable norms of the type "nobody is allowed to" or "everybody can?" Even then such proposals could never hope to prove their validity—no longer on formal grounds, but rather because of their material specifications. Indeed, while the alternatives that can be refuted easily as regards their claim to moral validity on simple formal grounds can at least be practiced, the application of those more sophisticated versions that would pass the universalization test would prove for material reasons to be fatal: even if one would try, they simply could never be put into effect.

There are two related specifications in the libertarian property theory with at least one of which any alternative theory comes into conflict. According to the libertarian ethic, the first such specification is that aggression is defined as an invasion of the *physical* integrity of other people's property.[28] There are popular attempts, instead, to define it as an invasion of the *value* or *psychic integrity* of other people's property. Conservatism, for instance, aims at preserving a given distribution of wealth and values, and attempts to bring those forces which could change the status quo under control by means of price controls, regulations, and behavioral controls. Clearly, in order to do so property rights to the value of things must be assumed to be justifiable, and an invasion of values, *mutatis mutandis*, would have to be classified as unjustifiable aggression. Not only conservatism uses this idea of property and aggression; redistributive socialism does, too. Property rights to values must be assumed to be legitimate when redistributive socialism allows me, for instance, to demand compensation from people whose chances or opportunities negatively affect mine. And the same is true when compensation for committing psychological, or what has become a particularly dear term in the leftist political science literature, "structural violence" is requested.[29] In order to be able to ask for such compensation, what one must have done—affecting my opportunities, my psychic integrity, my feeling of what is owed to me—would have to be classified as an aggressive act.

Why is this idea of protecting the value of property unjustifiable? First, while every person, at least in principle, can have full control over whether or not his actions cause the *physical* characteristics of something to change, and hence also can have full control over whether or not those actions are justifiable, control over whether or not one's actions affect the *value* of somebody else's property does not rest with the acting person, but rather with other people and their sub-jective evaluations. Thus no one could determine *ex ante* if his actions would be qualified as justifiable or unjustifiable. One would first have to interrogate the whole population to make sure that one's planned actions would not change another person's evaluations regarding his own property. And even then nobody could act until universal agree-ment was reached on who is supposed to do what with what, and at which point in time. Clearly, for all the practical problems involved one would be long dead and nobody could argue anything any longer, long before this were ever accomplished.[30] But more decisively still, this position regarding property and aggression could not even be effectively *argued*, because arguing in favor of any norm implies that there is conflict over the use of some scarce resources, otherwise there would simply be no need for discussion. However, in order to argue that there is a way out of such conflicts it must be presupposed that ac-tions must be allowed *prior* to any actual agreement or disagreement, because if they were not, one could not even argue so. Yet if one can do this, and insofar as it exists as an argued intellectual position the posi-tion under scrutiny must assume that one can, then this is only pos-sible because of the existence of *objective* borders of property—borders which anyone can recognize as such on his own without having to agree first with anyone else with respect to his system of values and evaluations. Such a value-protecting ethic, too, then, in spite of what it says, must in fact presuppose the existence of objective property borders, rather than of borders determined by subjective evaluations, if only in order to have any surviving persons who can make its moral proposals.

The idea of protecting value instead of physical integrity also fails for a second, related reason. Evidently, one's value, for example on the labor or marriage market, can be and indeed is affected by other peo-ple's physical integrity or degree of physical integrity. Thus, if one wanted property values to be protected, one would have to allow phys-ical aggression against people. However, it is only because of the very fact that a person's borders—that is the borders of a person's property in his own body as his domain of exclusive control that another person is not allowed to cross unless he wishes to become an aggressor—are *phys-ical* borders (intersubjectively ascertainable, and not just subjectively fan-cied borders) that everyone can agree on anything independently (and, of course, agreement means agreement among independent decision-

making units!). Only because the protected borders of property are objective then, i.e., fixed and recognizable as fixed prior to any conventional agreement, can there at all be argumentation and possibly agreement of and between independent decision-making units. Nobody
could argue in favor of a property system defining borders of property
in subjective, evaluative terms, because simply to be able to say so
presupposes that, contrary to what theory says, one must *in fact* be a
physically independent unit saying it.

The situation is no less dire for alternative ethical proposals when
one turns to the second essential specification of the rulings of the libertarian theory of property. The basic norms of libertarianism were
characterized not only by the fact that property and aggression were
defined in physical terms; it was of no less importance that property
was defined as private, individualized property and that the meaning
of original appropriation, which evidently implies making a distinction
between prior and later, had been specified. It is with this additional
specification as well that alternative, non-libertarian ethics come into
conflict. Instead of recognizing the vital importance of the prior-later
distinction in deciding between conflicting property claims, they propose
norms which in effect state that priority is irrelevant for making such a
decision and that late-comers have as much of a right to ownership as
first-comers. Clearly, this idea is involved when redistributive socialism,
for instance, makes the natural owners of wealth and/or their heirs
pay a tax in order for the unfortunate late-comers to be able to participate in its consumption. And it is also involved, for instance, when the
owner of a natural resource is forced to reduce (or increase) its present
exploitation in the interest of posterity. Both times it only makes sense
to do what one does when it is assumed that the person accumulating
wealth first, or using the natural resource first, has thereby committed
an aggression against some late-comers. If they had done nothing
wrong, then the late-comers could have no such claim against them.[31]

What is wrong with this idea of dropping the prior-later distinction
as morally irrelevant? First, if the late-comers, i.e., those who did not
in fact do something with some scarce goods, had indeed as much of a
right to them as the first-comers, who *did* do something with the scarce
goods, then literally nobody would be allowed to do anything with
anything, as one would have to have all of the late-comers' consent
prior to doing what one wants to do. Indeed, as posterity would include one's childrens' children—people, that is, who come so late that
one could not possibly ask them—to advocate a legal system that does
not make use of the prior-later distinction as part of its underlying

property theory is simply absurd in that it implies advocating death but must presuppose life to advocate anything. Neither we, our forefathers, nor our progeny could, do or will survive and say or argue anything if one were to follow this rule. In order for any person—past, present or future—to argue anything it must be possible to survive now. Nobody can wait and suspend acting until everyone of an indeterminate class of late-comers happens to come around and agree to doing what one wants to do. Rather, insofar as a person finds himself alone, he must be able to act, to use, produce, and consume goods straightaway, prior to any agreement with people who are simply not around yet (and perhaps never will be). And insofar as a person finds himself in the company of others and there is conflict over how to use a given scarce resource, he must be able to resolve the problem at a definite point in time with a definite number of people instead of having to wait unspecified periods of time for unspecified numbers of people. Simply in order to survive, then, which is a prerequisite to arguing in favor or against anything, property rights can not be conceived of as being timeless and nonspecific regarding the number of people concerned. Rather, they must necessarily be thought of as originating through acting at definite points in time for definite acting individuals.[32]

Furthermore, the idea of abandoning the prior-later distinction would simply be incompatible with the non-aggression principle as the practical foundation of argumentation. To argue and possibly agree with someone (if only on the fact that there is disagreement) means to recognize the prior right of exclusive control over one's own body. Otherwise, it would be impossible for anybody to first say anything at a definite point in time and for someone else to then be able to reply, or vice versa, as neither the first nor the second speaker would be a physically independent decision-making unit anymore, at any time. Eliminating the prior-later distinction, then, is tantamount to eliminating the possibility of arguing and reaching agreement. However, as one can not argue that there is no possibility for discussion without the prior control of every person over his own body being recognized and accepted as fair, a late-comer ethic that does not wish to make this difference could never be agreed upon by anyone. Simply *saying* that it could be, would imply a contradiction, as one's being able to say so would presuppose one's existence as an independent decision-making unit at a definite point in time.

Hence, one is forced to conclude that the libertarian ethic not only can be justified, and justified by means of *a priori* reasoning, but that no alternative ethic can be defended argumentatively.

Notes

1. See Ludwig von Mises, *Human Action*, 3rd rev. ed. (Chicago: Contemporary Books, 1966), p. 357ff.; idem, "Profit and Loss," in *Planning for Freedom* (South Holland, IL: Libertarian Press, 1974), esp. p. 116. In this essay Mises takes a somewhat different, one might say, a proto-Rothbardian position.

2. See Murray N. Rothbard, *Man, Economy, and State* (Los Angeles: Nash Publishing, 1972), chap. 10, esp. pp. 604-14.

3. Ibid., p. 607.

4. Ibid., p. 614. See also Walter Block, "Austrian Monopoly Theory: A Critique," *Journal of Libertarian Studies* 1 (Fall 1977): 271-81; Hans-Hermann Hoppe, *Eigentum, Anarchie und Staat* (Opladen: Westdeutscher Verlag, 1987), chap. 5; idem, *Theory of Socialism and Capitalism* (Boston: Kluwer, 1988), chap. 9.

5. See Rothbard, *Man, Economy, and State*, pp. 883-90; idem, "The Myth of Neutral Taxation," *Cato Journal* (Fall 1981): 519-65.

6. Mises, of course, is by no means a completely orthodox public goods theorist. He does not share their and the public choice theorists' commonly held naive view of the government being some sort of voluntary organization. Rather, and unmistakably so he says "the essential feature of government is the enforcement of its decrees by beating, killing, and imprisoning. Those who are asking for more government interference are asking ultimately for more compulsion and less freedom," (*Human Action*, p. 719). On this see also the refreshingly realistic assessment by Joseph Schumpeter, (*Capitalism, Socialism and Democracy* (New York: Harper and Bros., 1942), p. 198), that "the theory which construes taxes on the analogy of club dues or the purchase of a service of, say, a doctor only proves how far removed this part of the social sciences is from scientific habits of minds." Nor does Mises overlook, as they almost invariably do, the multitude of fallacies involved in today's fashionable economic literature on "externalities," (*Human Action*, pp. 654-661). When nonetheless Mises's position is classified as orthodox here, this is due to the fact that he, in this respect not differing from the rest of the public goods theorists, dogmatically assumes that certain goods (law and order, in his case) cannot be provided by freely competing industries; and that he, too, with respect to law and order at least, "proves" the necessity of a government by a *non sequitur*. Thus, in his "refutation" of anarchism he writes: "Society cannot exist if the majority is not ready to hinder, by the application or threat of violent action, minorities from destroying the social order. This power is vested in the state or government," (ibid, p. 149). But clearly, from the first statement the second one does not follow. Why cannot private protection agencies do the job?! And why would the government be able to do the job better than such agencies?! Here the reader looks in vain for answers.

7. On the specific problem of a free market provision of law and order see Murray N. Rothbard, *For A New Liberty*, rev. ed. (New York: Collier, 1978), chap. 12; idem, *Power and Market* (Kansas City: Sheed Andrews and McMeel, 1977), chap. 1; also G. de Molinari *The Production of Security*, Occasional Paper No. 2 (1849; reprint, New York: Center for Libertarian Studies, 1977).

8. Rothbard, *Man, Economy, and State*, p. 887; see on the above also Walter Block, "Public Goods and Externalities: The Case of Roads," *Journal of Libertarian Studies* 7 (Spring 1983): 1-34; Hans-Hermann Hoppe, *Eigentum, Anarchie und Staat*, chap. 1; idem, *Theory of Socialism and Capitalism*, chap. 10.

9. On this see Mises, *Human Action*, pp. 153-55.

10. For Rothbard's Mises-critique see Murray N. Rothbard, *The Ethics of Liberty* (Atlantic Highlands, N.J.: Humanities Press, 1982), pp. 205-12.

11. For various "cognitivist" approaches towards ethics see, Kurt Baier, *The Moral Point of View: A Rational Basis of Ethics* (Ithaca, N.Y.: Cornell University Press, 1958); M. Singer, *Generalization in Ethics* (New York: A. Knopf, 1961); P. Lorenzen, *Normative Logic and Ethics* (Mannheim: Bibliographisches Institut, 1969); S. Toulmin, *The Place of Reason in Ethics* (Cambridge: Cambridge University Press, 1970); F. Kambartel, ed., *Praktische Philosophie und konstruktive Wissenschaftstheorie* (Frankfurt/M.: Athenaeum, 1974); Alan Gewirth, *Reason and Morality* (Chicago: University of Chicago Press, 1978).

12. On the natural rights tradition see, J. Wild, *Plato's Modern Enemies and the Theory of Natural Law* (Chicago: University of Chicago Press, 1953); Henry Veatch, *Rational Man: A Modern Interpretation of Aristotelian Ethics* (Bloomington, Ind.: Indiana University Press, 1962); idem, *For An Ontology of Morals: A Critique of Contemporary Ethical Theory* (Evanston, Ill.: Northwestern University Press, 1971); idem, *Human Rights: Fact or Fancy?* (Baton Rouge, La.: Louisiana State University Press, 1985).

13. Alan Gewirth, "Law, Action, and Morality," in Rocco Porreco, ed., *Georgetown Symposium on Ethics: Essays in Honor of Henry Babcock Veatch* (New York: University Press of America, 1984), p. 73.

14. See the discussion in Veatch, *Human Rights*, pp. 62-67.

15. To disassociate myself from the natural rights tradition is not to say that I could not agree with its critical assessment of most of contemporary ethical theory—indeed I do agree with Veatch's complementary refutation of all desire—(teleological, utilitarian) ethics as well as all duty—(deontological), ethics, ibid., chap. 1. Nor, then, do I claim that it is impossible to interpret my approach as falling in a "rightly conceived" natural rights tradition after all (see also footnote 17 below). What is claimed, though, is that the following approach is clearly out of line with what the natural rights approach has actually come to be, and that it owes nothing to this tradition as it stands.

16. See K. O. Apel, "Das Apriori der Kommunikationsgemeinschaft und die Grundlagen der Ethik," vol. 2, *Transformation der Philosophie* (Frankfurt/M.: Suhrkamp, 1973); also Jürgen Habermas, "Wahrheitstheorien," in H. Fahrenbach, ed., *Wirklichkeit und Reflexion* (Pfullingen: Neske, 1974; idem, *Theorie des kommunikativen Handelns*, vol. 1 (Frankfurt/M.: Suhrkamp, 1981), pp. 44ff; idem, *Moralbewusstsein und kommunikatives Handeln* (Frankfurt/M.: Suhrkamp, 1983).

17. Of course, then, since the capability of argumentation is an essential part of human nature—one could not even say anything about the latter without the former—it could also be argued that norms which cannot be defended effectively in the course of argumentation are also incompatible with human nature.

18. Methodologically, this approach exhibits a close resemblance to what Gewirth has described as the "dialectically necessary method," (*Reason and Morality*, pp. 42-47)—a method of *a priori* reasoning modelled after the Kantian idea of transcendental deductions. Unfortunately though, in his important study Gewirth chooses the wrong starting point for his analyses. He attempts to derive an ethical system not from the concept of argumentation but from that of action. However, surely this cannot work, because from the correctly stated fact that in action an agent must, by necessity, presuppose the existence of certain values or goods, it does not follow that such goods then are universalizable and hence should be respected by others as the agent's goods by right. (Gewirth might have noticed the ethical "neutrality" of action had he not been painfully unaware of the existence of the well-established "pure science of action" or "praxeology" as espoused by Mises. And incidentally, an awareness of praxeology also might have spared him many mistakes that derive from his faulty distinction between "basic," "additive" and "non-subtractive" goods (ibid, pp. 53-58).) Rather, the idea of truth, or of universalizable rights or goods only emerges with argumentation as a special subclass of actions,

but not with action as such, as is clearly revealed by the fact that Gewirth, too, is not engaged simply in action, but more specifically in argumentation when he wants to convince us of the necessary truth of his ethical system. However, with argumentation being recognized as the one and only appropriate starting point for the dialectically necessary method, a libertarian (i.e. non-Gewirthian) ethic follows, as will be seen.

On the faultiness of Gewirth's attempt to derive universalizable rights from the notion of action see also the perceptive remarks by Alasdair MacIntyre, *After Virtue: A Study in Moral Theory* (London: Duckworth, 1981), pp. 64-5; Habermas, *Moralbewusstsein und kommunikatives Handeln*, pp. 110-11; and Veatch, *Human Rights*, pp. 159-60.

19. See the works cited in footnotes 11 and 12 above.

20. See the works cited in footnote 16 above.

21. It might be noted here that only because scarcity exists is there even a problem of formulating moral laws; insofar as goods are superabundant ("free" goods) no conflict over the use of goods is possible and no action-coordination is needed. Hence, it follows that *any* ethic, correctly conceived, must be formulated as a theory of property, i.e., a theory of the assignment of rights of exclusive control over scarce means. Because only then does it become possible to avoid otherwise inescapable and unresolvable conflicts. Unfortunately, moral philosophers in their widespread ignorance of economics have hardly ever seen this clearly enough. Rather, like Veatch (*Human Rights*, p. 170), for instance, they seem to think that they can do without a precise definition of property and property rights only to then necessarily wind up in a sea of vagueness and ad-hoceries.

On human rights as property rights see also Rothbard, *The Ethics of Liberty*, chap. 15.

22. John Locke, *Two Treatises on Government*, edited by Peter Laslett (Cambridge: Cambridge University Press, 1970), esp. vols. II, V.

23. On the non-aggression principle and the principle of original appropriation see also Rothbard, *For a New Liberty*, chap. 2; idem, *The Ethics of Liberty*, chaps. 6-8.

24. This, for instance, is the position taken by Jean-Jacques Rousseau, when he asks us to resist attempts to privately appropriate nature-given resources by, for example, fencing them in. He says in his famous dictum " 'Beware of listening to this impostor; you are undone if you once forget that the fruits of the earth belong to us all, and the earth itself to nobody.' " "Discourse upon the Origin and Foundation of Inequality Among Mankind," Jean-Jacques Rousseau (*The Social Contract and Discourses*, edited by G. Cole [New York: 1950], p. 235). However, to argue so is only possible if it is assumed that property claims can be justified by decree. Because how else could "all" (i.e., even those, who never did anything with the resources in question) or "nobody" (i.e., even those not, who actually made use of it) own something—unless property claims were founded by mere decree?!

25. Rothbard, *The Ethics of Liberty*, p. 32; on the method of *a priori* reasoning employed in the above argument see also, idem, *Individualism and the Philosophy of the Social Sciences*, (San Francisco: Cato Institute, 1979); Hoppe, *Kritik der kausalwissenschaftlichen Sozialforschung. Untersuchungen zur Grundlegung von Soziologie und Okonomie* (Opladen: Westdeutscher Verlag 1983); idem "Is Research Based on Causal Scientific Principles Possible in the Social Sciences?" *Ratio* 1 (1983); idem, *Theory of Socialism and Capitalism*, chap. 6.

26. On the problem of deriving "ought" from "is" see W. D. Hudson, ed., *The Is-Ought Question*, (London: Macmillan, 1969).

27. See Rothbard, *The Ethics of Liberty*, p. 45.

28. On the importance of the definition of aggression as *physical* aggression see also Rothbard, ibid., chaps. 8-9; idem, "Law, Property Rights and Air Pollution" *Cato Journal* (Spring 1982): 60-3.

29. On the idea of structural violence as distinct from physical violence see D. Seng-haas, ed., *Imperialismus und strukturelle Gewalt* (Frankfurt/M.: Suhrkamp, 1972).

The idea of defining aggression as an invasion of property *values* also underlies both the theories of justice of John Rawls and Robert Nozick, however different these two authors may have appeared to be to many commentators. For how could Rawls think of his so-called difference-principle ("Social and economic inequalities are to be arranged so that they are . . . reasonably expected to be to everyone's—including the least advantaged one's—advantage or benefit," (from John Rawls, *A Theory of Justice* (Cambridge, Mass.: Belknap Press 1971), pp. 60-83); ibid., p. 75ff, as justified, unless he believes that simply by increasing his relative wealth a more fortunate person commits an aggression, and a less fortunate one then has a valid claim against the more fortunate person only because the former's relative position in terms of value has deteriorated?! And how could Nozick claim it to be justified for a "dominant protection agency" to outlaw competitors, regardless of what their actions would have been like? (Robert Nozick, *Anarchy, State and Utopia* (New York: Basic Books, 1974), pp. 55f.) Or how could he believe it to be morally correct to outlaw so-called non-productive exchanges, i.e., exchanges where one party would be better off if the other one did not exist at all, or at least had nothing to do with it (as, for instance, in the case of a blackmailee and a blackmailer), regardless of whether or not such an exchange involved physical invasion of any kind (ibid., pp. 83-6), unless he thought that the right to have the integrity of one's property *values* (rather than its physical integrity) preserved existed?! For a devastating critique of Nozick's theory in particular see Rothbard, *The Ethics of Liberty*, chap 29; on the fallacious use of the indifference curve analysis, employed both by Rawls and Nozick, idem, *Toward a Reconstruction of Utility and Welfare Economics*," Occasional Paper No. 3 (New York: Center for Libertarian Studies, 1977).

30. See also Rothbard, *The Ethics of Liberty*, p. 46.

31. For an awkward philosophical attempt to justify a late-comer ethic see James P. Sterba, *The Demands of Justice* (Notre Dame: Notre Dame University Press, 1980), esp. pp. 58ff, 137ff; on the absurdity of such an ethic see Rothbard, *Man, Economy, and State*, p. 427.

32. It should be noted here, too, that only if property rights are conceptualized as private property rights originating in time, does it then become possible to make contracts. Clearly enough, contracts are agreements between enumerable physically independent units which are based on the mutual recognition of each contractor's private ownership claims to things acquired prior in time to the agreement, and which then concern the transfer of property titles to definite things from a definite prior to a definite later owner. No such thing as contracts could conceivably exist in the framework of a late-comer ethic!

7

Welfare Economics:
A Modern Austrian Perspective

0315
0240

Israel M. Kirzner

Among the most notable of Murray Rothbard's many contributions
to the literature of modern Austrian economics, is surely the
major paper on utility and welfare theory that he wrote for the 1956
Mises Festschrift.[1] This writer can personally attest to the excitement
engendered by the lucid manner in which this paper deployed Austrian insights to illuminate fundamental theoretical issues (concerning
which contemporary economics was floundering), and by the characteristic erudition which Rothbard poured into that single essay.
Whether or not one fully accepted Rothbard's conclusions, it was impossible not to glimpse the power of consistent Misesian thinking
which that paper so excellently exemplified. The present paper, written
thirty years later, seeks to reexamine a small part of the terrain covered
by Rothbard's essay. In offering a modern Austrian perspective on welfare economics we shall be emphasizing some of the same basic Austrian
tenets that Rothbard so rightly insisted on thirty years ago. While our
perspective may not entirely dovetail with some of Rothbard's conclusions, we venture to hope that our observations concerning welfare
economics be judged to be in the same subjectivist, methodologically
individualistic tradition that Rothbard's work has so valuably carried
forward for so many years.

Some Observations Concerning Welfare Economics

Welfare economics has, in its numerous incarnations, sought to offer
criteria by which it might be possible scientifically to evaluate the economic merits of specific institutions, pieces of legislation or events.
Such evaluation would have to transcend the narrow economic con-

77

cerns of specific individuals whose interests might be involved, and to express, somehow, a perspective flowing from the economic interests of all individuals in society. As we shall see, Austrian economists have been particularly sensitive to the difficulties that must beset such an undertaking. Indeed, many of the difficulties have been recognized again and again by the economics profession at large, and it is for these reasons, of course, that welfare economics has undergone so many attempted reconstructions "from the ground up."

We shall briefly survey the more important of these attempts from a perspective that seeks consistently to apply the following (related) Austrian concerns: (a) methodological individualism: we shall refuse to recognize meaning in statements concerning the "welfare of society" that cannot, in principle, be unambiguously translated into statements concerning the individuals in society (in a manner which does not do violence to their individuality); (b) subjectivism: we shall not be satisfied with statements that perceive the economic well-being of society as expressible in terms (such as physical output) that are unrelated to the valuations and choices made by individuals; (c) an emphasis on process: we shall be interested in the economic well-being of society not merely in terms of its level of economic well-being (however defined), but also in regard to the ability of its institutions to stimulate and support those economic processes upon which the attainment of economic well-being depends.

Welfare Economics—Some Highlights of its Past

a) During the period of classical economics it was, of course, taken for granted that a society was economically successful strictly insofar as it succeeded in achieving increased wealth. Adam Smith's *Inquiry into the Nature and Causes of the Wealth of Nations* expressed this approach to the economics of welfare simply and typically. It was taken for granted that a given percentage increase in a nation's physical wealth (with wealth often seen as consisting of bushels of "corn") meant a similar percentage increase in the nation's well-being. From this perspective a physical measure of a nations' wealth provides an index of that nation's economic success, regardless of its distribution. A bushel of wheat is a bushel of wheat. Clearly this notion of welfare offends the principles of methodological individualism and subjectivism; it was swept away by the marginalist (subjectivist) revolution of the late nineteenth century.

b) Marshall and Pigou sought to preserve certain central elements of the classical approach, while avoiding the trap which sees well-being as identified with (or directly proportional to) physical wealth itself. They focused attention not on goods themselves, but on the *utility* of those goods. In principle a nation's physical wealth, given its pattern of distribution, corresponded to a given level of aggregate utility. Moreover they believed this aggregate to be measurable, in principle, by the "measuring rod of money." They sensed no problem in conceiving of "aggregate utility"; they thought of utility as something that could be compared and aggregated across individuals. They certainly did not see utility as associated uniquely with an individual act of choice; rather they saw it as a kind of psychological shadow that closely followed physical wealth. Its central advantage over wealth, as an index of well-being, was that it incorporated the refinement of diminishing marginal utility. It was no longer acceptable to consider a bushel of wheat to be identical, welfare-wise, with each other bushel of wheat; the margin of consumption by the individual must be considered. But it was still considered valid to treat one dollar's worth of utility as entirely equivalent to a second dollar's worth of utility.

This approach to welfare economics is clearly unacceptable to economists who have absorbed the Misesian (and Rothbardian) lessons concerning the true meaning of utility in economic analysis. Utility is, for Austrians, not a quantity of psychological experience, it is merely an index of preferability as expressed in acts of choice. To attempt to aggregate utility is not merely to violate the tenets of methodological individualism and subjectivism (by treating the sensations of different individuals as being able to be added up); it is to engage in an entirely meaningless exercise: economic analysis has nothing to say about sensations, it deals strictly with choices and their interpersonal implications.

c) The approach to welfare economics that has, of course, been central to economics for the past half-century, is that which revolves round the notion of Pareto-optimality. A change is seen as enhancing the economic well-being of society if it renders some of its members better-off (in their estimation) without rendering any others worse-off. This approach certainly avoids the problems of interpersonal comparisons of utility, and would thus seem to be consistent both with the methodological individualism and with the subjectivism that Austrians insist upon. Several points need, however, to be noticed.

While the notion of Pareto-optimality is indeed concerned with the individual members of society it nonetheless reflects a supra-individual conception of society and its well-being. After all, a Pareto-optimal move is considered to advance the well-being *of society*—considered as a whole. Otherwise it is not at all clear what is added (to the bald observation that the change is preferred by some and objected to by none) by the judgement that the move is "good for society." Indeed the Pareto-criterion turned out to become an integral element in the development of the idea that society faces an "economic problem"—that of allocating its resources among its competing goals, in the most efficient manner. Societal inefficiency in resource allocation came to be identified with sub-optimality according to the Pareto criterion. Now this notion of society facing its economic problem in the resource-allocation sense arose, as is well-known, as an extension of the concept of individual economizing behavior that was articulated so definitively by Lionel Robbins in 1932.[2] But, as has before been recognized, this extension is in fact an illegitimate extension, not at all faithful to the spirit of Robbins's formulation. Robbins was concerned to identify the economic problem facing the *individual*. It is the individual who has goals and who deliberately deploys his perceived resources in order to most efficiently achieve his goals, as far as is possible. To transfer this important concept of individual allocative choice, to society as a whole is, at best, to engage in metaphor. Society, as such, neither possesses goals of its own nor deliberately engages in allocative choice. Insofar as the idea of Pareto-optimality came to reinforce the faulty and misleading notion of society's "economic problem," it was part of an approach to the analysis of economic welfare that fell grievously short of consistent adherence to the principle of methodological individualism.

Hayek and the Critique of Welfare Economics

It was against this mainstream notion of society and its purported allocative problem that Hayek's famous 1945 paper[3] was directed. Hayek's attack might, it is true, be seen as not being *primarily* against the welfare notion that was embedded in the idea of society's economic problem. Hayek focused on the circumstance of dispersed knowledge. The relevant information that "society" would have to possess in order to solve its economic problem is widely dispersed. Society is thus simply not in a position to address its supposed economic problem (even if, for the sake of discussion, this societal allocative task could be held to be meaningful). Hayek's critique might thus be seen as emphasizing the problems obstructing the practical solution of a nation's economic problem, rather than as a critique of the standard conception of that problem itself. But Hayek's paper constituted, nonetheless, a profound—if indirect—critique of the very meaningfulness of societal efficiency as developed, for example, in the Paretian context.

For once it is recognized that the relevant information *is* inevitably and definitely dispersed among many minds, it is impossible to avoid the conclusion that the notion of social efficiency is correspondingly devoid of meaning. Social efficiency must refer to the extent to which the allocation of social resources corresponds to the priorities implied in the relative urgencies of social goals. But in order for the notion of "social resource" to be meaningful, and in order for the notion of "relative urgencies of social goals" to be meaningful, it must, at least in principle, be possible to imagine a single mind to which the relevant arrays of social resources and social objectives are simultaneously given. Hayek's insight concerning dispersed knowledge was, in effect, to deny such a possibility. Thus dispersed knowledge turns out to be not merely a phenomenon that constitutes a practical difficulty with which would-be planners must grapple; it turns out to be a phenomenon (not necessarily the only one) that robs the very concept of social efficiency of its meaningfulness, even in principle. To choose, *presupposes* an integrated framework of ends and means; without such a presumed framework allocative choice is hardly a coherent notion at all.[4] Hayek's insight into the subjectivism of knowledge and information has thus decisively dislodged the foundations of Paretian welfare economics, at least insofar as those foundations have been held to support the concept of social choice and social efficiency. (More recent extensions by Hayek and others of this subjectivism of information to encompass also Polanyi's idea of "tacit knowledge"—knowledge incapable of being deliberately communicated to others—have rendered these damaging implications for standard welfare economics even more destructive.)[5]

Coordination as a Hayekian Welfare Criterion

Several writers have, pursuing the implications of these Hayekian insights, seen the concept of "coordination" as offering a normative yardstick consistent with these subjectivist and methodologically individualistic insights.[6] As discussed, the notion of social choice (and thus of the efficiency of such choice) has been fatally undermined (except at the level of metaphor). If Jones (who prefers Smith's food to his own enjoyment of a day's leisure) fails to trade with Smith (who prefers the labor of Jones over his own food), we may not be able to say that society has failed to efficiently allocate the food and labor time among Jones and Smith—but we could surely still say that Jones and Smith have failed to coordinate their activities and their decisions. It seems plausible and intuitively appealing to perceive coordination—permitting each agent to achieve his goals through the simultaneous satisfaction of the goals of the other agent—as constituting a desideratum transcending the individual goals of the respective agents. Failure to achieve coordination might thus be seen as a failure of the social apparatus to achieve a supra-individual result—but such a judgment relies not at all on any notions inconsistent with subjectivism or with methodological individualism.

It is of course true that the fulfillment of the coordination norm appears to be formally equivalent to the fulfillment of the Paretian welfare criterion. Any sub-optimal situation (in the Paretian sense) clearly corresponds to the failure of a pair of potential market participants to trade with one another on feasible, mutually attractive terms—in other words, it corresponds to a failure to achieve coordination. But, unlike the Paretian norm, the coordination norm escapes interpretation as a yardstick for social efficiency in social-allocative choice. Coordination does not refer to the well-being achieved through its successful attainment; it refers only to the dovetailing character of the activities that make it up.

Thus Hayek's emphasis on the dispersed character of knowledge appears to provide not merely the definitive critique of standard Paretian welfare economics, but also the basis for an alternative normative yardstick, one thoroughly consistent with the tenet of methodological individualism. Scope for this new normative yardstick is provided precisely by the circumstance of dispersed knowledge. Fragmented knowledge is responsible for activities that are *not* mutually coordinated. The "social" problem faced by Hayek's economic society is precisely that of overcoming the discoordination to be expected to flow out of such fragmentation. There is a deeper issue here. If one abstracts from the fragmented character of information, if one treats all existing information as if it were known to all market participants, one is, of course, abstracting from the possibility of discoordinated activities. With the Hayekian "economic problem" assumed to be out of the way, in this fashion, it might seem that the standard (Paretian) economic problem comes back into its own, invulnerable to Hayekian strictures. The problem facing society would, on such assumptions, appear to reduce to that of achieving Paretian optimality in respect of the relevant social objectives, in the face of its limited resources. But, surely, if we assume away the dispersed character of information, the standard economic problem facing society presents no challenge at all. If we can assume that what is known to one is known to all, then (averting our gaze from the remaining quibbles which the methodological individualist might have against the concept of social efficiency) it seems difficult to imagine the possibility of any social allocation of resources that might be pronounced socially *inefficient*. Given perfect mutual knowledge it appears obvious that all possible Pareto-optimal moves *must have already been implemented*. To imagine otherwise would be to imagine that agents deliberately refrain from taking advantage of available opportunities known by them to exist. Knowledge of all such opportunities, and knowledge of all relevant transaction costs, must appear inevitably to lead to Pareto-optimality (given these transaction costs)—achieved either through market activity or through centralized organization (with this later choice itself determined by comparison of the respective transaction costs). Thus Hayek's insights concerning fragmented knowledge might appear to provide not merely a critique of standard welfare criteria, and also a substitute yardstick (in terms of the coordination norm)—they might appear at the same time to salvage welfare economics from the extinction to which it would be doomed by the inevitability of perpetual optimality. But the situation is not quite so simple.

Hayek in the Panglossian World

The truth is that many of the observations made in the preceding sections of this paper might seem to be vulnerable to serious challenge. Such challenges, it would seem, can be launched at several distinct levels—with the challenges stemming precisely from the paralysis arising from the inevitability optimality. On the one hand it might appear that the circumstance of fragmented knowledge does *not* salvage welfare economics from the extinction spelled by perpetual optimality. Further it might be argued that Hayek's insights in fact deepen the perplexities created by such Panglossian concerns. We shall in the present section develop these challenges. In subsequent sections we shall rebut these challenges, showing how the observations made in the preceding sections in regard to Hayekian welfare economics *can* be defended (despite the challenges developed in the present section). Moreover we shall use our discussion to point out a novel sense in which "coordination" offers a normative criterion that escapes Panglossian paralysis. (It will be in the context of this latter discussion that we shall deploy the third Austrian tenet referred to at the outset of this paper, that of maintaining a concern with *processes* rather than exclusively with states of affairs.) We turn now to develop the apparent challenges to Hayekian welfare economics referred to at the outset of this section.

The difficulties that we must face up to, in considering the Hayekian thesis of dispersed knowledge and information, consist in the fact that, from a mainstream perspective, the Hayekian "knowledge problem" might appear not to be a problem at all, in the relevant sense.[7] To point out that knowledge is scattered in society is, it might be argued (contrary to our earlier assertions), not necessarily to note that standard welfare analysis is inapplicable—it is merely to point out that such standard welfare analysis is to be carried on in the context of a hitherto unsuspected cost, the cost of ascertaining and of communicating information. Dispersal of knowledge and information indeed introduces new costs for the acquisition of the knowledge necessary for economic choice. But surely the presence of a novel class of costs does not, in principle, render inapplicable the standard criteria for the evaluation of social efficiency.

Moreover, once it is recognized that the fragmentation of information complicates standard welfare analysis without vitiating it, it seems appropriate to point out that the Panglossian paralysis referred to earlier offers as serious threats to a "coordination"-based approach to welfare analysis, as it does to the mainstream approach. After all any discussion of Jones and Smith "coordinating" their activities must refer to a potential for coordination in the context of the relevant resource constraints confronting the respective parties. Surely then, the availability and costliness of information-acquisition must be counted in as part of these "relevant resource constraints." If engineer Jones, Sr., and farmer Smith can exchange engineering services for food, with mutual gain, it may seem that only a coordination failure could prevent such exchange from taking place. But it will not constitute a coordination failure if Jones, Jr., schoolboy, refrains from enrolling in an engineering program on his graduation from high school if the costs of the training program are too high. Similarly, it might appear, all coordination "failures" attributable to Hayekian knowledge fragmentation, turn out not to be failures at all once one properly considers the cost of searching for the information needed to bridge the dispersed knowledge gaps. If Jones, Sr., and Smith fail to engage in mutually gainful exchange, as a result of knowledge dispersal, they are not, it might be contended, acting sub-optimally, from a social point of view; they are fully taking advantage of each other's availability in the context of their limited knowledge of each other's situation. To pronounce this state of affairs to be socially inefficient or "uncoordinated" might seem to be succumbing to a temptation warned against in elementary economics, viz. that of pronouncing welfare judgments without regard to resource scarcities. Participants in an economy can be counted upon to engage in mutually gainful exchange transactions, insofar as their knowledge permits. Moreover, insofar as participants are aware of worthwhile possibilities for learning useful information that may reveal as yet unexploited opportunities for mutual gain, they can surely be counted upon to engage in such useful learning. It does seem, then, that in a world of dispersed information as in a world of omniscience, sub-optimality or states of discoordinatedness cannot be postulated to exist (if one properly includes the costs of information-acquisition).

Indeed it might be contended that it is precisely Hayek's dispersed information insights that are capable of focusing needed attention on the costs of learning and of knowledge-communication. Once the paralyzing assumption of perfect knowledge has been dropped it becomes impossible to avoid grappling with the economics of learning and communication. Our contention thus far is that, once such economics of learning and communication has been taken into account, Panglossian perpetual optimality paralysis sets in once again. At all times agents will be engaging in the optimal mix of decisions (including decisions to learn and to communicate). No pair of decisions can be pronounced uncoordinated, given the costs of learning.

Dispersed Knowledge, Optimal
Ignorance and Genuine Error

We shall discover, however, that these contentions are invalid. The Panglossian paralysis we have found to afflict mainstream welfare economics is *not* a threat to the Hayekian coordination approach. It is *not* the case, we shall see, that Hayek's fragmentation of information does nothing more than to complicate matters through the introduction of a new cost. Rather the dispersal of knowledge creates scope for a genuinely fresh approach to normative analysis. This is so because such dispersal of knowledge necessarily involves not merely new costs (of learning and communication) but also the very real possibility of what we may call *"genuine error."* This writer has elsewhere argued[8] that genuine error, so often exorcised form economic analysis, in fact deserves a central place in that analysis. Genuine error occurs *where a decision-maker's ignorance is not attributable to the costs of search, or of learning or of communication.* In such cases the decision-maker's ignorance is *utter* ignorance—i.e., it is a result of his ignorance of available, cost-worthy, avenues to needed information (which includes, of course, the possibility of his being altogether ignorant of the very existence of valuable information). At the level of the individual decision-maker we may describe his activity as having been sub-optimal when he subsequently discovers himself to have inexplicably overlooked available opportunities that were in fact worthwhile. He cannot "condone" his faulty decision-making on the grounds of the cost of acquiring information, since the information was in fact costlessly available to him. He can account for his failure only by acknowledging his utter ignorance of the true circumstances (i.e., of his ignorance of the availability of relevant information at worthwhile low cost). Such utter ignorance cannot be explained in cost-benefit terms; it is simply a given.

Two implications of the phenomenon of utter ignorance, of genuine error, may be noticed. First the injection into economic reasoning of the possibility of genuine error, introduces a degree of "looseness" into our understanding of economic processes that is of great importance. It is no longer true that the configuration of exogenous variables, tastes, resource availabilities and technological possibilities, unambiguously marks out the course of individual activities. This is so because while these data do mark out the optimal opportunities, we cannot be confident that such optimal opportunities will be known to the relevant decision-makers—even if we make provision for deliberate processes of search and learning. We cannot be sure that available processes of search and learning are known to those who might benefit therefrom. The second implication (flowing from recognition of the phenomenon of genuine error) is that we must now recognize the possibility of corrective actions within an economy, that are not to be traced to shifting cost patterns. Corrective action may be set off by the sudden ("entrepreneurial") discovery by a market participant of a hitherto unperceived opportunity for pure profit. Let us now return to examine Hayek's dispersed information.

We objected that the introduction of the need for costly search, learning and communication (forced upon us by Hayek's insight) does not really threaten the mainstream economizing view. The fragmentation of knowledge, we pointed out, merely introduced an additional cost-dimension—that of mobilizing and centralizing scattered bits of information. We now see that the fragmentation of knowledge is likely to affect matters far more seriously and fundamentally. *The fragmentation of knowledge injects into the picture scope for genuine error, resulting from utter ignorance.* Pursuing once again the line of reasoning introduced earlier in this paper (and subsequently challenged in the preceding section) the circumstance of dispersed and fragmented knowledge compels us not merely to recognize a practical difficulty to be encountered in seeking to address society's allocative-efficiency problem—this circumstance undermines the very meaningfulness of such a social "economic problem." Given the scope for genuine error which we see to be implicit in the circumstance of dispersed information, we now see that this circumstance indeed erodes the meaningfulness of the concept of social allocative efficiency. Before we can even begin to contemplate what we may mean by social allocative efficiency we must somehow confront the problem of overcoming that utter ignorance which obstructs the relevancy of the efficiency concept for social policy. It is here that the norm of "coordination" is to be perceived in a fresh light, rather different from that coordination-norm discussed earlier in this paper.

Coordination and Coordination[9]

We must distinguish carefully between (a) a possible norm of coordination in the sense of a coordinated state of affairs, and (b) a possible norm of coordination in the sense of the ability to detect and to move towards correcting situations in which activities have until now been discoordinated. The distinction between these two possibilities corresponds to the two different meanings of the word "coordination": the word may refer to the activities being carried out when these activities are indeed dovetailing with one another; alternatively it may refer to the process through which initially clashing, discoordinated activities, are somehow being hammered out in a manner such as to approach a more smoothly dovetailing pattern of activities. The discussion earlier in this paper implicitly referred to coordination only in the first of these two senses. (It is for this reason that we were able to note formal equivalency between the coordination norm and the norm of Pareto-efficiency.) We wish now to draw attention to the possible relevance of the second coordination norm for a modern Austrian approach to welfare economics. Once we have identified genuine error as a culprit responsible for a failure of a society's economic system to successfully fulfill its functions, we have placed ourselves in a position to appreciate the meaning of this second coordination norm. Absent the phenomenon of utter ignorance, we have seen, our *first* coordination concept (like its Paretian counterpart) turned out to be of little normative interest. After all, we noted, given the absence of utter ignorance, all activities must be carried on in optimal fashion. Even if some activities are being carried out "erroneously," because of incomplete information, we saw, we could hardly describe these activities as being sub-optimal or "wrong"—after all, they took advantage of every scrap of information it was judged worthwhile to lay one's hands on. In this sense the world is, at all times, at a Pareto-optimum, in a state of full coordination—the best of all possible worlds, given the costs of change. But injection of the possibility of genuine error arising out of simple utter ignorance introduces us to the possibility of *genuine* discoordination—and to the possibility of evaluating the institutional environment in terms of its potential to inspire genuine discovery (of opportunities previously overlooked as a result of utter ignorance). Thus a norm of coordination looms into center stage in the sense of permitting us to ask what potential a society's economy possesses to inspire such pure discovery of its earlier genuine errors. Such an approach to welfare economics is made possible by our escape from the Panglossian world; that escape was, in turn, made possible by our emphasis on genuine error (arising out of utter ignorance); we have seen in this paper that scope for genuine error is widened most considerably by the circumstance of dispersed and fragmented information identified by Hayek. It is for this reason that we see Hayek's criticisms of standard approaches to welfare analysis as opening the door, at the same time, towards the possible reconstruction of normative economics along truly Austrian lines, that is, in a manner fully consistent with (a) subjectivism, (b) methodological individualism, and (c) an emphasis on dynamic processes.

Notes

1. Murray N. Rothbard, "Toward a Reconstruction of Utility and Welfare Economics," in Mary Sennholz, ed., *On Freedom and Free Enterprise* (Princeton: Van Nostrand, 1956), pp. 224-62.

2. Lionel Robbins, *An Essay on the Nature and Significance of Economic Science* (London: Macmillan, 1932).

3. Friedrich A. Hayek, "The Use of Knowledge in Society," *American Economic Review* 35 (September 1945).

4. Cf. J. M. Buchanan, "What Should Economists Do?" *Southern Economic Journal* 30 (January 1964).

5. See Friedrich A. Hayek, *Law, Legislation and Liberty.* vol. 3, *The Political Order of a Free People* (Chicago: University of Chicago Press, 1979), p. 190.

6. Israel M. Kirzner, *Competition and Entrepreneurship* (Chicago: University of Chicago Press, 1973), chap. 6; Gerald P. O'Driscoll, Jr., *Economics as a Coordination Problem* (Kansas City, Kans.: Sheed Andrews and McMeel, 1977).

7. See also Israel M. Kirzner, "Economic Planning and the Knowledge Problem," *Cato Journal* 4 (Fall 1984): 407-18.

8. Israel M. Kirzner, *Perception, Opportunity and Profit,* (Chicago: University of Chicago Press, 1979), chap. 8; idem, *Discovery and the Capitalist Process* (Chicago: University of Chicago Press, 1985).

9. See also Israel M. Kirzner, "Prices, the Communication of Knowledge, and the Discovery Process," in Kurt R. Leube and Albert H. Zlabinger, eds., *The Political Economy of Freedom: Essays in Honor of F. A Hayek* (Munich: Philosophia Verlag, 1984).

8

Why Murray Rothbard Will Never Win the Nobel Prize!

0329

Gary North

M ark Skousen insists that Murray Rothbard ought to win the Nobel Prize in economics. I think so too, but for his professional contribution which categorically bars an economist from ever winning the Nobel Prize in economics: *clarity*. Murray Rothbard has an addiction: clear, forthright writing. He says what he thinks, and he explains why he thinks it, in easily followed logic. He does not use equations, statistics, and the other paraphernalia of the economics priesthood. He simply takes his readers step by step through economic reasoning, selecting the relevant facts—relevant in terms of the economic logic he sets forth—and drawing conclusions. He gives readers his operating presuppositions; he then marshals the evidence and reaches conclusions. It is an old-fashioned procedure, and decidedly out of favor these days. If you doubt me, pick up a copy of *American Economic Review* (let alone *Econometrica*), turn to any page randomly, read it three times to yourself, and offer a brief summary to your wife. Understand, this can be done with Rothbard's books.

Rothbard's ability to communicate the truths of economics to reasonably intelligent non-economists is not the sort of skill which impresses the Nobel Prize Committee members. If they can understand anything, and especially if they can understand it rapidly on the first reading, they are unimpressed. What impresses them is an economics book which cannot be understood even after three or four readings, and when its conclusions are at last grasped, they prove to be utterly inapplicable to the real world. (If you think I am exaggerating, take a look at any page of the book by the 1983 economics prize winner, Gerald Debreu, *Theory of Value: An Axiomatic Analysis of Economic Equilibrium*, which was in its eighth printing in 1979—a testimony to the horrors of graduate study in economics. The only hint of reality in the entire book appears on page 29, the words, "No. 2 Red Winter Wheat.")[1]

Furthermore, Rothbard does something which is absolutely unacceptable in academia in general and the economics profession in particular. He uses italics. Yes, when he thinks that something is important, he underlines it. How gauche! How utterly unscientific! One is supposed to allow the reader the option of missing the whole point—an option which reputable scholars exercise frequently, if not continually.

Furthermore, in an age of positive economics—"facts speaking for themselves"—Rothbard has adopted Ludwig von Mises's use of *apriorism*: he deduces economic truths from a handful of axioms of human action, meaning human choice. He goes so far as to say that economic facts cannot disprove a logically formulated economic theorem. "The only *test* of a theory is the correctness of the premises and of the logical chain of reasoning."[2] I can remember reading one review of *America's Great Depression* in a professional journal in which the reviewer must have spent over half his alloted space criticizing this Misesian methodological principle, and he spent the remainder criticizing the book's conclusions, namely, that the great depression was created by government monetary policy, and was prolonged by government price restraints (floors) that impeded the readjustment of prices and markets. To summarize: Rothbard's *presuppositions* concerning the proper methodology of economics have been unacceptable, and so have his *conclusions* concerning the economic effects (not to mention immoral effects) of State intervention into the economy.

He is also afflicted with another professional weakness: historical curiosity. He continues to involve himself in detailed detours to his professional career as an economist, especially in the area of U.S. history,[3] and worst of all, *revisionist* U.S. history. He believes that there have been a series of conspiracies against the public welfare—conspiracies that have used the rhetoric of democracy to hide machinations of special-interest groups of power-seekers and monopoly-seekers. These conspirators have invariably used the State to achieve evil goals.

Then he takes it one step farther, thereby committing the ultimate academic *faux pas*: he believes that the State can be used *only* to attain evil goals. It is not simply that conspirators have used (and continue to use) the State to do evil against the public welfare; it is that to use the State in any way is automatically to become a conspirator against the public welfare.

Then he compounds this indiscretion; in his popular writings, he uses pejorative adjectives. For example, it is difficult to imagine a Rothbard article dealing with any aspect of the modern welfare-warfare State in which he fails to tag at least one monopoly-milking participant or policy with the adjective "monstrous." This is considered bad form among the academics. People are supposed to be given a legitimate benefit of the doubt. Rothbard replies, in effect, "Not when it's impossible to doubt their illegitimate benefits." He is especially outraged by the whole Progressive movement (1890-1918), the movement which dominated American politics in the era in which the State became the supposed engine of public welfare in the United States. He concludes that the Progressives' rhetoric of democracy was in fact a vast smoke screen for massive theft by the State's newly trusted beneficiaries. In short, he concludes, the Progressive movement was monstrous.

Then, just to make sure that his exile to the academic fringe is secured, he argues that the almost universal hostility of scholars to conspiracy theories of history is basic to the growth of the State.

> It is also particularly important for the State to make its rule seem *inevitable*: even if its reign is disliked, as it often is, it will then be met with the passive resignation expressed in the familiar coupling of "death and taxes." One method is to bring to its side historical determinism: if X-State rules us, then this has to be inevitably decreed for us by the Inexorable Laws of History (or the Divine Will, or the Absolute, or the Material Productive Forces), and nothing that any puny individuals may do can change the inevitable. It is also important for the State to inculcate in its subjects an aversion to any outcropping of what is now called "a conspiracy theory of history." For a search for "conspiracies," as misguided as the results often are, means a search for motives, and an attribution of individual responsibility for the historical misdeeds of ruling elites. If, however, tyranny or venality or aggressive war imposed by the State was brought about *not* by particular State rulers but by mysterious and arcane "social forces," or by the imperfect state of the world—or if, in some way, *everyone* was guilty ("We are *all* murderers," proclaims a common slogan), then there is no point in anyone's becoming indignant or rising up against such misdeeds.[4]

Goodbye, Nobel Prize.

Out of Touch

It is not simply his economic conclusions that have sealed his fate with the Nobel Committee, as well as the with his professional colleagues. It is also his commitment to the methodological past. It is not simply that he is a self-conscious *apriorist*; Marxists are *apriorists*, too. Thomas Kuhn has made one variant of *apriorism* nearly respectable.[5] Rothbard's problem is that he forthrightly follows in Mises's *a priori* footsteps, an indication that he is behind the times. It is not simply that he is arguing that everyone has to make a series of unprovable fundamental assumptions about the way the world works, and then he must necessarily interpret all factual evident in terms of these "pretheoretical" assumptions. It is rather that Rothbard argues that there are assumptions concerning human action that are "apodictically certain" (to use Mises's phrase)—assumptions about human action that are inescapably true at all times. The economist, says Rothbard, is supposed to use these axioms to interpret historical events and statistical data. Rothbard is therefore a non-relativistic *apriorist*. He claims to have found truth, in an era in which scholars are supposed to be professionally limited to the mere quest for truth.

This backward-looking proclivity on Rothbard's part is indicative of his disrespectful attitude—not disrespectful toward the dead, but disrespectful toward the trendy. If one is an economist, one should respect present academic trends. To be "with it" is always best in the eyes of the profession. Being "with it" is indicated in part by textbook royalties and in part by the publication of zero-price articles in professional journals. The articles are officially more important,[6] but the textbooks are unofficially more important. The articles prove that an economist is a professional, but nobody actually reads them—and nobody is expected to. The textbook proves that an economist is accepted, thereby reducing the likelihood of the author's deviant ideology. ("Nobody ever got fired for assigning Samuelson's *Economics*." And its corollary: "Nobody ever got fired because he hadn't read Samuelson's *Foundations of Economic Analysis*.")

Officially, textbooks are considered to be inferior scientific production.[7] Nevertheless, high textbook royalties are considered a test of competence. Understand, textbook royalties are not the same as book royalties. Book royalties are always highly suspect by professional economists, because people *voluntarily* buy books. A sincere professional is not to appeal to the off-campus rabble, after all. Textbooks are completely different from books. Textbooks are assigned by professionals to students who would not read them under any known stimulus other than the fear of flunking out of school. Thus, it is the profession, not the rabble, which determines textbook royalties. Textbooks are "in"; books are "out" (*ceteris paribus*).

Galbraith and Rothbard

John Kenneth Galbraith has fallen afoul of this unwritten rule, even though the profession generally approves of his many conclusions regarding the necessity of State action to improve the performance of the economy. A lot of clicking of tongues and throat-clearing goes on behind closed professional doors when Galbraith's name is mentioned. Sometimes it is done in public, as when UCLA Professor William R. Allen publicly resigned his membership in the American Economic Association because Galbraith was elected president (an honorary position) one year. He alienates his professional colleagues when he writes that "only someone who is decently confusing can be respected" by his peers and by the public, and then goes on to assert, almost Mises-like, that "In the case of economics there are no important propositions that cannot, in fact, be stated in plain language."[8]

Galbraith is a lot like Rothbard in many ways, especially stylistically. He writes clearly. He writes real books. He has not written a professional journal article in decades. He never wrote a textbook. He uses ridicule in his speeches and essays. He is also a bit of a conspiracy theorist, even going so far as to publish the details of otherwise private meetings of those who make plans for the rest of us.[9] Most of all, he shuns mathematics. He even wrote that the reason why mathematics is employed extensively by economists is primarily sociological, not methodological. Mathematics is in fact a *guild screening device.* "The oldest problem in economic education is how to exclude the incompetent." Mathematical competency is therefore "a highly useful screening device." Worse, he said this in a mass-market paperback book.[10]

This was not such a revolutionary statement in itself. Former Austrian economist Fritz Machlup[11] had written a decade earlier: "Even if some of us think that one can study social sciences without knowing higher mathematics, we should insist on making calculus and mathematical statistics absolute requirements—as a device for keeping away the weakest students."[12] But Machlup had said this in a presidential address to a regional economics society, not in a mass-market paperback book.

But then Galbraith went too far—way, way too far. He displayed some of the profession's dirtiest linen in public. He blew the whistle on the guild's professional journals. He admitted the following in a foot-note—worse, a footnote not at the back of the book, where few people would read it, but at the bottom of the page, where anyone might read it: "The layman may take comfort from the fact that the most esoteric of this material is not read by other economists or even by the editors who publish it. In the economics profession the editorship of a learned journal not specialized in econometrics or mathematical statistics is a position of only moderate prestige. It is accepted, moreover, that the editor must have a certain measure of practical judgment. This means that he is usually unable to read the most prestigious contributions which, nonetheless, he must publish. So it is the practice of the editor to associate with himself a mathematical curate who passes on this part of the work whose word he takes. A certain embarrassed silence covers the arrangement."[13]

Like Galbraith, Rothbard has never written a textbook. Worse, he has not written professional journal articles since the early 1960s. He has written books instead. He has not honored the rules of the scientific game. Books are written for people, not scientists. A scientist writes articles, not books. Kuhn comments with respect to the natural sciences: "No longer will his researches usually be embodied in books addressed, like Franklin's *Experiments . . . on Electricity* or Darwin's *Origin of Species*, to anyone who might be interested in the subject matter of the field. Instead they will usually appear as brief articles addressed only to professional colleagues, the men whose knowledge of a shared paradigm can be assumed and who prove to be the only ones able to read the papers addressed to them."[14]

Clearly, Rothbard and Galbraith are professionally out of touch. But Galbraith's conclusions were far more acceptable to non-economists who publish the popular literary magazines and books. The royalty money poured in. Rothbard had to content himself with being readable, even though not that many people read what he wrote. Neither scholar was professionally "with it," but Galbraith was ideologically "with it," and that made a lot of financial difference.

Pioneers

The only professional excuse for not being "with it" is being dead. A few people are granted posthumous recognition by the economics profession because they were "pioneers." But the Nobel Committee does not award prizes posthumously. Furthermore, evidence suggests that the Nobel Committee hates pioneers—not just the economics subcommittee, but the whole Nobel Prize establishment. In any case, the Nobel Committee only awards its prizes to living figures. (Some of us were more than a little suspicious when F.A. Hayek received the Nobel Prize for 1974, the year after the death of Ludwig von Mises, who provided Hayek with his major economic theorems,[15] and for which Hayek was awarded the prize. Admittedly, Hayek put these ideas into a form which was more acceptable to "scientific economists." For example, in his youth, he once used six graphs in an essay.[16] Admittedly, he never did it again. Mises, in contrast, never once adopted such tactics to appeal to his peers. He assumed that one graph is worth a thousand methodologically illegitimate words.)

Am I exaggerating concerning the Nobel Committee's conservatism? Consider Albert Einstein's prize in physics. Do you think it was granted for his theory of general relativity, the theory which transformed twentieth-century thinking?[17] Not a chance! He was granted the Prize for his 1905 essay on the photoeffect. The Committee informed him specifically that the award was *not* being given for his work on relativity.[18] Too controversial, too radical, you understand. Furthermore, he was given the award in 1922 retroactively for 1921, the year in which nobody got the award. Talk about the second-class honor! ("Gee, Al, we have this extra money lying around, so we got to thinking. . . .") And then, just to make the whole thing utterly preposterous, it turned out that Einstein's essay on the photoeffect really *was* his most revolutionary contribution to pure physics. "It is a touching twist of history that the Committee, conservative by inclination, would honor Einstein for the most revolutionary contribution he ever made to physics."[19] Mistakes do happen.

Rothbard continues to cite Professor Mises in his writings. This is another totally unacceptable methodological strategy in the eyes of the Nobel Committee. It is acceptable to cite favorably the writings of certain living authorities, but not dead ones, and especially not a dead one whose ideas were rejected by his contemporaries because he was a backward-looking defender of free market institutional arrangements. It is sometimes permissible to announce discoveries that are based on the long-ignored findings of some historical figure, but you are not to base your presentation on the same kinds of evidence that this historical figure offered. You are to dress up your discovery in modern garb, preferably the use of stochastic functions, and then refer briefly in a footnote to the dead originator's "preliminary but undeveloped findings." You cannot then be accused of stealing his ideas, nor can you be accused of attempting to revive discarded ideas. Safety first.

Let us consider a recent example. These days the "rational expectations" school is very "in." (By the time the ink dries on this page, it
may be "out." Fads come and go rapidly in economics.) Keynesian
"fine-tuning" of the economy is "out" in the eyes of the younger "comers" in economics.[20] What do the rational expectations ("rat-ex") people
say? They say that Keynes did not give sufficient attention to people's
expectations concerning the future. People respond to government
economic policies in terms of what they expect in the future, which
means that they respond differently than economic planners expect. In
other words, Keynes did not take into account *human action*. But "rat-
ex" economics are exceedingly careful not to footnote Mises,[21] Jacob
Viner,[22] or Frank H. Knight[23] in their criticism of Keynes, despite the
fact that all of the former used similar arguments against him fifty
years ago. To cite them favorably would indicate that this sort of argument was well known back in the 1930s and 1940s, implying that their
now-tenured and graying colleagues had their heads in the ideological
sand for half a century. This would open them up to the standard
response of tenured gray-heads: "You are backward-looking and have
not fully mastered the tools of modern economic analysis."

To deflect this sort of criticism, the "rat-ex" proponents dress up
their arguments with lots of mathematical symbols. Viner, Knight,
and Mises generally wrote in English rather than mathematics. They
were "bucking the mathematical trend" in economics, which has increased steadily since the days of Cournot (1838). Bronfenbrenner's
comment seems appropriate: "The question is whether certain of our
fellow economists may not have elevated mathematical and statistical
virtuosity to the status of ends in themselves."[24] The "rat-ex" economists are prime examples of this trend. With respect to the previous
work of anti-Keynesians of the 1930s, they have adopted the rule set
forth by another important philosopher who was also overlooked by
the Nobel Committee, the late Satchel Paige: "Don't look back; something may be gaining on you."

To put it bluntly, the secret of success in academic economic circles
has as much to do with style as it does with content. This is not a new
development; it has ever been true. Murray Rothbard has the unique
distinction of being consigned to the professional outer darkness for
both the style *and* content of his writing, an honor he shares with
Mises. Mises, however, wrote his first book in 1906 and his most important book, *The Theory of Money and Credit*, was published in 1912,
in the era in which mathematics had not yet triumphed in economic
discourse. Rothbard's stubbornness in writing exclusively in English

can be viewed by his academic peers as perverse intransigence, rather than a mere stylistic carryover from a now-bygone era. Mises had an excuse; Rothbard doesn't. Besides, Mises is dead; Rothbard isn't.

Poor Timing

So, from the start of his career, Rothbard was stylistically condemned and methodologically condemned, and his conclusions were also condemned. Now, just for the record, let us consider the words, "from the start of his career." Consider when Rothbard's Ph.D. was granted by Columbia University. He entered the academic world of New York City, where in those days he was determined to remain, in the not-too-promising year of 1956. It was the Eisenhower era, and the Keynesian Revolution was consolidating its hold on every university in the land, with the exception of the University of Chicago, which was steadily falling under Milton Friedman's influence. Rothbard's commitment to Austrian economics was even more of an anomaly in 1956 than it is now. The post-Keynesian interest in neo-Austrianism[25] was two decades away.

The least opportune time to challenge an academic guild is during its consolidation phase. You need to do it during its self-doubt phase, when younger scholars and innovative outsiders to the guild are asking hard questions that the prevailing paradigms of the guild can no longer handle. Perhaps the paradigms could never handle these questions, but few people were asking the tough questions, or at least few people inside the guild were listening. But when observable reality presses against the guild's paradigms, members can no longer suppress inquisitiveness along paths that were previously unexplored or even unofficially (but nonetheless effectively) roadblocked.[26]

For example, the great depression smashed the paradigms of non-Austrian free market neoclassical economics, allowing the Keynesians entry into the fold, and the success of the post-war economic recovery seemed to validate the Keynesian vision of a depression-free economy.[27] The Full Employment Act of 1946 was considered a landmark for the Keynesians and a tombstone for the pre-Keynesian neoclassical school. Walter Heller, the Chairman of President Kennedy's Council of Economic Advisors, modestly refereed to it as "the nation's economic Magna Carta."[28] The Kennedy years were understood as the crown of glory to the Keynesian (Samuelson) synthesis. The coronation came in the December 31, 1965 issue of *Time*: "U.S. Business in 1965." It was a lengthy story on how Keynesian economic policies have brought permanent prosperity tot he United States. It even quoted Milton Friedman: "We are all Keynesians now."

That was the high-water mark. As Hegel said (somewhere or other): "The owl of Minerva flies only at dusk." The intellectual capstone of an era becomes its tombstone. The "great inescapable truths" that govern historical reality are delivered to a self-confident world just about the time that the confidence begins to erode. So it was with Dr. Heller. The next year, 1966, brought the beginning of the Keynesian price inflation. Gardner Ackley, President Johnson's chairman of the Council of Economic Advisors, had put it well at the end of 1965: "We're learning to live with prosperity, and frankly, we don't know as much about managing prosperity as getting us there."[29]

Nevertheless, Walter Heller remained confident, one of the truly high-flying owls of his day. "Economics has come of age in the 1960s," he announced in the opening sentence of page one of his 1966 book.[30] "The economist 'arrived' on the New Frontier and is firmly entrenched in the Great Society."[31] But that's not all, folks!

> The significance of the great expansion of the 1960s lies not only in its striking statistics of employment, income, and growth but in its glowing promise of things to come. If we can surmount the economic pressures of Vietnam without later being trapped into a continuing war on inflation when we should again be fighting economic slack, the "new economics" can move us steadily toward the qualitative goals that lie beyond the facts and figures of affluence.[32]

> The promise of modern economic policy, managed with an eye to maintaining prosperity, subduing inflation, and raising the quality of life, is indeed great. And although we have made no startling conceptual breakthroughs in economics in recent years, we *have*, more effectively than ever before, harnessed the existing economics—the economics that has been taught in the nation's college classrooms for some twenty years—to the purposes of prosperity, stability, and growth.[33]

> But the record of the 1961-1966 experience in putting modern economics to work is not to be read solely in the statistics of sustained expansion or in critics confounded. An important part of the story is a new flexibility in the economic thinking of both

liberals and conservatives. Both have been dislodged from their previously entrenched positions, their ideological foxholes, by the force of economic circumstance and the impact of policy success.[34]

Into this era of "non-ideological" confidence came Murray Rothbard, Ph.D. in hand, the most ideologically committed zero-State academic economist on earth. He faced an entrenched guild which was convinced of its own wisdom, its own openness, and its own flexibility. Of course, flexibility did not mean absolute flexibility. It meant an open welcome to those who defended flexibility, and an inflexibly closed door to those who did not. Heller's language revealed just how "open" he was: "In political economics, the day of the Neanderthal Man—indeed, the day of the pre-Keynesian Man—is dead."[35] Somehow, the vision of Murray Rothbard, hunched over, dressed in animal skins, club over his shoulder, and dragging Joey by her hair back to his cave, seems a bit far-fetched, but this is the image Heller wanted to convey to the public. This was the proper mental image concerning "doctrinaire" economists. Their day was over. In 1966.

> The success of expansionary policy, then, especially in the form of the tax cut, has undermined the position and thinned the ranks of the dug-in doctrinaire on both the left and the right. Minds have opened, and the area of common ground has grown. Doubters, disbelievers, and dissenters remain. Some vaguely feel it's "too good to be true." Others cling to beliefs too long cherished to flee before mere facts. But they are increasingly outside the main body of economic policy consensus.[36]

It *was* too good to be true. What followed was at least mildly disturbing to the faithful Keynesian victors: the price inflation and rising interest rates of 1968-69, the recession of 1969-71, back-to-back federal deficits of $25 billion each (big money in those days) in 1971 and 1972, the price and wage controls of 1971-73, the recession of 1975, the coming of double-digit price inflation in 1978-80, the worst recession(s) in 40 years in 1980, and 1981-82, and the $200 billion annual federal deficits after 1982. These unpleasant events did not fit the glowing Keynesian paradigm. It has become the Keynesians's turn to experience academic and professional barbs quite similar to those experienced by the tenured economists of 1938. The "young Turks" started raising doubts about everything that stalwart "non-ideological" men had always held sacred. They started calling into question both the theories and alleged successes of the Keynesian synthesis. Gray hair once again became a distinct liability in the economics classroom.[37] By 1972, the Union for Radical Political Economics (New Left, Marxists) was growing fast on campuses throughout the U.S.,[38] indicating an end to "the end of ideology." By 1975, a new group of young, bright neo-Austrian economists at last surfaced. By 1980, they had become influential in one local university, George Mason University, in Fairfax, Virginia, on the very edge of Washington, D.C.

But some things do not change, certainly not old tunes sung by aging economists. There was Walter Heller, in the middle of Jimmy Carter's economic debacle, writing such essays as "Balanced Budget Fallacies" (*Wall Street Journal*, March 16, 1979) and "An Anti-Inflationary Tax Cut" (*Wall Street Journal*, Aug. 2, 1979). The Full Employment Act of 1946 had become the Magna Carter. Yet Heller continued to issue the Keynesians's S.O.S.: Same Old Solutions. Who had become the Neanderthal Man by 1979? Galbraith's 1973 comment is correct—ironically delivered to the press at the meeting of the American Economic Association at which Heller had become president-elect: "Economists, like generals, usually fight the last war. On great matters they're like the gooney bird—it flies backward to see where it came from."[39]

The problem facing Murray Rothbard in 1956 was that he was on the wrong side of the trade in the academic pit, selling Keynesianism short while the market boomed upward for almost two decades. By the time the Keynesian market had begun to slide, in the mid-1970s, he was 50 years old.[40] This is not to say that he had been wasting his time for two decades. He helped influence a group of younger economists, just as Mises had guided him: not as a grade-granting professor in some prestigious graduate school, but at his informal private seminars. Mises at least had received some formal recognition, for the William Volker Fund had supported him at New York University, and had provided scholarship money for some of his students. At least Mises had been given the opportunity to have formal graduate-level lectures every Monday evening (1945-1964), as well as a graduate seminar on Thursday evenings (1948-1969). Rothbard did not have even this much formal recognition. Mises was granted only "visiting professor" status for 24 years in a third-rate university which was staffed overwhelmingly with nonentities.[41] Rothbard wound up teaching at Brooklyn Polytechnic, where there is no graduate program in economics, or even an undergraduate degree in economics.

Pariahs and Scientific Revolutions

Why bring up these unattractive details in a *Festschrift*? Because, first, they were the facts of academic life in the post-war era, up until the 1970s. Second, because they illustrate an ignored side of the history of economics—indeed, the history of scientific breakthroughs generally: the fact that the revolutionaries who set the academic agenda usually do it outside the classroom.

The modern university curriculum would be very different without the contributions of Karl Marx, Charles Darwin, Sigmund Freud, and Albert Einstein, three humanist Jews and a hypochondriac, none of whom was welcome in a major university during his lifetime. Darwin was too sick and weak to teach,[42] but no university ever asked him. Dr. Marx held only temporary editing jobs, always just before the authorities shut down his periodicals, and for his whole life he was shunned by academic world. (Engels put him on the dole for the last 20 years of his life.) Freud was not asked to teach at the University of Vienna, despite his world-famous reputation. (Mises suffered the same fate as Freud: the University of Vienna ignored him.) Einstein was a clerk in the Swiss patent office when he made his major theoretical breakthroughs, including his essay on the photoeffect. Yet the textbook scholars who occupy today's college classrooms wind up building their lectures around Darwin and his heirs, or Marx and his heirs, or Freud and his heirs, or Einstein and his heirs. (If classroom economists were smarter, they would pay more attention to Mises and his heirs.)

My point is simple: those who make revolutionary intellectual breakthroughs generally get into major university classrooms only posthumously. I write this to cheer up Murray Rothbard on his 60th birthday. Think of all he has to look forward to after he is dead. But he can forget about the Nobel Prize. It is not awarded posthumously.

Rothbard became the leader, at least for a decade, of younger scholars who were not impressed with Keynesianism, Marxism, or the University of Chicago's monetarism. This is not to say that they adopted his entire approach to economics, any more than he adopted Mises's entire approach. Mises was a self-conscious Kantian; Rothbard regards himself as an Aristotelian. Mises was a nineteenth-century classical liberal who wrote favorably concerning military conscription during wartime.[43] To make his position clear, he added these words to *Human Action* in the 1963 edition: "He who in our age opposes armaments and conscription is, perhaps unbeknownst to himself, an abettor of those aiming at the enslavement of all."[44] Rothbard opposes not only the conscripting State but also every non-conscripting State. Mises wanted free banking without government interference; Rothbard wants 100% reserve banking mandated by . . . ? (This one has always baffled me. Private law courts, I suppose.) Mises was an ethical utilitarian; Rothbard is a natural rights absolutist. Rothbard is not happy with the "hermeneutics" of the younger neo-Austrian scholars who have followed Ludwig Lachmann and G. L. S. Shackle into their kaleidic universe of entrepreneurial indeterminism, but that is the way of academic life. Students do not always develop in ways hoped for by teachers.

Rothbard published three economics books in 1962 and 1963: *The Panic of 1819*, his doctoral dissertation; *Man, Economy, and State*, his magnum opus; and *America's Great Depression*. Columbia University Press published the first, and it was well received in the journals. Like most monographs, it sank without a trace. The other two were openly ideological, and were not well received, but for a generation of neo-Austrian readers who did not begin with Mises's fat tomes, these books were vital, especially *Man, Economy, and State*. They opened up Mises's deductivist and subjectivist economics to necessarily self-taught students who found Mises's less structured presentations foreboding. In a movement which could survive only by the printed word, Rothbard wrote the clearest words available.

The question is: Can the Austrian school make a comeback? Can it become the wave of the future, despite its position as a trickle out of the past? One hopeful sign is its growing popularity in non-professional circles. Perhaps a dozen or more "hard money" newsletter writers officially claim to be followers of Austrianism. Even more impressive is the heavy reliance Paul Johnson placed on Rothbard's *America's Great Depression* in his eloquent history of the twentieth century, *Modern Times*. He follows Rothbard's narrative concerning the causes of the great depression and those who made it possible.

But what about inside the profession? Will a generation of younger economists embrace Austrianism? It depends on several factors, the most important of which is this: What will voters demand from politicians? If voters finally get fed up with the planned economy, almost certainly because the planners have created an economic catastrophe, then today's odd-ball economic theories may gain a hearing, *if they can be put into the common man's language*. Here, in my view, is the soft underbelly of today's orthodox economists. With few exceptions, their ideas cannot simultaneously be defended academically and popularly. Without his graphs and equations, the conventional economist is about as effective as Superman in a Kryptonite mine. Liquidity preference will not play in Peoria. Neither will government-mandated 3% to 5% steady monetary growth forever.

What am I arguing is that revolutions in economic thought are not endogenous variables within the economics profession; they are exogenous variables. Economists will supply professionally acceptable evidence for whatever line of argument is selling well to those who pay economists' salaries. Furthermore, few of them are entrepreneurs. They are not going to prepare for the next ideological wave which hits the public and the politicians. Thus, remarkable opportunities for pure entrepreneurial profit now exist. When the bad stuff hits the stochastic fan next time, the present occupants of the endowed chairs will offer the public a choice of deodorizers, not shovels. I think that the real market will be in shovels.

If the Austrian economic tradition should survive intact despite its present methodological disintegration, and if it should eventually gain the foothold on campus which it has never really enjoyed, then much of the credit (with 100% reserves, of course) will have to go to Rothbard's essays in persuasion. This scientific revolution, should it come, will have been produced by Mises, who was denied a full professorship for over six decades, except for six years in Geneva (1934-40), by F. A. Hayek, who suspects he was blackballed in secret session by the University of Chicago's economics department,[45] and by Murray Rothbard, who has been denied formal access to graduate students throughout his career.

Nobel Prize-Losing Insights

What are Rothbard's unique major intellectual contributions? Economists will differ. To some of them I return year after year, without which I would be substantially impoverished. Others are curiosities, but delightfully outrageous socialist balloon-poppers. Each one is worth a professional journal article, except that Murray refuses to write professional journal articles.

1. The impossibility of applying the calculus (infinitely small steps) to human action.[46]

2. The impossibility of total utility.[47]

3. The relevance of choice and the irrelevance of indifference curves.[48]

4. The impossibility of a universal vertical monopoly (no economic calculation).[49]

5. Neighborhood and even household tariffs ("Buy Jones!").[50]

6. The distinction between entrepreneurship (overcoming uncertainty) and gambling (deliberately created risk).[51]

7. Who bears the tax burden of sales taxes (not just consumers).[52]

8. Tax exemptions are not implicit subsidies.[53]

9. The nonsense of "the ability to pay" arguments.[54]

10. The non-neutrality of any known tax.[55]

11. Bureaucrats pay no taxes.[56]

12. The refutation of the single tax.[57]

13. Bribery as a market tool.[58]

Consider his critique of economic reasoning based on the indifference curves. This is the selected approach of Sir John Hicks and his followers. Hicks, it should be recalled, was the co-winner of the Nobel Prize in 1972. Rothbard wrote in 1956: "Indifference can never be demonstrated by action. Quite the contrary. Every action necessarily signifies a *choice*, and every choice signifies a definite preference. Action specifically implies the *contrary* of indifference. . . . If a person is really indifferent between two alternatives, then he cannot and will not choose between them. Indifference is therefore never relevant for action and cannot be demonstrated in action."[59] (Notice this early use of italics. He was afflicted at age 30.)

But it is not simply his general statement of the problem of indifference cures which sticks in the mind. It is his classic example.

The indifference theorists have two basic defenses of the role of indifference in real action. One is to cite the famous fable of Buridan's Ass. This is the "perfectly rational" ass who demonstrates indifference by standing, hungry, equidistant from two equally attractive bales of hay.[60] Since the two bales are equally attractive in every way, the ass can choose neither one, and starves therefore. This example is supposed to indicate how indifference can be revealed in action. It is, of course, difficult to conceive of an ass, or a person, who could be *less* rational. Actually, he is not confronted with *two* choices but with *three*, the third being to starve where he is. Even on the theorists' own grounds, this third choice will be ranked lower than the other two on the individual's value-scale. He will *not* choose starvation.[61]

Buridan's Ass has been in the economic literature since the late-medieval scholastic era. If nothing else, Murray Rothbard ought to go down in history as the economist who at last, after 600 years, kicked Buridan's Ass into action.

Conclusion

There are a lot of articles I would like Murray Rothbard to write. There is a lot of foundational work which still needs his insightful efforts, if only to clear up lingering confusions and doubts. I would list the following possibilities, just in case he has a lot of extra time on his hands:

1. If the economist cannot make interpersonal comparisons of subjective utility (Lionel Robbins's 1932 position, before Roy Harrod got him to capitulate in 1938), as Rothbard insists,[62] then how can he be certain that "the free market maximizes social utility"?[63] What is "social utility" in an epistemological world devoid of interpersonal aggregates?

2. If "*in human action there are no quantitative constants*,"[64] and therefore no index number is legitimate,[65] then how can we say that monetary inflation produces price inflation? What is price inflation without an index number? What is an index number without interpersonal aggregation?

3. If we cannot define "social utility," or price inflation, then how can we know that "money, in contrast to all other useful commodities employed in production or consumption, does not confer a social benefit when its supply increases"?[66] How can we legitimately say anything about the aggregate entity, "social benefit"?

4. If we also cannot make inter*temporal* comparisons of personal subjective utility, let alone intertemporal comparisons of social utility,[67] how can we avoid the seeming nihilism of the Lachmann-Shackle "Impregnable self-contained isolation"?[68]

5. If it is illegitimate to use the calculus in economics, because its infinitesimal gradations are not relevant to human action, should we continue to use Euclidian lines in our expositions of economics? Why not use discrete dots or small circles to replace Alfred Marshall's famous scissors?

6. If Mises's methodological construct of the Evenly Rotating Economy hypothesizes a world in which all participants have perfect fore-

knowledge, thereby denying the possibility of human action,[69] how can such a mental construct ("ideal type") serve as a useful guide to the realm of human action? How can the zero-human action world of "equilibrium" be related logically to the real world of human action?

With respect to the decision by the Nobel Committee concerning future answers to these questions, there need be no sense of urgency. There is plenty of time. Don't call them; they'll call you.

Just like they called Mises.

Notes

1. Gerald Debreu, *Theory of Value: An Axiomatic Analysis of Economic Equilibrium* (New Haven: Yale University Press, 1959).
2. Murray Rothbard, *America's Great Depression* (Kansas City, Kans.: Sheed and Ward, [1963] 1972), p. 4.
3. He even went so far as to write a five-volume history of colonial America prior to the U.S. Constitution, thereby demonstrating that he is interested in history, although only four volumes are published: *Conceived in Liberty* (New Rochelle, N.Y.: Arlington House, 1975-79). Writing five volumes on an era of U.S. history which seldom gets two hundred pages in even large U.S. history textbooks is probably deemed by his economist colleagues as an excessive curiosity concerning U.S. history.
4. Murray N. Rothbard, *For a New Liberty: The Libertarian Manifesto*, rev. ed. (New York: Collier, 1978), p. 57.
5. Thomas Kuhn, *The Structure of Scientific Revolutions* (Chicago: University of Chicago Press, 1962).
6. A. W. Coats, "The Role of Scholarly Journals in the History of Economics: An Essay," *Journal of Economic Literature* IX (1971): 29-44; John J. Siegfried, "The Publishing of Economic Papers and Its Impact on Graduate Faculty Ratings, 1960-1969," ibid. X (1972): 31-49.
7. Coats, ibid., p. 20.
8. *Annals of an Abiding Liberal*, cited by "Adam Smith," *New York Times*, 30 September 1979.
9. He is generally acknowledged as the anonymous "John Doe" who wrote the *Report from Iron Mountain on the Possibility and Desirability of Peace* (New York: Dial Press, 1967). He unquestionably wrote "The Day Khrushchev Visited the Establishment," *Harper's* (April 1971).
10. Galbraith, *Economics Peace and Laughter*, edited by Andrea D. Williams (New York: New American Library, 1972), p. 43.
11. Machlup was formerly an Austrian economist in both senses: at one time, he was a follower of Mises, and he lived in Austria. He received his doctorate from the University of Vienna in 1923, and came to the United States in 1933. He edited *Essays on Hayek* (Hillsdale, Mich.: Hillsdale College Press, 1976).
12. Fritz Machlup, "Are the Social Sciences Really Inferior?" *Southern Economic Journal* 27 (January 1961): 182.
13. Galbraith, *Economics Peace and Laughter*, pp. 44n, 45n.
14. Kuhn, *Structure of Scientific Revolutions*, p. 20.

15. The impossibility of socialist economic calculation, the monetary theory of the trade cycle, the impossibility of "neutral money," and the structure of production over time.

16. F. A. Hayek, *Prices and Production* (London: Routledge & Kegan Paul, [1931] 1960), Lecture II.

17. Paul Johnson begins his account of "modern times" with an account of the astronomical observation which is regarded as the experimental confirmation of Einstein's theory of relativity. He writes (somewhat apocalyptically): "The modern world began on 29 May 1919. . . ." *Modern Times: The World from the Twenties to the Eighties* (New York: Harper and Row, 1983), p. 1.

18. Abraham Pais, *"Subtle is the Lord . . ." The Science and the Life of Albert Einstein* (New York: Oxford University Press, 1982), p. 503.

19. Ibid., p. 511.

20. Susan Lee, "The un-managed economy," *Forbes*, 17 December 1984.

21. "Lord Keynes considered credit expansion an efficient method for the abolition of unemployment; he believed that 'gradual and automatic lowering of real wages as a result of rising prices' would not be so strongly resisted by labor as any attempt to lower money wage rates. However, the success of such a cunning plan would require an unlikely degree of ignorance and stupidity on the part of the wage earners," Ludwig von Mises, *Human Action: A Treatise on Economics* (New Haven, Conn.: Yale University Press, 1949), p. 771.

22. "In Keynes's analysis perfect and active competition is assumed, and prices are supposed to fall immediately and in full proportion to the fall in marginal variable costs. . . . What I understand to be the current doctrine is different. It looks to wage-reductions during a depression to restore profit-margins, thus to restore the investment-morale of entrepreneurs and to give them again a credit status which will enable them to finance any investment they may wish to make," Viner, "Review of Keynes's *General Theory of Employment, Interest and Money*," *Quarterly Journal of Economics* 51 (1936-37); reprinted in *Critics of Keynesian Economics*, Henry Hazlitt, ed. (Princeton: Van Nostrand, 1960), p. 60.

23. "In the first two chapters of book IV, which bear directly on the incentive to invest, the main point emphasized is the speculative element involved in any decision to produce durable wealth. . . . My criticisms of Mr. Keynes's treatment of anticipation, apart from the exasperating difficulty of following his exposition, would be that he does not follow through in accord with the importance and universality of the speculative aspect of capital production (and, in a lesser degree, capital-maintenance) in real life," Frank Knight, "Review of the *General Theory*," *Canadian Journal of Economics and Political Science* (February 1937); reprinted in Hazlitt, *Critics of Keynesian Economics*, p. 83.

24. Martin Bronfenbrenner, "Trends, Cycles, and Fads in Economic Writing," *American Economic Review* LVI (May 1966): 538.

25. I use "neo-Austrianism" because, as I argue below, there are no longer any disciples of Mises's original synthesis among younger scholars. They are all Rothbardians, Kirznerians, or Lachmannians. Hans Sennholz of Grove City College in Pennsylvania is, to my knowledge, the only pure Misesian remaining within the economics profession.

26. Kuhn, *Structure of Scientific Revolutions*.

27. Byrd L. Jones, "The Role of Keynesians in Wartime Policy and Postwar Planning, 1940-1946," *American Economic Review, Papers and Proceedings* LXII (May 1972).

28. Walter Heller, *New Dimensions of Political Economy* (New York: Norton, 1966), p. 59.

29. *Time*, 31 December 1965, 67B.

30. Heller, *New Dimensions*, p. 1.

31. Ibid., p. 2.
32. Ibid., p. 58.
33. Ibid., p. 116.
34. Ibid., p. 79.
35. Ibid., p. 14.
36. Ibid., p. 83.
37. An enlightening discussion of the five steps that produce an academic revolution in economics is provided by Harry Johnson, "The Keynesian Revolution and the Monetarist Counter-Revolution," in Elizabeth S. Johnson and Harry G. Johnson, eds., *The Shadow of Keynes: Understanding Keynes, Cambridge and Keynesian Economics* (Chicago: University of Chicago Press, 1978), chap. 14.
38. "The Unorthodox Ideas of Radical Economists Win a Wider Hearing," *Wall Street Journal*, 11 February 1972; *Business Week*, 18 March 1972.
39. *Business Week*, 6 January 1973, 57.
40. "Theory deserts the forecasters," *Business Week*, 29 June 1974, 50-59.
41. An exception is Professor Israel Kirzner.
42. "Passing much of his intellectual life on a sofa, Darwin believed, with an almost missionary strenuousness, in easy and comfortable reading. At times he found every unnecessary movement, and even the weight of a book, intolerable. His remedy was surgery on the book. With a ruthless, unbibiophile hand he dismembered heavy and dignified tomes, in order to read them in light and manageable sections," William Irvine, *Apes, Angels and Victorians: Darwin, Huxley, and Evolution* (New York: McGraw-Hill, 1955), p. 165.
43. "The only way to stop Hitler would have been to spend large sums for rearmament and to return to conscription. The whole British nation, not only the aristocracy, was strongly opposed to such measures," Ludwig von Mises, *Omnipotent Government: The Rise of the Total State and Total War* (New Haven, Conn.: Yale University Press, 1944), p. 189.
44. Ludwig von Mises, *Human Action* (New Haven, Conn.: Yale University Press, 1963), p. 282.
45. He was subsequently hired as a full professor in the University of Chicago's interdisciplinary Department of Social Thought.
46. "Toward a Reconstruction of Utility and Welfare Economics," in Mary Sennholz, ed., *On Freedom and Free Enterprise: Essays in Honor of Ludwig von Mises* (Princeton: Van Nostrand, 1956), p. 233. A reprint has been issued by Liberty Press, Indianapolis.
47. Ibid., pp. 233-35.
48. Ibid., pp. 236-38; Murray N. Rothbard, *Man, Economy, and State* (Los Angeles: Nash Publishing, 1970), pp. 265-67.
49. *Man, Economy, and State*, pp. 547-48.
50. Ibid., p. 722; idem, *Power and Market: Government and the Economy* (Menlo Park, Calif.: Institute for Humane Studies, 1970), p. 36.
51. *Man, Economy, and State*, pp. 500-1.
52. *Power and Market*, pp. 66-70.
53. Ibid., p. 104.
54. Ibid., p. 110.
55. Ibid, pp. 117-19.
56. Ibid., p. 118.
57. Ibid., pp. 91-100.
58. *Power and Market*, pp. 57-58.
59. "Toward a Reconstruction," p. 237.

60. He refers us to Schumpeter's *History of Economic Analysis* (New York: Oxford University Press, 1954), p. 94n.

61. "Toward a Reconstruction," p. 238.

62. Ibid., pp. 245-46.

63. *Power and Market*, p. 13.

64. *Man, Economy, and State*, p. 739.

65. Ibid., p. 740.

66. Rothbard, "The Case for a 100 Per Cent Gold Dollar," in Leland B. Yeager, ed., *In Search of a Monetary Constitution* (Cambridge, Mass.: Harvard University Press, 1962), p. 121.

67. "It is not possible, however, for an observer scientifically to compare the social utilities of results on the free market from one period of time to the next. As we have seen above, we cannot determine a man's value-scales over a period of time. How much more impossible for all individuals!" Rothbard, "Toward a Reconstruction," p. 255.

68. Ludwig Lachmann, *Capital, Expectations, and the Market Process: Essays on the Theory of the Market Economy* (Kansas City, Kans.: Sheed Andrews and McMeel, 1977), p. 83.

69. "But in the evenly rotating economy there is no choosing. . . . It is a world of soulless unthinking automatons; it is not a human society, it is an ant hill," Mises, *Human Action*, p. 248.

9

Economic Efficiency and Public Policy

E. C. Pasour, Jr.

A great deal has been written about the wasteful habits of U.S. citizens. Individual decision makers and business entrepreneurs are alleged to be inefficient. Consumers are frequently criticized for driving large cars, keeping their homes too warm in the winter, and so on. Workers are said to operate below their potential because of ignorance or lack of motivation. Business entrepreneurs are accused of wasting money in many different ways, including wasteful advertising and unproductive mergers.

Allegations of economic inefficiency are not restricted to editorial writers and other such observers of the business scene. Hundreds of economic studies purport to measure efficiency (or inefficiency). However, Professor Rothbard demonstrates that the efficiency of human action measured against the conventional economic norm is a "chimera."[1] Moreover, as shown below, the inability of economists to measure economic efficiency is but one aspect of the more general problem that public policy can not be prescribed on the basis of marginal efficiency rules.

This paper first explores the implications of uncertainty and subjectivism in identifying examples of economic inefficiency. It is shown that neither economists nor other outside observers can identify inefficient behavior as is widely assumed in the conventional theory of the firm, including x-efficiency theory. It is further shown that efficiency measurements of group activities present an even greater challenge than efficiency measurements of individual actions. These findings are shown to be consistent with Rothbard's argument that the advocacy of public policy must be based on ethical considerations rather than on marginal efficiency rules.[2] The implication is that the focus of interest in economic analysis should be less on the outcome of the resource allocation process and more on the rules and institutions that permitted individuals to engage in mutually beneficial exchange. The challenge to economists is to further the understanding of this system, including the operation of the market process as it is fueled by subjectivist expectations of actors operating under conditions of uncertainty.

Economic Efficiency and the Perfect Competition Norm

Economic efficiency is conventionally defined as the ratio of the value of output to the value of inputs. Although there is general agreement among economists that efficiency must be measured in value terms, there is little recognition of the problems posed by subjectivism in making efficiency measurements.

Any test of efficiency must be based on some standard of comparison. The efficiency standard commonly used in economics is "perfect competition." Perfect competition requires price-taking behavior and perfect markets.[3] The features of a "perfect market" are perfect communication, instantaneous equilibrium, and costless transactions.

The forbidding requirements of perfect competition mean that it is useless as a norm in measuring the efficiency of actions of real world actors. If perfect competition is used as a standard, no individual or market operating in the real world of change and uncertainty will be judged to be efficient. The decision maker judged against the standard of perfect competition would be considered efficient only if he had perfect knowledge. On this basis, real world decision makers are *never efficient* because they are not omniscient.[4]

The conventional static perfect competition approach to the measurement of efficiency assumes away uncertainty and knowledge problems confronted by decision makers as they must operate in a constantly changing environment. However, it is not appropriate to use a model that assumes away problems facing the decision maker in assessing the performance of that individual. Thus, it is clearly inappropriate to measure the performance of an actor against the efficiency standard of perfect competition. Moreover, economists have yet to describe efficiency under real world conditions of uncertainty where knowledge is costly.[5] Inefficiency in a meaningful sense implies both that a superior outcome is attainable and that the expected benefits of achieving this arrangement exceed the expected costs.[6] However, the individual decision maker operating in an environment shrouded with uncertainty is motivated by costs and returns that are inherently subjective. The problems posed by uncertainty and subjectivism in identifying inefficient behavior on the part of other economic actors are described below in several different contexts.

Inefficiency of Individual Decisions

The first example is taken from the traditional economic theory of the firm. Consider the classical case of production involving a single variable input. As the number of cattle on a given amount of pasture (other resources being fixed) is increased, for example, the ratio of cattle to land eventually becomes so large that overgrazing results in a smaller amount of production than would be produced with a smaller number of cattle. Production under these conditions in conventional neoclassical theory is considered "irrational" or "inefficient" because an increase in the amount of the variable input results in a decrease in output. Thus, static neoclassical production theory holds that inefficient entrepreneurial behavior can be determined in this situation on the basis of production data alone.[7] However, the inefficiency conclusion fails to take into account problems posed by time and uncertainty.

The most profitable number of cattle to have on a given amount of pasture in any time period cannot be determined independently of expected costs and returns in future periods.[8] The decision maker presumably is interested in maximizing wealth over time—not in obtaining the most income in a single period. The entrepreneur may, therefore, have "too many" cattle on pasture in the current period because he expects cattle prices to be higher in a future period. If cattle prices *are* expected to be higher in future periods, "overgrazing" in the current period may be consistent with wealth maximization over time. Consequently, inefficient entrepreneurial behavior cannot be identified on the basis of production data alone. And, since expected costs and returns are inherently subjective (as shown below), there is no reason to expect the decision maker and the economist (or other outside observer) to assess the profitability of cattle management decisions in the same way. Thus, the outside observer cannot identify inefficient input use in situations involving production over time.

A second, and closely related, example is "x-inefficiency."[9] Leibenstein focuses on the difference between actual and potentially higher worker output attributable to factors such as ignorance, inertia, and custom. The shortfall in output arising from these factors is labelled "x-inefficiency." Consider the farmer who doesn't produce the most profitable amount of corn—choosing to go fishing instead of weeding at a crucial time because it is his custom to fish on that day each year.

The corn producer might be labelled x-inefficient. Again, however, it cannot be concluded on the basis of observable data that the farmer is inefficient.[10] The farmer doesn't seek maximum profits from corn—he seeks instead the most overall satisfaction, and income from corn production is only one element affecting his wealth or state of mind. The farmer can devote more time to corn production only by reducing leisure or by diverting time used for some other purpose. Moreover, in the present example, leisure may be valued more highly by the farmer than the amount of corn foregone. And, as shown below, the outside observer cannot objectively measure the costs and returns that influence choice. Here, again, observable data are not sufficient to assess the efficiency of the decision maker.

It may be contended that the decision maker in the above example was "x-inefficient" because he had "too little" information about the costs and benefits associated with alternative courses of action. However, the outside observer faces problems similar to those described above in determining when another person has too little knowledge. The decision maker acquires information on the basis of expected costs and returns that vary from person to person. Thus, problems facing the outside observer in identifying inefficient behavior are similar, whether the issue is amount of labor to devote to corn production or amount of resources to devote to acquisition of knowledge. This problem is rooted in the subjective nature of the costs and benefits that influence individual choice.

Implications of Subjectivism

The conclusion that an outside observer cannot identify another decision maker's inefficiency follows from the subjective nature of opportunity cost. The opportunity cost of an action is the expected value of the alternative sacrificed as a result of the action taken. Since the opportunities foregone are not actually experienced, the value of the rejected course of action hinges on the decision maker's anticipations.[11] Consequently, opportunity cost is inherently subjective and distinct from data that can be objectively measured by an outside observer. The problem in attempting to determine choice-influencing cost is not one of measurement. The real problem is that the information needed is knowledge of subjective tradeoffs that are nowhere articulated.[12] The conclusion is that an outside observer cannot identify another person's inefficient behavior since the expected value of the costs and benefits that determine choice are unique to the economic actor.[13]

It is often alleged that the actor's decision would have been different if the chooser had possessed more information. This is correct but irrelevant in identifying inefficiency. After a choice is made, retrospective calculations of what the cost would have been if the actor had had additional information can not be relevant to that prior choice situation.[14]

Inefficiency of Group Decisions

The conclusion (of the preceding analysis) that the outside observer cannot measure the efficiency of another person's actions is not generally accepted in welfare economics. However, some economists who agree that inefficiency and waste cannot be detected at the individual level, attempt to measure economic efficiency at the "societal level."

The problem of identifying real world inefficiencies, however, is even greater at the group level than at the individual level. If the outside observer cannot assess the efficiency of an individual acting alone, such measurement is likely to be even more unfeasible when that individual acts as a member of a group. In assessing the efficiency of group actions, not only is there the problem that costs and benefits are subjective, these values are noncomparable from person to person.[15] Hayek vividly describes the implications of subjectivism for empirical measurements in conventional welfare economics:

> The childish attempts to provide a basis for "just" action by measuring the relative utilities or satisfactions of different persons simply cannot be taken seriously. . . . the whole of the so-called "welfare economics," which pretends to base its arguments on inter-personal comparisons of ascertainable utilities, lacks all scientific foundation.[16]

Despite the misgivings of Hayek and other analysts skeptical of the usefulness of welfare economics as a basis for public policy, the social efficiency approach continues to be widely used for policy purposes—including pollution problems related to air, land, and water. Consider the classic example of the operation of a business firm that pollutes a nearby stream. In the conventional Pigouvian approach, it is recommended that a per unit tax equal to the difference between "marginal private cost" and "marginal social cost" be levied on the firm to induce it to consider the full ("social") cost in making production and output decisions.[17] However, a difference between private cost and social cost is simply postulated since neither private cost nor "social cost" can be measured objectively.[18] The economist cannot measure the relevant private cost because the perception of the satisfaction foregone at the moment of choice is the only sense in which cost influences choice. Furthermore, once it is recognized that cost is subjective to the individual and that costs to different people are incommensurate, it follows that "social cost" cannot be objectively measured and that ". . . net social benefit is an artificial concept of direct interest only to economists."[19]

It is no more feasible for the economist to identify inefficiencies in group decisions relating to pollution (or other) problems than it is to detect inefficiencies in actions of individuals. Despite this fact, economists continue to identify numerous examples of alleged "market failure," including pollution and other "externalities," monopoly, imperfections in the capital market, lack of information, and so on. In every purported example of individual or market inefficiency, however, the finding is wholly in terms of the observer's estimate of the value scales of other people.[20]

Consider, for example, the rate of return on public investment in agricultural research. There is a widespread view that the level of public investment in agricultural research and educational activities is "too low." This opinion is based on the results of cost-benefit studies which show that the rates of return to past public investments of this type have been quite high. Ruttan, for example, cites a host of empirical rate-of-return estimates of publicly funded research and educational activities that are in the 30 to 40% range. Because these rates apparently are higher than returns from competing investments, Ruttan concludes there is inefficiency or underinvestment in the elective choice process.[21]

The underinvestment conclusion in the case of public investment in agricultural research can be challenged on a number of grounds.[22] Rates of return on public investment are subject to all of the problems of the "net social benefit" approach discussed above. Moreover, the high rate of return estimates in this case are suspect even if one overlooks the problems arising because costs and returns are noncomparable between individuals. First, about half of agricultural research is now privately funded. If the rate of return were, in fact, relatively high, one might expect the competitive process to bring about entry until the rate of return is similar to that of other investments of similar risk.[23]

Second, rate of return estimates on publicly funded activities are not comparable with private rates of return because state and federal research agencies pay no taxes. If a correction were made for taxes paid by private-sector firms, the rates of return on publicly funded research would appear much less impressive.[24]

Third, rate-of-return estimates from publicly funded research fail to consider the misallocation of resources resulting from taxation. These estimates implicitly assume that $1 of government expenditures has an opportunity cost of $1.[25] Taxation to finance public expenditures, however, causes distortions in product and input markets so that the opportunity cost of $1 of public expenditures is actually more than the $1 collected from taxpayers. Thus, the rate of return estimates on public expenditures are biased upward because they fail to take into account this misallocation of resources.[26]

Fourth, it is important in policy advocacy to distinguish between *ex post* and *ex ante* costs and returns. Empirical rate of return studies are necessarily based on *ex post* data. Yet, investment choices are based on *expectations* of costs and returns. And, as demonstrated in the above examples, the economist has no way to measure the *ex ante* costs and returns that influence collective choice decisions. The opportunity cost of an additional expenditure of $1 billion by the federal government on agricultural research must take into account the value of the sacrificed alternatives in the private sector from tax collections and the opportunity cost of alternative public expenditures. The estimated return on such investments, however, is highly subjective. For example, what is the potential payoff from a $1 billion expenditure on prisons, law enforcement, and so on when there are no market price signals? It cannot be concluded that there is underinvestment in one area unless its rate of return is higher than that from other spending alternatives.

In summary, the social rate of return concept is subject to all the problems of social cost. In each case, choice-influencing costs are subjective and cannot be observed. Moreover, even if costs were given or known for different people, the magnitudes are incommensurable. Therefore, any efficiency measurements by an economist must be wholly in terms of the observer's estimates of the value scales of other people.[27]

Existence versus Measurement of Efficiency

The conclusion that neither the economist nor any other outside observer can make meaningful efficiency measurements, however, does not mean that all individuals and markets are efficient in the sense that there is no scope for improvement. At each instant, decisions are not perfectly coordinated because knowledge is imperfect and the decision-making process is permeated with uncertainty. The partial ignorance and inconsistent plans mean that there are opportunities for individuals to better their lot. In a market context, imperfect coordination provides profit opportunities for alert entrepreneurs.[28] Indeed, the market process is a reflection of how individuals search for opportunities that are present only when markets are in disequilibrium. Thus, even though an outside observer can neither identify inefficiency in the actions of other parties not specify actions that would necessarily improve their welfare, we can be confident that such opportunities frequently exist.

Much of the confusion related to efficiency measurements is associated with the neglected role of the entrepreneur.[29] There is no role for entrepreneurship when data are assumed given to the decision maker. In this case, the choice problem is reduced to mathematical calculation. Under real world conditions of uncertainty, however, data on means and ends are not given and a key entrepreneurial function is to determine what they are.

In retrospect, decision makers' actions often are incorrect. Actions are based on expected costs and returns, but expectations frequently are not realized. Kirzner defines an action as inefficient ". . . when one places oneself in a position one views as less desirable than an equally available alternative state."[30] In this sense, inefficiency results from error since the rational actor would not knowingly act to worsen his lot. Inefficiency defined in this way, however, is not helpful in assessing the efficacy of the actions taken by the decision maker. Any standard applicable only after the event is useless as a guide to choice.[31]

Success in decision making, however, sometimes is evaluated on the basis of results. Although this criterion is useful for some purposes, it is not a good measure of the correctness of decisions. If an economic actor undertakes to do something entailing uncertainty, he considers the chance of gain is worth the risk and whether he ultimately succeeds or fails has no relevance to this preference.[32]

Moreover, the relationship between purposeful behavior and success is ambiguous in a world of uncertainty. Success quite often is due to chance or unforseen circumstances rather than to superior foresight.[33] Decisions are based on expectations and the future is not only unknown but unknowable. Consequently, human action, including the allocation of resources between uses, is an individual decision process continuously unfolding in time.[34] As shown below, recognition of the implications of uncertainty and subjectivism is likely to have a profound influence on the economist's approach to public policy questions.

Marginal Analysis, Economic Efficiency and Public Policy

The marginal efficiency conditions of economics in their briefest form ". . . are that the marginal rates of substitution between any two commodities or factors must be the same in all their different uses."[35] The fact that an independent observer cannot measure the costs and benefits that motivate choice suggests that marginal analysis cannot be used by economists for policy prescription. These efficiency conditions nevertheless are useful to the individual decision maker. If the potential chooser is aware of these conditions, he will weigh alternatives more carefully in terms of their opportunity cost and search more diligently for superior alternatives.[36] Thus, knowledge of economic efficiency conditions can help the chooser make "better" choices as evaluated by the decision maker's own standards.

As Hayek stresses, however, these efficiency conditions do *not* provide the solution to public policy issues. The reason is that the data necessary to apply such rules for the whole society are never given to a single mind. Consequently, marginal efficiency rules are not useful as guides to public policy. In reality, economic analysis intended to guide public policy frequently overlooks functions and requirements of entrepreneurial decision making and the costs necessary to carry out those functions.

Neoclassical monopoly theory is a good example of the failure to take into account the functions and requirements of entrepreneurial decision making. The problem of how to identify monopoly generally is downplayed in economic analysis. In conventional theory, competition implies that sellers have no influence on price, and the firm facing a negatively sloped demand curve is regarded as a monopolist.[37] If every firm facing a negatively sloped demand curve were regarded as a monopoly, however, many firms operating under highly competitive conditions, including Grandma Moses, would be classified as monopolists. Yet, if monopoly in this traditional approach is not identified with a downward sloping demand curve, any demarcation of how inelastic demand must be for the seller to be considered a monopolist must be purely arbitrary.

The alternative suggested by the Austrians is to consider competition as a dynamic *process* rather than as a situation in which demand is perfectly elastic. Monopoly power is then defined in terms of restrictions on the market process rather than on the basis of the slope of the demand curve facing the seller. And, as Rothbard suggests, effective restrictions on the competitive market process are almost invariably the result of government intervention.[38]

Conventional monopoly theory is not consistent with the nature of the entrepreneurial market process.[39] Alleged monopoly "profits" may be merely returns to entrepreneurship. A seller operating under competitive conditions, for example, may acquire a short-run advantage over other sellers through entrepreneurial ingenuity. Entrepreneurial profits are likely to be beneficial rather than harmful, however, since entrepreneurship fuels the market process. Thus, any appropriate model of the market process must permit above-average returns to alert entrepreneurs. Worcester describes why it is crucial to take a long-run view in assessing the effects of returns to entrepreneurial activity.

> A longer run view of what may seem to be excessive profits or losses is appropriate because every successful penetration of the unknown (that is) successful because of artful foresight, scientific estimation, or plain luck gives the entrepreneur an edge . . . that can be classified as a monopoly return.[40]

The conclusion is that marginal efficiency conditions do not enable the economist to identify harmful monopoly power.[41] Similar problems arise in other attempts to use marginal analysis for policy-making purposes.[42]

What does the conclusion that economic analysis is not suitable for policy making imply for the role of the economist? If it is recognized that marginal efficiency rules do not provide answers to economic policy questions, the focus of the economist changes. Marginal efficiency rules are concerned with the outcome of the resource allocation process, assuming that the necessary information is available to apply these rules. If such information is not available to policy makers, interest then is less on the *outcome* of the resource allocation process and more on the rules of the game and the operation of the market process itself.

An economist's view of the importance of uncertainty and subjectivism generally will, therefore, determine or greatly influence the approach taken in economic analysis. The market is most accurately viewed as a ceaseless process of discovery and information dissemination in which no single individual or planning board can know the future relative scarcity of goods and services.[43] Thus, providing a stable institutional framework and letting adjustments of actions by private economic actors occur on their own is likely to be the best way to ensure the increase and dissemination of knowledge.

If resource allocation by economic actors is viewed as a decision process unfolding over time, marginal efficiency conditions of static equilibrium receive much less attention by the economist in analysis of public policy issues. Instead, focus is placed on development of institutions and rules that permit individuals to engage freely in actions that are mutually beneficial.[44] This implies that for resolution of public policy questions the expected payoff is likely to be higher from additional work on the nature and operation of these institutions and rules than from further refinements either in equilibrium theory or in quantitative techniques of economic analysis.[45]

The proposed approach is consistent with what Buchanan refers to as the "morally relevant" approach in economics. In this view, a logical goal in public policy is to develop an institutional framework that maximizes the scope for mutually beneficial behavior. A discussion of the specific characteristics of this framework is beyond the purview of this paper. This approach emphasizing the institutional framework is markedly different from the one that attempts "to control other people's behavior with increasing efficiency" by measuring costs and benefits on an aggregate basis.[46]

Reductions in economic regulations that hamper the market process cannot be vindicated on the basis of comparisons of changes in income (or utility) of consumers and producers because the gains and losses are incommensurable. Thus, economic theory is not a substitute for ethical analysis in resolving public policy problems. A more promising approach is to consider economic freedom on the same level as freedoms guaranteed under the First Amendment. If economic freedom is considered an ethical issue, restrictions of economic freedom are bad because individuals have the *right* to engage in voluntary mutually beneficial exchange. The conclusion is that policy recommendations inevitably involve value judgments.[47]

The economist can play an important role in explaining the operation of the decentralized market economy and the effects of market impediments. Not only can knowledge of economics help make individual decisions more intelligible, but expertise in the market process is also useful in tracing out the direct and indirect effects of public policies.[48] Much work remains to be done in exploring the implications of uncertainty for the operation and explanation of systematic market processes in which individual choice is inherently subjective.[49]

Conclusions and Implications

Economic efficiency inevitably involves valuation. Therefore, efficiency measurements require the use of a standard of comparison. When the commonly used perfect competition norm is used to measure efficiency, all decision makers operating under real-world conditions will be inefficient. Moreover, no one has developed an efficiency norm that is helpful in assessing the efficiency of decisions made under real-world conditions of uncertainty. Economic efficiency, then, is not useful as a touchstone of public policy.

Choice is motivated by opportunity cost, which is inherently subjective. Consequently, any efficiency measurement by an outside observer must be wholly in terms of the observer's estimates of the value scales of other people. Therefore, the economist as an outside observer cannot measure or identify other decision makers' inefficiencies because of the subjective nature of the costs and benefits that influence choice.

Rothbard's correct assessment that efficiency is a chimera does not suggest that economists have no useful role in improving public policy. The existence of uncertainty and the subjective character of economic data do mean that the economist cannot use marginal analysis to select "optimal" public policies. However, economists can provide a useful service in explaining the workings of the market economy, including the consequences of free markets and the effects of different types of government intervention.[50] Economists often fail to criticize harmful government programs on the grounds that it is not politically feasible to abolish them. The only serious defense of a policy recommendation hinges on whether the policy is good instead of whether it is realistic under the current political climate.[51]

Murray Rothbard's numerous contributions have increased public understanding of the benefits and requirements of a free society. None of these works, however, is likely to have a larger and more lasting impact than his analysis of the uses and misuses of economics in the public policy arena. Rothbard's contribution to public policy will become more widely recognized if and when uncertainty and subjectivism are taken seriously in economic analysis.

Notes

1. Murray N. Rothbard, "Comment: The Myth of Efficiency," in Mario J. Rizzo, ed., *Time, Uncertainty, and Disequilibrium* (Lexington, Mass.: D. C. Heath, 1979), p. 90.
2. Murray N. Rothbard, *The Ethics of Liberty* (Atlantic Highlands, N.J.: Humanities Press, 1982).

3. Jack Hirshleifer, *Price Theory and Applications* (Englewood Cliffs, N.J.: Prentice-Hall, 1984), pp. 418-19.

4. In another sense it can be argued that individuals are always efficient. Under traditional economic assumptions where each individual is assumed to behave consistently with the postulate of constrained maximization, economic inefficiency presents a contradiction in terms (S. N. G. Cheung, "A Theory of Price Control," *Journal of Law and Economics* 17 (1974): 53-71). That is, if the decision maker is assumed to maximize subject to the constraints faced, the individual is then necessarily efficient in the sense that the action selected is *ipso facto* at least as good as any feasible alternative (E. C. Pasour, Jr., "Economic Efficiency and Inefficient Economics: Another View," *Journal of Post Keynesian Economics* 4 (1982): 454-59). This argument is consistent with the Mises view that human action is necessarily rational because individuals always act to improve their situation (Ludwig von Mises, *Human Action* 3rd ed. (Chicago: Henry Regnery, 1966), p. 19).

5. Harold Demsetz, "Information and Efficiency: Another Viewpoint," *Journal of Law and Economics* 12 (1969): 1-22.

6. E. C. Pasour, Jr. and J. B. Bullock, "Implications of Uncertainty for the Measurement of Efficiency," *American Journal of Agricultural Economics* 57 (1975): 335-39.

7. Edgar K. Browning and J. M. Browning, *Microeconomic Theory and Applications* (Boston: Little, Brown and Co., 1983), p. 169.

8. Louis DeAlessi, "The Short Run Revisited," *American Economic Review* 57 (1967): 450-61.

9. H. Leibenstein, "Allocative Efficiency vs. 'X-Efficiency,'" *American Economic Review* 56 (1966): 392-415.

10. George J. Stigler, "The Xistence of X-Efficiency," *American Economic Review* 66 (1976): 213-16.

11. James M. Buchanan, *Cost and Choice* (Chicago: Markham Publishing, 1969).

12. Thomas Sowell, *Knowledge and Decisions*, (New York: Basic Books, 1980).

13. "When it is understood that a reckoning of cost . . . depends upon the forecasting of events and outcomes of the future, and when it is understood that any individual is uniquely situated in relation to past events on which such forecasts are based, it becomes clear that the result of the reckoning is dependent for what it is upon the unique knowledge and attitude (towards uncertainty or risk) of the unique and uniquely situated individual who calculates it, and that the validity, correctness or authoritativeness of an overriding calculation by somebody else would often be dubious in the extreme," (G. F. Thirlby, "Economists' Cost Rules and Equilibrium Theory," in James M. Buchanan and G. F. Thirlby, eds., *L. S. E. Essays on Cost* (London: Weidenfeld and Nicolson, 1973), pp. 280-81).

14. Gerald P. O'Driscoll, Jr. and Mario J. Rizzo, *The Economics of Time and Ignorance* (New York: Basil Blackwell, 1985), p. 48; such calculations may, of course, influence actions in future choice situations.

15. Rothbard, *The Ethics of Liberty*, p. 204.

16. F. A. Hayek, *Law, Legislation and Liberty*, vol. 3, *The Political Order of a Free People* (Chicago: University of Chicago Press, 1979), p. 201.

17. For a comprehensive critique of the social efficiency approach to pollution problems, see Murray N. Rothbard, "Law, Property Rights, and Air Pollution," *Cato Journal* 2 (1982): 55-99.

18. ". . . static maximizing models cannot explain (rationalize) suboptimality; they can merely postulate it. Either an equilibrium is suboptimal in an irrelevant and unexplained sense, or it is optimal in an explained but trivial sense. Statist welfare economics thus self-destructs" (O'Driscoll and Rizzo, *The Economics of Time and Ignorance*, pp. 89-90).

19. Stephen C. Littlechild, "The Problem of Social Costs," in Louis M. Spadaro, ed., *New Directions in Austrian Economics*, (Kansas City, Kans.: Sheed Andrews and McMeel, 1979), p. 9. Lionel Robbins explains why prices and incomes before and after an event cannot be used to compare the satisfactions of different persons involved, ". . . whenever we discuss distributional questions, we make our own estimates of the happiness afforded or misery endured by different persons or groups of persons. But these are *our* estimates. There is no objective measurement conceivable" (Lionel Robbins, "Economics and Political Economy," *American Economic Review* 71 (1981): 5).

20. James M. Buchanan, "Positive Economics, Welfare Economics, and Political Economy," *Journal of Law and Economics* 2 (1959): 126.

21. "There is little doubt that a level of expenditures that would push rates of return to below 20 percent would be in the public interest" (Vernon W. Ruttan, "Bureaucratic Productivity: The Case of Agricultural Research," *Public Choice* 35 (1980): 531.

22. E. C. Pasour, Jr. and M. A. Johnson, "Bureaucratic Productivity: The Case of Agricultural Research Revisited," *Public Choice* 39 (1982): 301-17.

23. It is frequently contended that privately funded agricultural research is not feasible because the fruits of this research are "public goods." However, developers of new technology generally can appropriate the returns from new plant varieties, new machinery, and information through patents, copyrights, and fees. Thus, public funding of agricultural research generally cannot be justified on the basis of public goods theory.

24. Glenn Fox, "Is the United States Really Under-investing in Agricultural Research?" *American Journal of Agricultural Economics* 67 (1985): 806-12.

25. Fox, ibid.

26. Ronald H. Coase, "The Theory of Public Utility Pricing and Its Application," *Bell Journal of Economics* 1 (1970): 113-28.

27. Buchanan, "Positive Economics, Welfare Economics, and Political Economy."

28. Israel M. Kirzner, *Perception, Opportunity, and Profit* (Chicago: University of Chicago Press, 1979).

29. Ibid.; Israel M. Kirzner, *Competition and Entrepreneurship* (Chicago: University of Chicago Press, 1973).

30. Kirzner, *Perception, Opportunity, and Profit*, p. 120.

31. G. L. S. Shackle, *Epistemics and Economics* (Cambridge: Cambridge University Press, 1972).

32. Ronald H. Coase, "Business Organization and the Accountant," in James M. Buchanan and G. F. Thirlby, eds., *L. S. E. Essays on Cost* (London: Weidenfeld and Nicolson, 1973), 104-05.

33. Armen A. Alchian, "Uncertainty, Evolution, and Economic Theory," *Journal of Political Economy* 58 (1950): 211-21.

34. Jack Wiseman, "Economics, Subjectivism and Public Choice," *Market Process* 3 (1985): 14-15.

35. F. A. Hayek, *Individualism and Economic Order* (Chicago: University of Chicago Press, 1948), p. 77.

36. James M. Buchanan, *What Should Economists Do?* (Indianapolis, Ind.: Liberty Press, 1979), p. 41.

37. Milton Friedman, *Price Theory* (Chicago: Aldine Publishing, 1976), p. 126.

38. "It is clear that the term 'monopoly' applies only to governmental grants of privilege, direct or indirect" (Murray N. Rothbard, *Power and Market* (Kansas City, Kans.: Sheed Andrews and McMeel, 1977), p. 79).

39. E. C. Pasour, Jr., "Monopoly Power, Taxation, and Entrepreneurship" in *Taxation and the Deficit Economy*, Dwight R. Lee, ed., (San Francisco: Pacific Institute for Public Policy Research, 1986), pp. 381-405.
40. Dean A. Worcester, "On the Validity of Marginal Analysis for Policy Making," *Eastern Economic Journal* 8 (1982): 83-8.
41. Rothbard, *The Ethics of Liberty*.
42. "Economic analysis suitable for policy must provide a negative answer to the first and a positive answer to the second of these questions: (1) Is any unavoidable task ignored or excluded by assumption? (2) Has an equally skeptical investigation been made of the viable alternatives?" (Worchester, "On the Validity of Marginal Analysis for Policy Making," p. 87).
43. Karl-Heinz Paqué, "How Far is Vienna from Chicago?" *Kyklos* 38 (1985): 412-34.
44. Leland B. Yeager, "Economics and Principles," *Southern Economic Journal* 42 (1976): 392-415.
45. "The social action which the study of economics has as its function to guide, or at least to illuminate, is essentially that of 'rules of the game,' in the shape of law, for economic relationships" (Frank H. Knight, *On the History and Method of Economics* (Chicago: University of Chicago Press, 1956), p. 174).
46. James M. Buchanan, "The Related But Distinct 'Science' of Economics and Political Economy," *British Journal of Social Psychology* 21 (1982): 97.
47. Murray N. Rothbard, "Value Implications of Economic Theory," *The American Economist* 17 (1973): 35-40. "Economics cannot be purged of moral content if it is to be concerned with the question of welfare; and economists must be concerned with this question, at least implicitly and indirectly, if economics is to be anything more than an intellectual game" (G. Warren Nutter, "Economic Welfare and the Welfare Economics," in *The Methodology of Economic Thought*, Warren J. Samuels ed., (New Brunswick, N.J.: Transactions Books, 1980), p. 395-96).
48. Kirzner, *Perception, Opportunity, and Profit*.
49. Israel M. Kirzner, review of *The Economics of Time and Ignorance* by Gerald P. O'Driscoll, Jr. and Mario J. Rizzo, *Market Process*, 3 (1985): 1-17.
50. Rothbard, *Power and Market*, pp. 256-61.
51. Ibid.; and Clarence Philbrook, "'Realism' in Policy Espousal," *American Economic Review* 43 (1953): 846-59.

10

Comparable Worth: Theoretical Foundations

Ellen Frankel Paul

Comparable worth is sweeping the country. In 25 states, studies are currently being conducted on wage disparities between men and women and how they might be rectified, while five other states have already implemented comparable worth schemes. A bill calling for a comparable worth study of the Federal bureaucracy passed the House of Representatives in 1984.

Court cases have also leant some encouragement to the supporters of comparable worth. *County of Washington v. Gunther*, decided by the Supreme court in 1981, breathed new life into the comparable worth movement, opening the door for suits under Title VII of the Civil Rights Act of 1964 that would allow claims of something more than "equal pay for equal work," the standard set in the Equal Pay Act of 1963.[1] In 1985, the United States District Court for the Western District of Washington decided a case, *American Federation of State, County and Municipal Employees (AFSCME) v. State of Washington*, which invigorated the movement even more.[2] In this case, Judge Tanner held that the State of Washington, which had instituted a series of comparable worth studies beginning in 1974, had to implement these findings. The plaintiffs, the class of those in women-dominated job classifications, were awarded back pay, injunctive relief and a declaratory judgment that the state was in violation of Title VII. The *AFSCME* case seemed to fulfill the promise held out to comparable worth advocates by *Washington v. Gunther*. However, that promise may prove illusory, as the Ninth Circuit Court of Appeals overturned on appeal the decision of the District Court.[3]

"Comparable worth," "comparable work," or the currently more fashionable "pay equity" is usually defined as the requirement that employers pay the same salaries to women in female-dominated job categories that they pay to men in male-dominated job categories who are performing work of comparable value to their employers. Although the definitions differ from advocate to advocate, what is clear is that the term "comparable worth" encompasses much more than equal pay for equal work. It is not sufficient, comparable worth activists argue, for women to be paid the same salaries for the same or substantially the same work. The Equal Pay Act, they contend, does not go far enough. If 80 percent of the women in the United States work in jobs which are 70 percent dominated by women,[4] then something more must be done to alleviate their lot than simply securing them equal pay for equal work. Women earn a mere 64 percent of the salaries of males who likewise work full-time. Something must be radically amiss in a market system that produces such patent inequities, they conclude.

The market, for the comparable worth advocates, is corrupted by discrimination, for nothing else can sufficiently explain the discrepancies between women's wages and men's. As Joy Ann Grune, former Executive Director of the National Committee on Pay Equity, one of the leading activist groups, wrote:

> Culture, history, psychiatry, and social relations all have a role in wage discrimination, as they do in other legal rights issues. They contribute to the creation and maintenance of a gender-based division of labor in the market economy that is old, pronounced, and pays women less.[5]

The market, Grune contends, will not spontaneously eliminate this alleged discrimination. Even when an employer acts to set wages with a non-discriminatory intent, if that employer uses prevailing market standards as his guide, those wages will reflect the prior discriminatory evaluations of other employers. Thus, remediation is necessary by government actions to break this chain of perpetuated inequities. Comparable worth, while it began in the public sector and has enjoyed its greatest successes there, is not a concept to be limited to government employment. Rather, its proponents wish to extend its purview eventually to all employment. In one state, Pennsylvania, legislation is pending which would do precisely that, apply comparable worth standards to private employment as well as public.

As an alternative to the allegedly defective market mechanism for setting wages, comparable worth would employ "objective" standards. For example, the state of Washington engaged the consulting firm of

Norman Willis & Associates when it performed its first comparable worth study in 1974. The Willis study utilized a methodology similar to that used in comparable worth studies by other consulting firms. Each employment classification was assessed on the basis of four factors: (1) Knowledge and Skills (job knowledge, interpersonal communication skills, coordinating skills), (2) Mental Demands (independent judgment, decision making, problem solving requirements), (3) Accountability (freedom to take action, nature of the job's impact, size of the job's impact), and (4) Working Conditions (physical efforts, hazards, discomfort, environmental conditions).[6] Evaluation committees assessed job classifications on these four criteria and awarded points to each. Comparable jobs, then, were those that achieved approximately the same overall point scores. In this way, such disparate jobs as secretary, nurse, surveyor, highwayman, etc., could be compared. This methodology attempts to replace subjective and, hence, discriminatory market decisions with objective, nondiscriminatory assessments by trained evaluators.

Comparable worth's opponents have attempted to dispute the inference which the proponents draw from the raw data, i.e., that the wage disparity between the sexes can only be explained by discrimination on the part of employers. June O'Neil of the Urban Institute argues that the 64 percent figure for women's work as compared to men's is flawed because it defines full-time employment as 35 hours or more, thus ignoring the fact that full-time women work 9 to 10 percent fewer hours than men. She thinks a better statistic is hourly earnings. On this basis, women in 1983 earned 72 percent of what men earned. However, as O'Neil points out, this figure may mask some significant progress. Women in the 20 to 24 year-old age bracket earn 89 percent of their male peers' earnings. O'Neil further points out that this gap has narrowed in recent years, with women in this same age-group earning only 81 percent of the male salary in 1979. Furthermore, as Thomas Sowell has pointed out, single women between the ages of 25 and 64 earn 91 percent of the income of men. Single men and single women are more nearly alike in their earning power than married men and married women. This leads O'Neil to speculate that factors other than discrimination account for the disparity in earnings between men and women. She enumerates several factors: women have lower investments in schooling; women currently employed have worked 60 percent of the time while men have worked almost continuously. These two factors alone can explain about half the earnings differential between the sexes, O'Neil contends. Other factors can explain most of the rest: women's expectations are different from men's, particularly in regard to their roles in the family; given these disparate roles, women prepared in high-school and college for homemaking tasks, and this is particularly true of middle-aged women and older women.[7]

O'Neil and other critics have pointed to additional problems with comparable worth. It would be too expensive to implement with a price tag somewhere around $300 billion. It would disrupt the American economy, increase inflation, drive up unemployment, and make American products less competitive on world markets. It would have a particularly adverse impact on women's employment prospects. It would penalize employers for wage-setting acts over which they have little control, thus violating one of the principles of our legal system—that individuals should be penalized only for actions in which they are at fault.[8] And pay equity for women would hurt blue-collar men, and blue-collar women also, because Willis-type schemes seem to favor education and other easily measured skills over manual labor.

In this paper, I do not wish to explore these objections to comparable worth. The comparable worth activists are right in one respect, I think. Justice and equity must prevail over considerations of efficiency. If right lies on the side of comparable worth, then comparable worth should prevail. Where I differ with those who endorse comparable worth, is that I strongly believe that justice and equity do not direct us to supplant market decisions by the decrees of experts. For, I am afraid, despite the assurances of some comparable worth advocates, that the decrees of experts is what comparable worth would involve in practice. The first section of this paper is devoted to an examination of the philosophical assumptions of the comparable worth position; the second section will present some arguments to show why, in a general way, the market ought to be appealing; and the final section will discuss why the market should be particularly appealing to those concerned with the welfare of women.

The Philosophical Assumptions of Comparable Worth

If we examine some of the philosophical assumptions of the comparable worth position (and I use the term "philosophical" rather loosely to include moral and economic assumptions), the idea of paying people according to such a scheme will seem much less attractive. I freely concede that, at least on the surface, the notion of comparable worth and even more of "pay equity" seems alluring and just. However, it involves accepting some assumptions which I take to be highly dubious and endorsing a view of equality which is contrary to our American tradition, unpersuasive as an ideal, and incapable of being put into practice without chaotic results.

Comparable Worth and Intrinsic Value

Comparable worth depends on an intrinsic value theory or an objective-value theory. It assumes that the worth of jobs to employers can be measured on an objective scale. If we leave aside, for the time being, the consideration of whether any given set of people can impartially implement such a system, the notions of intrinsic-value or objective value themselves are defective.

Intrinsic or objective value theories are by no means new. St. Thomas Aquinas and other medieval theorists endorsed a notion of "just price," and this intrinsic-value view was exemplified in the guild system which set prices not only for the labor of guild members but also for their products. The classical economists of the nineteenth century, and Karl Marx too, argued for an objective theory of value— the labor theory of value. Normally, the classical economists contended, the price of commodities depends upon the amount of labor spent on bringing them to market. Market forces, such as scarcity or a temporary shift in demand, could modify this price, so that the market price would fluctuate around this norm. The theory had numerous problems. The principal problem was that it could not explain everyday market phenomena. For example, why is the price of water negligible while the price of diamonds is substantial: water has great use value to sustain life while diamonds have only a frivolous, ornamental function. The labor theory of value fell in the late nineteenth century to a more sophisticated theory, one which did not claim that value was derivative from any objective quality, but rather that value depended upon the subjective judgments of people in the marketplace, and the supply of the good in question.

This marginal utility theory of value had several noteworthy advantages over its objective, labor-theory competitor. It solved the water-diamond "paradox." Diamonds are priced higher than water because people are willing to pay more for them. Diamonds are relatively scarce compared to water, hence the marginal unit of diamonds commands a higher price than the marginal unit of water. If water suddenly became scarce, people would value it higher and be willing to pay more to acquire it, and its price would rise. Also, the marginal theory explained what the labor theory could not, that is, how prices are set for everyday commodities in the market.

Despite Marx's abhorrence of this fact, labor power is as much a commodity as anything else. The price of any particular kind of labor is set by the same criteria as anything else. The market price equates supply and demand; each laborer is paid the equivalent of his contribution to the enterprise. Marginal utility theory, thus, overcame another problem inherent in a labor theory of value: that every factor of production—labor, land, entrepreneurship—required a different theory to explain how its price was set.

Now, what bearing does all of this have on comparable worth? Comparable worth shares with the labor theory of value a desire to discern some objective characteristic of worth or value apart from the valuations of actual buyers. For comparable worth it is no longer the hours of labor embodied in a thing which sets its value, but rather that the value of labor itself can be determined by assessing the knowledge and skills, mental demands, accountability, and working conditions that characterize each job. But there is no intrinsic value to any job. A job has value to someone who creates it and is willing to pay someone to do it. The price for that job is set by the market, which is nothing more than an arena for averaging the demands for labor of each particular kind by numerous employers. It is an impersonal process. In most cases, employers and potential employees do not know each other before the process is begun. It is impersonal in another way, also. No individual employer can exercise much influence over the price of labor of the kind he needs. Only in the rarest of cases, where no alternative employers are available to willing workers, will any one employer have an impact on the overall job market. (Such influence characterizes centrally planned and government owned economies much more than it does market economies.)

If an employer, through discriminatory motivation or any other reason, wishes to pay less than the prevailing wage for a certain kind of labor, one of three things will normally happen: he will get no takers; he will get fewer takers than he needs; the quality of the applicant pool will be lower than the job requires. On the contrary, if he wishes to pay more, he will get many applicants and some of them will be of higher quality than normal in that job classification. In the former case, the employer jeopardizes his business by presumably making his products less marketable and his operation less efficient; in the latter case, the employer may benefit his business if his more skilled employees produce a better product that the consumers are willing to pay a higher price to acquire, but the consumer may not be willing, and then the business would be jeopardized. Thus, employers are, in the normal case, pretty much tied to paying prevailing market wages.

If jobs have no intrinsic worth, as I have argued, then the comparable worth position has been severely wounded, for it bases its case on precisely such an assumption. All commodities, labor included, are worth what buyers are willing to pay for them and what sellers are willing to take in order to part with them. Furthermore, if jobs have no intrinsic worth, they cannot be compared on any objective scale. In fact, we cannot even say that a plumber who makes $10 an hour is worth the same to his boss as a teacher who earns the same wage is worth to his employer. Such comparisons are vacuous. I am not even convinced that a comparison of worth based on differences in salary can be made within the same firm or that any correlation exists between use value (utility) and salary. Firm X may desperately need an efficiency expert and be willing to pay $100,000 per year for one, but if efficiency experts are plentiful, firm X may only have to pay $20,000. The use value (or utility) to firm X of the efficiency expert does not seem to correlate with his salary. Value and worth are moral terms which do not seem to equate all that well with price or salary which are economic terms and depend on the available supply and the demand for particular labor. Who is to say that Michael Jackson is worth thousands of times more than an emergency room nurse because he earns several million dollars each year and the nurse earns a pittance? The question doesn't make any sense.

The problem with comparable worth is similar to the problem of making interpersonal comparisons of utility. While each person can order his own preferences, these separate preference orders cannot be equated. Similarly, different jobs cannot be equated on any objective scale. Even the market cannot equate the worth of one job with another.

Thus, any attempt to employ supposedly objective job-assessment criteria must be inherently discretionary; the judgments of bureaucrats would be forcibly substituted for the assessments of those who are the actual purchasers of labor services. It is unavoidable since there is no intrinsic value to any job. The impersonal forces of the market would have to be replaced by subjective judgments of "experts" regarding the value of different jobs. Even if these "experts" were bereft of all tastes—which is, of course, impossible—they could not implement a system of objective measurement. We all have tastes, and it has been observed by other critics of comparable worth that its advocates tend to staff the consulting firms and oversee the studies. But the problem with comparable worth, as I have argued, lies deeper than that. There is no intrinsic value to any job, and hence they cannot be measured or compared.

Comparable Worth and the Market

Most proponents of comparable worth argue that comparable
worth is not an alternative to the market, that it is like other correc-
tives to the market that have been instituted by government in recent
years. I will contend that this is false. Comparable worth, unlike the
Equal Pay Act, Title VII, or affirmative action, cannot be grafted onto
the market. Rather, the market and comparable worth emanate from
two entirely different normative assessments about individual action.
The market exemplifies the assumption that individual consumers
ought to be sovereign, that there desires ought to rule the economy.
Comparable worth assumes that individuals ought not be the final ar-
biters of economic life. Some individuals, rather, should place their
judgments above those of the rest of their countrymen. These
"experts" will insure that wage decisions are made on equitable, non-
prejudicial grounds.

The Equal Pay act said to employers that you cannot pay women
less than you pay men for the same job. Title VII of the Civil Rights
Act of 1964 said to employers that you cannot discriminate in hiring,
promotion, compensation, etc., between men and women. And affirmative action said to employers that you must try to advance women,
as historic victims of discrimination, to positions in which they had
been under-represented. All of these mandates interfered with employers' rights. All limited employers' freedom. Formerly, an employer
could hire women if he liked, pay whatever he liked, and use any criteria for hiring that he wished.[9]

But comparable worth is different. Instead of employers determining their wage scales by evaluating their demand for a certain type of
labor and the supply of it on the market, "expert" boards would have
to examine the jobs in each firm or government bureau and set wage-
scales according to the comparability of different jobs. While most
comparable worth advocates do not envision one wage board doing
this for the entire country—as the National War Labor Board tried to
during World War II[10]—it is obvious that some national standards
would have to evolve, either by legislative decree or judicial interpretation. Even if there were many boards rather than one, this would still
prove problematical on several grounds, in addition to the ones previously adumbrated in the sub-section on intrinsic worth.

The very reason for having "expert" boards to assess jobs rather
than the market is to eliminate subjectivity and, thus, prejudice. But
can the boards accomplish this? I think not. All people have preju-

dices, and if that is too harsh a term, all have tastes. Consulting firms have proven more sympathetic to white-collar than blue-collar jobs in their comparable worth studies. This is not surprising. What is to insure that a board acts impartially? (I do not wish to concede, here, that such would be a theoretical possibility.) Will we need another board to assess the fairness of the first, and yet another to judge the fairness of the second? We seem to be caught in an infinite regress situation.

Furthermore, the institution of a comparable worth scheme nationwide would depend not only on a universal standard and pay boards but, more problematically, on a static view of the economy. Let us suppose that comparable worth were put into effect and operated at time T_1 to the satisfaction of its supporters. What would immediately happen at time T_2? A myriad of events would occur to upset the carefully crafted design. Consumer choices, preferences for jobs, availability of resources, etc., would change. This indicates that the comparable worth wage boards would have to be a permanent fixture of our economy. As soon as "pay equity" were achieved, it would be upset in the next instant. Thus, the pay boards would have to constantly disrupt the economy, causing massive uncertainty, instability, and the impossibility of any rational planning on the part of businesses, workers, or consumers. The only way out of this bind would be an attempt to freeze the economy. But of course, this is impossible. Thus, comparable worth cannot be operationalized. As Robert Nozick pointed out, any attempt to impose one pattern of distribution as the just pattern, must require perpetual interferences with human freedom of action.[11]

Thus, the market and comparable worth seem to be mutually exclusive. Either we have market-set wages or we have wages set by administrative boards and courts. The former has the advantage, since it works. The latter has the fault that it cannot be operationalized without producing chaos.

Discrimination

Comparable worth proponents believe that the market for women's work has been distorted by centuries of prejudice. The market devalues the work of women, and hence it should be supplanted. The work of June O'Neil seems pretty compelling, and it shows that the market for women's labor operates just like other markets. But leaving this aside, there is something else fundamentally flawed about this line of argument.

Comparable worth cannot eliminate discrimination from the labor market, and neither can any other scheme, including the market. The purpose of any hiring process is precisely *to* discriminate. It is not only skills that a personnel director looks for in hiring an applicant. Such intangibles as personality, looks, motivation, etc., play a factor. Just as any employer discriminates in hiring, so the wage boards or the consulting firms would impose their tastes and value judgments.

One kind of discrimination that is invidious is government-imposed discrimination. *Apartheid* is an excellent example. What makes this kind of discrimination so odious is that it is government imposed, and hence nearly inescapable. Discrimination on the market is haphazard and usually escapable. If you don't like the wages or the conditions in one firm you can join another or start your own. The comparable worth consulting firms, and what I see as the inevitable wage boards, court appointed masters, or judicial "wage boards" denote more the *apartheid* model and less the market kind of discrimination. The standards would be government mandated and inescapable except by leaving the country.

If discrimination is irremediable, why should we prefer comparable worth to the market, with all of the problems attendant upon comparable worth that I have already documented?

Equality of Opportunity vs. Equality of Results

The market as it currently operates in the United States embodies a conception of equality that political theorists call equality of opportunity. All positions in society ought to be open to everyone, without any artificial barriers of race, nationality, sex, etc., being placed in anyone's way. Where the actual world departs from this model, government intervenes to guarantee the rights of those who have been discriminated against. While equality of opportunity has its problems—it interferes with personal freedom—it is preferable to the view of equality embodied in the comparable worth position.

Equality of results, or some looser variant of it, seems to be the vision embraced by comparable worth's adherents. As I have argued earlier, the attempt to operationalize such a principle (as Nozick argued) is doomed to failure. Life will always intervene to upset the carefully balanced apple cart. Even if this were not so, I do not think that equality of results is an appealing moral objective. It is contrary to our American tradition, going back to Locke and the natural law theorists, of treating each person as an individual. Equality of results demands that each person be treated as a component of an organic society; the parts must be rewarded so that the entire organism will be just. But this is merely an historical argument about Western traditions, and is not in itself compelling. However, it is based upon a realization that individuals are different—they have disparate talents, needs, desires, and tastes. These differences cannot be denied. Any attempt to fit such heterogenous beings into one scheme to judge "worth," would involve a massive amount of paternalism. If individuals freely hiring on the market and individuals freely offering their services, determine that dogcatchers are "worth" more than nurses, and the board thinks otherwise, then the wishes of countless employers and workers will be ignored.

Equality of opportunity is more appealing than equality of results because it gives more respect to the wishes of individuals, and it just attempts to guarantee that the process of selection is fair. It does not require making independent assessments of the value to society or to a firm of the work of baseball players, laundresses, plumbers, or secretaries. It leaves such decision to the marketplace.

I have argued that several of the key assumptions upon which the case for comparable worth lies are fallacious or cannot be operationalized without producing chaos. (1) Jobs have no intrinsic worth or value, and, therefore, they cannot be objectively measured nor compared. (2) Comparable worth operates on principles that are antithetical to the market. Thus, one must choose either the market or comparable worth. (3) Discrimination is irremediable, and it cannot be eliminated by comparable worth schemes. In fact, comparable worth if implemented might exacerbate the problem of discrimination by replacing the choices of millions of individuals by the views of "experts." (4) Finally, equality of opportunity is preferable on many grounds to the alternative embodied in comparable worth—equality of results.

Why the Market is Appealing

Markets are impersonal. If secretaries and nurses on average receive lower salaries than accountants and auto mechanics, it is not because any one group of experts has determined that the latter are more worthy than the former. It is simply a function of supply and demand. While individual employers may operate their businesses as idiosyncratically as they like (within, of course, the current labor and civil rights laws of the United States), they follow discriminatory wage policies at their peril. If fewer women choose to become nurses and secretaries, these occupations will receive higher remuneration in the future.

Markets express consumer sovereignty. Employers are consumers of labor, but they are also intermediaries between the ultimate consumers of their products and their laborers. Employers produce goods by combining various factors of production, and they hope that these goods will mesh with what consumers want. They do so as efficiently as their competitors or else they are soon out of business. Thus, comparable worth is not simply an attempt to replace the decisions of employers with the decisions of wage boards. Comparable worth seeks ultimately to replace the decisions of consumers themselves with the judgments of "experts."

Markets are efficient. In contrast to centrally planned economies which have proven notoriously inefficient, market systems produce bounties undreamt of in past centuries. Comparable worth seems to require wage boards, and with all the constant disruptions and inefficiencies such boards would cause, a movement to explicit central planning of the economy would be the logical next step. Something would have to provide a "cure" for the dislocations caused by continuous comparable worth evaluations by boards, and since the market is out, central planning seems inevitable.

Markets are just. In a market system, everyone is free to produce what he likes, to trade with other willing partners, and to give or bequeath his wealth to anyone he chooses. It is based on a simple and just principle—that those who produce are entitled to the products of their labor. Comparable worth would deprive employers of the right to freely dispose of their holdings. It would give that right either to consulting firms, boards, or judges.

Markets allow freedom of exit and entry. If an individual does not like the terms of employment offered to him, if he thinks the proffered wage is too low, he (and, of course, she) is perfectly free to seek another employer or strike out on his own. No one is perpetually tied to a job, as has been the practice off and on in some centrally planned economies. If one feels that as a secretary one is being discriminated against in relation to office managers, one can acquire new skills and become an office manager or go into a different occupation.

The Market and Women

Why should the market system appeal to women? The market has proven remarkably adaptable to the huge influx of women into the workplace in the last few decades. In 1960 only 38 percent of women worked, while 1983 saw an increase to 53 percent.[12] Many of these women were formerly homemakers with minimal job skills. Employment opportunities have multiplied to meet this rising demand by women for work outside of the home. With relatively little dislocation, the market has expanded to provide jobs for women who now want to or need to work. Also, as aspirations of women have changed in the last fifteen years, as a result in no small part to the women's movement, women pioneers entered formerly male professions. Today, the pioneering phase is over, and it is no longer cause for discussion or even much notice when a woman is a lawyer, doctor, politician, business executive, coal miner, or truck driver.

We ought not dwell upon the past. If women of another generation wanted to remain at home with their children, it is foolish to blame "society" for the results. For society is nothing more than the attitudes and expectations of men and women who inhabit it at any particular time. If men formerly saw women primarily as homemakers, so did women. Today, it is not only the attitudes of women that have changed, but the perception of women by men. It does not require any elaborate empirical study to observe that younger men hold vastly different expectations of women, and their wives, than did their fathers and grandfathers.

Rather than bemoaning "societal" values of past generations, or seeking an unattainable goal of eliminating all discrimination, or trying to overturn our market system, women ought to encourage each other to become prepared for better jobs and to take risks by becoming entrepreneurs. Comparable worth is a detour that will not aid women, and if fully implemented it will destroy our market system and all the abundance it produces.

Notes

1. *County of Washington v. Gunther*, 452 U.S. 161 (1981). While *Gunther* gave hope to comparable worth proponents, it was not an endorsement of the concept, nor was it a clear signal that comparable worth claims would fall under Title VII. The decision sets no criteria for what claims in addition to "equal pay for equal work" might fall under Title VII. It is certainly not a decision that sets definitive standards, as the dissenters pointed out. However, the majority at several points in the decision disclaimed any relation of their decision to the comparable worth theory. For example, at 757: "We emphasize at the outset the narrowness of the question before us in this case. Respondents' claim is not based on the controversial concept of "comparable worth. . . ."" For comments on the meaning and impact of *Gunther* see: Comment, "Civil Rights-Employment Discrimination-Sex Based Compensation Discrimination," 28 *New York Law School Law Review* 149 (1983); Janice R. Bellace, "Comparable Worth: Proving Sex-Based Wage Discrimination," 69 *Iowa Law Review* 655 (1984); Judith Anne Pauley, "The Exception Swallows the Rule: Market Conditions as a 'Factor Other than Sex' in Title VII Disparate Impact Litigation," 86 *West Virginia Law Review* 165 (1983); Charles Waldauer, "The Non Comparability of the 'Comparable Worth' Doctrine: An Inappropriate Stan-

dard for Determining Sex Discrimination in Pay," 3 *Population Research and Policy Review* 141 (1984); Sndra Hard, Paula Murray, and Bill Shaw, "Comparable Worth: A Legal and Ethical Analysis," 2 *American Business Law Journal* 417 (1984).

2. *American Federation of State, County, and Municipal Employees v. State of Washington*, 578 F. Supp. 846 (1983). Many court decisions, however have been unsympathetic to comparable worth pleas, both prior to and since *Gunther*. Among these are: *Lemons v. City and County of Denver*, 17 FEP cases 906 (D. Col. 1978), affirmed 620 P. 2d 228 (10th cir.), *cert. denied*, 449 U.S. 883 (1980); *Christensen v. State of Iowa*, 563 F. 2d 353 (8th Cir. 1977); *Power v. Barry County*, 539 F. Supp. 721 (W.D. Mich. 1982); *Spaulding v. University of Washington*, 35 FEP cases 217 9th Cir. 1984), affirming 35 FEP cases 168 (W.D. Wash. 1981); *Plemer v. Parsons-Gilbane*, 713 F. 2d 1127 (CA 5, 1983); *Connecticut State Employees Association v. State of Connecticut*, 31 FEP Cases 191 (D. Conn. 1983); *EEOC v. Affiliated Foods, Inc.*, 34 FEP Cases 943 (W.D. Miss. 1984). In this last case, the court pointed to the Supreme Court's disclaimer in *Gunther* that "Respondents' claim is not based on the controversial concept of 'comparable worth'" (at 958).

3. *American Federation of State, County, and Municipal Employees v. State of Washington*, 770 F. 2d 1401 (1985). Despite the appeals court's ruling, the state of Washington settled with the union, granting women employees nearly $500 million in compensatory salary increases by 1992.

4. *Who's Working for Working Women*, National Committee on Pay Equity and the National Women's Political Caucus, 1984.

5. Joy Ann Grune, "Pay Equity is a Necessary Remedy for Wage Discrimination," in *Comparable Worth: Issues for the 80s*, A Consultation of the U.S. Commission on Civil Rights, June 6-7, 1984, p. 165.

6. *AFSCME v. Washington*, *supra* note 2, at 854 n. 9.Discrimination," in *Comparable Worth: Issues for the 80s*.

7. June O'Neil. "Comparable Worth: An Interview with June O'Neil," Manhattan Report on Comparable Worth, Vol. IV. no. 4, 1984; idem, "An Argument Against Comparable Worth," in *Comparable Worth: Issues for the 80s*, pp. 177-180.

8. Daniel Leach, *Comparable Worth: Issues for the 80s*, p. 92.

9. I do not intend to ignore the Wagner Act and minimum wage laws which had already greatly circumscribed employers' latitude in compensating employees.

10. See: *County of Washington v. Gunther*, at 185 n.l., Rehnquist dissent.

11. Robert Nozick, *Anarchy, State, and Utopia* (New York: Basic Books, 1974), Part II.

12. *The Female-Male Earnings Gap: A Review of Employment and Earnings Issues*, Women's Bureau, Office of the Secretary, U.S. Dept. of Labor, Report No. 673 (1982).

11

Three National Treasures: Hazlitt, Hutt, and Rothbard

Llewellyn H. Rockwell, Jr.

T o most Americans, economists don't leap instantly to mind as treasures, let alone national treasures. Whether making arrogant and fallacious mathematical predictions; filling the minds of college students with the wrong-headed Keynesian and socialist ideas; or giving a theoretical cover to State inflation, taxation, regulation, and spending—the typical economist is not a friend of liberty.

But all this is a perversion of the pure science of economics as exemplified by the Austrian school and its greatest exponent, Ludwig von Mises. Professor Mises was not only the twentieth-century's greatest creative force in economics, he was also a radiant champion of liberty.

There is a Japanese custom naming great achievers as living national treasures. Scott Stanley of Conservative Digest once asked me to name our three living national treasures in economics. I told him that three men stand out as great economists in the Misesian tradition: Henry Hazlitt, W. H. Hutt, and Murray N. Rothbard.

Henry Hazlitt

Henry Hazlitt's career as an economist and journalist spans more than seven decades. An outstanding teacher of the economics of freedom, he did pathbreaking theoretical work, and made the ideas of Austrian, free-market economics accessible to everyone. One of the most quotable economists of all time, his writing sparkles. And his clear and sprightly style seems—like his commitment to freedom—only to grow stronger with the passing years.

One of his chief accomplishments is the masterful *Economics in One Lesson* written in 1946. This small volume has educated millions (in

139

eight different languages) toward an understanding of the free market and Austrian economics. It destroys the arguments of socialists and interventionists as it explains the truth. Although it was written more than 40 years ago, there is still no better way to start learning good economics. But the book is shunned by most economists. And no wonder. If Hazlitt were followed, interventionist politicians and their intellectual bodyguards in the academic world would be unemployed.

If it's not bad enough that he defied the economics establishment, his airtight case for the free market is accessible to the layman, and that's anathema to the economics establishment. Thumb through any issue of a top economics journal and you'll know why Hazlitt's book is considered heretical. Not because it doesn't make sense, but because it does; not because it isn't logical, but because it is; not because it isn't true to life, but because it is.

Translate their jargon into English, and we find most economists beginning with such axioms as "let's assume everybody knows everything" or "nobody knows anything" or "people never change their minds" or "all goods are identical." Men and women are stripped of their individuality to make them fit into mechanistic computer models, and the economy is seen as static, or at best a series of shifting static states, without elaboration or the process of change. Deductions from such axioms must, of course, be false.

Hazlitt, like Mises, starts with the assumption that individuals act, that they do so with a purpose, and that as conditions change, their plans change. He makes no separation between "microeconomic" and "macroeconomic," terms commonly used to give the impression that different principles and laws apply to the whole economy than apply to individuals. So that while it may be justified to talk about purposive action, decisions on the margin, and subjective valuations at the individual level, this is of no relevance for the macro-managers in government. But Hazlitt is a methodological individualist, and thus recognizes that the economy must be analyzed from the standpoint of individual action.

Most economists are notorious justifiers of special-interest legislation because they ignore what Hazlitt so eloquently charts in *Economics in One Lesson*: the unseen and long-run effects of government policy. To Hazlitt, as an Austrian school economist, "economics consists in looking not merely at the immediate but at the longer effects of any act or policy; it consists in tracing the consequences of that policy not merely for one group but for all groups."

Central bank inflation of the money supply, for example, lowers interest rates initially, but leads to higher interest rates and lower purchasing power in the long run, not to speak of the business cycle of booms and busts. Inflation may benefit the government and those who get the new money first, but it hurts everyone else.

Although a formidable scholar, Hazlitt did not spend his career in a university. He was a working journalist of whom H. L. Mencken once said: "He is one of the few economists in human history who could really write." Born in 1894, Hazlitt went to work in 1913 as a reporter for the *Wall Street Journal*. He was also an editorial writer for the *New York Times* and a columnist for *Newsweek*.

As a very young man, Hazlitt read the Austrian economists Carl Menger, Eugen von Böhm-Bawerk, and Philip Wicksteed. But the main influence on him was Ludwig von Mises. And in 1940 Hazlitt helped—with the late Lawrence Fertig—to raise funds for a job for Mises at New York University. At a time when every second-rate European Marxist and historicist was getting a professorship at Harvard or Princeton, Mises was blackballed by U.S. universities as "dogmatic," "intransigent," and "right-wing." Eventually Hazlitt and Fertig were able to persuade NYU—where Fertig was a trustee—to allow Mises to teach as an unpaid visiting professor.

Mises and Hazlitt became close friends and he later arranged the publication of Mises's *Omnipotent Government, Theory and History, Bureaucracy,* and the monumental *Human Action* by Yale University Press.

During Hazlitt's years at the *New York Times* he wrote about the troubles that would flow from the Keynes-designed Bretton Woods monetary agreements. (His insightful editorials are collected in *From Bretton Woods to World Inflation* [1983].) Bretton Woods, which Supply-Siders wrongly look back on with nostalgia, guaranteed—as Hazlitt predicted—a world of paper money inflation. It also gave us the International Monetary Fund (IMF) and the World Bank, still major funders of statism.

As Hazlitt has argued, only a true gold standard, with the dollar redeemable in gold domestically as well as internationally, qualifies as sound money. And institutions like the IMF and World Bank only benefit governments and banking interests at the expense of the American taxpayer and the poor in other countries.

Another Hazlitt masterpiece is the *Failure of the "New Economics"* (1959). Here Hazlitt produced what no one else has ever attempted: a line-by-line refutation of Keynes's *General Theory*. The book is a patient and meticulous shattering of Keynes's fallacies, contradictions, and muddled thinking.

A Renaissance man in the Mises tradition, his output includes 25 books—on economics, philosophy, politics, history—plus a novel and hundreds of persuasive columns and articles.

The Bretton Woods system did break down, of course, as Hazlitt had predicted. But when, many years before, the publisher of the *New York Times* asked him to reverse his position and endorse Keynes's phony gold standard, he resigned rather than do so. That act of courage and principle exemplifies his whole life.

W. H. Hutt

It's possible for a student of economics to go all the way through graduate school without once hearing the name William H. Hutt. Yet his scholarship, bravery, and dogged adherence to economic truth make him a hero.

Hutt, now a visiting professor at the University of Dallas, has labored quietly and with little acclaim for more than 60 years. He is responsible for major breakthroughs in economic theory, a dozen books, and hundreds of articles. Among his most important works are the *Theory of Collective Bargaining* (1930), *Economists and the Public* (1936), *Economics of the Colour Bar* (1964), *The Strike-Threat System* (1973), and *A Rehabilitation of Say's Law* (1975).

Born in 1899, Hutt graduated from the London School of Economics. He published his first major academic article in 1926, refuting the charge that the Industrial Revolution impoverished workers, when in fact it raised their standard of living dramatically. He went on to become the great defender of working people and scholarly opponent of their enemy: labor unions.

Many books had been written about labor unions, usually from a leftist perspective, yet no comprehensive theory of collective bargaining had ever been advanced. Hutt did this while teaching at South Africa's University of Cape Town. In his *The Theory of Collective Bargaining*, which Ludwig von Mises called "brilliant," Hutt exploded the still-common myth that the interests of labor and management naturally clash, a disguised version of Karl Marx's theory of exploitation. On the contrary, Hutt said, the free market brings harmony. Only government intervention—such as laws favoring labor unions against employers and non-union workers—creates conflict.

Hutt also proved that collective bargaining and other union activities depress wages for non-union workers and the poor. He showed how much better off all countries would be if government-sponsored union activities were banned.

Unlike "liberals" and socialists, Hutt recognized that unionization's equal wage structure is destructive. Paying everyone the same, regardless of contribution, destroys the incentive to improve. He is also an articulate opponent of the violence endemic to unions, and he has shown that it is necessarily an integral part of their functioning.

These ideas, of course, did not sell well in the 1930s. But that never hindered Hutt. He took on another statist idol: J. M. Keynes. While Hazlitt was fighting Keynesianism in the U.S., Hutt did the same in the British world.

Economists and the Public was published in the same year as Keynes's *General Theory*, 1936. Hutt's book was already in page proofs when Keynes's book appeared, but he inserted a warning about the dangers of Keynesianism. In the book, Hutt sought to explain why the obviously superior free market was under attack, and why economists were held in such disrepute. The problem, he stated, was that neither economists nor the public understood the nature and effect of competition, and that only unfettered competition protects the general interest against the government and its interests. In "An Interview with W. H. Hutt," Hutt said that far from being a destructive force, competition is the "sole principle of coordination in a complex world" and the greatest liberator of the poor, a class which Marxists and Keynesians claim to love, but succeed only in increasing.

In the late 1930s Hutt also unveiled his concept of "consumer sovereignty," which influenced Ludwig von Mises. In the free market, Hutt said, consumers have the right to buy or not to buy, and therefore producers play a subservient role. The only path to success in a free market is for the producer to serve the consumer. In a statist economy, consumers have no voice, producers don't know what to produce, and pleasing politicians becomes the road to riches.

In 1939, Hutt delivered another blow to Keynesianism with the *Theory of Idle Resources*, which exploded Keynes's theory of unemployment. Keynes had entirely misunderstood how economic resources are allocated. Hutt showed that a resource like labor can be idle only through government intervention that raises its price higher than the community can afford, in light of other demands. This is why minimum wages and unions are so destructive: they inhibit flexibility in the price of labor. With completely free labor markets (i.e., without government intervention or union control), all unemployment is voluntary. Perhaps a laborer wants to use time searching for another job, or he is holding out for a higher wage. To say that unemployment in free labor markets is not voluntary, Hutt conclusively showed, that all human wants are satisfied, which is to deny that scarcity exists. With this observation, Hutt destroyed the rationale for macro-managing labor policy, and for any government programs to "save jobs."

Not satisfied with attacking Keynesianism, in 1964 Hutt wrote the first detailed critique of South Africa's racial apartheid in the *Economics of the Colour Bar*, criticizing the South African government's pro-labor union socialism and interventionism as giving an opening to Communism. Unless the market were freed from State intervention, he showed, there would be bloodshed and a destruction of freedom for everyone. He pleaded for blacks to be given a chance to own their own businesses, and to seek and hold any jobs they were capable of holding, without State discrimination.

Hutt showed that South Africa's economic apartheid was designed largely to protect white labor union members from black competition. The free market, he said, offers the only hope to minorities and the disadvantaged, and for a free society in South Africa. Government controls benefit only loot-seeking special interests.

The Economics of the Colour Bar—which anticipated Walter Williams's analysis of race and government—is a triumph of the union of theory and policy. This is something most economists shun as "unscholarly." But Hutt makes no secret of his desire to influence public opinion toward laissez-faire. For this, he was banned from working in South Africa.

As Ludwig von Mises wrote, W. H. Hutt "rank(s) among the outstanding economists of our age." That he is not ranked as such by the mainstream shows only its deficiencies; it in no way detracts from his magnificent achievements and courage.

Murray N. Rothbard

Ludwig von Mises was the greatest economist and defender of liberty in the twentieth century. In scholarship and in passion for freedom, his rightful heir is Murray N. Rothbard.

Rothbard was born in New York City in 1926. He received his Ph.D. from Columbia University, and studied for more than 10 years under Mises at New York University. However, his degree was delayed for years, and he came close to not receiving it at all, because of the unprecedented intervention of a faculty member.

Rothbard's dissertation—*The Panic of 1819*—showed how the Bank of the United States, the Federal Reserve's ancestor, caused the first American depression. This offended Professor Arthur Burns, later chairman of the Federal Reserve under Nixon, who was horrified by Rothbard's anti-central bank and pro-gold standard position.

Rothbard eventually got his Ph.D., and he began writing for the libertarian Volker Fund in New York. Like his great teacher Mises, Rothbard's views prevented him from getting a teaching position at a major American university. Finally he was hired by Brooklyn Polytechnic, an engineering school with no economics majors, where his department consisted of Keynesians and Marxists.

He worked there, in a dark and dingy basement office, until 1986, when—thanks to free-market businessman S. J. Hall—he was offered a distinguished professorship of economics at the University of Nevada, Las Vegas.

But this lack of a prestigious academic base did not prevent Rothbard, any more than it had Hazlitt, Hutt, or Mises, from reaching a wide audience of scholars, students, and the general public. Rothbard is the author of hundreds of pathbreaking scholarly articles and 16 books, including *Man, Economy, and State* (1962), *America's Great Depression* (1963), *Power and Market* (1970), *For a New Liberty* (1973), *Conceived in Liberty* (1976), *The Ethics of Liberty* (1982), and *The Mystery of Banking* (1983).

In *America's Great Depression*, an authoritative revisionist history of that economic debacle, Rothbard uses Austrian trade cycle theory to show that Federal Reserve inflation created the boom of the twenties and the bust of the thirties. Continued assaults on the market from Hoover and FDR—in the form of plant closing laws, taxation, agricultural intervention, price controls, et al.—prevented a liquidation of malinvestments made during the boom, and prolonged and deepened the depression. This book also contains the clearest and most convincing explanation of the Austrian theory of the trade cycle for students.

Both *The Panic of 1819* and *America's Great Depression* use theoretical tools drawn from the great tradition of Austrian economics, including Carl Menger's theory of the development of monetary institutions, Eugen von Böhm-Bawerk's theory of capital and the time-preference theory of interest, and Mises's methodology and trade cycle theory. Rothbard solved several theoretical problems in each, and wove them together to create a formal praxeological model. He succeeded not only in explaining cyclical fluctuations caused by central bank intervention, but also in making the case for the gold coin standard, no central bank, 100% reserves, and laissez-faire.

After Rothbard's masterful integration, economists can no longer dismiss recessions and depressions as an "inevitable" part of the market economy. Instead, it is clear, they are caused by central bank inflation, and the corresponding distortion of interest rates, malinvestment of capital, theft of savings, and price increases that go with it. Government, of which the central bank is only an arm, is the real source of business cycles.

Though it is still practiced almost universally within neoclassical industrial organization and price theory, Rothbard refuted the fallacy of separating monopoly prices from competitive prices. The distinction between the two only exists in the world of neoclassical pricing models, where businessmen charge higher and higher prices in the inelastic portion of the consumers' demand curve. But these static models have nothing to do with the dynamic market process. Rothbard showed that a free economy has only one kind of price: the free-market price, thus destroying the entire neo-classical and Keynesian justification of anti-trust policy. Monopolies do exist, Rothbard shows, but only when government erects a barrier to entry into the market by granting some firm or industry a special privilege. The real monopolies included are admitted ones like the Post Office, somewhat obscured ones like electric power companies, and worst of all, the least-questioned one, the Federal Reserve.

In 1956, Rothbard made the first formidable advance in the field of utility and welfare since the marginal revolution in the 1870s with his article "Toward a Reconstruction of Utility and Welfare." Building on Menger's work, he showed that utility is something that we can know only by observing individual preferences revealed through human action. Utility, a strictly ordinal and subjective concept, cannot be aggregated, and thus there can be no total utility. This insight removes the foundation from most modern utility and social welfare theory, which, although disguised, usually relies on interpersonal comparisons of subjective utility.

Not only does Rothbard's advance affect the pure theory of utility and welfare, but also the policies so often justified by neoclassical welfare models: redistribution of wealth, progressive taxation, and State planning. When individuals are free to trade and demonstrate their subjective preferences without interference from government, each party expects to benefit from the exchange or else they would not exchange in the first place. Rothbard thus deduces that free markets maximize utility and welfare, whereas government intervention, by the very fact that it is forcing people to behave in ways in which they otherwise would not, can do nothing but diminish utility and welfare.

It was this foundation that allowed Rothbard to integrate a rigorous theory of property rights with a scientific theory of economics. Today, others within the Chicago school are trying to do the same through studies in rights, ethics, and the means to utility optimization. But until they accept the theory of utility and welfare as taught by Rothbard, and ground their analysis in the pure logic of action, they will not succeed.

In his great work *Man, Economy, and State*, Rothbard provides a rigorous defense of economic science. It is a treatise covering the whole subject, and is the last such magnum opus. In it, clearly and logically, Rothbard deduces the whole of economics from its first principles. It is a tour-de-force unmatched in modern economics.

In his *Power and Market*, originally part of *Man, Economy, and State*, he develops a comprehensive critique of government coercion. He developed three useful categories of intervention: autistic, binary, and triangular. Autistic intervention prevents a person from exercising control over his own person or property, as with homicide or infringements on free speech. Binary intervention forces an exchange between two parties, as in highway robbery or income taxes. Finally there is triangular, in which the government forces two people to make an exchange or prohibits from doing so, as in rent control or minimum wages. He carefully outlines the bad effects of every possible intervention in the economy, refutes moral objections to the market, and develops the first and only praxeological critique of all types of taxation, showing that taxes are never neutral.

Rothbard also broke new ground in attacking government statistics. Because the government lacks the knowledge generated by the market, it must collect millions of statistics to plan the economy, which of course it is ultimately unable to do. Among Rothbard's least favorite statistics is the "trade deficit," which is only considered a problem because government keeps the figures. Thank goodness, he has noted, that trade statistics aren't kept on Manhattan and Brooklyn. "Otherwise we'd hear cries from Brooklyn politicians about the dangerous trade deficit with Manhattan."

Another statistic he dislikes is GNP. This number counts welfare payments and all other government spending as "productivity." His own alternative, PPR or Private Product Remaining (for producers), shows a much clearer picture by subtracting government spending from the economy. He has also—with Professor Joseph Salerno—constructed an Austrian alternative to the Federal Reserve's money supply statistics, which are constructed without regard for theoretical consistency.

Not only is he a brilliant economist, he is also a master of narrative political history, as his four-volume colonial history of the United States, *Conceived in Liberty*, shows; and a great philosopher in the individualist tradition, as demonstrated in the *Ethics of Liberty*. His current project is a massive history of economic thought from an Austrian per-spective, commissioned by investment advisor and Austrian econo-mist Professor Mark Skousen, which covers the ancient Greeks to the present. Judging by the chapters so far, this will be the greatest study of its kind ever written.

Rothbard is a writer of singular power, whose words fairly glisten on the page. Like Mises, he has inspired millions with his vision of the free society. In the academic world, where devotion to principle is as popular as it is in Washington, he has carried the torch of pure Misesianism.

Three Giants

Like Mises, these three giants exhibit extraordinary ability, courage, personal gentleness, and an unbending adherence to principle. In an age when loot-seeking is the norm among politicians—governmental and academic—Hazlitt, Hutt, and Rothbard have held high the ban-ner of truth and freedom. They have faced immense pressure to retreat, but never wavered. Today they are still at work extending the scholarship of freedom. Despite the barriers they have faced in the past, today their influence is spreading. And it will continue to do so. In their fight for liberty and the free market, they have one asset the other side cannot match: the truth.

An earlier version of this article appeared in *Conservative Digest*.

Selected Bibliography

Henry Hazlitt

Economics in One Lesson. New Rochelle, N.Y.: 1946. Reprint. Arlington House, 1979.

The Failure of the "New Economics." Princeton: Van Nostrand, 1959. Reprint. Lanham, Md.: University Press of America, 1983.

The Critics of Keynesian Economics. Princeton: Van Nostrand, 1960. Reprint. Lanham, Md.: University Press of America, 1983.

Time Will Run Back. New Rochelle, N.Y.: Arlington House, 1966. Reprint. Lanham, Md.: University Press of America, 1986.

Man vs. Welfare State. New Rochelle, N.Y.: Arlington House, 1969.

The Foundations of Morality. Princeton: Van Nostrand, 1969.

The Conquest of Poverty. New Rochelle, N.Y.: Arlington House, 1973.

The Inflation Crisis, and How to Resolve It. New Rochelle, N.Y.: Arlington House, 1978.

From Bretton Woods to World Inflation. Chicago: Regnery Gateway, 1983.

William H. Hutt

The Theory of Collective Bargaining. Washington, D.C.: Cato Institute, [1930] 1977.

Economists and the Public. London: Jonathan Cape, 1939.

The Theory of Idle of Resources. London: Jonathan Cape, 1939.

Plan for Reconstruction. London: Kegan Paul, 1943.

Keynesianism: Retrospect and Prospect. Chicago: Regnery, 1963.

The Economics of the Colour Bar. London: Deutsch, 1964.

Politically Impossible . . . ? London: Institute of Economic Affairs, 1971.

The Strike-Threat System. New Rochelle, N.Y.: Arlington House, 1973.

A Rehabilitation of Say's Law. Athens, Ohio: Ohio University Press, 1975.

The Keynesian Episode: A Reassessment. Indianapolis, Ind.: Liberty Press, 1979.

"The Factory System of the Early Nineteenth Century." *Economica* (March 1926).

"The Concept of Consumers' Sovereignty." *Economic Journal* (March 1940).

"The Yield on Money Held." In *On Freedom and Free Enterprise*, edited by Mary Sennholz, Princeton: Van Nostrand, 1956.

"Every Man A Capitalist." *Policy Review*, 1982.

"An Interview with W. H. Hutt." In *An Economist for the Long Run*, edited by Morgan Reynolds. Chicago: Regnery Gateway, 1986.

Murray N. Rothbard

The Panic of 1819. New York: Columbia University Press, 1962.

Man, Economy, and State: A Treatise on Economic Principles. 2 vols. Los Angeles: Nash Publishing, [1962] 1979.

Power and Market. Menlo Park, Calif.: Institute for Humane Studies, 1970.

America's Great Depression. Kansas City, Kans.: Sheed and Ward, 1963. Reprint. New York: Richardson and Snyder, 1983.

The Essential Ludwig von Mises. South Holland, Ill.: Libertarian Press, 1973. Reprint. Washington, D.C.: Ludwig von Mises Institute, 1983.

The Mystery of Banking. New York: Richardson and Snyder, 1983.

What Has Government Done to Our Money? Larkspur, Colo.: Pine Tree Press, 1964.

Conceived in Liberty. 4 vols. New Rochelle, N.Y.: Arlington House, 1975, 1975, 1976, 1979 respectively.

For a New Liberty. New York: Macmillan, 1973.

The Ethics of Liberty. Atlantic Highlands, N.J.: Humanities Press, 1982.

Ludwig von Mises: Scholar, Creator, Hero. Auburn, Ala.: The Ludwig von Mises Institute, 1988.

"Toward a Reconstruction of Utility and Welfare Economics." In *On Freedom and Free Enterprise*, edited by Mary Sennholz. Princeton: Van Nostrand, 1956.

"In Defense of 'Extreme Apriorism.'" *Southern Economic Journal* 23, no. 3 (January 1957).

"The Case for a 100 Percent Gold Dollar." In *In Search of a Monetary Constitution*, edited by Leland B. Yeager. Cambridge, Mass.: Harvard University Press, 1962.

"Praxeology, Value Judgments, and Public Policy." In *The Foundations of Modern Austrian Economics*, edited by Edwin G. Dolan. Kansas City, Kans.: Sheed and Ward, 1976.

"New Light on the Prehistory of the Austrian School." In *The Foundations of Modern Austrian Economics*, edited by Edwin G. Dolan. Kansas City, Kans.: Sheed and Ward, 1976.

"The Austrian Theory of Money." In *The Foundations of Modern Austrian Economics*, edited by Edwin G. Dolan. Kansas City, Kans.: Sheed and Ward, 1976.

"Law, Property Rights, and Air Pollution." *Cato Journal* (Spring 1982).

"The Laissez-Faire Radical: A Quest for the Historical Mises." *Journal of Libertarian Studies* 5, no. 3 (Summer 1981).

"The Federal Reserve as a Cartelization Device." In *Money in Crisis*, edited by Barry Siegel. San Francisco: Pacific Institute for Public Policy Research, 1984.

"The Case for a Genuine Gold Dollar." In *The Gold Standard: An Austrian Perspective*, edited by Llewellyn H. Rockwell, Jr. Lexington, Mass.: Lexington Books, 1985.

"The Origins of the Federal Reserve." In *Central Banking and the Federal Reserve*, edited by Llewellyn H. Rockwell, Jr. Auburn, Ala.: The Ludwig von Mises Institute, forthcoming.

12

Murray Rothbard as
Investment Advisor

Mark Skousen

> Practical men, who believe themselves to be quite exempt from
> any intellectual influences, are usually the slaves of some defunct
> economist.
>
> John Maynard Keynes

I t may seem inappropriate to cast Murray Rothbard as an investment
advisor, since by profession he is an academic economist who is largely
disinterested in personal investment strategies. Nevertheless, Professor
Rothbard has been the ideological mentor of most of the major investment advisors, writers and entrepreneurs in the "hard money" movement, including Harry Browne, Gary North, Jerome F. Smith, John
Pugsley, Julian Snyder, James U. Blanchard, III, Richard Band, and
myself. Others, such as Howard Ruff and Douglas R. Casey, have been
influenced by Rothbard indirectly through the writings of Harry
Browne. Rothbard's writings, especially those published in the early
1960s, greatly affected their way of looking at the effects of government
economic policy on the financial world. His popular works provided
the theoretical foundation for investing in precious metals, foreign currencies, and other "hedges" against inflation or monetary crises.[1]

There are, of course, other "free market" economists who also
greatly contributed to the hard-money movement. Alexander P. Paris
mentions Friedrich A. Hayek, current leader of the "Austrian" school
of economics.[2] James Dines credits the French economist Jacques
Rueff.[3] Donald J. Hoppe says he was influenced by E. C. Harwood,
who founded the American Institute for Economic Research in Great
Barrington, Massachusetts, and Dr. Elgin Groseclose, author of *Money
and Man*, a book which Hoppe considered a "classic."[4] In addition to

151

Rothbard, Gary North credits Ludwig von Mises, F. A. Hayek, and Hans Sennholz.[5] Hans Sennholz, both an academic economist and avid speculator, was influenced by Wilhelm Röpke and Ludwig von Mises. John Pugsley praises, in addition to Rothbard, the works of Henry Hazlitt, especially his *Economics in One Lesson*; "I probably would never have written this book [*Common Sense Economics*] but for his inspiration."[6] Harry Browne acknowledges the influence of several other economists besides Rothbard, including Hazlitt, Mises and Milton Friedman.[7]

But it is apparent from hard-money books and articles that Rothbard has had the broadest appeal and is the chief intellectual architect of the hard-money movement. Harry Browne says, "Rothbard has had far greater influence than Mises on the popular 'hard money' investment community, although some writers have read only Rothbard's popular pamphlets and pay him lip service." Undoubtedly it was Rothbard's ability to write to laymen in a lucid, practical fashion that made him so influential. As one of the members of the hard-money movement, Larry Abraham, states, "Murray Rothbard is the best popularizer of the 'Austrian' school of economics who has ever lived."

Are Economists Superior Investors?

While Professor Rothbard's theoretical and historical writings have had a significant impact on hard-money investment advisors, this fact does not mean that he considers himself an investment counselor or even a gifted speculator. Rothbard freely admits that his investment advice, which he occasionally proffers, has been wrong from time to time. Moreover, he has suffered incredibly bad luck in the stock market, according to his own account. For example, in 1956, he bought shares in Shell Oil, only to see the value of the stock plummet when Egypt nationalized the Suez Canal the very next day. On another occasion, he bought some cheap "junk" bonds, only to see them delisted the following week. Investment advisor Douglas R. Casey says that he once called Rothbard in the mid-1970s and tried to talk him into buying South African gold shares, which at the time were selling at bargain prices, but he wasn't interested. Rothbard says he has primarily lost money based on "inside tips" from brokers. He has since then become much more conservative, putting most his savings into money market funds and a few gold coins.

Of course, some economists have done well as investors. The British economist John Maynard Keynes was considered an astute foreign currency speculator, "dealing in rupees, the dollar, the French franc, the German mark, and the Dutch florin." He made several highly profitable trades, often while "still in bed in the morning."[8] However, the belief that Keynes was a consistent profiteer taking advantage of sources inside government is probably mistaken. Like most speculators, he also lost money frequently. He almost went bankrupt in 1920, when he shorted the German mark, and took severe losses in the 1937 stock market collapse.[9] Still, Keynes became well-to-do and considered financial success a sign of a "versatile genius." In his *Essays in Biography*, Keynes praised Sir Isaac Newton as not only a preeminent scientist, but a successful investor who survived the South Sea Bubble fiasco and died a rich man.[10]

There is no evidence to indicate that the financial performance of economists is any better than other professions. Some contemporary economists, such as Paul A. Samuelson and Milton Friedman, have become wealthy, but they have done so primarily because of their business—through teaching, writing, and lecturing—not from their investments. Indeed, if one evaluates Rothbard's financial performance in terms of his own business, which also comes from teaching, writing, and lecturing, he would be rated highly successful compared to the average income level of academic economists.

One might think, initially, that sound economic theory should lead to correct economic predictions, which, in turn, should result in superior personal money-making strategies. Certainly, that is the implication of the hard-money investment advisors. Jerome Smith, for example, writes on the value of using sound economic principles:

> Its application permits us to determine where we are, approximately, in any given cycle and, more importantly for investment decisions, what the next stage of the cycle is, approximately when it will begin, and its probable impact on various investment categories. . . . Austrian economists have developed techniques of economic analysis which allow them to understand these secondary effects of government intervention and, based on microeconomic analysis of the impact of these interventions on acting individuals, to forecast the range of distorting and damaging consequences that follow the obvious immediate impact.[11]

Economists' Ability to Forecast

However, there are many reasons why economic analysis may not lead to correct economic forecasts or sound investment advice. There could be a sizeable slip twixt the "theoretical" cup and the "investment" lip.

Making predictions and investment decisions depend on a complex set of factors. Hayek has written:

> The value of business forecasting depends upon correct theoretical concepts. . . . Every economic theory . . . aims exclusively at foretelling the necessary consequences of a given situation, event or measure. The subject-matter of trade cycle theory being what it is, it follows that ideally it should result in a collective forecast showing the total development resulting from a given situation under given conditions. In practice, such forecasts are attempted in too unconditional a form, and on an inadmissibly over-simplified basis: and, consequently, the very possibility of scientific judgments about future economic trends today appears problematical, and cautious thinkers are apt to disparage any attempt at such forecasting.[12]

Forecasting is extremely difficult because financial data, such as interest rates, the inflation rate and the prices of commodities, stocks and other investments, are determined by a myriad of supply and demand factors, both major and minor, which are constantly undergoing change. The markets are in continual disequilibrium, and, in fact, as Ludwig Lachmann states, "Relative prices change every day . . . a price system implying a uniform rate of profit and wage cannot exist. The forces tending to bring it about will always be weaker than the forces of change."[13]

Take interest rates as an example. Why is the movement of interest rates difficult to predict? Because they depend on both the supply and demand for money. Suppose, for instance, that the Federal Reserve starts a massive inflation. If the government has not previously been inflationary, interest rates may drop as the supply of money increases. However, the drop in interest rates is only temporary. As nominal incomes increase, the demand for money rises, which pushes interest rates up. This is the general scheme of events.

Economics may properly determine the *direction* that interest rates may take, but it is extremely difficult to determine *when* interest rates will start changing direction and *by how much*. As Rothbard notes, such decisions are "quantitative" in nature, while economics can only properly deal with "qualitative" changes. "There are no constant numerical relations in human action, and therefore there are no coefficients that can be included . . . that are not simply arbitrary and erroneous. Economic theory is and can only be qualitative—not quantitative."[14] It's up to professional speculators and entrepreneurs to try to predict and profit from "quantitative" changes.

The whole scenario can change radically, too, if the government has inflated in the past and the general public starts to anticipate the effects of high prices. The result may be an immediate rise in interest rates when the government starts inflating again. Inflationary expectations play a major role in determining interest rates, both long and short term.[15]

The outlook for inflation is another case in point. Rothbard, in the various introductions to his book, *America's Great Depression*, has consistently pointed out the inflationary nature of government policies. In the perennial "inflation-deflation" debates that go on at investment seminars, Rothbard has consistently been on the inflationist side, arguing that higher consumer prices are practically inevitable: "As long as the Federal Reserve has the unlimited power to inflate, and the will to inflate, it will not stop inflating. It's inevitable. Even in the deep recession of '82, we still had inflation. Sometimes more inflation, sometimes less. But always inflation."[16]

But Rothbard has not pretended to know the *rate* of inflation, nor by how much it will vary from year to year. One of the principal reasons why the rate of inflation is difficult to predict, as Rothbard clearly demonstrates, is that the central bank's fiat monetary system affects both relative prices and the production of various goods and services. There can be no scientific way to measure a "general price level." One can only look at "relative" prices as they relate to the structure of production, from capital goods to final consumer products. The monetarists' Quantity Theory of Money and alleged long-run neutrality of money is rejected.[17] Monetary inflation, no matter how large or small, causes a business cycle and malinvestments, particularly in the capital goods markets. Because of malinvestments, it's possible to have both a "recession" and an "inflation" at the same time. Rothbard was the first economist to offer a practical explanation of the phenomenon of "inflationary recession." As Rothbard states,

> . . . the prices of consumer goods always tend to rise, relative to the prices of producer goods, during recessions. The reason that this phenomenon has not been noted before is that, in past recessions, prices have generally fallen. . . . But, in the last few decades, monetary deflation has been strictly prevented by government expansion of credit and bank reserves. . . . The result of the government's abolition of deflation, however, is that gen-

eral prices no longer fall, even in recessions. . . . Hence, the prices of consumer goods still rise relatively, but now, shorn of general deflation, they must rise absolutely and visibly as well.[18]

The Importance of Timing

Timing is critical in making investment decisions. Rothbard's outlook for continued inflation might suggest investing in gold and other inflation hedges, yet a fall in the rate of inflation can have an adverse effect on "inflation hedges" for many years. For example, when inflation was generally rising in the 1970s, gold rose to nearly $850 an ounce by January, 1980, only to fall back to under $300 an ounce when the rate of inflation significantly dropped during the first half of the 1980s.

In short, investing is an art, not a science. It requires unusual skill and keen interest, and the ability to forecast accurately based on assessing a myriad of supply and demand factors and investment psychology.

Given the complexity of the economic and financial world, it is not surprising that economists have made serious blunders in their predictions and investment advice. Perhaps the most egregious prediction was made by Yale economist Irving Fisher, when he stated, "stock prices have reached what looks like a permanently high plateau. . . . I expect to see the stock market a good deal higher than it is today within a few months" on October 16, 1929, a few days prior to the stock market crash.[19]

Even in recent times, sophisticated econometric programs developed by economists in conjunction with high-speed computers have not fared well. The record of most of them in predicting the future of the economy has been dismal.[20]

How about the "Austrian" economists? It's difficult to assess their ability to make predictions. Early in his career, Ludwig von Mises was offered a high position at the Credit Anstalt, the largest bank in Austria, but he refused because he expected a great "crash" to be coming and he didn't want his name associated with it. He was proven correct when Credit Anstalt went bankrupt and precipitated the depression in Europe in the 1930s.[21]

In recent times, however, the forecasts of "Austrian" economists have been mixed. They were largely correct in their predicting higher inflation, higher interest rates, the fall of the dollar, and the rise in the prices of gold and silver in the late 1960s and 1970s. But in large measure they failed to see the reduction in inflation and interest rates in the 1980s. As Hans Sennholz, professor of economics at Grove City College, admits, "The 1980s took us by surprise."

It is no wonder, as financier Bernard Baruch once remarked, that "I think economists as a rule . . . take for granted they know a lot of things. If they really knew so much, they would have all the money and we would have none."[22] Rothbard says practically the same thing: "If someone were really able to forecast the economic future, he wouldn't be wasting his time putting out market letters or econometric models. He'd be busy making several trillion dollars forecasting the stock and commodity markets."[23]

The Mind of the Speculator

Recent research, particularly by Eastern schools of thought, has shown that the world of investing is distinct from the academic world of economic analysis. The analytical and deductive mind, used by economists, is separate from the intuitive and emotional mind. Bennett W. Goodspeed makes this point in his intriguing book, *The Tao Jones Averages*:

> Looking at the brain and how it operates, it is interesting to see that we have two brains within our neocortex: a left and right hemisphere. Furthermore, each person is dominated by either one side or the other. . . . our left hemisphere, which controls the right side of the body, is analytically oriented. It reasons logically and sequentially and is responsible for our speech. It is adept at math, accounting, languages, science, and writing. . . . Our right-brain hemisphere, which controls the movements of the left side of the body, is unique. It operates non-sequentially, is intuitive, artistic, has feelings, is gestalt-oriented (sees the forest and not just the trees), and controls our visual perceptions.[24]

According to Goodspeed, left-brain oriented professions include most lawyers, editors, doctors, scientists, researchers and analysts, dancers, politicians, and entrepreneurs.[25] The point of Goodspeed's book is that a successful investor must use both sides of the brain effectively, relying on both in-depth research and analysis (left brain) and intuitive feelings (right brain).

Interestingly, Rothbard's method of reasoning is primarily *a priori*,[26] which fits the "left brain" analytical side, while successful investing usually requires a strong "right brain" artistic approach, according to Goodspeed. This may be one explanation of why Rothbard has shown little interest in giving investment advice or speculating in the markets.

Charles Hession, in his biography of John Maynard Keynes, argues that Keynes was both a creative economist and successful speculator because he was in essence "dual-minded," in a similar sense described by Goodspeed.

> In modern analyses of creativity there is a pronounced tendency to conceive it as a rhythmic process involving an interplay between opposite aspects of the mind. . . . more recently, students of the lateral functioning of the brain have stressed that it is the polarity and integration of the two hemispheres, the complementary workings of the intellect and of intuition, which underlie creative achievement. . . ."[27]

Hession goes further to suggest that Keynes' androgynous behavior was, in part, responsible for this creative ability, combining "the masculine truth of reason and the feminine truth of imagination."[28] Goodspeed's thesis also suggests that the left-brained analytical side is usually more developed in males and the right-brained intuitive side is usually more developed in females, and that men or women who adopt both sides of the brain might be more creative and entrepreneurial.[29]

Rothbard also recognizes the necessity of skill and intuition to be successful in business or finance. "Forecasting on the market is the function of the entrepreneur, and entrepreneurship in the final analysis is an art rather than a science, a matter of intuition, hunch, and deep insight into the slice of the market that the entrepreneur knows and is dealing with."[30]

The Personal Goals of the Economist

The study of finance and business is not the same as the study of economics. They are related fields, but being knowledgeable in economics does not make one an expert in finance. An academic economist may be totally engrossed in the theory of interest rates, inflation, or foreign trade, while showing little interest in the investment vehicles which profit from movements in interest rates, inflation and foreign trade. Some economists such as Keynes find the markets intriguing, others like Rothbard find them uninteresting.

An academic economist can certainly use the principles of economics to make investment decisions, but it is purely a voluntary decision which many economists eschew. In fact, many well-known economists such as Milton Friedman refuse to give investment advice when asked publicly. If there is one thing economists recognize, it's the fact that time is a scarce commodity and one cannot do everything in this lifetime. Therefore one must allocate his time to achieve his most desired goals. These goals are not always materialistic.

As successful short-term traders know, keeping track of your speculative investments is a full-time job and can keep you from achieving many other non-pecuniary goals you may have. The troubles and sorrows connected with substantial wealth can be counter-productive.

Being "rich" does not necessarily mean financial wealth. It can mean richness in wisdom, creative ideas, and charity toward mankind. Rothbard spends most of his time working on books and articles that will live far beyond his time. They are "classics" which will be read a hundred years from now, far after the dust gathers on today's popular titles. As economist Leon Walras once commented, "If one wants to harvest quickly, one must plant carrots and salads; if one has the ambition to plant oaks, one must have the sense to tell oneself: my grandchildren will owe me this shade."

In conclusion, perhaps Murray Rothbard would agree most with his teacher, Ludwig von Mises, who told his new wife, Margit, "If you want a rich man, don't marry me. I am not interested in earning money. I am writing about money, but will never have much of my own."[31]

Hard-Money Response to Monetary Crises: Assessing Rothbard's Impact

Rothbard wrote a series of books and pamphlets which were published in the early 1960s which had a great impact on the hard-money movement. There were several major economic events which triggered the creation of the hard-money movement: the silver coin shortage in the United States in 1963-64, the dollar crisis in 1968-71, and the inflation crisis and commodity shortages of the 1970s.

Rothbard's popular works appeared a few years prior to this series of economic crises. The first book, *Man, Economy, and State*, published in 1962, was a treatise on economic principles and appealed primarily to a small group of dedicated followers who had some form of economic training.[32] In fact, most regard it as a graduate text in its degree of difficulty. Nevertheless, the book had a tremendous impact because it elucidated the principles of the free market, following in the footsteps of Rothbard's teacher, Ludwig von Mises, and his magnum opus, *Human Action*. Moreover, *Man, Economy, and State* offered a full-scale critique of Keynesian economics, practically the only type of economic doctrine being taught in colleges in the 1960s. It was a breath of fresh air. When first exposed to Rothbard's magnum opus, the reaction of students of free-market economics seemed like Paul A. Samuelson's when he had read Keynes's *General Theory*: "Bliss was it in that dawn to be alive, but to be young was very heaven!"

As far as popularity was concerned, the next two works were far more significant for the intelligent layman. *America's Great Depression*, a revisionist history of the Great Depression in the 1930s, came out a year later, in 1963.[33] It explained in lucid terms the basics of a business cycle and why government monetary inflation was the cause of booms and busts, not the free market. It also offered a devastating critique of Keynesian and other business cycle theories. Investment writer John Pugsley wrote, "Dr. Rothbard's *America's Great Depression* was both shocking and exciting in its revelation of the causes of the economic debacle in the thirties. I have always been impressed by careful scholarship and adherence to scientific principles, and Dr. Rothbard's book was a fine example of both."[34]

Rothbard's next work, a 60-page pamphlet called *What Has Government Done to Our Money?*, published in 1964, probably had the greatest impact of any short work.[35] What *The Communist Manifesto* was to Marxists, Rothbard's *What Has Government Done* was to the hard-money movement. The booklet was highly influential because for the first time it explained in simple, understandable terms what money is all about. It took away the mystique of the dollar and foreign currencies. It explained the creation of money all the way from barter to the modern fiat money system. It showed the ill-effects of government's meddling with money, why central banking was inflationary, and the monetary breakdown of the West. Finally, he demonstrated that the only stable monetary system was a return to a pure gold standard.

Financial writer Gary North recalls the influence Rothbard's works, especially *Man, Economy, and State*, had on him during the silver coin shortage in 1963-64. Rothbard's writings demonstrated how going off the gold standard allowed the government to be more and more inflationary. Meanwhile, the government had established a controlled price for silver at $1.29 an ounce. As inflation worsened, a shortage of silver coins was inevitable. This was interpreted by many free-market economists as an example of Gresham's Law, which stated that "bad money drives out good money." It was named after Sir Thomas Gresham, founder of the English Royal Exchange, who lived in the sixteenth century during the reign of Queen Elizabeth I. According to Gresham's Law, if the government made two commodities equal in price, the overvalued ("bad") commodity will circulate, while the undervalued ("good") commodity will disappear. If two coins of equal nominal value are circulating, the one with the highest intrinsic value will be hoarded and the one with the lower intrinsic value will be spent. As John Pugsley states, "When you find you have a silver quarter and a copper plated quarter, you'll naturally follow Gresham's Law by keeping the silver and spending the copper."[36]

North states, "In 1962, I read Rothbard's *Man, Economy, and State*. After reading his section on Gresham's Law, I knew that silver dimes and quarters would gradually become scarce, and I started hoarding the coins. In the fall of 1963, the crisis hit and silver coins disappeared from the big cities. The U.S. Mint had to introduce non-silver coins in 1964 to avert a nationwide shortage of small coins."[37]

After the silver coin shortage of 1963-64, the conservative publishing house, Arlington House, under Neil McCaffrey, began publishing a series of books on hard-money topics. One of the most popular books in 1966 was *Wooden Nickels*, by William F. Rickenbacher, who discussed the "decline and fall of silver coins" in America, and how to profit from it. Rickenbacher said he had been influenced by Henry Hazlitt and Elgin Groseclose. He recommended buying silver coins and silver mining stocks.[38] This book was followed by another in 1968, *Death of the Dollar*, in which Rickenbacher predicted the "inevitability" of more inflation, a devaluation of the dollar, and a rise in the dollar price of gold. In the final chapter, he recommended investing in collectibles, rare coins, real estate, gold and silver shares, and silver coins.[39]

By far the most popular financial book published by Arlington House was Harry Browne's *How You Can Profit from the Coming Devaluation* in 1970. It reached the *New York Times* bestseller list, and eventually sold nearly half a million copies (including paperback). Browne's book took a more direct investment approach than Rickenbacher's and also came at a more opportune time; the dollar was reaching a crisis stage in the foreign exchange markets in the early 1970s at the time when Browne's book was published. In his breakthrough work, Browne correctly predicted the devaluation of the U.S. dollar and the rise in the price of gold. "The greatest influence on my thinking at the time was Rothbard," Browne said. In the "acknowledgements" section of the book, Browne credits Rothbard: "In the field of money, the most important help has come from the writings of Murray Rothbard." He cites several of Rothbard's works: *What Has Government Done to our Money?*, *America's Great Depression*, and the *Panic of 1819*. Using principles developed by Rothbard and other free-market economists,

Browne concluded that the fixed exchange rate system and the fixed gold price ($35 an ounce) were in essence forms of price controls. Therefore, a run on gold and the dollar were almost inevitable, which in turn could only mean an "official devaluation," according to Browne. The devaluation occurred in 1971, soon after Browne's book came out.

Browne used Gresham's Law as an investment tool. "A good example of this took place in the United States during 1964 and 1965. The dollar was continuing to depreciate rapidly. American citizens couldn't legally own gold. But silver coins were available. At that time, the value of the silver in a silver coin was slightly less than the face value of the coin (a silver quarter had about 23 cents worth of silver in it). But the silver had value; the paper was intrinsically worthless. Consequently, the silver coins became scarce. Pretty soon it became almost impossible to keep the cash register stocked with dimes, quarters, or half-dollars. It reached a point where the government (after having tried to flood the market with 300 million ounces of new silver coins) gave up and switched to copper-nickel tokens."[40]

Browne also noted, "Gresham's Law can't tell us how soon a given reaction will occur. It's a mistake to take a general principle and try to predict specific short-term market activity from it."[41]

Based on Mises, Rothbard, and other Austrian economic thinkers, Browne applied these principles to the financial situation and concluded in 1970, "Because its only alternative is deflation, a devaluation is an overwhelming probability."[42] Browne says he was "lucky." In his *Devaluation* book, he declared, "I expect a devaluation to occur sometime between this coming Saturday and the end of 1971."[43]

As a result of the devaluation of the dollar, Browne expected a fall in stock prices ("With a good selection of stocks, a short seller might do surprisingly well at this time") and a rise in gold ("gold bullion is a prime beneficiary of devaluation"). He recommended buying North American and South African gold shares, silver ("Silver bullion is one of the best all-around investments. . . ."), and Swiss francs ("The only currency to be recommended is the Swiss franc").[44]

Browne's *Devaluation* book was the first in a series of Arlington House books under the category, "Dollar Growth Library." Llewellyn H. Rockwell, Jr. was the senior editor in charge of the financial books. In 1971, Arlington House published *Panics and Crashes, and How You Can Make Money Out of Them*, by Harry D. Schultz. It also published two books by Donald J. Hoppe, entitled *How to Buy Gold Coins* and *How to Buy Gold Stocks and Avoid the Pitfalls*.[45]

Harry Browne followed with another financial book in 1974, entitled *You Can Profit from a Monetary Crisis*, which also became a bestseller.[46] Again, he acknowledged several books by Rothbard. In it, he argued that continued inflation in the 1970s would mean further rises in the prices of gold, silver and Swiss francs. His expectations proved to be correct in the late 1970s. "All of these events were probable according to my understanding of economics, but no one could predict exactly when they would happen. The timing was very fortuitous."

Following the official devaluation of the dollar and the closing of the gold window on August 15, 1971, a whole industry was created. The mid-1970s witnessed a tremendous increase in "hard money" books, newsletters, seminars, coin companies, survival retreats, food storage, and related businesses. In 1974, Robert D. Kephart, former publisher of *Human Events* and long-time follower of Austrian economics, began the first mass-audience investment letter, called the *Inflation Survival Letter*. Of course, many hard-money activities took place prior to these events, but the monetary crises, the OPEC oil embargo and commodity shortages of the early 1970s gave great impetus to the movement. Harry Schultz claimed to have sponsored the first hard-money investment seminar in 1967. James U. Blanchard, III, a free-market devotee and admirer of Rothbard, began his famous New Orleans investment conferences in 1974. There are several financial advisors who claim to be the "original gold bug," including Harry Schultz, James Dines, and Joe Granville, because they recommended buying gold shares in the late 1950s. However, Hans Sennholz and E. C. Harwood were two hard-money investment advisors who bought gold shares as early as 1950. Sennholz wrote several articles in *Human Events* in 1959 and 1960 predicting higher gold and silver prices. He also was one of the first hard-money investment counselors to invest in real estate.

Another well-known investment counselor and writer is Jerome F. Smith, who formed the ERC Publishing Co. in West Vancouver, British Columbia, in the early 1970s and helped investors open Swiss bank accounts. Smith has high regard for Rothbard and the "Austrian" school of economics: "Murray Rothbard has advanced economic science, in my view, more than any other living economist."[47] Smith's most famous book was *Silver Profits in the Seventies*, which argued that silver was greatly undervalued at the time because of inflationary pressure and annual figures indicating net consumption of silver throughout the 1970s. He predicted, "silver will double in price and then double again."[48]

Another writer influenced by Rothbard and the Austrian economists is Alexander P. Paris, who wrote *The Coming Credit Collapse* in 1974, analyzing the debt and banking crisis, and the significance it would have on investments. Paris wrote, "My view of the business cycle and the cause of the recessions is a simple one and is based upon the role of money and credit in the economy. It is also strongly based on theories of the Austrian school of economics. . . ."[49]

John A. Pugsley also wrote a hard-money investment book in 1974, entitled *Common Sense Economics*, which sold over 200,000 copies by mail order. He argued that the financial survivors of these turbulent years would only be "a more astute minority who will succeed because they have taken the time to understand the causes of the world's economic turmoil."[50]

Based on this economic analysis, Pugsley developed a "rational portfolio," which included an emphasis on gold and other inflation hedges: "I believe that the demand for gold from, private holders will increase dramatically in the next few years as currency inflation accelerates."[51]

The Inflation-Deflation Debate

A recurring debate within the hard-money movement has been over the question of whether the economy would suffer a serious deflation, or the continuation of inflation. The debate went on throughout the 1970s and continues even more fiercely in the 1980s. Murray Rothbard has been in the center of this battle for over 10 years. The principal "deflationists" have been C. Vern Myers, John Exter, Don Hoppe and James Dines. The "inflationists" have been led by Rothbard, Jerome Smith, James Blanchard and Howard Ruff, among others.

The deflationists argued that business, consumer and government debt were reaching such dangerous levels that a recession would lead to worldwide bankruptcies, a banking crisis, and a financial panic. The government would not be able to stop it. Official efforts would be futile, like "pushing on a string," because the demand for cash in a banking crisis would exceed the ability of the government to supply it. The deflationists have pointed to the sharp drop in commodity prices at various times to prove that deflation was "imminent."[52]

Rothbard wrote at least three articles for investment newsletters responding to the deflationists' arguments, covering the past 10 years. The timing of the articles is helpful in examining Rothbard's views on the subject. His first article was written for *Inflation Survival Letter*, in 1975, at the bottom of the 1973-75 inflationary recession; the second

for *World Market Perspective*, in 1979, at the height of double-digit inflation; and the third for *Jerome Smith's Investment Perspectives* in
November 1984, during the "disinflationary" era.

In the first article, written in 1975, Rothbard makes a strong case
for higher inflation ahead, despite the "inflationary depression" at
hand. The Federal Reserve, Rothbard maintained, "can stop any deflationary process from taking hold, and can ensure that inflation will
continue." This is because the U.S. and the world are no longer on a
gold standard, so that "restraints on Fed inflationary manipulation
have been removed." He concluded, "[i]f, as seems likely, the current
depression is substantially over by next year, this recovery will add further fuel to the fires of accelerated inflation."[53]

In 1979, writing for *World Market Perspective*, Rothbard acknowledged that the Federal Reserve can precipitate a major recession or depression. "The deflationists see correctly that our Keynesian policies of
inflationary bank credit, propelled by the Federal Reserve System,
have brought and will continue to bring about recessions. . . ." Rothbard refers back to the 1973-75 recession, noting that "inflation,
though indeed stamped down to 6 or 7 percent per year, was yet not reversed." Using Austrian economic analysis, Rothbard showed how the
deflationists have been misled by declines in industrial commodity
prices. He explained how it's perfectly natural for consumer prices to
rise relative to commodity or wholesale prices during a recession. But
Rothbard also raised the possibility that the "inflationist mentality"
could be reversed.

> It is certainly theoretically possible that power in Washington
> will soon be assumed by sound-money men dedicated to stop-
> ping inflation in its tracks. . . . the last few years have seen a no-
> table economic education on the part of the public. Most people
> now believe that federal spending and deficits are in some im-
> portant way a cause of chronic inflation, and are putting pres-
> sure on the politicians to reduce or slow down their spending
> and deficits. Even the money printing process as a source of in-
> flation is becoming known among the public. . . . Already the
> Carter Administration has slowed down, though in no way
> stopped, the rate of inflating because of this public pressure.

Nevertheless, Rothbard dismissed the possibility of lower inflation:
". . . until hard-money trends among the public take hold and become
more institutionalized in organized political pressure—inflation will

probably continue to grow. Furthermore, it might even accelerate, because we have in the last few years gotten to the dangerous point where the public expects continued inflation. . . ."[54]

Finally, in late 1984, in the midst of a lower inflation environment, Rothbard responded to the question, "Is it really true that inflation is finished?" He stated, "I am notoriously leery about making forecasts in economics, but I am confident in repeating the same thing I have been saying, over and over, for several decades: Don't you believe it! Inflation is here to stay, a permanent feature of the economic landscape. No one can predict the precise percentage of price rise from year to year, but the direction—inflation—is here and will not be altered." Rothbard noted that, if by deflation is meant a fall in *consumer* prices, it won't happen. He expressed great skepticism about President Ronald Reagan's "supply side" economics and the possibility of a return to some kind of gold standard. He noted that Congress, under the Monetary Control Act of 1980, gave the Federal Reserve increased power to "buy any asset whatever, even foreign currencies and shares of stock" to avoid a monetary crisis. Rothbard concluded, ". . . inflation is going to be permanent in the United States and throughout the world."[55]

Rothbard's Critique of the Kondratieff Cycle

Part of the deflationists' argument involved the use of what is called the "Kondratieff Cycle," frequently expounded by investment writers such as Donald J. Hoppe, Julian Snyder, Jim McKeever and Bert Dohmen-Ramirez. Rothbard has been sharply critical of this cycle theory, and of cycle theories in general.

The Kondratieff cycle theory is named after the Russian economist Nikolai D. Kondratieff, who in the 1920s researched the proposal that Western business cycles go through a periodic "long wave" lasting approximately 50-60 years. The Great Depression of the 1930s represented a major cyclical point of reference for predicting the next depression. According to Kondratieff advocates, the next depression would be 50-60 years later—some proponents suggested the 1973-75 recession as a starting point, while others keep moving the date upward into the 1980s.[56] Rothbard criticized the Kondratieff long-wave theory in both specific and general terms. In an article published in the *Inflation Survival Letter* in 1978, Rothbard demonstrates that the economic data does not fit the 50-60 year cycle. For example, the 1896-1940 trough-to-trough cycle lasted only 44 years. Moreover, Rothbard notes that Kondratieff only observed the "long wave" two and one-half times: "The idea of even hypothesizing, much less proclaiming, the existence of a cycle on the basis of only two-and-a-half observations must strike the unbiased observer as breathtaking in its presumption."

On a more general level, Rothbard criticizes the whole notion of cycle analysis:

> Correct business cycle theory is qualitative; it cannot predict the length or the intensity of any particular cycle. Specifically, the length of the boom period depends on how long the government authorities are willing to keep inflating the money supply at a rapid pace. It is manifestly absurd for economists or historians to claim that they can forecast precisely *when* the monetary authorities will stop or slow down their inflationary policies. This depends on complex qualitative political and psychological factors than manifestly cannot be squeezed into some predictable set of numbers.[57]

Still, despite Rothbard's and others' devastating critiques, the Kondratieff wave theory is still espoused by investment writers. Recently, for example, financial advisor Bert Dohmen-Ramirez suggested that the early 1980s was the "depression" which Kondratieff predicted. "I have often referred to the Kondratieff Wave (K-Wave), which is the long-term, 52 to 56-year, economic wave. I believe we are presently at the end of that wave and that the K-Wave crash (which many analysts are still expecting) occurred in 1980, when all the tangible assets collapsed."[58]

Rothbard's stinging criticism of wave or cycle theory could also apply to other recent cycle theories. For example, during the first half of the 1980s, some hard-money writers and analysts (especially Mary-Anne and Pamela Aden, chart analysts from Costa Rica) predicted that gold and silver would skyrocket by 1986, based on a so-called "six year" cycle in gold and silver prices (gold and silver reached previous highs in 1974 and 1980). Forecasts of $2,000 to $4,000 per ounce for gold were made frequently. Although Rothbard did not comment publicly on the six-year gold cycle theory, he expressed grave skepticism about technical analysts who forecast higher prices based purely on "cycle" theory. As Rothbard stated in 1979, "Computer models can only embody *past* quantitative linkages. But there is no guarantee that these same linkages and ratios will hold in the near or far future. Ratios and trends change. It is no great thing simply to extrapolate past trends into the next year: anyone can do this with a ruler, and there is no need for high-speed computers. The real trick is to forecast sudden changes and reversals of trends; and econometricians have been spectacularly unsuccessful in doing so."[59] In 1982, when the six-year gold cycle became popular, Rothbard stated that "expectations are purely subjective, and cannot be captured by the mechanistic use of charts and regressions."[60]

Rothbard and the Financial Markets in the Eighties

Rothbard and the "inflationist" camp expected inflation to worsen in the 1980s. In 1979, Rothbard suggested that, barring the government adopting an anti-inflation policy, "the prognosis ahead can only be for more, and ever more, inflation."[61] Jerome Smith, Hans Sennholz, Howard Ruff, Jim Blanchard, Doug Casey and other hard-money investment writers expected double-digit inflation to worsen in the 1980s. Jerome Smith, for instance, wrote in 1979, "the accelerating double-digit inflation rate of the 1970s (now around 15 percent) will lead to triple-digit inflation and destruction of the dollar (and all dollar-tied national currencies) in the 1980s."[62] Doug Casey, in his bestselling book, *Crisis Investing*, argued that an "inflationary depression" was inevitable, based on "Austrian" malinvestment theory of the business cycle. Casey suggested that "a hyperinflation seems almost inevitable."[63]

But higher inflation didn't materialize—in fact, the "Reagan Eighties" have so far been characterized by a reduction in inflation and a gradual decline in interest rates, following the severe 1981-82 recession. At that point, some hard-money investment advisors parted company with the "inflationists."

Harry Browne's views on the markets changed in the early 1980s, departing from Rothbard's inflationist viewpoint. In the book, *Inflation Proofing Your Investments*, Browne and co-author Terry Coxon developed one potential scenario in which the demand for money might rise substantially, offsetting the rise in the money supply and resulting in a "high interest, low inflation" environment.[64] But, according to Browne, Rothbard read the chapter in manuscript and thought such a possibility to be "remote." "He felt very strongly that deflation wasn't politically possible," Browne said. "I'm philosophically more in harmony with Ludwig von Mises, who was agnostic, skeptical, and non-political."

Despite the decline in interest rates and inflation in the 1980s, Rothbard has been staunchly critical of the monetary and fiscal policy of the Reagan Administration and the Federal Reserve. In 1981, he commented, "there is no Reagan Revolution. There is no budget cut; there is no tax cut. The whole *brouhaha* is sound and fury, signifying nothing. Nothing is happening." Rothbard noted that Reagan's budget showed an increase in government spending, not a decrease. Also, despite a reduction in the highest tax bracket from 70% to 50%, and a reduction in long-term capital gains rates to 20%, the tax bill for most Americans was going up, if one includes Social Security levies. As far as monetary policy is concerned Rothbard criticized Federal Reserve chairman Paul Volcker for achieving "neither stable nor slow monetary growth so far. . . . Federal Reserve actions, and the resulting money supply, have been unprecedentedly erratic and volatile." He added that ". . . the Reagan program of gradually reducing the rate of money growth until a 'moderate' level is achieved is not going to work. Gradualism won't work, now less than ever." Nevertheless, Rothbard noted that a "disinflationary psychological impact" had already begun in the United States in 1981, with incredibly high deregulated interest rates and the dramatic drop in precious metals prices and other commodities. Rothbard was critical of his friends in the hard-money movement who were sympathetic with Reagan: "James Sinclair asserts that Reagan, Regan and Volcker have been saying exactly the right things, which are exactly the *wrong* things for gold, and my old friend Dr. Mark Skousen persists in claiming significant future reductions in inflation and improvements in the economic climate." Rothbard summarized by stating:

> "The bottom line is that the Reagan program is all talk and no action. In short order, the market will discover this, will realize that all we are getting is retread Nixon-Ford economics, and inflation will resume its accelerating course. The interesting question is: will my friends in the hard-money movement wake up before, or later than, the market?"[65]

Actually, a case can be made to explain the disinflationary phenomenon of the 1980s using "Austrian" principles of economics. F. A. Hayek and other Austrian economists have shown that fiat money inflation is inherently unstable, creating a boom-bust cycle. A monetary inflation inevitably leads to a recession, even if the central bank adopts a monetarist rule by expanding the money stock at a steady rate equal to average GNP growth. In fact, according to Hayek, the only short-term way to postpone a recession is to *accelerate* monetary growth (which of course can only result in a worse disaster in the long run, eventually leading to what Mises called the "crack up" boom).[66] A corollary of this principle can be applied to the monetary policy of the eighties: if, after a "tight" money policy and severe recession, the government expands the money supply at a rate *equal* to the previous monetary inflation, general consumer prices will rise by an amount *less* than the previous rate (assuming that the recession is strong enough to break the inflationary psychology). Moreover, in order to reignite consumer price inflation to the previous high level, the Federal Reserve would have to reinflate at a more rapid rate. Why? Because the tight money policy and severe recession have left the capital goods industry in a precarious financial state, many of them close to bankruptcy. In general, with a high debt exposure, the capital markets are in a more vulnerable position than at the beginning of the previous cycle. The level of "malinvestment" in the economy has grown as a result of the inflationary policy of the government. Thus, the "mal-invested" capital markets require substantially greater resources to bring them out of their dangerous financial condition. Under this burden, the chances of reigniting an artificial boom, accompanied by sharply higher prices, are reduced.

Monetary policy in the first half of the 1980s appears to bear this out. The Federal Reserve under Carter expanded the money supply at double-digit rates, anywhere from 10% to 13% depending on which definition of money you look at. The Federal Reserve under Reagan has expanded the money supply at similar rates. The result has been less consumer price inflation under Reagan than under Carter. Admittedly, there are other significant factors at work which keep inflation down— e.g., the tight money in the early 1980s, the deregulation of the banking industry, the reduction of marginal tax rates, the collapse of OPEC, and the worldwide psychological impact of Reagan's conservative image. But the point is that, under Austrian analysis, the Federal Reserve under Reagan would have had to expand the money supply at significantly higher levels than it has been doing in order to reignite the fires of price inflation to equal the double-digit levels of the 1970s. And so far it has not done so.[67]

Despite the drop in interest rates and inflation in the 1980s, Rothbard takes a long-term view. In a 1985 interview, he said that "we will certainly see a reacceleration of inflation and interest rates. . . . I can't predict the exact time frame. . . . but certainly over the next few years. . . . We've been in a permanent inflation for the last 50 years, and I don't see any sign that it's ending. The money supply has been going up about 10%, depending on which figures you look at. It's inevitable that prices will start reaccelerating again as the economy heats up. And when they do start to move, they will do so quickly. People have been lulled to sleep by the rhetoric of the Reagan administration." He considered Volcker "less inflationary than Arthur Burns, but he's certainly no hero of the free market. The Reagan administration has been attacking Volcker for not being inflationary enough. In that sense, he's keeping monetary growth down. But based on any absolute criteria, the guy's an inflationist." When asked about the bull market in stocks, with the Dow at 1,300 at the time, he responded, "That's only 30% higher than it was in 1966. Consumer prices have tripled since then. I'd hardly call it a boom." He did, however, suggest that the stock market could go higher.[68]

The Prospects for Another Economic Crisis

Unlike an investment advisor, who has to be concerned about the short-term shifts in public psychology and trends in the financial markets, Rothbard is an academic economist who can take the long-term view. Despite good economic news in the mid-1980s—low inflation, falling interest rates, and a bull market in stocks—Rothbard points out that serious fundamental problems still exist. Consumer inflation is maybe 4% but—"Four percent was considered so terrible in 1971 that Nixon put on a wage and price freeze," notes Rothbard. The Federal Reserve still governs a totally fiat monetary system, which is both inflationary and economically destructive. As Rothbard states, "Since the Fed is no longer limited by gold restraints, it can now print dollars in unlimited amounts, unhampered by domestic statute or international obligations."[69] And the Federal government continues to run huge deficits and is always looking for ways to increase revenues. So the wise investor, while taking advantage of the temporary goods news in traditional investment vehicles such as stocks and bonds, must be prepared for the bad economic news that Rothbard eventually foresees. Rothbard's viewpoint may not be a popular one today, but in the words of Josh Billings, "As scarce as truth is, the supply has always been in excess of the demand."

Notes

1. Sources, unless otherwise indicated, are based on private interviews with individuals in the hard-money movement. Each has had the opportunity to review references to them, but only I am responsible for any conclusions reached in this paper. I also wish to thank Robert D. Kephart for the use of his extensive library in preparation of this paper.
2. Alexander P. Paris, *The Coming Credit Collapse* (New York: Arlington House, [1974] 1980), p. x.
3. James Dines, *The Invisible Crash* (New York: Random House, 1975), p. xiv.

4. Donald J. Hoppe, *How to Buy Gold Coins* (New York: Arlington House, 1970), pp. 17, 19-20.

5. Gary North, *How You Can Profit From the Coming Price Controls* (Durham, N.C.: American Bureau of Economic Research, 1978). See also his *Introduction to Christian Economics* (Nutley, N.J.: The Craig Press, 1973), pp. 107-23.

6. John A. Pugsley, *Common Sense Economics* (Costa Mesa, Calif.: Common Sense Press, [1974] 1976), pp. v-vi.

7. Harry Browne, *How You Can Profit from the Coming Devaluation* (New York: Macmillan, 1974); *Inflation-Proofing Your Investments* (New York: William Morrow & Co., 1981), co-authored with Terry Coxon, is dedicated to Rothbard, Mises, Hazlitt and Friedman.

8. Charles H. Hession, *John Maynard Keynes* (New York: Macmillan, 1984), pp. 174-75, 212.

9. Ibid., pp. 174-75, 305.

10. John Maynard Keynes, *Essays in Biography*, in *The Collected Writings of John Maynard Keynes*, vol. X, A. Robinson and D. Moggridge, eds. (London: Macmillan and Cambridge University Press, 1951).

11. Jerome F. Smith, "Charter Issue: Understanding the Business Cycle," *Jerome Smith's Investment Perspectives* (October 1983): 1-2.

12. Friedrich A. Hayek, *Monetary Theory and the Trade Cycle* (London: Jonathan Cape, 1933), pp. 41, 36n.

13. Ludwig M. Lachmann, *Capital, Expectations, and the Market Process* (Kansas City, Kans.: Sheed Andrews and McMeel, 1977). pp. 31-32.

14. Murray N. Rothbard, "Foreword," in James B. Ramsey, *Economic Forecasting—Models or Markets?* (San Francisco: Cato Institute, 1977), p. x.

15. Interview with Murray N. Rothbard, *Predictions* (April 1985), p. 6-7.

16. Murray N. Rothbard, "The Inflation-Deflation Debate," *World Market Perspective* (January 1985), p. 2.

17. Murray N. Rothbard, *Man, Economy, and State* (Los Angeles: Nash Publishing, [1962] 1970), pp. 727-37.

18. See Murray N. Rothbard, "Introduction to Second Edition," *America's Great Depression* (New York: Richardson and Snyder, [1963] 1983), pp. xxv-xxxviii.

19. Irving Fisher, *New York Times*, 16 October 1929. Quoted in *Oh Yeah?*, compiled by Edward Angly (New York: Viking Press, 1931), an amusing compilation of predictions about the economy and the stock market during the 1929-1931 depression.

20. Ramsey, *Economic Forecasting*.

21. Margit von Mises, *My Years with Ludwig von Mises* (Cedar Falls, Iowa: Center for Futures Education, [1976] 1984), pp. 23-24.

22. James Brant, *Bernard M. Baruch* (New York: Simon Schuster, 1983), p. 324.

23. Quoted in Ramsey, *Economic Forecasting*, p. xii.

24. Bennett W. Goodspeed, *The Tao Jones Averages: A Guide to Whole-brained Investing* (New York: Penguin Books, 1983), pp. 22-23.

25. Ibid., p. 30.

26. Rothbard, "In Defense of Extreme Apriorism," *Southern Economic Journal*, 23, no. 3 (January 1957): 314-320

27. Hession, *John Maynard Keynes*, pp. 105-06.

28. Ibid., p. 107.

29. Goodspeed, *The Tao Jones Averages*, pp. 117-18. This "dual-minded" theory does not justify, in my mind, a proclivity toward deviate sexual behavior as a prerequisite to creativity or financial success, as Hession seems to characterize Keynes.

30. Ramsey, *Economic Forecasting*, p. xi.

31. Margit von Mises, *My Years*, p. 24.
32. Rothbard, *Man, Economy, and State* (Princeton: Van Nostrand, 1962; reprint, Los Angeles: Nash Publishing, 1970).
33. Murray N. Rothbard, *America's Great Depression*, (Princeton: Van Nostrand, 1963; 2nd ed., Los Angeles: Nash Publishing, 1972; 3rd ed., New York: New York University Press, 1975; 4th ed., New York: Richardson and Snyder, 1983).
34. Pugsley, *Common Sense Economics*, p. v.
35. Murray N. Rothbard, *What Has Government Done to Our Money?* (Larkspur, Colo.: Pine Tree Press, 1964; 2nd ed., San Rafael, Calif.: Libertarian Publishing, 1982).
36. Pugsley, *Common Sense Economics*, p. 118.
37. Cf. Gary North, *How You Can Profit From the Coming Price Controls*, p. 2.
38. William F. Rickenbacher, *Wooden Nickels* (New York: Arlington House, 1966), pp. 145-47, 154-55.
39. William F. Rickenbacher, *Death of the Dollar* (New York: Arlington House, 1968).
40. Harry Browne, *How You Can Profit from the Coming Devaluation*, pp. 88-89.
41. Ibid., p. 89.
42. Ibid., p. 124.
43. Ibid., p. 125.
44. Ibid., pp. 148, 154-59, 162.
45. Harry D. Schultz, *Panics and Crashes and How You Can Make Money Out of Them* (New York: Arlington House, 1971); Donald J. Hoppe, *How to Buy Gold Coins*; idem., *How to Buy Gold Stocks and Avoid the Pitfalls* (New York: Arlington House, 1972).
46. Browne, *You Can Profit from a Monetary Crisis*.
47. *Jerome Smith's Investment Perspectives* (November 1984).
48. Jerome Smith, *Silver Profits in the Seventies* (West Vancouver, B.C.: ERC Publishing, 1972). Smith's book was updated in 1982; idem, *Silver Profits in the Eighties* (New York: Books in Focus, 1982). Smith calls his letter, "The Investment Advisory Newsletter Based on the Austrian School of Economics."
49. Alexander P. Paris, *The Coming Credit Collapse*, p. 198.
50. Pugsley, *Common Sense Economics*, p. xii.
51. Ibid., pp. 108-09.
52. The most popular deflationist book was C. Vern Myers, *The Coming Deflation* (New York: Arlington House, 1979).
53. "Inflation or Deflation?" *Inflation Survival Letter* (4 June 1975).
54. "Inflation or Deflation—Which Way?" *World Market Perspective* (19 July 1979).
55. "What's Ahead? Resurging Inflation or Sudden Deflation?" *Jerome Smith's Investment Perspectives* (November 1984).
56. For an in-depth critique of the Kondratieff cycle theory, see John A. Pugsley, "The Long Wave: Should We Praise or Bury Kondratieff?" *Common Sense Viewpoint* (November 1982).
57. "The Kondratieff Cycle Myth," *Inflation Survival Letter* (14 June 1978); see also, "The Kondratieff Cycle: Real or Fabricated?" *Investment Insights*, (August and September 1984).
58. Bert Dohmen-Ramirez, "The Long-Term Wave Phenomenon," *Wellington's Capital* (January 1986), p. 7.
59. Murray N. Rothbard, "Ten Most Dangerous Economic Fallacies of Our Time," *Personal Finance* (21 March 1979); see also my critique of the six-year gold cycle theory in *Personal Finance* (9 December 1981).
60. Rothbard, *America's Great Depression*, p. x.

61. "Inflation or Deflation—Which Way?" *World Market Perspective* (19 July 1979), p. 7.
62. Ibid., p. 1. See also Jerome F. Smith, *The Coming Currency Collapse—And What You Can Do About It* (New York: Books in Focus, 1980).
63. Douglas R. Casey, *Crisis Investing* (Los Angeles: Stratford Press/Harper and Row, 1980), pp. 39-62, 278. See also Howard Ruff, *How to Prosper During the Coming Bad Years* (New York: Times Books, 1979).
64. Harry Browne and Terry Coxon, *Inflation-Proofing Your Investments*, pp. 45-83.
65. Rothbard, "The Reagan Budget Fraud," *World Market Perspective* (19 March 1981).
66. F. A. Hayek, *Monetary Theory and the Trade Cycle*, pp. 111-32, 212-26. For a more complete explanation of Hayek's monetary theory of the business cycle, see his *Prices and Production* (New York: Augustus M. Kelly, [1931] 1967).
67. Written extensively on this subject in my newsletter, *Forecasts & Strategies* (September 1985 and March 1985). In order for my thesis to occur, it is essential that the inflationary psychology be broken. If not, the result might be more price inflation, not less.
68. *Predictions* (April 1985). By the summer of 1987, however, Rothbard had turned bearish on the stock market. In a private letter to a money manager, he suggested that a tight-money policy by the Federal Reserve could send stocks "plummeting" (Mark Skousen, *The Great Crash of 1987: Prelude to Financial Disaster?* [Potomac, Md.: Phillips Publishing, 1988], p. 7).
69. "Inflation or Deflation—Which Way?" *World Market Perspective* (19 July 1979), p.2.

13

Utility and the
Social Welfare Function

0222
0242
0240

Leland B. Yeager

The Issues

Murray Rothbard's judiciously skeptical but creative interests in utility theory, welfare economics, interpersonal utility comparisons, inequality and egalitarianism, Pareto optimality as a supposed evaluative device, philosophy and particularly ethics, and the relation between value judgments and positive economics date back to some of his earliest writings (his 1956, for example). His interests in these topics have inspired or reinforced my own.

Here I try to rethink some related issues. My discussion largely takes the form of a sympathetic but not wholly concurring review of writings by an economist who shares several of Rothbard's philosophical interests, John C. Harsanyi (see the references, especially 1976, Chapter V). Rothbard may well think that Harsanyi takes interpersonal utility comparisons and the social-welfare function too seriously and that his rejection of egalitarianism is incomplete and insipid. Although Harsanyi treats inherently fuzzy concepts as if they were sharp, doing so can have heuristic value, helping to clarify certain ethical issues. As for egalitarianism, Harsanyi was focusing on one narrow aspect or application of it and was not aspiring to as comprehensive a critique as Rothbard offers.

Rothbard may also be unhappy with some of my specific judgments. (I am still trying to make up my mind on some points.) I can only hope that he will find my discussion on the whole compatible with or complementary to what he has written.

Harsanyi has argued that the very meaning of utility, coupled with compelling postulates of rationality and with individualist (nonauthoritarian) values, practically demands a social-welfare function whose

175

maximand is the arithmetic average of the utilities of individuals. The required premises of Bayesian rationality are transitivity of preference, each person's aim to maximize his own expected utility, and the sure-thing principle, meaning that if a person would have made a particular risky choice and if the reward for being right is increased, then the person would still make the same choice. A social-welfare function incorporating individualistic values would approve of any change in circumstances benefitting one or more persons and harming none.

No one supposes that a single "correct" social-welfare function objectively exists for society as a whole. Each person who cares about such matters has his own SWF. Harsanyi is merely examining the characteristics of any defensible SWF embodying humanitarian and individualist values. He stipulates, however, that the evaluator is applying his social or ethical preferences rather than his own subjective preferences. Instead of trying to promote social arrangements favoring persons with his own particular characteristics, he is adopting a detached, "moral," point of view. He disregards knowledge of any abilities and tastes distinctively his own, including any especially high or low degree of risk aversion. Such an evaluator, Harsanyi argues, would opt for the criterion of maximum average utility.

Some critics say that this criterion is not egalitarian enough. Harsanyi replies that the critics either are mistaken or are applying nonindividualistic values. This is the issue I want to focus attention on.

Strange as it may seem to say so at this point, the version of utilitarianism that most appeals to me turns out not vulnerable to James Buchanan's well-based strictures against the idea that economics concerns techniques of maximization (strictures implied by much that Murray Rothbard also has written). I ask the reader to be patient, until later on, with language nevertheless seeming to suggest that utilities are measurable and interpersonally comparable and that social welfare is a maximizable function of them.

The Charge of Incoherence

First, let us get a subsidiary issue out of the way. David Gauthier (1978, 1982, 1985) has raised an objection to the criterion of average utility as assessed by Harsanyi's impartial evaluator. The evaluator would imagine himself as each of the various members of society, each with his own particular characteristics and tastes and social position, and would estimate the utility experienced by each one under each of the alternative sets of social arrangements being compared. The arrangements recommended would be those expected to yield highest average utility.

Gauthier objects that such a choice, instead of being made on the basis of any single self-consistent utility function, is made on the basis of a hodge-podge of diverse and even divergent functions. It is made in the absence of the conditions necessary for individual choice and so must be incoherent. It reflects no particular point of view. No actual person, aware of his own identity, would have to consider its implementation rational and fair.

Although Gauthier makes repeated and lengthy stabs at stating this objection, I confess I do not see its force. I am tempted to dismiss it with "So what?" or "Where is the incoherence?" (Goldman 1980, pp. 386-388, also seems unconvinced by Gauthier's argument.) True enough, Harsanyi's disinterested evaluator, akin to Adam Smith's (1759/1976) benevolent and impartial spectator, has an incomplete utility—or welfare—function. He merely prefers whatever set of social arrangements will give diverse individuals the best opportunities to achieve satisfaction as they themselves feel it. But such a function suffices for the purpose at hand. A smoothly operating system of social cooperation is conducive to people's successfully seeking satisfaction in many different specific ways.

Gauthier presses the objection just noted to clear the grounds for his own supposedly "contractarian" approach. Explaining why that approach seems unsatisfactory to me would be irrelevant to our present topic.

The Charge of Insufficient Egalitarianism

Egalitarian critics of the average-utility criterion (e.g., Rawls 1971, Sen 1973) would prefer a more to a less nearly equal distribution of utilities even at the cost of a somewhat lower level. As Gauthier says (1982, p. 154), Harsanyi fails to distinguish adequately between utilities themselves and their welfare significance or ethical worth. A given increment to the already high utility level of a fortunate person may well count less socially than the same increment to an unfortunate person's low level.

Harsanyi does not reject an egalitarian slant in assessing different distributions of *money or goods and services.* (He recognizes diminishing marginal utility of income or wealth.) He does not consider and so does not deny the invasions of personal rights, the impairment of production, and other consequences that would flow from efforts to implement such a slant. He focuses on a narrower and more technical aspect of egalitarianism. When distributions of *utilities* are at issue, a further egalitarian slant rests, he says, either on a logically indefensible *double*

adjustment for distribution or on rejection of the individualist postulate that only individuals' preferences are to count. He gives a similar
answer to egalitarian criticisms (considered below) based on aversion
to the risk associated with dispersed prospective utilities.

I keep changing my mind on whether Harsanyi or his critics are
right on this issue of double adjustment. The puzzle illustrates Harsanyi's own point (1976, p. 64) that social scientists encounter not only
(1) formal or logical problems and (2) empirical problems but also (3)
conceptual-philosophical problems. By confessing my wavering on the
type-3 problem under discussion here, I am trying to invite comments
that will bring it closer to solution.

Average versus Maximin

Harsanyi defends the average-utility criterion partly by contrasting it
with the maximin criterion of John Rawls (1971). Rawls recommends
social arrangements to maximize the welfare (strictly, the index of "primary goods") of the least-well-off stratum of the population. But this
criterion could call for odd, counterintuitive policies—allocating a
scarce drug to a poor patient precisely because he is poor rather than
to a rich patient whose medical need is greater (Harsanyi 1976, p. 72),
or sticking with a dismal job to avoid the slight risk of a plane crash on
the way to an inviting new job (Harsanyi 1975, p. 595).

Rawls's attempt to swat down such counterexamples with a micro/
macro distinction fails. It just is not reasonable to formulate policies by
paying overriding attention to the most unfortunate persons or the worst
conceivable outcomes. In many cases, the maximin and maximum-
average criteria may not call for appreciably different policies, and
maximin may then be a convenient simplification. When they do
clash, though, the average criterion makes better sense (Harsanyi 1975,
pp. 595-596).

Interpersonal Comparisons

The required interpersonal comparisons can be made in a rough and
ready way. It is not nonsensical to imagine myself in the position of
another person, with his values and tastes, and consider how my utility
would then be affected by some event or set of circumstances (perhaps
a distribution of income or wealth). We make such judgments all the
time. Harsanyi (1976, pp. 75-76) offers the example of two five-year-old
boys. One seems happy and able to derive joy even from little presents;

the other seems morose and hard to cheer up. To which one should Harsanyi give a little present he happens to have in his pocket? He would give it to the boy likely to get more utility from it (unless he saw reasonable hope that receiving presents and other signs of attention might benefit the morose boy's personality and happiness in the long run).

Expected Utility

Harsanyi's argument also depends on recognizing that the utility of a "lottery ticket"—a set of risky outcomes with associated probabilities—is the weighted average of the utilities of its possible outcomes, the weights being the probabilities of those outcomes. Two "tickets" having the same weighted average have the same overall desirability, regardless of the probability distribution of the particular outcomes. Suppose I attach 50 utils and 0.2 probability to outcome A, 30 utils and 0.5 probability to outcome B, and 70 utils and 0.3 probability to outcome C. The expected utility of the set, or ticket, is therefore $0.2 \times 50 + 0.5 \times 30 + 0.3 \times 70 = 46$ utils. A different ticket offers outcomes whose utilities and probabilities are 30 and 0.2 for A, 40 and 0.3 for B, and 56 and 0.5 for C, giving the same weighted average of 46 utils. I am therefore indifferent between the two sets. When, however, two sets have different weighted averages, a rational chooser prefers the one with the higher average, no matter how "unequal" its distribution of individual utilities may be.

This argument concerns the *utilities* and not the amounts of income or wealth associated with outcomes. Suppose an experimenter offers you a choice between two free lottery tickets, each offering a 50 percent chance of prize A *plus* a 50 percent chance of prize B. With ticket 1, A is $4900 and B is $5100. With ticket 2, A is $1 and B is $9999. Although the two tickets are equal in expected *dollar* value, you might definitely prefer ticket 1.

Unlike the dollar amounts of possible individual outcomes, their utilities do represent what significance the individual attributes to the dollar amounts. Utility is the sort of thing of which more or less *means* better or worse from the standpoint of the affected person.

You may object that a person cannot measure the utilities and estimate the probabilities of chancy outcomes. But a person making a decision in an uncertain situation cannot avoid trying to do so, however rough his estimates must be. Suppose you are deciding whether to accept a new job far away or to keep your old job and home. Either choice, either "ticket," offers a whole range of possible outcomes, but you must assess them as best you can. Or suppose an experimenter offers you a choice between two lottery tickets. One pays you $1000 if candidate A wins an election and nothing if he loses; the other tickets pays $500 if rival candidate B wins and nothing if he loses (compare Harsanyi 1976, p. 78). You will not refuse both free tickets; and in choosing between them, you rationally must consider what significance you would attribute to each amount of money and what you think each candidate's chances are.

Harsanyi is not inventing these aspects of choice in uncertain situations; he is just calling attention to them. Numerical examples exaggerate the precision with which people can estimate utilities and probabilities, but doing so is legitimate to clarify the issue.

Societies as Lottery Tickets

Harsanyi applies the reasoning just described to a hypothetical evaluator choosing among alternative types of society, in each of which he would be a person selected at random, enjoying or suffering his fate in accordance with that person's utility function and position in life. Harsanyi's device for thus envisioning an impartial choice resembles Rawls's "original position" behind a "veil of ignorance," but it is free of the latter's pretense of contract and other implausible features.

In assessing alternative types of society, Harsanyi's impartial evaluator employs the weighted-average-utility criterion as he would do in choosing among lottery tickets. The weights or probabilities are presumably proportional to the number of persons likely to be in each slot. If each person is considered to occupy a slot of his own, the weights are equal. (The criteria of average and total utility do not diverge, of course, if the population can be taken as given.)

Egalitarianism Again

In reply to critics urging a more egalitarian criterion, Harsanyi argues that their views involve either a mistake or refusal to count only the preferences of individuals. He is not criticizing an egalitarian bias in assessments of distributions of money or goods and services; he is referring to distributions of *utilities*.

The average-utility criterion already takes account of any nonproportionalities between levels of utility and levels of income or wealth experienced by individuals. People's feelings about distribution itself are likewise reflected in their utilities. If people would feel uncomfortable living in a society with a very rich minority, then their discomfort is expressed in the lowness of their utilities, which holds down the average.

To insist on further egalitarianism in the social-welfare function would be to adjust twice, illegitimately, for feelings about inequality. An evaluator who does so must be taking as his supreme criterion or ultimate moral value something other than the well-being experienced by individuals. He must, as Harsanyi says (1976, p. 68), be willing to sacrifice humanitarian considerations to his own egalitarian views. That is what it means for an evaluator to attribute diminishing marginal social significance to the utilities of persons.

Consider a state of affairs in which, all things considered, including the pattern of distribution, 99 persons enjoy 50 utils each and the 100th person enjoys 80. To prefer a more egalitarian society in which the 99 retain their 50 utils and the 100th has his utility chopped down to 55 is an extreme example of abandoning the individualistic postulate. Such a SWF makes the well-being of the 100th person affect social welfare perversely, negatively. The evaluator employing that SWF wants to obtrude his egalitarian feelings onto the members of society in a way going beyond his perhaps being one of those members.

Why should the welfare criterion be the arithmetic mean of individual utilities rather than, say, their geometric mean? Suppose that three slots exist, the probabilities of occupying each being equal and the associated utilities being 50, 60, and 70. The arithmetic mean is 60, their geometric mean 59.44. Now the original utilities change to 60, 60, and 59. Their total falls by 1 util and their arithmetic mean by ⅓ util; yet their geometric mean rises slightly, to 59.66. The change is for the worse by Harsanyi's criterion, for the better by the more egalitarian geometric criterion. Why the disagreement? Harsanyi would insist on the very meaning of utility. Loss of one unit is just that, a loss. It is either irrational or anti-individualistic to attribute less significance to a unit of utility when enjoyed by a higher-utility person than when enjoyed by a lower-utility person.

The geometric-mean criterion is not so extremely egalitarian that a cut in the utility of the best-off person, other utilities unchanged, could raise the social-welfare score. Neither is any of a family of functions conveniently given by a formula adapted from Alexander (1974, p. 611): Social welfare is the A'th root of the arithmetic mean of the A'th powers of the utility levels of the individual members of society. When $A = 1$, the criterion is simply the arithmetic mean. An A greater than 1 is anti-egalitarian: inequality biases the welfare score upward from the mean. An A smaller than 1 gives an egalitarian bias. A function with an extremely negative A might be called quasi-Rawlsian, since it yields a welfare score almost as low as the lowest of the individual utilities. A different type of function, such as one according the standard deviation of utilities a negative influence on the welfare score, is required to represent so egalitarian an attitude that an unaccompanied cut in the utilities of the best-off persons could count as an improvement.

Adjustment for Risk

Something further must be said about risk. James Sterba (1980, pp. 47-50) offers the example of persons behind Rawls's veil of ignorance who expect equal chances of belonging to the Privileged Rich or to the Alienated Poor. Under social arrangement A, expected utilities are 55 for the Rich and 10 for the Poor, with an arithmetic mean of 32.5. Under arrangement B, expected utilities are 40 and 20, with a mean of only 30.

Sterba recognizes that the utility numbers are supposed to take the diminishing marginal utility of income or wealth already into account. Yet, he asks, might not people reasonably consider the chance of having 55 utils under arrangement A rather than 40 utils under B insufficient to outweigh the danger of having only 10 utils rather than 20? Might it not be reasonable to play safe by choosing B despite its lower expected utility? Remember, a person is going to wind up definitely belonging to the Rich or to the Poor and will never experience average utility. To choose according to the average-utility criterion, persons would have to think of themselves as destined to live, seriatim, integral parts of the lives of many randomly selected individuals. That criterion curiously expects persons to think of themselves as parts of "average persons."

Sen (1973) had already presented a similar argument for making social welfare depend not only on the mean but also, inversely, on the dispersion of individuals' utility levels. Harsanyi (1976, pp. 72-73) sees a close formal similarity between Sen's argument and the utility-dispersion argument about lottery tickets. On that view, the desirability of a lottery ticket should depend not only on its expected (mean) utility but also on risk as reflected in some measure of dispersion among the utilities of its possible outcomes.

Yet, Harsanyi continues, that argument is notoriously fallacious. True, a similar argument would be valid if references to the *money values* of possible prizes replaced references to their utilities.

But the argument does not carry over from possible money outcomes to their utilities. ". . . the utility of any possible money income is measured by the decision makers' von Neumann-Morgenstern utility function, which already makes appropriate allowance for his attitude toward risk. For instance, if he has a negative attitude toward risk, then his utility function will display decreasing marginal utility for money. . . . Thus, his risk aversion will already be fully reflected in the utilities he assigns to various possible incomes and, therefore, also in his expected utility associated with the lottery ticket. Hence, it would be *unnecessary* and *inadmissible* double-counting if we made an allowance for the decision maker's risk aversion for a second time, and made his utility for a lottery ticket dependent, not only on its expected utility, but also on the dispersion in achievable utilities" (Harsanyi 1976, pp. 73-74).

Sen's utility-dispersion argument about social welfare falls, says Harsanyi (1976, pp. 74-75), to essentially the same objection. So, then, does Sterba's. It illegitimately transfers a mathematical relation, nonlinearity, from money amounts to utility levels.

For Harsanyi, the issue is not merely mathematical but also moral. When we measure utility changes affecting two different persons as being of the same size, we mean that those changes involve human needs of equal urgency. It would be unfair and often inhumane discrimination to maintain, as a matter of principle, that satisfaction of one person's needs should socially count less than satisfaction of the other's no more intense needs. (Recall Harsanyi's example, 1975, p. 75, of the scarce life-saving drug.)

Is it irrational to prefer being a person selected at random in a society with lesser expected mean utility than being a person at random in an alternative society with a greater dispersion of individual utilities? As I read him, that is just what Harsanyi says. If the chooser would be unhappy about winding up as a relatively disadvantaged person, especially in a highly unequal society, then he already takes these feelings into account in assessing individual utility levels and their mean. He already discounts the higher individual utilities for the risk of not receiving them, much as one might discount future utilities in terms of present ones. The lowness of the low utilities already takes full account of the danger of winding up with them, especially as members of a highly unequal distribution. With risk and risk aversion thus already taken into account, taking them into account again would be an illegitimate double adjustment. (Remember that Harsanyi conceives of the chooser as applying ethical rather than personal preferences: he lacks or disregards knowledge of his own *distinctive* characteristics, including any especially high or low degree of risk aversion.)

What Conception of Utility?

I confess to gnawing doubt. Harsanyi avowedly employs the von Neumann-Morgenstern conception of measurable utility, which is defined in the context of decisions under risk. Is he eliding some necessary distinction between utility so conceived and utility in the ordinary or more intuitive sense? Is he eliding a distinction between the utilities of chances and the chances of utilities? I suspect he is and that his doing so is connected with the particular conception of utility he employs.

Consider two lottery tickets. One bears a 50 percent chance of $490 plus a 50 percent chance of $510, while the other bears 50-50 chances of nothing or $1100. Expected dollar values are $500 for the first ticket, $550 for the second. On the von Neumann-Morgenstern conception, but only on that conception, the choice between those tickets is the same as the choice between (a) a 50 percent chance of the utility of $490 plus a 50 percent chance of the utility of $510 and (b) a 50 percent chance of the utility of nothing plus a 50 percent chance of the utility of $1100.

On a more nearly traditional conception, one must distinguish between utilities of chances and chances of utilities. On the more nearly traditional conception, whereby utility means subjectively perceived satisfaction, it is not necessarily irrational to prefer the lottery ticket affording not only the lesser expected dollar value but also the lesser expected utility score. I might attribute 490 utils to $490 and 508 utils to $510, averaging 499 utils as the utility score of a 50-50 chance of winning one or the other of those prizes. And I might attribute zero utils to zero dollars and 1040 utils to $1100, giving 520 as the expected utility score. Yet even though the second ticket offers a higher expected utility score than the first, I might rationally prefer the first instead because of my risk aversion and the greater riskiness of the second ticket.

The distinction deserves emphasis: "Measurable utility in the von Neumann-Morgenstern sense bears little resemblance to the measurable utility that was discarded during the past two decades" (Strotz 1953, p. 181). ". . . the von Neumann-Morgenstern measure is convenient and manageable for the class of problems involving risk, but it need not prove convenient for all classes of utility problems that may conceivably arise. Nothing rules out the usefulness of another measure for another purpose" (Strotz 1953, p. 194).

William J. Baumol acknowledges the argument that von Neumann-Morgenstern utility calculation already take the dispersion of lottery prizes into account and that adjustment for the dispersion of their *utilities* would be an illegitimate double adjustment (1965, chapter 22, esp. p. 520 and footnote). But, he says, it is generally (though not universally) agreed that no relation holds between von Neumann-Morgenstern and neoclassical utility theories. VN-M theory is concerned with predicting choices between lottery tickets, not with cardinal utility in the old-fashioned sense of introspective pleasure intensity (Baumol 1965, chapter 22, esp. pp. 523-524).

The upshot is that the vN-M conception, making expected or average utility the criterion of rational choice, does indeed already take account of risk aversion in cases of dispersed possible outcomes expressed in utility terms. It does so in such a way that further adjustment for risk would be double adjustment, and illegitimate. But it does so by its special definition of utility. When utility is understood as subjectively experienced satisfaction instead, it is not so clear that allowance for dispersion and risk is illegitimate and that rationality practically demands the criterion of maximum expected or average utility.

Choosing (or recommending) a kind of society, as already suggested, resembles choosing between alternative lottery tickets. If rationality requires choosing the ticket or the society affording maximum average expected von Neumann-Morgenstern utility, then rationally employing the person-at-random criterion is equivalent to employing the von Neumann-Morgenstern criterion.

Perhaps it is not true that as between, say, Sterba and Harsanyi, one is right and the other wrong. They may be talking at cross-purposes. Sterba is saying that maximum average classical utility is not the correct criterion, and Harsanyi is not necessarily disagreeing. He is calling for maximum average vN-M utility instead, which does take full account of risk and risk aversion.

Admittedly, though, I am unsure about this conclusion. I have changed my mind before and may well change it again. I especially invite attention to the issue.

Operationality and Heuristics

How does all this bear on the choice among types of society, sets of social arrangements? How does it matter, in practice, what particular conception of utility the social philosopher might have vaguely in mind? Can one distinguish, operationally, between operating with one conception of utility and another? Is there any way of really measuring and comparing and making calculations with the utilities of different persons?

Operationally, of course not. Our theorizing as if we could measure and compare and calculate is best interpreted as a device for sharpening our thinking about—as a stylization of—what we can in fact do. What we can do is make an intuitive stab at estimating utilities and their average. This stab, though the best we can do, is so very rough and ready that the question whether we are adequately allowing for risk sinks into nonoperationality.

Harsanyi, as I interpret him, takes this approach. When he shifts to a level of discourse more nearly operational than that of the mathematics of utility and social-welfare functions, he in effect recommends the good-society or comparative-institutions criterion: What set of social arrangements would offer the most appealing menu of prospects (unavoidably, uncertain prospects) for individuals in their various possible roles in life? Which arrangements, which menu of prospects, would most appeal to an evaluator consulting his ethical preferences rather than his own distinctive preferences?

Such an evaluator, practically by definition, is contemplating equal chances of being the occupant of each of the possible slots in society. He contemplates the least fortunate and most fortunate and in-between occupants and tries to imagine how he would feel being each of them. If in a particular kind of society he would feel miserable as a member of the least fortunate stratum, that assessment counts against that society.

F. A. Hayek proposes a similar criterion. True, he does not envision maximizing any aggregate or average of numerical measures (but neither does Harsanyi, except heuristically, if my interpretation is correct). "The conception of the common welfare or of the public good of a free society can . . . never be defined as a sum of known particular results to be achieved, but only as an abstract order which as a whole is not oriented on any particular concrete ends but provides merely the best chance for any member selected at random successfully to use his knowledge for his own purposes" (Hayek 1967, p. 163). The aim in developing or altering rules of just conduct "should be to improve as much as possible the chances of anyone selected at random" (Hayek 1976, pp. 129-130). "The Good Society is one in which the chances of anyone selected at random are likely to be as great as possible[.] . . . we should regard as the most desirable order of society one which we would choose if we knew that our initial position in it would be decided purely by chance. . . . the best society would be that in which we would prefer to place our children if we knew that their positions in it would be determined by lot" (Hayek 1976, p. 132, where one sentence appears in italics as a section heading). (Similar formulations by Hayek occur in his 1978, pp. 62-63, and 1976, p. 114; compare Vickrey 1961.)

If Harsanyi's and Hayek's (and Vickrey's) formulations sound like Rawls's criterion of choice behind a veil of ignorance, the similarity goes to show that such a criterion need not be a distinctively contractarian one.

Understood literally, I cannot recommend the criterion of the maximum of the average of measurable and interpersonally comparable utilities. Yet I do like the criterion of the sort of society in which an impartial evaluator would prefer to be a member chosen at random. The latter way of looking at things is a device, an expedient, for handling the fact that measurement and comparison are not really possible. As in the examples of deciding whether to move to a new job or which of two free bets on an election to accept, one unavoidably must act *as if* one could assign utilities and probabilities to the outcomes. The maximum-average and person-at-random criteria thus boil down to practically the same thing. The former is an exaggeration, a stylization, to focus our thought.

The numerical immeasurability of classical utility—subjective experiences—does not wholly discredit the concept. It is not meaningless to say that average utility would be lower or higher than it is in the United States today if circumstances were changed in specified ways. One could even meaningfully say more: As compared with the level *and distribution* of individual utilities in the United States today, specified changes would make the level-cum-distribution less or more satisfactory. And it not a meaningless judgment, though certainly one difficult to implement, to say that the criterion of institutions and policies should be whatever is likely to yield the most satisfactory level-cum-distribution of the utilities of individual persons.

A question might still seem to arise about the choice between maximum average utility on the one hand and lesser average utility associated with a more nearly equal distribution on the other hand. While the question may arise with the classical conception of utility, it does not arise, if Harsanyi is right, with the von Neumann-Morgenstern conception; and applying the criterion of maximum average vN-M utility is equivalent in practice to the person-at-random criterion.

It seems reasonable to conjecture, furthermore, that this average-versus-distribution question just dissolves on the level of discourse concerned with social institutions. Is it possible to specify a set of institutions that would yield greater average utility but a lesser degree of equality and an alternative set that would yield a lesser average but a greater degree of equality? We can, of course, conceive, at one extreme, of a complete absence of redistributive measures (other than, perhaps, private charity) and conceive, at the other extreme, of egalitarian measures involving punitively progressive taxation. But persuasive arguments suggest that either extreme policy would result in lesser average utility—or less attractive prospects for the person considered at random or even for members of the worst-off stratum—than some intermediate policy. Such arguments would enlist facts and theory from various fields of knowledge. Similar considerations would still apply, if less decisively, to comparisons between alternative nonextreme policies. We would never obtain all the detailed factual and theoretical knowledge necessary to say that one policy would yield more utility more unequally distributed while another would yield less utility less unequally distributed. Further information and reasoning would always remain relevant to assessing alternative sets of social institutions. We would never, I conjecture, have to make a sheer value judgment on a clear-cut tradeoff between utility and equality.

Positive research in economics, political science, psychology, and other disciplines into the probable operating properties and consequences of alternative institutions and policies contributes to and even constitutes the rough and ready measurement that utilitarians can carry out. Even regarding redistributionary policies, room remains for positive research into operations and consequences. We should beware of classifying unsettled issues as purely ones of tastes or values; we should not give up prematurely on positive research. As Harsanyi suggests (1975, p. 82), "the most important sources of moral disagreements are disagreements about what conditional or unconditional predictions—whether deterministic or probabilistic predictions—to make about future empirical facts."

Another indication that the utilitarian criterion is not meaningless is that it contrasts with conceivable alternatives—Rawlsian maximin, Nietzschean perfectionism, deontology, and others.

Political Economy and Operations Research

The foregoing discussion makes contact, I hope, with an important insight expressed by James Buchanan (for example 1979, especially selections 1, 2, and 4). The problem investigated by economists and tackled by policymakers is not properly seen as that of maximizing a social-welfare function—or anything else. It is not analogous to a problem in engineering or business administration, where the decisionmaker does pursue a rather definite objective. The economic problem is quite different. It is one of easing cooperation among millions, indeed billions, of distinct persons and easing coordination among their plans and activities as each of them pursues goals of his own. Each may be trying to maximize something—his own satisfaction, his own profit— and the concept of maximization is fruitful in economic theory. Yet no definite thing exists whose aggregate or average "society" or the policymaker may properly (except perhaps metaphorically or heuristically) be said to be trying to maximize.

What the policymaker is concerned with instead, ideally, is improving laws and institutions that affect how well diverse persons can coordinate their own efforts. (Compare Vining 1984.) While it can be useful in some strands of theory to speak of maximizing social welfare or average utility, such language really serves little more than a heuristic purpose. It reminds us of what the ultimate criterion of tinkering with rules and institutions is—utility or satisfaction, conceived of, however, not as an actual aggregate but as something experienced by each person in his own way. One who uses such language for heuristic purposes is not necessarily exposing himself to Buchanan's strictures.

Social cooperation—to adopt a term much used by Herbert Spencer, Ludwig von Mises, and Henry Hazlitt and a concept going at least as far back as Thomas Hobbes and David Hume—becomes the criterion of institutions and policies. A system of social cooperation is a means so essential to the effective pursuit of happiness by individuals in their own diverse ways that it may be regarded almost as an end in its own right. Operationally, the average-utility criterion of policy is pretty much the same thing as the criterion of serving social cooperation.

Conclusion

Rationality does not flatly require maximizing average utility, unless, perhaps, utility is interpreted in the sense of von Neumann and Morgenstern. When classical utility is meant, James Sterba may have a valid point about the possible rationality of preferring a distribution with a slighter dispersion at the cost of a lower average level. However, this consideration does not much impugn Harsanyi's criterion of what the person taken at random would prefer. Operationally, we cannot distinguish between maximizing expected average utility and adopting the choice of the person considered at random. Described either way, this version of utilitarianism is practically equivalent to what is sometimes called the good-society or comparative-institutions approach to assessing social arrangements. Comparing alternative sets of institutions, enlisting positive analysis, is as close as we can come, operationally, to "measuring" utilities and social welfare.

I hope Murray Rothbard agrees. What he and I might disagree on is whether utilities have any proper place in the appraisal of alternative sets of social institutions, whether some version or other of utilitarianism is an acceptable philosophical stance. Rothbard, as I understand him, might insist, instead, on conformity with personal rights as the supreme test. But is there any real clash? Recognition and respect for rights, instead of being taken as undiscussibly axiomatic, can be defended as serving utility, human well-being. But that is material for some further discussion.

The author is Ludwig von Mises Distinguished Professor of Economics at Auburn University. He thanks Roger Garrison for suggesting that the present topic might be suitable for the *Festschrift*. He thanks Will Carrington Heath, in particular, for thoughtful written comments on an earlier draft.

References

Alexander, Sidney. "Social Evaluation through Notional Choice," *Quarterly Journal of Economics* (November 1974): 597-624.

Baumol, William J. *Economic Theory and Operations Analysis*. 2nd ed. Englewood Cliffs, N.J.: Prentice-Hall, 1965.

Buchanan, James M. *What Should Economists Do?* Indianapolis, Ind.: Liberty Press, 1979.

Gauthier, David. "Bargaining and Justice." *Social Philosophy & Policy* 2 (Spring 1985): 29-47.

_____. "On the Refutation of Utilitarianism." In *The Limits of Utilitarianism*, edited by Harlan B. Miller and William H. Williams, 144-63. Minneapolis: University of Minnesota Press, 1982.

_____. "The Social Contract: Individual Decision or Collective Bargain?" In *Foundations and Applications of Decision Theory*, vol. 2., edited by C. A. Hooker, J. J. Leach, and E. F. McClennan, 47-67. Dordrecht and Boston: Reidel, 1978.

Goldman, Holly Smith. "Rawls and Utilitarianism." In *John Rawls' Theory of Social Justice*, edited by H. Gene Blocker and Elizabeth H. Smith, 346-94. Athens, Ohio: Ohio University Press, 1980.

Harsanyi, John C. "Can the Maximin Principle Serve as a Basis for Morality? A Critique of John Rawls's Theory." *American Political Science Review* 69 (1975): 594-606.

_____. "Cardinal Welfare, Individualistic Ethics, and Interpersonal Comparisons of Utility." *Journal of Political Economy* 63 (August 1955): 309-21. Reprinted in *Economic Justice*, edited by Edmund S. Phelps, selection 10, 266-85. Baltimore: Penguin, 1973.

_____. *Essays on Ethics, Social Behavior, and Scientific Explanation*. Dordrecht and Boston: Reidel, 1976.

_____. "Morality and the Theory of Rational Behavior." *Social Research* 44 (1977): 623-56.

_____. "Rule Utilitarianism and Decision Theory." *Erkenntnis* 11 (1977): 25-53.

_____. "Rule Utilitarianism, Equality, and Justice." *Social Philosophy & Policy* 2 (Spring 1985): 115-27.

Hayek, Friedrich A. *Law, Legislation and Liberty*. vol. 2, *The Mirage of Social Justice* Chicago: University of Chicago Press, 1976.

_____. *New Studies in Philosophy, Politics, Economics, and the History of Ideas*. Chicago: University of Chicago Press, 1978.

_____. *Studies in Philosophy, Politics and Economics*. Chicago: University of Chicago Press, 1967.

Rawls, John. *A Theory of Justice*. Cambridge: Belknap Press of Harvard University Press, 1971.

Rothbard, Murray N. *Egalitarianism as a Revolt Against Nature and Other Essays*. Washington, D.C.: Libertarian Review Press, 1974.

_____. *The Ethics of Liberty*. Atlantic Highlands, N.J.: Humanities Press, 1982.

_____. *Freedom, Inequality, Primitivism and the Division of Labor*. Menlo Park, Calif.: Institute for Humane Studies, 1971.

_____. *Man, Economy, and State*. 2 vols. (continuous pagination). Princeton: Van Nostrand, 1962.

_____. "Toward a Reconstruction of Utility and Welfare Economics." In *On Freedom and Free Enterprise*, edited by Mary Sennholz, 224-62. Princeton: Van Nostrand, 1956.

Sen, Amartya K. *On Economic Inequality*. Oxford: Clarendon Press, 1973.

Smith, Adam. *The Theory of Moral Sentiments*. (Originally published in 1759.) Indianapolis, Ind.: Liberty Classics, 1976.

Sterba, James P. *The Demands of Justice*. Notre Dame: University of Notre Dame Press, 1980.

Strotz, Robert H. "Cardinal Utility." *American Economic Review* 43 (May 1953): 384-97. Reprinted in *Readings in Microeconomics* (the version cited here), edited by David R. Kamerschen, 180-194. Cleveland and New York: World, 1967.

Vickrey, William S. "Risk, Utility and Social Policy." *Social Research* (Summer 1961). Reprinted in *Economic Justice*, edited by Edmund S. Phelps, selection 11, 286-297. Baltimore: Penguin, 1973.

Vining, Rutledge. *On Appraising the Performance of an Economic System*. New York: Cambridge University Press, 1984.

1. *Murray at one and one-half years old.*

2. *A sixteen year old Murray with his parents in 1941.*

3. *Murray earned his Ph.D. in 1956 from Columbia University and had this picture taken to forestall his parents who wanted a picture taken in his cap and gown.*

4. & 5. At a dinner given by the National Taxpayer's Union in 1973, Murray was presented with one of five bound volumes of Benjamin Tucker's Liberty *magazine. Top left, left to right, Professor W. H. Hutt, James Dale Davidson (founder of the National Taxpayer's Union), Murray, and Henry Hazlitt; top right, James Dale Davidson and Murray.*

6. From left to right, Ralph Raico, Murray, George Reisman, Robert Hessen, and Leonard Liggio in August 1955.

7. This picture was taken at a dinner given in honor of Ludwig von Mises in 1955; at right, Murray and F. A. Harper, founder of the Institute for Humane Studies.

8. *Murray in 1962.*

9. *On a trip by the York River in 1967.*

10. *This picture was taken in 1965, in Orange, Virginia, as the Rothbards took their first trip to the South.*

11. Murray with Robert Kephart, founder of Audio-Forum and the Personal Finance *newsletter, in August 1979.*

12. Murray and JoAnn Rothbard in 1979, take a few minutes to vacation in Florida.

13. Murray in a thoughtful moment.

14. Happy Sixtieth Birthday, Murray!

15. Rothbard responds with appreciation to the papers delivered in his honor at the Mises Institute Conference, Man, Economy, and Liberty, that accompanied the surprise birthday party for his sixtieth birthday.

16. Murray lectures on the foundations of the Austrian school at a Mises Institute seminar in Washington, D.C.

17. The classic Rothbard! Picture taken in 1978 at a meeting of the board of the Cato Institute.

Part 2

Philosophy

14

Freedom and Virtue Revisited

Murray Rothbard
0322
0315

Douglas J. Den Uyl

Q: How many Libertarians does it take to screw in a light bulb?
A: None. The free market will do it.

For me it is both a pleasure and an honor to be associated with this volume of essays paying tribute to Murray Rothbard. I was introduced, figuratively and literally, to Professor Rothbard by some businessmen in Milwaukee who were reading *Man, Economy, and the State* at an economics discussion group. Later that same year, Professor Rothbard spoke to the Wisconsin Forum where I met him for the first time in person. The meeting came at a time when I was getting over the fact that Ayn Rand was not God. Since Rothbard was *persona non grata* with the Randians, I expected to meet a man I would not like. Instead, I found a warm, human and humorous man whose personality I found engaging. It was only a matter of time before I developed an affection for him.

My willingness to pay tribute to Murray Rothbard goes deeper than personal affection. In the first place his passion for liberty is infectious. My spirits with respect to the prospects and case for liberty have been lifted more than once by reading Rothbard. Secondly, his intellect is penetrating. I have learned from him. But most important from my point of view is the fact that Rothbard and I come at the defense of liberty from the same Aristotelian or teleological eudaimonistic framework.[1] He is thus not only a friend and mentor, but an intellectual partner.

I wish to pay tribute to Professor Rothbard by discussing some themes and issues related to the topic of liberty and virtue. We have both published essays on this topic. In my own case, I wrote a piece entitled "Freedom and Virtue" some years ago, a revised version of which was later reprinted.[2] With respect to Rothbard, I shall focus upon one of his perhaps lesser known recent articles entitled, "Frank S. Meyer: The Fusionist as Libertarian Manqué."[3] The topic of the connection, if any, between liberty (or freedom) and virtue interests me greatly; but forums for exploring it are rare, because in today's world one is compelled to spend time just defending the legitimacy of liberty alone.

Some Preliminary Observations

In my own piece on freedom and virtue, I argue that coercion is necessarily destructive of moral agency and that moral agency must be present for virtue to be present. I take moral agency to refer neither to "intention" alone (e.g., the supposed immorality of Jimmy Carter's "lusting in his heart"), nor simply to the behavior or "action" of the agent. As Aristotle understood,[4] moral agency involves both elements linked together by the purpose of the agent. Coercion obliterates one or both elements of moral agency (not to mention the link between them). It can force a behavior that is "good," but at the expense of the presence of a good intention. It can effectively destroy intention altogether (whether good or bad) by forcing actions (either good or bad) which are performed simply because they are forced and for no other reason. Finally, by severing the connection between intention and action, coercion can encourage good intentions which result in evil (i.e., harmful) actions. This last point is so because the separation tends to create the illusion that the manner in which the action is undertaken (e.g., coercively) is not a factor in determining the moral character of the action.[5] Thus, if the intention is "sincere" "heartfelt" "compassionate" or whatever, that is enough to qualify it as "good." The means by which the intention is fulfilled becomes a practical, not a moral matter.

Since coercion destroys moral agency, a necessary condition for virtue is freedom (or liberty). The social side of my argument, therefore, was that for a "society" to be virtuous, it must also be free. This, of course, does not say that freedom is a sufficient condition for virtue. It is not. But whatever further sufficient conditions there may be for attaining virtue, they cannot come at the expense of the necessary condition. This implies that although a free society cannot be totally immoral (because basic rights are respected), it may be a society whose citizens adhere to a minimalist (i.e., simply rights respecting) form of virtue. Higher levels of moral excellence could be ignored. This thesis raises questions that I do not address in my previous article, and shall only partially address here. The main question, of course, is whether the free society has much of a prospect of going beyond a minimalist morality. This question is uninteresting to those libertarians who are either moral skeptics or moral minimalists,[6] but within an Aristotelian framework the question is real, because social and political life is taken to be a component in the development of moral perfection for Aristotle.

The Rothbard article comes at the question of freedom and virtue from a different perspective. In the first place, the main thesis of that article was that Frank Meyer was, in virtually all essential respects, a libertarian and not a fusionist. In the second place, the article shows that there really is not much common ground between libertarians and conservatives. The connection between freedom and virtue is less the topic than the two theses just mentioned. Nevertheless, six theses about the relationship between freedom and virtue are contained in the Rothbard article.

What follows, therefore, depends first upon the assumption that the basic argument of my first article is correct. In other words, I shall not be offering an additional defense of my original thesis here. Secondly, I shall be ignoring the main themes of Rothbard's article and focusing instead upon the six underlying theses about freedom and virtue. These six theses will be section topics for what follows. I consider what I say below to be a schematic presentation of issues related to the six theses and not as a definitive treatment. But given the paucity of libertarian literature on this topic, a schematic treatment may be sufficient to encourage further exploration of the relationship between liberty and virtue.

Virtue and the State

The first of the six theses in Rothbard's essay argues that the state is not an appropriate instrument for promoting virtue. The argument here is similar to my own as I sketched it above. In addition, Rothbard—referring to Hayek's chapter in *The Road to Serfdom* "Why the Worst Get on Top"[7]—shows how those in positions of state power are likely to have precisely the kinds of characters one concerned with virtue would not want to encourage. It hardly seems appropriate, then, to have such people lead a crusade for moral excellence. Yet if we grant Rothbard his point, as we should, who or what remains to encourage the development of moral excellence?

There are two stock libertarian answers to this question: (1) persuasion, and (2) the market. Beginning with the second one, we see here the application of the old joke with which I began this essay. Most people do not see the market as encouraging much of anything with respect to morality, and if we understand the market in a literalist fashion, they are right. For if most people's desires and goals are base, the market will provide the mechanism for satisfying those desires and goals. Yet advocates of free markets have a deeper insight into what markets do than is offered by the literalist interpretation. As Hayek has shown often enough, the market encourages some not inconsiderable social values—namely, order and cooperation. Furthermore the demands and rigors of the market place tend to encourage numerous virtues such as prudence, honesty, independence, thrift, and diligence. The stock answer, therefore, goes some distance in dispelling the myth that in advocating the market one is not advocating anything morally positive.

But does the stock answer go far enough? It may be the case that the virtues encouraged by the market order are offset by a number of vices. One must be careful here. Some things that are often touted as vices may not be, for example commercialization. Moreover, certain forms of self-destructive behavior might be permitted by the market, but in no way encouraged. Suppose, for the sake of argument only, that taking certain drugs caused in all users the type of irrational addiction depicted on television. A free society would permit such addictions, but it is unlikely that they would be encouraged by market forces. If the actions were truly self-destructive, the costs of engaging in them would be high and thus contrary to the virtues admitted to be encouraged by the market. Yet so as not to appear too ideological, let us remain open to the possibility that maybe there are some vices encouraged by the market. If so, we are nevertheless forced to concede that they must be vices consistent with the virtues admitted to be encouraged by the market.

I believe that finding such vices will not be as easy as first appearances might suggest. The usual list, e.g., lust (pornography leading to sex crimes or the degradation of women), greed, selfishness, materialism, and so on, all seem to be increasing as society's commitment to the free market is decreasing. If there are aspects of these "vices" that really are vices, it is unclear how the market encourages them. If an individual must bear the costs of these actions him or herself—without a guaranteed income or state supported detoxification centers—what encouragement can there be for such short-sighted hedonic pursuits? In this respect there seems to be a general confusion between what is permitted and what is encouraged. The free society may permit many vices, but it hardly follows from that that it encourages them.

Even if we grant that the free market might encourage some vices that are not counteracted by its virtues, it seems to me that the stronger argument against the second stock response is that the market *ignores* certain virtues. One virtue often mentioned is charity, but the case here is not compelling. The freest societies have often been the most generous. Indeed our own society seems quite prone to any and all schemes for sharing wealth, and I take this to stem as much from the generosity of the citizens as from the cunning of politicians. The argument here must therefore rest with those virtues that concern moral perfection and not the ordinary virtues that require little more than an appropriate attitude to acquire. These virtues of perfection might include those most often associated with the liberal and fine arts: the development of one's mind, encouragement of true artistic excellence, the encouragement of friendships based on significant and lasting values, and so on. The market fails to encourage these values, so the argument goes, because the market is a mechanism for catering to the masses of men, and these values stand apart from or go beyond what is ordinary and has mass appeal.

Sometimes the inference is drawn that the market *discourages* these values by appealing to the lowest common denominator in society. But this inference is false. The free market distributes resources according to their most valued uses. It may be that the bulk of society values goods that have little to do with moral perfection, thus commanding a large share of resources. Other "higher" values, however, are neither ignored nor discouraged. The resources devoted to these higher values are impartially distributed by the market in proportion to their value. If values were to change, so would the distribution of resources. The market does not discourage these values, although its impartiality may do little to encourage them.

The idea that the market ignores certain virtues has been noted by Leo Strauss.[8] If we look to the origins of defenses of commercial societies through the eyes of such thinkers as Montesquieu, we find that the market order encourages what Strauss calls the "liberal virtues" at the expense of the "severe and restrictive" virtues. Peace, humanity, comfort, cooperation, and freedom are encouraged by the market order. Courage, self-denial, justice (as opposed to "fairness" or benevolence), and discipline are ignored or discouraged. Let us concede, for the sake of argument, both that the highest levels of moral perfection are not necessarily encouraged by a society grounded in libertarian principles and that such a society may be prone to ignoring the "restrictive virtues." Would this concession imply that libertarianism ignores virtue? I think not. In the first place, it is a complete non sequitur to suppose that corrective action on the part of the state is required if we made this concession. It may, for example, be the case that the link between virtue and the state is the real problem here, and not the degree to which virtues are or are not present in society. Indeed, I would argue that it is precisely the collectivist perspective on virtue—required when one thinks of virtue in terms of state action—that destroys moral perfection. Even if the coercive methods of the state were not at issue, the collectivist understanding of virtue would be.[9] It makes little difference whether the virtues in question are "liberal" or "restrictive."[10] What is latent within libertarian social theory is the idea that virtue is not a collective phenomenon at all. But to grasp this point we must look at the remaining themes discussed in our other sections.

With respect to the first stock response, persuasion, little needs to be said. Persuasion is the means we must use to achieve our end (virtue). As an answer to our question, however, persuasion tells us nothing about whether anyone in a free society is likely to undertake the effort to persuade others. Yet if Aristotle is correct in believing us to be social animals, it would seem that our very sociality would serve to encourage concern for the actions of others. And clearly such concern is manifest in both free and unfree societies—a person's actions are constantly being evaluated by neighbors, peers, colleagues, superiors, and others. The difference, then, is that in a society where *only* persuasion is allowed as a means for altering behavior, we might predict an increase in that technique over one where subtle and not-so-subtle forms of coercion are also permitted.

Liberty, Politics and Ethics

Rothbard's second argument is that libertarianism is a political philosophy and not an ethical doctrine. Elsewhere in the same volume in which Rothbard's essay appears, Tibor Machan takes a similar position. While Rothbard and Machan may both believe that the only plausible defense of liberty can be given from a particular moral theory, libertarianism may be, and has been, defended from a variety of moral perspectives. Advocating libertarianism as a social doctrine in no way implies that one is advocating that individuals become libertines. This point is effective in defusing the conservative's tendency to equate the libertarian with the libertine. It is also used by Rothbard (and Machan) to show that there is no necessary incompatibility between libertarianism and a concern for virtue. If we accept this argument (as we must), a difficulty arises. If there is no necessary incompatibility between libertarianism and a concern for virtue, then there would appear to be no necessary *compatibility* either. For since libertarianism as a strictly political doctrine is logically distinct from moral theories which may be concerned with virtue, it seems difficult to draw anything more than a contingent connection between liberty and virtue. Indeed, libertarianism would seem to be best characterized as indifferent to virtue.

The claim about the indifference of libertarianism to virtue ignores my argument that virtue and coercion cannot be connected to each other. Therefore, the relationship between the two is not as contingent as first appearances might suggest. But my argument only presents a necessary or formal connection, not a substantive one. To make the substantive case we need to say something more about the fallacious belief that if something is not directly advocated by a political doctrine, that doctrine must therefore be indifferent to it. I shall refer to this fallacy as the "fallacy of advocacy." In general the fallacy of advocacy is committed when one assumes that there is a necessary connection between what people *say* is, will be, or ought to be the case and what *actually* is, will be, or ought to be the case. Economists, for example, have long known that what people say they believe in or will do has little bearing on how they actually behave. And in political theory, if a doctrine has no explicit provision for state supported welfare it does not follow that believers in that doctrine have no concern or compassion for the poor. Indeed, precisely the opposite might be true—that is, it may be that concern for the poor is precisely what attracts a person to that political theory in the first place.[11]

The version of the fallacy of advocacy we are dealing with here is the negative side of the fallacy. The failure of libertarianism to explicitly include a place for virtue as a principle of its political conclusions does not, in other words, give one grounds for claiming that libertarianism is indifferent to the issue. One would have to show in addition that there are features of libertarianism which are incompatible with a substantive concern for virtue. Oddly enough it is the very feature of libertarianism that allows it to be advocated from different moral perspectives (and even moral skepticism) that links the political doctrine to a substantive conception of the nature of virtue. To understand this, one must keep in mind that virtue is something that must be achieved and can thus be lost. If we recognize that the achievement of virtue implies the possibility of vice, we must also recognize that the same soil which nurtures the flower of virtue may also nurture the weed of vice.

The tenuous and contingent character of virtue is correlated to a central component of libertarianism—individualism. Values are pursued, gained, and lost by individuals, and it is only individuals that can have values, not collectivities. Virtue, being the pursuit or possession of good values, must also be achievable only by individuals. The individualist perspective may be arguable, but it does constitute a core component of libertarian political theory. And if virtue (again arguably) must be understood along individualist lines, collective efforts to secure virtue would constitute a virtual contradiction in terms. Virtue is solely and exclusively an achievement of individuals. Collective action, if it can do anything at all, can only lay the foundation for the achievement of virtue.

For the libertarian that foundation is the protection of individual rights. Efforts to go beyond that foundation by collectively prescribing appropriate courses of action may achieve conformity of behavior, but not virtue. Virtuous actions are willed for their own sake by the agent undertaking them. Appropriate behavior without the corresponding understanding and will of the individual agent is not sufficient for producing virtue. Thus even if the state, *per impossible*, could non-coercively direct or encourage appropriate forms of behavior, there would still be no virtue because of the missing intentional component on the part of the individual agent. That intentional component must be supplied by the individual agent himself.

If the Strausseans are correct and modernity is at least partly characterized by the belief that state efforts to secure and promote virtue along the lines advocated by Plato and Aristotle were failures, then libertarianism must here side with modernity. What I have been arguing is that it is not just the coercive techniques of state action that are incompatible with virtue, but also the collectivist presupposition that stands behind those techniques. Just as economic prosperity cannot be achieved on collectivist principles, so also must collectivism fail with respect to moral prosperity. Conservatives cannot create productive life styles or humane sexuality by wars on drugs and pornography any more than liberals can create compassion and charity by redistribution schemes. All that can be accomplished by such collective efforts is a restriction on the opportunity for vice which simultaneously restricts the opportunity for virtue. In the end such efforts promote not moral excellence, but a drab form of moral mediocrity and conformity.

We are now in a position to realize that the Rothbardian claim that libertarianism is a political doctrine and not necessarily incompatible with a concern for virtue does not imply indifference to virtue. What is implied is that virtue must be understood in light of two libertarian principles—freedom and individualism. If both principles are substantively connected with virtue, then so is libertarianism. This would be true even if libertarianism permits non-rights violating vices. And it would be true even if advocates of libertarianism say they have no interest in virtue but in liberty alone. For what is at issue here is not whether certain virtues are more or less promoted by certain social arrangements, but whether virtue is more properly understood within the context of basic libertarian principles than in other contexts. In the last analysis, then, the debate is not over who cares about virtue, but rather over what constitutes the very nature of virtue. Conservatives, like their leftist enemies, incorporate collectivist premises in their model of virtue. Libertarians reject those premises at the outset.

Virtue and Community

Rothbard's third argument concerns the relationship between virtue and community. Here Rothbard argues that virtue can be linked to community, but only if a community is understood to be the free and voluntary association of individuals. If the two principles mentioned in the last section—freedom and individualism—are abandoned, then Rothbard would argue that we are not speaking of true human communities. Conceptions of community which hold that the value of the individual is subservient to the collective, or which argue for the organic and metaphysically primary nature of communities over individuals, or which define appropriate roles for individuals in terms of contributions to the collective, all fail to constitute true human communities. There is significant mutuality among persons only when those persons freely associate under mutually agreeable terms. The "human" nature of this significant mutuality is defined by the centrality of choice and judgment. Respect for persons is shown by grounding communities in individual judgment and choice. And since virtue must be achieved by individual judgment and choice, virtue and community are connected by the same conception of personhood.

Little needs to be added to this conception of community, persons, and virtue. Either one finds the perspective attractive or not. I shall not offer a further defense of this perspective, but instead treat an issue that may underlie it. For it seems to me that a certain conception of ethics stands at the core of both the Rothbardian treatment of the relation between individuals, communities and virtue and the apparent belief that libertarian political theory does not emphasize the virtue of community enough. If we can isolate some different approaches to ethics, we can perhaps isolate which approach is most compatible with libertarianism and how that approach may affect the concept of virtue.

Consider the following definition of ethics or morality by a noted contemporary moral theorist:

> Morality is a set of categorically obligatory requirements for action . . . that are concerned with furthering the interests . . . of persons or recipients other than or in addition to the agent or the speaker.[12]

Moral philosophers today are likely to debate the first part of this definition, viz., whether morality is best thought of in terms of categorical obligations. The last part of the definition would seldom receive comment or disagreement. But it is precisely this last part that is at issue here. Notice that the definition implies that morality is, in the first instance, essentially concerned with standards on how to behave towards others. One might, *additionally*, consider oneself too, but the self is an addendum to the basic moral enterprise. Now this is certainly an accurate way of conceiving of ethics in the modern era. Yet it is quite incorrect to conclude that the nature of ethics itself is essentially focused upon the other. There is another tradition.

Antiquity (e.g., Plato and Aristotle) seem to take the self as the basic object of ethics, with our behavior towards others being a function of the requirements for self perfection. Unlike the preceding definition, ethics is *essentially* a theoretical investigation of the principles of self-improvement and only secondarily and derivatively an investigation of interpersonal relations. Let me illustrate this with an example from Plato that I use in my introductory courses in philosophy. Plato defines justice as having one's soul in proper order.[13] I ask my students if this definition means anything to them. They always say no, because they think of justice as being essentially concerned with rules about appropriate behavior *towards others*. I point out to my students that for Plato how we behave toward others is a function of what we are like inside. Thus the first and primary object of ethics (justice) is self-perfection or the development of character. If our character is properly developed, our actions towards others will be appropriate as well. The same point could be made about Aristotle who devotes an entire Book (Book II) of the *Nichomachean Ethics* to character development. From Plato's perspective, no amount of rules on how to behave towards others, however obligatory, can replace the central role of self-perfection. Even the excessive propagation of rules found in Plato's *Laws* seem to reflect Plato's misguided belief that such rules will help in the quest for *self-perfection* or the development of character, and not because these rules are dictated by a deontic theory of categorical obligation.

Modern philosophy, however, reversed the emphasis. Ethics became primarily concerned with others and only secondarily concerned with self. Morality became thoroughly infused with the social. The two leading ethical theorists of the modern era, Kant and Mill, labor mightily, and probably in vain, to keep some semblance of self-perfection within the scope of their ethical theories. Moreover, the ordinary citizen in the modern world has a difficult time distinguishing ethics and law. There are, nevertheless, some good reasons for the modern position. Antiquity gave a more or less significant role to the state with respect to the development of self—Plato being one of the more extreme examples, but Aristotle is not to be excluded. Modernity discovered that societies organized to promote virtue were dismal failures. Virtue was lacking, especially among those in charge of promoting it; and the value of freedom was often forgotten. It became more plausible to argue that the state was not the appropriate instrument for promoting virtue. The state should instead focus upon interpersonal conflict and freedom—ends it could reasonably accomplish.

The modern position on the state's ability to secure virtue is, of course, correct, but it carries with it a fatal flaw. Despite the criticism of the state as an inappropriate vehicle for promoting virtue, the modern era never really severed the connection between state and virtue. At best modernity simply lessened the number of kinds of virtues the state could control. One tendency was to associate virtue with interpersonal relations and ignore self-perfection. States and communities could do little about self-perfection; but since they could observe interpersonal relations, virtue came to be ever increasingly understood in interpersonal terms. Arguments then developed about the degree to which states or communities should control interpersonal relations. Liberalism answered by saying "only to a small degree," while various forms of statism answered "to a large degree." Neither answer challenged the proposition that morality is essentially concerned with interpersonal relations.

The other main tendency was moral skepticism and/or relativism. Since states and communities were so unsuccessful in securing virtue, and since vice was everywhere to be found even in the face of efforts to wipe it out, perhaps there are no general principles of virtue (or vice) after all. Perhaps we can say no more about virtue than that, if it has any meaning at all, it must refer to keeping society going by not allowing people to harm one another. This sort of minimalism and/or skepticism is at the heart of much of both classical and modern liberalism.[14]

The implications of libertarianism in this connection are quite interesting. As a political theory it would agree that the state is not suited to the promotion of virtue. If there is a role for the state, it would rest with the resolution of interpersonal conflict and the maintenance of liberty. Yet insofar as libertarianism is not understood in terms of the skepticism and relativism that are so much a part of the traditional defense of liberalism, the individualism of libertarianism may render its political theory most compatible with the conception of ethics found in antiquity. In short, libertarianism can be understood as a modern political theory based upon a classical moral perspective.

All that remains, then, is the question of the role of virtue with respect to community (as opposed to state). If libertarianism understands community in the way described at the beginning of this section, then it must also be the case that virtue is not a communal concept but an individualist concept. This means that virtue is not a phenomenon achieved by or descriptive of communities, but rather it is an achievement of individuals. The role of community is secondary. It serves to make possible the achievement of self-perfection. In this sense communities serve individuals, not individuals communities. In answer to our opening question, therefore, libertarianism does not stress the virtues of community because communities do not have virtues. Individuals may achieve virtues that concern relations with others, and the environment of one's community may be more or less conducive to virtue; but the point of emphasis is the individual, not the community. It is for this reason that the explicit focus of libertarianism upon the individual is, given the perspective outlined above, simultaneously a focus upon virtue and community.

Virtue and Reason

Rothbard's fourth argument concerns Meyer's attempt to fuse reason and tradition. In an effort to reconcile conservatives and libertarians, Meyer attempted to give equal weight to the value of reason and tradition. Rothbard counters by arguing that this violates the law of excluded middle. Either reason reigns supreme over tradition or vice versa. One cannot have it both ways, and Rothbard argues for the supremacy of reason over tradition. In other words, traditions are valuable only insofar as they are rational.

Rothbard's argument is correct so far as it goes, but it raises an issue he does not address and which could place his thesis in jeopardy. Suppose, for example, that what is considered rational is itself a function of tradition, or more broadly, culture. That is to say, reason is itself a product of culture so that there can be no rational perspective beyond one's culture from which to evaluate that culture. The standards of rationality, in other words, are themselves reflections of the cultural forces surrounding the rational agent. Reason, in some sub-ultimate sense, could still reign supreme over tradition because tradition could be seen as arational cultural forces in need of criticism and evaluation. But in the end, standards of criticism and evaluation would themselves be a function of culture and best understood in historicist fashion.

We need not look to conservatives or various Marxist theorists to find the thesis about reason just mentioned. The position seems to be the one adopted by F. A. Hayek. Hayek argues that we are essentially rule governed creatures whose rules—some of which are not even known but which guide us "tacitly"—are themselves the product of cultural evolution.[15] There are no grounds for believing reason escapes or stands outside of these evolutionary forces. In addition, Hayek argues for the extremely limited role of reason. Reason for Hayek is essentially a formal process perhaps best exemplified by logic. Following Hume and Kant, reason has only a limited role to play in human affairs. The limited role of reason translates socially into Hayek's doctrine of universal and negative rules. Universality, as Kant showed in his moral theory, is a central feature of the nature of reason. Negativity is made plausible by the limited power of reason in the face of evolutionary forces.

But what is to keep the essential components of reason from themselves being swallowed up by culture? In Hayek, as in Hume, I see nothing to prevent this. Here Kant understood the problem better than most. If reason is itself to retain any independence of culture, we must make what Henry Veatch calls a "transcendental turn."[16] Hence Kant locates reason in a noumenal order that remains untouched by the vicissitudes of the phenomenal order, including culture. If the transcendental turn is not made in some way, only two alternatives remain—radical historicity (where what is, is a function of one's conceptual system and one's conceptual system is itself the product of culture) or a return to the essential tenets of classical realism. Now the merits of these alternatives are well beyond the scope of this essay. We might, however, bring this outline of approaches closer to home by making one further comment.

Because classical liberalism and libertarianism are so closely allied on many political and social issues, the historical figures libertarians are often most familiar with are also the intellectual fathers of classical liberalism (e.g., Hume). In ethics this means problems tend to be examined from a certain perspective. It is still common among libertarians to see the chief theoretical problem in ethics to be how to derive an "ought" from an "is." Thus, defenders of natural law (or rights) theory are attacked by their Humean or positivist counterparts for their failure to bridge the gap between "is" and "ought." How to rationally justify, or even find, any "oughts" in reality is often seen to be the central problem. Unfortunately, this issue is now old fashioned. The problem now is not how to derive "ought" from "is" or find values in a world of facts, but rather whether we can derive "is" from "ought" or discover any facts in a world of values.[17] In other words, if the standards of reason itself are essentially culture bound,[18] combating radical historicity becomes the main task. And the main thesis of this historicity is that all facets of evaluation (whether in science or ethics) are value laden.

I have obviously not "proven" anything in these remarks. I have sought only to identify a trend—one that thinkers like Hayek are participating in. If I have identified the trend correctly, the task will become one of fending off this radical historicism if, that is, one wishes to defend the rational primacy of liberty. Various efforts to this effect have begun. Among some economists, for example, the strategy has been to adopt a form of essentialism that would embarrass even Plato. We are told that there are certain fixed ends that all human beings possess to the same degree. Economics describes the way people try to pursue that same set of ends under different conditions. What look like different choices based on the premise of a diversity of values are really best described as the economics of trying to pursue the *same* values under different circumstances.[19] Yet another alternative, however, suggests itself. That one is to return to classical realism in all the main philosophical areas of metaphysics, epistemology, and ethics.[20] It is this alternative that Rothbard seems to have adopted.

The Rothbardian thesis that reason stands superior to culture, tradition, or whatever seems predicated upon a philosophy that locates reason at the core of the theory. Modern efforts to abandon classical realism and yet still retain the centrality of reason seem vulnerable to the onslaught of historicism. It is Rothbard's insight (along with those of Ayn Rand and others) that some fixed values and truths are necessary if liberty is to be defended. While this is my own view as well, my argument here has simply been to suggest that the basic tenets of classical philosophy may deserve the attention Rothbard and others have bestowed upon it.

Liberty, Virtue and Order

Rothbard's fifth thesis is that liberty, far from creating chaos and disorder, is actually conducive to order itself. This thesis is a mainstay of both liberalism and libertarianism; and as Rothbard himself notes, the thesis has been given added support in recent years by Hayek's analysis of "spontaneous orders." Yet assuming the truth of the connection between order and liberty, the question arises as to what, if anything, does order have to do with virtue? To this question the answer must be "very little."

If virtue is as we have conceived it—that is, achieved by individuals according to teleological eudaimonistic standards of self-perfection—then the value of order must be instrumental at best. What seems evident about conservatives is that order is taken as an end, not a means. However, if we use Aristotle's simple test for distinguishing ends in themselves from means or intermediate ends, we can see that order is not an end in itself. Aristotle held that something was a final end if it was sought for its own sake and not for the sake of anything else. Can this be said about order? It would seem that order is valuable because of what it makes possible. Order generally signifies peace, and peace allows the productive aspects of human nature to flourish. Order makes planning possible; the security it provides allows for long run plans to be conceived and undertaken. Order provides the kind of stability necessary for social relationships between individuals to be nurtured. But whether one is speaking of peace, planning, or stability, the value of each is a function of what is contributed to human perfection. Order does not seem to be valuable in its own right. Indeed, order is not even a necessary condition for virtue, since at least certain virtues can be, and often are, exhibited in times of disorder and social chaos.

Order tends to nurture virtue by creating those conditions under which virtue is most likely to flourish. But, of course, the *kind* of order one has will also have a bearing on the promotion of virtue. A free order is conducive to virtue; an imposed order is not. As we have argued here and elsewhere, if there is disorder and conflict present in society, the solution does not come through an imposition of rules of conduct. That is order for the sake of order and is bought at the price of what *is* a necessary condition for virtue, namely liberty. We must not confuse a favorable environment for the production of virtue with virtue itself.

Our argument implies that order, like virtue itself, must be endogenous rather than exogenous. Exogenous efforts to dictate order through formalized rules of conduct imposed by an instrument like the state (as opposed to procedural principles designed to encourage endogenous forms of cooperation), can actually produce disorder and conflict. It is at this juncture that tradition factors in so importantly. What is traditional is not necessarily virtuous nor rational, but it may be extremely significant with respect to what is orderly. The position is expressed best by James Buchanan.

> It is in this context that some of the behavioral changes of the 1960s raise fundamental and disturbing issues for social stability. As noted, individuals have lived, one with another, under the implicit behavioral rules that were respected by all, or nearly all, persons in community. But one of the instruments employed by the participants in the counterculture involved the explicit flaunting of traditional codes of conduct, the direct and open disregard for what had previously been considered to be acceptable standards for elementary "good manners." This placed stresses on the ordered anarchy that still describes much of ordinary social life in our society, stresses which were evidenced by calls for "law and order," for formalization and enforcement of rules that were previously nonexistent.[21]

The increased efforts to solve conflicts through the formalization of all rules of conduct has the effect of generating more conflicts over the rules themselves, of generating bureaucratic institutions to execute and monitor those rules, and of instilling a sense of alienation from the rules on the part of citizens. Buchanan correctly describes the present day situation as "constitutional anarchy"—disorder in the face of numerous rules and regulations.[22]

Traditions are endogenous rules of order. They cannot be flaunted without jeopardizing the environment most conducive to human perfection. But to say this is simply to recognize the important value of tradition. It in no way compels us to treat tradition and order as virtues or ends in themselves. Tradition and order are valuable because they serve individuals in achieving self-perfection and not because they are objects of self-perfection itself.

Conclusion

In the final section of Rothbard's paper the issues of elitism and populism are discussed. Conservatives, Rothbard argues, have within their ranks those who favor rule by an elite (e.g., Kirk and Wilhelmsen) and those who are drawn to more populist outlooks (e.g., Wanniski). The various schools of thought within conservatism do not concern us here, but Rothbard goes on to suggest that for libertarians the "masses" are neither inherently good nor inherently bad. This position reflects the individualist character of virtue we have spoken of above. The masses are neither virtuous nor vicious because such terms are not applicable to collectivities.

But the question of the masses raises an old issue in moral and social theory. Is it true, as Aristotle seemed to believe, that there is natural superiority among men? Or is Hobbes more correct in believing that men are by nature equal? The first thesis suggests that virtue is likely to be attained only by the few who, by their superior natures, already have a leg up in the quest for virtue. The second thesis suggests that virtue may be attained by almost anyone who makes the effort. Rothbard argues that libertarians tend more towards the equality position than the elitist one. The reasons for this probably stem from the original reaction of modernity to antiquity. Early liberalism held that "all men are created equal" and possessed equal rights. Antiquity seemed to give additional rights to those few of naturally superior powers and talents.

Yet in light of what we have argued for in this paper, the issue of whether people are equal by nature or unequal is irrelevant. In the first place, equality of basic rights must holds because of the metaethical thesis that natural (or human) rights apply to persons as such. The *kind* of person one is, whether by nature or nurture, is not a determining factor with respect to natural rights. If we add to the metaethical point our claim about the state not being a suitable instrument for the promotion of virtue, then natural superiority would be relevant only if it had some bearing on the protection of legitimate rights. By the same token, the natural equality of man would only be relevant if it gave a reason to treat all inequalities as aberrations of nature in need of correction. It seems to me that both these positions fail to justify the conclusions commonly drawn from them. Natural superiority is not a necessary precondition for protecting basic rights, and the equality of human nature does not imply that inequality is somehow illegitimate. The first is largely an administrative issue; the protection of rights might be achieved equally well without men and women of superior talent. The second could only be true if equality precluded differences in talent, effort, desire, taste, and so on, which is clearly not the case.

What does seem to be true empirically is that virtue is relatively rare. Perhaps it is the exceptional character of virtue that leads us to regard its qualities as virtuous in the first place. Yet whatever the reason for its rarity, liberty demands that we face squarely the prospect that a society may be peopled with relatively less men and women of virtue than with more. No mechanism—whether it be markets, democracy, progressive socialism, or whatever—can guarantee more rather than less virtue. The modern eras attempt to replace the rule of virtuous men and women with mechanism or "systems" of social order as a means for controlling vice or promoting virtue, no more guarantees virtue than antiquity's efforts to institute the rule of the wise. Both approaches make the mistake of thinking that virtue is essentially a social problem. Embedded within libertarian social theory is the alternative. Virtue is essentially a problem for individuals. Whether the society in which one lives has more or less virtue is irrelevant to one's obligation to pursue it.

I wish to thank Douglas Rasmussen for some helpful suggestions on an early draft of this paper. My understanding of the metaphysical and epistemological issues related to the topic of this paper owes much to his influence.

Notes

1. See, for example, the first two chapters of *The Ethics of Liberty* (Atlantic Highlands, N.J.: Humanities Press, 1982).
2. "Freedom and Virtue," *Reason Papers* 5 (1979); reprinted in *The Libertarian Reader*, edited by Tibor Machan (Totowa, N.J.: Rowman and Littlefield, 1982); also reprinted in *The Main Debate*, edited by Tibor Machan (New York: Random House, 1986).
3. The essay can be found in *Freedom and Virtue: the Conservative/Libertarian Debate*, edited by George W. Carey (Lanham, Md.: University Press of America, 1984).
4. *Nichomachean Ethics*, book II, chap. 4, 1105a30-35.
5. Douglas Rasmussen has reminded me that the term "moral" here stands not only in opposition to "amoral" but also to "immoral." Self-directedness, in other words, is not only a necessary condition for an action being moral, but is itself necessarily a constituent of the morally good.
6. "Moral minimalists" being those libertarians who, like their welfare state liberal counterparts, equate morality essentially with rights—there being fewer rights for the libertarian.
7. F. A. Hayek, *The Road to Serfdom* (Chicago: University of Chicago Press, 1944.
8. Leo Strauss, *Natural Right and History* (Chicago: Chicago University Press, 1974), p. 300.
9. It is here that a great debt is owed to Ayn Rand's novels; for she, more than anyone else, has severed the connection between moral perfection and the collectivist premise that had always been tied to it.
10. With regard to the "restrictive virtues," the promotion of these by the state is usually achieved at the price of the liberal virtues (e.g., Sparta vs. Athens). On the face of it, this would be too high a price to pay. In any case, it is presumably the presence of *both* types of virtues that we desire.

11. The fallacy cuts both ways, however. Critics of libertarianism might argue that although the doctrine claims to respect individual rights, the society libertarians envision does not in fact do so. We must keep separate the issues of what is the case from what is claimed to be the case, as the next paragraph indicates. The fallacy of advocacy simply argues that saying X (or not) does not make X (or not X) so.

12. Alan Gewirth, *Reason and Morality* (Chicago: University of Chicago Press, 1978), p. 1.

13. *Republic*, Book IV, 443d-e.

14. The latter sees itself as offering a different interpretation on what it means to be harmed, and not as expanding the state's role in the direct promotion of morality or virtue.

15. F. A. Hayek, *Law Legislation and Liberty*, vol. 1 (Chicago: University of Chicago Press, 1973), chap. 1.

16. Henry B. Veatch, *For an Ontology of Morals* (Evanston, Ill.: Northwestern University Press, 1971), pp. 49-56.

17. Given the Kantian position that we cannot know things in themselves and that therefore what X is is a function of our conceptual system, the question we face is what conceptual system to adopt? Contemporary philosophers from Quine to Feyerabend seem to answer this question in terms of what values we have. But then which value system should we adopt? For a useful discussion of these matters see, Douglas Rasmussen, "Ideology, Objectivity, and Political Theory," (Paragon Press, 1986). Kant's own belief that he had discovered a *fixed* conceptual scheme was, of course, threatened by non-Euclidean geometry.

18. And we find this thesis advanced from diverse sources. See *Post-Analytic Philosophy*, edited by John Rajchman and Cornel West (New York: Columbia University Press, 1983).

19. George J. Stigler and Gary S. Becker, "De Gustibus Non Est Disputandum." *The American Economic Review* (March 1977).

20. The central tenets of classical realism are: (1) existence exists independently of our awareness of it; (2) we can come to know the nature of existent things; and (3) that ethics is essentially concerned with self-actualization. For some realist perspectives in one or more of these categories see Douglas Rasmussen, "Quine and Aristotelian Essentialism," *The New Scholasticism* 58 (Summer 1984): 316-35; David Kelley, *The Evidence of the Senses*, (Baton Rouge: Louisiana State University Press, 1986); Henry Veatch, *For an Ontonology of Morals*, pp. 49-56; David Norton, *Personal Destinies* (Princeton: Princeton University Press, 1976); Douglas Den Uyl and Douglas Rasmussen, *The Philosophic Thought of Ayn Rand* (Champaign, Ill.: University of Illinois Press, 1984), chaps. 1, 4, 8.

21. James Buchanan, *The Limits of Liberty* (Chicago: University of Chicago Press, 1975), p. 20.

22. Ibid., pp. 7, 14.

15

Particular Liberties
Against the General Will

Antony Flew

In one of the most valuable and most characteristic chapters of a work in which he was not always at his best Bertrand Russell described Jean-Jacques Rousseau (1712-78) as "the father of the romantic movement, . . . the inventor of the political philosophy of pseudo-democratic dictatorships. . . . Ever since his time . . . reformers have been divided into two groups, those who followed him and those who followed Locke."[1] Since the author of *For a New Liberty* and *The Ethics of Liberty* has devoted his life to defending, strengthening, and expanding the Lockean tradition of individual rights and limited, responsible government, I can think of no way of contributing to the present project either more appropriate or more likely to appeal to Murray Rothbard himself than by developing a critique of Rousseau's peculiar, distinctive, and catastrophically collectivist concept of the general will.

I

The true implications of the political thought of that founding father of the opposing tradition, and in particular the factitious justificatory possibilities of this grandiose yet elusive fiction, appear to have emerged only slowly. To this day they are often not adequately appreciated by the friends of liberty. For this there are various reasons.

In the period between its first publication and the beginnings of the great French Revolution *The Social Contract* seems to have been the least read of Rousseau's major works. And, although the entire revolutionary generation appears to have practiced a cult of Rousseau, at least in the earlier years, this devotion rarely if ever involved either

214

acceptance or even much knowledge of his distinctive political ideas.[2] It was only with the rise of the Jacobins that would-be despots and apologists for despotism began to recognize the conveniences of an inherently all-overriding collective General Will; the particular content of which might from time to time be discovered without reference—or even contrary—to the findings of vulgar and pedestrian countings of individual heads.[3]

When we do turn to *The Social Contract* it is easy to be misled, either by studying the work out of context, or by its stylistic adornments, or even by its title. For a start, that title is bound—one is tempted to say calculated—to suggest limited and responsible government. For how could there be contracts without reciprocal undertakings and acceptances of some limitations upon future behavior?

Then again, this is a quite extraordinarily flashy book, replete with epigram and paradox. Its opening sentence is as typical as it has been unforgettable: "Man is born free, yet everywhere he is in chains" (I[i], 17).[4] Then, on the following page, Grotius, once a respected establishment figure, is seen off in three short, decisive sentences: "Grotius denies that all human power is established for the benefit of the governed, citing slavery as an example. His usual method of reasoning is always to present fact as a proof of right. A more logical method could be used, but not one more favorable to tyrants" (I[ii], 18).[5] So how can the reader—especially the reader knowing something of the author's vagrant, feckless and dissident life-style—believe that he was anything but devoted to liberty, and a hater of despotism? (Perhaps indeed he was, but, like so many others later, he failed to grasp the concrete consequences of his own high abstractions and paradoxical sleights of mind.)

A third source of error is the failure to read *The Social Contract* as what it was, the climactic expression of Rousseau's political and social thinking. It is significant that, in both the editions most frequently employed in the English-speaking world, *The Social Contract* (1762) is placed before whatever *Discourses* are included in the same volume. But, in fact, all three of the *Discourses* were composed and published first: the *Discourse on the Arts and Sciences* in 1750; the *Discourse on the Origin of Inequality* in 1754; and the *Discourse on Political Economy* in 1765 (as an article in Volume V of the *Encyclopédie*). Certainly the last two *Discourses* provide valuable clues to the interpretation of *The Social Contract*.

(a) What, for instance, the former has to say concerning property in general and riches in particular is about as remote as could be from Locke. Thus Part II of the *Discourse on the Origin of Inequality* begins:

"The first person who, having enclosed a plot of land, took it into his head to say *this is mine* and found people simple enough to believe him, was the true founder of civil society. What crimes, wars, murders, what miseries and horrors would the human race have been spared, had some-one pulled up the stakes or filled in the ditch and cried out to his fellow men: "Do not listen to this impostor. You are lost if you forget that the fruits of the earth belong to all and the earth to no one!" (p. 140)[6]

Earlier, in distinguishing "natural or physical" from "moral or political inequality," Rousseau asserted: "This latter type . . . consists in the different privileges enjoyed by some at the expense of others, such as being richer, more honored, more powerful than they, or even causing themselves to be obeyed by them" (p. 118). The contention that one person's riches must always and necessarily be possessed "at the expense of," and hence through the exploitation of another has since, of course, become a fundamental, forever uncriticized, false assumption of all socialist thought.[7]

(b) The *Discourse on the Origin of Inequality* also warns us how the later talk of social contracts is to be construed: "Let us therefore begin by putting aside all the facts, for they have no bearing on the question. The investigations that may be undertaken concerning this subject should not be taken for historical truths, but only for hypothetical and conditional reasonings, better suited to shedding light on the nature of things than to pointing out their true origin. . . ." (pp. 118-19).

It would, therefore, be inept to fault Rousseau's account of the origin of private property by objecting that the words in which "this impostor" made his claim could not have been understood unless his society already possessed both an institution of private property and the vocabulary necessary for its operation.

(c) The spirits of libertarians may rise when they read that "it is a fundamental maxim of all political right, that peoples have given themselves leaders in order to defend their liberty and not to enslave themselves" (p. 152). Yet our spirits must surely fall again once account has been taken of the sentence immediately following: "*If we have a prince*, Pliny said to Trajan, *it is so that he may preserve us from having a master*" (p. 152; emphasis added). The difference, which for Rousseau was crucial, is explained earlier in the same paragraph: ". . . in the relations between men, the worst that can happen to someone is for him to see himself at the discretion of someone else . . ." (p. 152). It was, presumably, the peculiarities and the limitations of his own vagabond experience which led

Rousseau thus to rate as crucial the difference: between being compelled by a private person; and being compelled by agents of the state.

It is this obsessional and blinkering emphasis upon the supposedly supreme evil of private dependency which leads him to a perverse redefinition of "liberty." In the "Letter to the Republic of Geneva," prefacing the *Discourse on the Origin of Inequality*, Rousseau considers where he would have chosen to be born, had he been offered such a choice. In answering this question he says: "I would have wanted to live and die free, *that is to say*, subject to the laws in such wise that neither I nor anyone else could shake off their honourable yoke . . ." (p. 106, emphasis added).

This redefinitional manoeuvre is in large part to be explained, although certainly not by the same token to be excused, by the fact that these particular laws are supposed to be both in the best interests of, and somehow self-imposed by, every individual subject to them. That Rousseau is indeed appealing to these claims is made clear by the previous paragraph. His ideal birthplace would be "a country where the sovereign and the people could have but one and the same interest, so that all the movements of the machine always tended to the common happiness. Since this could not have come about unless the people and the sovereign were one and the same person, it follows that I would have wished to be born under a democratic government, wisely tempered" (p. 106).

Even where both these two claims were correct it ought to be obvious that those subject to the resulting laws, regulations and administrative orders would not, in respect of whatever was thereby mandated or forbidden, be free. If there is a law against it, with a penalty attached for disobedience, then I am precisely not free to disobey.[8] Russell was, therefore, entirely correct to condemn Rousseau's "misuse of the word 'freedom.' " For by thus making it mean "the right to obey the police, or something not very different" Rousseau was not offering something which might properly be called an alternative concept of freedom. Instead he was proposing to attach that honourable label to what is not freedom but its diametric opposite, constraint.[9]

In order to make out that in his ideal state the laws would be both in the interests of, or for the good of, and somehow self-imposed by, all those subject to them Rousseau employed another definitional manoeuvre. The immediately more relevant element in this exercise is to be seen most clearly in the *Discourse on Political Economy*. "The first and most important maxim of legitimate or popular government, *that is to say, of a government that has the good of the populace for its object, is* therefore, as I have said, to follow the general will in all things" (p. 168; emphasis added). It is no wonder that in March 1756, in a letter to Madame d'Epinay, Rousseau wrote: "Learn my dictionary, my good friend, if you want to have us understand one another. Believe me, my terms rarely have the ordinary sense."

The sinister significance of the passage emphasized in that quotation from the *Discourse on Political Economy* comes out clear and cruel when it is put in parallel with two statements made on behalf of contemporary "People's Democratic" regimes. The first of these statements was made by Janos Kadar, addressing the Hungarian National Assembly in 1957, the year after the ever-ready tanks of imperial normalization had first installed him in office: "The task of the leaders is not to put into effect the wishes and will of the masses. . . . The task of the leaders is to accomplish the interests of the masses. Why do I differentiate between the will and the interests of the masses? In the recent past we have encountered the phenomenon of certain categories of workers acting against their interests."[10] The second illustrative statement comes from a Vice-President of Tanzania: "Our government is democratic, because it makes its decisions in the interests of, and for the benefit of, the people. I wonder why men who are unemployed are surprised and resentful at the government . . . sending them back to the land for their own advantage."

II

There are signs in the two later *Discourses* that some notion of general will is moving to the centre of Rousseau's political thought. Thus, in the last sentence previously quoted, he reiterates that "the first and most important maxim of legitimate or popular government . . . is . . . to follow the general will in all things." In the *Discourse on the Origin of Inequality* he speaks of "the establishment of the body politic as a true contract between the populace and the leaders it chooses for itself"; and of how, "with respect to social relations, the populace has united all its wills into a single one" (p. 155). But later, in the *Discourse on Political Economy*, he speaks of a general will as attached to a kind of organism— something which must grow up naturally rather than be produced by contractual artifice: "The body politic . . . can be considered to be like a body that is organized, living and similar to that of a man." It is, therefore, "also a moral being which possesses a will . . ." (p. 166).

Before coming to grips with that notion as fully and finally deployed in *The Social Contract* we need to press two sharp points about these anticipations. First, that the organic analogy is downright incompatible with any idea of a contract. That idea, as was said before, is what must appeal to those who want only limited and responsible government, with heavy emphasis upon the rights of the individual against all comers—whether individual or collective. But in any organism organs are necessarily subordinate. They are not—unlike us humans—autonomous agents able to decide whether or not to serve and obey. It is a truth which—not very consistently—Rousseau himself stresses in the *Discourse on the Origin of Inequality* (p. 126). Nor, as Leninists so love to say, is it any accident that this organic analogy has become the traditional favourite of authoritarians advocating total and unconditional obedience. Consider, for instance, how in Shakespeare's *Coriolanus*, Menenius Agrippa labours to subdue the "mutinous citizens" (I[i]).

Second, notice that in the *Discourse on Political Economy*, Rousseau explains that all societies and corporations develop general wills distinct from, and sometimes contrary to, the private wills of their individual members: "Every political society is composed of other smaller and different societies, each of which has its interests and maxims. . . . The will of these particular societies always has two relations: for the members of the association it is the general will; for the large society it is a particular will . . ." (p. 166-67). This, as has often been remarked, is a sound sociological observation; notwithstanding that to make it here scarcely consists with the undertaking to put "aside all the facts, for they have no bearing on the question." Certainly all organization persons have abundant occasion to contrast corporate interests and policies with the private interests and policies of officers and members.

But Rousseau takes a further, more precarious step. Presumably because general wills are wills to promote the interests—and in that understanding—the good of the collectivities of which they are the general wills, he maintains that, at least in respect of those collectivities, they must be morally good. "The body politic . . . is also a moral being which possesses a will; and this general will, which always tends towards the conservation and well-being of the whole and each part, . . . is for all the members of the state, in their relations both to one another and to the state, the rule of what is just and what is unjust" (p. 166).[11] Suppose that we waive possible objections about the meaning of "morally good, at least in respect of these collectivities." Still we have to protest that here Rousseau seems himself to be arguing in the fashion so fiercely faulted in Grotius: "His . . . method of reasoning is . . . to present fact as a proof of right. A more logical method could be used, but not one more favourable to tyrants."

(a) The first sentence of *The Social Contract*, in a sort of preface to Book I, announces the object of the exercise: "I want to inquire whether there can be some legitimate and sure rule of administration in the civil order, taking men as they are and laws as they might be" (I, 17). Fair enough; and note it well. For we shall need to recall this splendidly forthright statement when it begins to emerge that the rule proposed—Submit always to the most general will—achieves inexpugnable sureness and legitimacy only at the cost of raising apparently insuperable difficulties for the determination, in particular cases, of what its concrete content is, and of how in actual practice revelations of that content are to be correctly applied.

Given the project propounded in that first sentence, the problem, as Rousseau sees it, is to "find a form of association which defends and protects with all common forces the person and goods of each associate, and by means of which each one, while uniting with all, nevertheless obeys himself alone and remains as free as before." This, he continues, "is the fundamental problem for which the social contract provides the solution" (I[vi], 24).

If we are ever to understand the rest of this book we have to begin by recognizing that and why the problem which Rousseau has here set himself must be insoluble. It cannot but be so. For contracts always and essentially involve mutual give and take. This is indeed a truth upon which in one particular case Rousseau himself has just been insisting. Thus, against Grotius, he has argued that no one could sell themselves into slavery. For that would be an "exchange" involving for one party all give and no take: "Do subjects then give their persons on the condition that their estate will also be taken? I fail to see what remains for them to preserve" (I[iv], 20).

But then, immediately, Rousseau goes on to promise an account of a "social contract" which is, allegedly, for all of us, all get and no give. To specify the problem in a manner making it necessarily insoluble is to guarantee that nothing offered as a solution can truly be such. We should, therefore, expect to find that any pseudo-solution generates grotesque paradox. And so we do!

(b) "The clauses of this contract," Rousseau assures us, "though perhaps they have never been formally promulgated, . . . are everywhere the same, everywhere tacitly accepted and acknowledged." Properly understood, they "are all reducible to a single one, namely the total alienation of each associate, together with all his rights, to the entire community." Every individual is supposed willingly to make, or to have made, this total and unconditional surrender to the totalitarian collective: "For . . . since each person gives himself whole and entire, the situation is equal for everyone; and, since the situation is equal for everyone, no one has an interest in making it burdensome for the others. . . . Finally, in giving himself to all, each person gives himself to no one. And since there is no associate over whom he does not acquire the same right that he should grant others over himself, he gains the equivalent of everything he loses, along with a greater amount of force to preserve what he has." The social compact is supposed in consequence to be "reducible to the following terms. *Each of us places his person and all his power in common under the supreme direction of the general will; and as one we receive each member as an indivisible part of the whole*" (I[vi], 24; emphasis added).[12]

It is very easy to see that we are here being deceived by pieces of ultra-swift sleight of mind. But it is not nearly so easy to spot how these quick tricks are taken. Soon however, as we reread the key paragraphs slowly, carefully, and calmly, objections do begin to make themselves felt. For a start, this whole superlatively fast-moving virtuoso performance of intellectual prestigiation proceeds at an excruciatingly aetherial level of abstraction. The moment we push down towards the everyday, pedestrian plane, populated by flesh and blood human beings, we have to notice that real people, though necessarily equal in their common humanity and consequent universal rights, are by nature rather rarely equal in anything else. We are also born into, or else in some other way acquire, all manner of different social relations, any of which may give rise to what we are so often asked to believe is an /or the most/ infamous thing, social inequality.[13] In particular, the universal and therefore equal human right to acquire and hold property is certainly not a right to be given "equal shares" by an all-taking and all-providing state.

In this somewhat more this-worldly perspective what becomes of the contention that, "since each person gives himself whole and entire, the situation is equal for everyone; and, since the situation is equal for everyone, no one has an interest in making it burdensome for the others"? For all persons having holdings which are below the local average—to say nothing of conspicuously underdeprived "liberal" (i.e., socialist) ideologues and other paid-up members of the New Class have an obvious interest (a class-interest) in Procrustean redistribution (from and to others).[14] So, remembering too that commitments made to other more particular associations are almost always partial, whyever should our commitment to the most fundamental and comprehensive association have to be thus total and unconditional? Whyever should we give ourselves "whole and entire" to an all-embracing and all-demanding collective rather than—more prudently and more modestly—agree to join with others in defending our and their rights by force of law?

The most central and the most fundamental objection, however, appeals to that greatest principle of practical wisdom, TANSTAFL—There Are No Such Things As Free Lunches! Allowed that, formally and superficially at any rate, Rousseau satisfies the requirement that any contract, to be a contract at all, must involve both parties in both giving and taking. For, "since there is no associate over whom he does not acquire the same right that he would grant others over himself, he gains the equivalent of everything he loses. . . ." Nevertheless there is no doubt but that the TANSTAFL principle is violated by the final clause in that sentence: "along with a greater amount of force to preserve what he has." The support of that "greater amount of force" neither is nor can be costless. Someone has to be compensated for the time and effort devoted to judicial and police work.

(c) "*Each of us,*" it is alleged, "*places his person and all his power in common under the supreme direction of the general will; and as one we receive each member as an indivisible part of the whole.*" This hypothetical, not to say fictitious, theoretical transaction is supposed then to generate a sort of instant Superman—remotely reminiscent of the more solid and visible figure constituting the original Frontespiece of *Leviathan*: "At once, in place of the individual person of each contracting party, this act of association produces a moral and collective body composed of as many members as there are voices in the assembly, which receives from this same act its unity, its common *self*, its life and its will" (I[vi], 24).

So now, what is the content of this general will and how is it to be identified? For, as we have seen, unless that content can be reliably determined the general will cannot serve as the promised "legitimate and sure rule of administration in the civil order." But, as is recognized rather rarely, Rousseau's claim to be operating with a genuinely applicable notion has to be—to put it no stronger—seriously prejudiced, unless this putative reality can be, at least in principle, confidently and positively identified. Rousseau himself, before attempting to offer directions on where some tolerably specific answer to these questions might be found, makes a stipulation which, though indispensable if he is to fulfill his project, is bound to make the problems of specification and identification even more intractable.

"This public person," Rousseau continues, "takes the name . . . *sovereign* when it is active" (I[vi], 265). This "sovereign, by the mere fact that it exists, is always what it should be" (I[vii], 26). Its will, therefore, being "the general will, is always right and always tends towards the public utility" (II[iii], 31).[15] The supporting argument runs thus: "since the sovereign is formed entirely from the private individuals who make it up, it neither has nor could have any interest contrary to theirs. Hence, the sovereign power has no need to offer a guarantee to its subjects, since it is impossible for a body to want to harm all its members, and, as we will see later, it cannot harm any one of them in particular" (I[vii], 26).

Of course we cannot see anything of the such, either later or at any other time. Maybe "it is impossible for a body to want to harm *all* its members." Yet everyone who has ever been actively involved in the affairs of any association must be able to cite plenty of instances in which the good of the organization called for heavy sacrifices of the private interests of *some* members. To deny, and to try to disprove, so manifest a truth is, and ought to be recognized as, the trademark of an utterly infatuated theoretician.

Furthermore, even if the sense of the general will necessarily "tends towards the public utility"—towards, that is to say, the public interest and hence in that understanding the public good—it will not be always and by the same token moral. For the public interest, and in this understanding the public good, may not only demand overridings of particular private interests and private goods within the collective in question. It may also urge both overridings of interests, and even violations of rights which are external to that collective.[16] Most dramatically, the national interest of one state may require harm without limit to another state and its citizens. Any argument from facts about interests to conclusions about morality also provides occasion to reiterate Rousseau's objection to Grotius: "A more logical method could be used, but not one more favourable to tyrants."

Obnoxious though it is to contend that "the sovereign power has no need to offer a guarantee to its subjects," this initial outrage is almost innocuous by comparison with the same chapter's concluding claim: "Thus, in order for the social compact to avoid being an empty formula, it tacitly entails the commitment . . . that whoever refuses to obey the general will be forced to do so by the entire body. *This means that he will be forced to be free*" (I[vii], 25, emphasis added).

That most notorious contention is sometimes glossed by reference to a later footnote: "In Genoa, the word *libertas* [liberty] can be read on the front of prisons and on the chains of galley-slaves. . . . In a country where all such people were in the galleys, the most perfect liberty would be enjoyed" (IV[ii], 82). Certainly Rousseau had a fair and true point there, albeit one obscured and distorted by his provocative and sensationalized form of expression. For the rights and liberties of citizens can be effectively guaranteed by law only where would-be violators are deterred by the threat of punishment, and where actual violations are regularly punished. Perhaps too it is just worth remarking that by forcing a child to study subjects which are initially uncongenial you really are ensuring that, in the future, that child will have a wider range of career possibilities to choose between. But the persistent defender does no justice either to Rousseau's honesty, or to his competence as a writer, if he suggests that he really meant something equally harmless when he said that the dissident "will be forced to be free." On what he actually said and therefore, presumably, meant the best comment is modelled on some famous words of a modern and funnier Marx: "It sounds absurd. But don't be misled. It is absurd."[17]

(d) Our final task is to review Rousseau's ruinously unsuccessful attempts to specify how in any particular case his general will is to be identified and its sense determined. At first it seems as if it is going to be the unanimous will of an assembly of all citizens, and that—as so often—Rousseau is thinking of some Classical city-state: "For either the will is general, or it is not. It is the will of either the people as a whole, or of only a part. . . . In the second case, it is merely a private will . . ." (II[ii], 30). This clear conclusion, however, is forthwith contradicted in a footnote: "For a will to be general, it need not always be unanimous. . . ."

Not a whit discomfited, it seems, Rousseau proceeds in the next chapter to insist that even unanimity would not be a sufficient criterion: "There is often a great deal of difference between the will of all and the general will" (II[iii], 31). This distinction is highly praised by Hegel (1770-1831): "Rousseau would have made a sounder contribution towards a theory of the State, if he had always kept this distinction in sight."[18] It was, surely, unfair so to suggest that Rousseau regularly failed to do this; although there are two opinions—Mine right and the other wrong!—about the soundness of what results from his success. Certainly persons seeing themselves as members of "parties of the vanguard" had, long before Hegel started to construct his *Logic*, become seized of the possibility that they were themselves privileged to discover the authentic sense of the general will; and that these revelations might be vouchsafed to them regardless of, or even contrary to, the verdicts of actual majority votes.[19]

Nevertheless, although even unanimity would not be a sufficient criterion, there is supposed to be—sometimes—magic in a mere majority: "There is often a great deal of difference between the will of all and the general will. The latter considers private interest and is merely the sum of private wills. But remove from these same wills the pluses and minuses that cancel each other out, and what remains as the sum of the differences is the general will" (II[iii], 31-2). What magic there seems to be is the mystery of mathematics. As so often now, in the age of computers, the only defense against deception is another acronymic principle—GIGO; which, being interpreted, is Garbage In, Garbage Out.

Rousseau also thinks to improve any electoral process which is admitted with various devices, none of which he even pretends to believe could be completely relied upon to yield the results desired, and most of which presuppose assumptions inconsistent with something previously asserted. Thus "The periodic assemblies I have spoken of earlier . . . which have as their sole object the preservation of the social treaty should always take place through two propositions . . . which are voted on separately:

"The first: *Does it please the sovereign to preserve the present form of government?*

"The second: *Does it please the people to leave its administration to those who are now in charge of it?*" (II[xviii], 78-9; manifestly these are, as teachers of the Latin language were wont to say, questions expecting the answer "Yes"!)

Once corruption has set in "the general will is no longer the will of all." Yet even the venal citizen "in selling his vote for money . . . does not extinguish the general will in himself; he evades it. The error he commits is that of . . . answering a different question from the one he was asked. Thus, instead of saying through his vote *it is advantageous to the state*, he says *it is advantageous to this man or that party* . . ." (IV[i], 80). But this is to assume, what before was sensibly denied, that, if only the responses are responses to the appropriate question, then they are bound to be correct. This same assumption is again, and rightly, rejected when, in the chapter immediately subsequent, Rousseau writes: "When a law is proposed . . . what is asked . . . is . . . whether or not it conforms to the general will. . . . Each man, in giving his vote, states his opinion on this matter, and the declaration of the general will is drawn from the counting of votes. *When, therefore, the opinion contrary to mine prevails, this proves merely that I was in error, and that what I took to be the general will was not so*" (IV[ii], 82; emphasis added).

Rousseau's last resort was to introduce the Legislator, summoned to fulfill in the supposedly ideal state of *The Social Contract* a function somewhat similar to that which, in the politics of France during the first two or three decades after World War II, General de Gaulle found for himself. "The Legislator," we are told, "is in every respect an extraordinary man in the state. If he ought to be so by his genius, he is no less so by his office, which is neither magistracy nor sovereignty. This office, *which constitutes the republic*, does not enter into its constitution" (II[vii], 39; emphasis supplied).[20]

It is, as was said a moment ago, the putative magic of mathematics which is conscripted to induce us to accept that, somehow, "the pluses and minuses" will "cancel each other out and what remains as the sum of the differences" must be—Hey Presto "the general will." Now, finally, we have a *deus ex machina* providentially wheeled out onto the stage in order to work the unfortunately essential miracle. Like "the fathers of nations," Rousseau, as the dramatist of political theory, is forced "to have recourse to the intervention of heaven" in order to provide the criterial wisdom which he cannot himself supply: "It is this sublime reason, which transcends the grasp of ordinary men, whose decisions the Legislator puts into the mouth of the immortals in order to compel by divine authority those whom human providence could not move. But not everybody is capable of making the gods speak or of being believed when he proclaims himself their interpreter. The great soul of the legislator is the miracle that should prove his mission" (II[vii], 61).

Notes

1. Bertrand Russell, *A History of Western Philosophy* (London, and New York: Allen and Unwin, and Simon Schuster, 1965), chap. XIX, pp. 684-85.
2. See Joan McDonald, *Rousseau and the French Revolution: 1762-1791* (London: Athlone, 1965), chapter V, *passim*.
3. See J. L. Talmon, *The Origins of Totalitarian Democracy* (London: Secker and Warburg, 1952; reprint, New York: Praeger, 1960). For Lenin's recognition of the Jacobins as proto-Bolsheviks see, for instance, his article "Enemies of the People," first published in *Pravda* in June 1917 and reprinted in R. C. Tucker, ed. *The Lenin Anthology* (New York: Norton, 1975), pp. 305-06. For an account of Russian Jacobinism before Lenin, see Tucker's Introduction, pp. xxvi-xxxxiii.
4. All references will be given, as here, by book and chapter followed by the page number from D. A. Cress, ed. and trans., *On the Social Contract: Discourse on the Origin of Inequality: Discourse on Political Economy* (Indianapolis, Ind.: Hackett, 1983).
5. See note 4, and compare the Everyman edition by G. D. H. Cole (London, and New York: J. M. Dent, and E. P. Dutton, 1913). Although after World War II this Everyman edition was reissued in a fresh format with a different pagination this costless opportunity to replace Rousseau's works into the order of their first publication was, regrettably, not taken.
6. References to this second *Discourse*, and to the third, will be to the page number in the edition described in note 4, above.

7. It is at this time the almost universal presupposition in the discussion of poverty in the "Third World." See P. T. Bauer, *Dissent on Development*, rev. ed. (Cambridge, Mass.: Harvard University Press, 1976), or any of his later writings; and compare Antony Flew, *Thinking about Social Thinking* (Oxford: Blackwell, 1984), pp. 120-22. To those truly concerned for the relief of man's estate, rather than with either the expiation of some perceived private guilt, or the retention of a reputation for anti-conservative compassion, it is a peculiarly obnoxious misconception. It obstructs the application of the vastly productive insights of that first and greatest masterpiece of development economics, Adam Smith, *An Enquiry into the Nature and Causes of the Wealth of Nations*.

8. Aficionados of Raymond Chandler's writing may recall an exchange in *The Big Sleep* between Anne O'Riordan and Philip Marlowe:

   "I had a gun. I wasn't afraid. There's no law against it."
   "Uh huh. Only the law of self-preservation."

9. Russell, *A History of Western Philosophy*, p. 697. We must, therefore, fault Sir Isaiah Berlin for an excess of liberal charity, betraying liberalism, in entitling his Inaugural Lecture "Two Concepts of Liberty." This is reprinted in his *Four Essays on Liberty* (Oxford: Oxford University Press, 1969).

10. For fuller references to the sources of both this and the following quotation, and for a discussion of "Wants or Needs: Choice or Command?", see Antony Flew, *The Politics of Procrustes* (London, and Buffalo: Temple Smith, and Prometheus, 1981).

11. I must not finish with this third *Discourse* without sharing and commending the apothegm: "Imposing a fine for work is a rather unusual way of abolishing idleness" (p. 187). It could serve as a motto for those urging, in the name of economic growth, the replacement of income by expenditure taxes.

12. Cress actually renders "la condition" as "the condition." I have changed this to "the situation"; which is, surely, at least equally faithful while fitting more smoothly into the present argument.

13. Compare "Sociology and Equality" in Antony Flew, *Sociology, Equality and Education* (London: Macmillan, 1976).

14. Here we have a welcome opportunity to recommend Robert Nisbet's superb critique of John Rawls's *A Theory of Justice*, an essay which recognizes Rawls as a new Rousseau, a *philosophe* rather than a philosopher. This appeared first in the *Public Interest* 35 (1976), but has since been reprinted in W. Letwin, ed., *Against Equality* (London: Macmillan, 1983). Compare also the critique of Rawls in *The Politics of Procrustes*, chaps. III-IV.

15. The original is "toujours droit." A better yet still not perfect translation would be "always upright." For Rousseau's point is that, although it may be mistaken on some point of act, the general will is always directed "towards the public utility."

16. This is something which in part and in his own way Rousseau recognizes when he notices that "... when ... partial associations come into being ... the will of each of these associations becomes general in relation to the state" (II[iii], 32).

17. For a properly cruel critique of one contemporary attempt to defend a similarly "positive" redefinition of "freedom" see "Freedom is Slavery: a Slogan for Our New Philosopher Kings," in A. P. Griffiths, ed., *Of Liberty* (Cambridge, England: Cambridge University Press, 1983).

18. See Hegel, *The Science of Logic*, section 163.

19. Compare again, Talmon, *The Origins of Totalitarian Democracy*. They ignored the remainder of that contradictory footnote, and much else: "... however, it is necessary for all the votes to be counted. Any formal exclusion is a breach of generality" (II[ii], 30).

20. The story is told that someone studying the frequency of the occurrence of the first person singular in the speeches of political leaders was puzzled by the low score achieved by the General. This perplexity was only resolved when the student noticed the extremely numerous employments of the expression "La France," and realized that this subject identified himself absolutely with his country.

16

In Defense of Rights

David Gordon

I f a recent work is to be believed, the entire basis of Murray Rothbard's political thought rests on myth. As even Macaulay's schoolboy knows, Rothbard's defense of libertarianism stands or falls with the notion of "natural rights." It is precisely this idea that L. A. Rollins, whose engaging and much discussed pamphlet *The Myth of Natural Rights*[1] I propose to examine, dismisses as unfounded.

What is a natural right? Rollins' definition of the term is one of the few items in his pamphlet not open to objection; " 'Natural Rights'. . . are rights that people are supposed to possess simply because they are human beings. Since natural rights are supposedly possessed simply because one is human, such rights are therefore considered to be universal: possessed by all people" (p. 1).

To show that natural rights, taken in the sense just mentioned, do not exist was, one would have thought, a broad and ambitious task. But Rollins's aim is more far-reaching still. He attempts to show that all morality is mythical. "But if one sees through the myth of morality, one realizes that one does not need a 'moral justification' (and that there *is* no 'moral justification') for anything one does or says . . . nothing is 'morally wrong' " (pp. 38-39). (This thesis is broader than one denying the existence of natural rights since one can have a moral theory, e.g., utilitarianism, that makes no use of rights. If, however, morality is rejected, natural rights go with it.)

But isn't it obviously wrong that "nothing is morally wrong"? To take a simple case, suppose someone, just for fun, kidnaps babies and eats them. What could be more evident than that the person is guilty of monstrous evil? Rollins himself discusses the Nazi mass murders of Jews during World War II. Surely these were morally wrong.

Rollins does not think so. He states: "the rejection of the idea of

natural rights entails the conclusion that the Nazis were neither 'justified' nor 'unjustified' in killing six million Jews" (p. 11). (I do not think
this is quite accurate as an expression of Rollins's thesis. One might
morally reject the Nazis's conduct without believing in natural rights:
it is rejection of morality, rather than just natural rights, that entails
Rollins's conclusion. It is clear, though, that he intends to embrace the
wider claim.)

What reasons does Rollins advance for his extraordinary claim?
First, he rightly points out that his rejection of morality does not entail
that it *was* moral for the Nazis to kill Jews: he casts aside altogether the
use of moral language. It isn't that Rollins wishes to propose a new
morality in which everything is morally permissible; he doesn't think
morality makes sense at all. It certainly doesn't follow, though, that
one has good reason to believe a proposition simply because there is
some absurd view which the proposition doesn't entail. Once more the
question arises: isn't it just obviously false that nothing is either moral
or immoral?

At the very least, Rollins needs to have powerful arguments if we
are even to take his radical claim seriously. In fact he has none which
withstand examination. (Here I refer only to his arguments directed
against morality as such, rather than those specifically aimed at the libertarian natural rights tradition.)

He lays great emphasis on the claim that one cannot prove something to be moral or immoral: "No matter how much I might gain
from murdering you, I 'must not' murder you. Why not? Simply
because I 'must not.' This 'must not' is unconditional and absolute.
But, as such, it is merely an arbitrary, unprovable assumption" (p. 11).

There is a trivial sense in which Rollins is incorrect, but this does
not affect his point. In one sense, it is quite easy to prove that "I must
not murder you": one simply derives it from the premise: "No one
ought to commit murder." But of course what Rollins means is that
one cannot prove that something is moral or immoral unless one appeals at some point in the argument to an unproved moral premise;
and it is the use of such a premise that introduces arbitrariness.

But why assume that a premise must rest on some other premise(s)
to escape the charge of arbitrariness? On the contrary, as Aristotle
long ago pointed out, one cannot go back to infinity in asking that the
premises of one's argument be justified by a new argument, the premises of that argument be justified by another new argument . . . etc.
Somewhere one must end with a premise which is both true and not in
need of further arguments. As Wittgenstein says, "Somewhere justifi-

cation must come to an end." (I don't mean to claim that it is a necessary condition for rational belief that either *p* is self evident or is derivable by argument from self-evident propositions. But this is, I think, a *sufficient* condition for rational belief in *p*.)

If this is right, why can't some moral propositions be self-evidently true or false? If they can be, an argument that appeals to one of these premises is *not* arbitrary: to assume that any appeal to moral axioms is dogmatic is to assume just the point at issue. When, in a passage from a review which Rollins is kind enough to quote, I claimed it to be obvious that slavery is wrong, I did not, as Rollins thinks, rely on an unprovable "hunch" of my own. I thought that this was an obvious truth, true regardless of how I or anyone else felt about it.

Of course, Rollins will have none of this. He cites a characteristically acute passage from Nietzsche, according to which philosophers "all pose as if they had discovered and reached their real opinions through the development of cold, pure, divinely unconcerned dialectic . . . while at bottom it is an assumption that they defend with reasons they have sought after the fact" (p. 42). Elsewhere Rollins claims that "natural law and natural rights are human *inventions* (not *discoveries*) intended to further the interests of the inventors" (p. 12).

No doubt it is true that people often use morality as a tool for their own purposes and allow their passions to color their judgment; and we owe much to Nietzsche's acute psychological insight in enabling us to see how these distortions arise. But it does not follow from the possibility that emotion or interest can bias one's judgment that there is no moral truth or falsehood. A defender of moral objectivity need only say that we should examine our judgments as closely as possible to see that they are as free as we can make them from such failings. (Note further that one way we can often show that someone is emotionally carried away or self-serving is to show that his judgments do not correspond to the truth as we see it.) Further, it does not follow from the fact that a belief is in someone's interest that it is false.

If someone regards appeals to self-evidence as irrational generally, rather than confining one's skepticism to morality, the result is chaos. All reasoning depends on certain principles: the laws of identity, non-contradiction, and excluded middle. (Fortunately, I will resolutely ignore here intuitionism, three-valued logic, "dialectics," etc.) These, as the basis of all proof, cannot be derived by arguments which do not presuppose at least one of them. If all appeals to self-evidence are to be rejected, is logic also to be thrown out as arbitrary and dogmatic? (Nietzsche, in some of his moods, seems to want to do just this.) If, on the other hand, Rollins holds back from this abyss of irrationality, he must recognize that there isn't a *general* reason for rejection of appeals to self-evidence. If so, he owes us some explanation of why moral judgments that seem to be self-evident really are not.

Rollins in fact makes some attempt to provide this. He states that "natural rights are mythical and are really fake or metaphorical rights" (p. 2). He obviously intends this characterization to apply to any moral claim. *Why* are natural rights unreal? Because, says Rollins, they do not have effects. To say, e.g., that you have a right against theft of your property will not in itself stop anyone from stealing it. Further, it is false that the failure to observe the rules of morality always has bad consequences. ("Bad" here does not mean "morally bad" but "contrary to one's non-moral interests.") There is no reason to think that all those who violate conventional morality lead unhappy lives.

Rollins's argument seems founded on misunderstanding. First, why is it a condition for a rule of morality to be true that it have some effect in the physical world? It is certainly true that the moral law against theft does not act as an invisible physical barrier impeding thieves. But who ever supposed that moral laws are some sort of physical force like gravitation? Nothing will physically stop one from drawing an invalid conclusion: people do it all the time. Does this show that logical laws are mythical or imaginary? Similarly, why is it a necessary condition for a moral law's being true that those who observe it fare better (in the non-moral sense) than those who do not? There are no bad consequences, so far as I can see, entailed by believing that one can square the circle; nevertheless this belief is logically false.

Of course, on some views of morality, e.g., egoist ones, it *is* a necessary condition for a moral rule to have just this consequence. But then at most Rollins has an argument against a particular view of morality rather than against morality as such. (I don't mean to suggest that ethical egoists have no adequate defense here: this is a topic for a different paper, most probably by another writer.)

It is in fact a general weakness of Rollins's pamphlet that it persistently confuses two different questions: are the judgments of morality capable of objective truth? and, why ought I, or anyone else, to follow these judgments in my own life? Rollins at one point asks: "Why should I refrain from violently interfering with Murray Rothbard's freedom simply because Murray Rothbard needs freedom? If I can advance my life by violent interference with Murray Rothbard's freedom, why should I care what Murray Rothbard needs?" (p. 27). The question of motivation (why ought Rollins to respect Rothbard's rights?)

seems entirely different from the question whether he does or does not have rights that ought to be respected. To reply to this that unless there is some non-moral reason to respect rights, the rights are just arbitrary, begs the question.

It is possible that I have misread the passage just cited. Perhaps Rollins is not claiming here that it is a necessary condition for a moral proposition to be true that one have a non-moral egoistic reason to accept it: rather, he may think that *Rothbard* holds this assumption and intend the point as an *ad hominem* argument against him. But regardless of how this passage should be construed, Rollins in many places *does* make just the assumption I am questioning (e.g., pp. 2, 4, 11).

Rollins has another argument against natural rights in particular and morality in general. There have been many disagreements about exactly which rights are "natural"; Rollins provides an extensive list of such conflicting views (p. 5). (Obviously the same point could be raised against any moral theory, not just rights-based ones.) But it doesn't follow from the existence of disagreement that objective truth does not exist. There are in philosophy of mind many conflicting views on perception, the conditions of knowledge, and the mind-body problem: does the existence of such conflicts in itself show that no solution to any of these problems is possible? Once more Rollins has begged the question: only if one first assumes that moral beliefs reflect irresolvably different standpoints need the existence of disagreement be taken as indicating the absence of truth. No doubt it is true that, even if there are true solutions to disputed moral questions, many will not accept them. But it isn't a requirement for a proposition to be true that everyone accept it. There are many true scientific theories that some people reject.

I suspect but cannot prove (and do not regard it as self-evident) that what is really bothering Rollins is that *he* does not see any force to the alleged dictates of morality. I have claimed that certain moral judgments are obviously true: but they certainly are not obvious to him. Fortunately, it is not an argument against a moral theory's truth that L. A. Rollins fails to believe it. That is a fact of purely biographical significance.

Before turning to another issue, I should like to clarify one point. When I have spoken of certain moral judgments being obviously or self-evidently true, I haven't meant to deny that there might be a moral theory explaining or systematizing such judgments (or deriving other moral judgments that are not evident). There have been philosophers, e.g., H. A. Prichard, who thought that one must simply see one's duty: no further explanation is possible and any attempt at one merely reduces morality to something else. But nothing I have said entails this view.

Rollins does not confine himself to presenting a case for moral skepticism. On the contrary, he gives a large number of specific arguments against writers who have argued for libertarian rights from an Aristotelian or Randian perspective. (Incidentally, even if one rejects entirely my suggestions about moral self-evidence, Rollins has not made his case against morality unless his arguments against the members of this school work. They claim, if I have understood them, to deduce morality from non-moral premises. Unless Rollins can show them wrong, he has not proved that morality is arbitrary.)

In the remainder of this paper, I should like to examine some of Rollins's arguments against a writer having a certain interest for readers of this volume—Murray Rothbard. I shall not cover all the points Rollins raises: merely a couple of particular interest. To begin with, Rothbard rests part of his argument for the self-ownership principle on what human beings need to survive and flourish. Rollins asks: "Why don't the survival needs of all other organisms generate 'rights' for those organisms? After all, they need freedom from violent interference with their survival activities as much as men do. Rothbard, however, clearly does not believe that animals have 'rights'" (pp. 28-29). I do not think Rothbard is guilty of inconsistency here. The argument against him (which originates with George Smith) assumes without proof that one must derive the premise that human needs entail certain rights from a more general premise that all organisms' needs generate rights. (See the quotation from Smith at the top of p. 16.) But why must one assume this? Is there anything odd or aberrant in starting with a premise dealing with human beings rather than deriving this as a conclusion from a premise about organisms? It may well be a good question to Rothbard how he would block an inference from an analogous premise to the conclusion that animals have rights based on their needs—but this is a separate point. (He might say, e.g., that only rational beings can have rights and that the question, what rights would animals have, if they could have rights, is empty.)

Finally, Rollins inquires of Rothbard why he claims that all human beings have the same rights. People are biologically very different (Rollins quotes (p. 35) an interesting passage from the biochemist Roger J. Williams elaborating this point): how then can they all have the same rights? But Rollins gives us not the slightest reason to think that rights-claims rest on assertions of biological equality. Further, even if they did, the fact that people are unequal in many respects does not preclude their being the same in others. And, for all Rollins has shown, it may be just these that generate claims to rights.

To sum up, both morality and Rothbard emerge from Rollins's attack unscathed.

Notes

1. L. A. Rollins, *The Myth of Natural Rights* (Port Townsend, Wash.: Loompanics Unlimited, 1983). All references to this work will be by the page number in parenthesis in the text.

17

Ethics vs. Coercion:
Morality or Just Values?

Tibor R. Machan

Government versus the State

"The state consists of full time professionals in coercion."[1] Murray Rothbard believes this and that is why he calls himself an anarchist. He is an opponent of coercion, ultimately on grounds of "a natural rights theory embedded in a wider system of Aristotelian-Lockean natural law and a realistic ontology and metaphysics."[2]

There is no question that all governments use force. And most of them are also coercive. To Murray Rothbard it seems self-evident that they must be. He admits, of course, that "in the libertarian tradition . . . either the state is to be abolished, or, if retained, . . . it be kept small and weighed down with fierce restrictions and greeted by permanent social hostility."[3] But since states persistently and inexcusably violate the rights of their citizens, as well as those of many foreigners, the former is the only just alternative.

Yet within the framework of Aristotelian-Lockean social philosophy the equivalent to governmental authority clearly has a role that by no means ought to be "greeted by permanent social hostility." How can Murray Rothbard nevertheless place himself in the company of these two famous defenders of government?

Throughout recorded history no government has managed to remain untarnished by coercion. Some, however, have approached giving full official recognition and protection to individual rights. Others have not even given lip service to the idea.

Now, in Rothbard's discussions of political theory, anarchism is usually defended in contrast to statism, not so much to the institution of government. He has, in short, argued for a "society without a state," which he claimed "might function successfully."[4] He is one of the few scholars who has argued, on essentially individualist grounds, not just for "limited" government but for anarchy. He took up the hardest case to tilt against, when he admitted that, "Surely, it is universally asserted, the state is at least vitally necessary to provide police protection, the judicial resolution of disputes and enforcement of contracts, and the creation of the law itself that is to be enforced."[5] In the face of this most plausible of views, Rothbard has persistently argued "that all of these admittedly necessary services of protection can satisfactorily and efficiently be supplied by private persons and institutions on the free market."[6]

Yet it is curious that Rothbard does not really argue against governments as such but against the state. Government is, of course, often identified with the state, but in the major statists of political theory—Plato, Hegel, Rousseau, Marx, Green, et al.—the state loomed far larger than government alone. I would argue—and have done so elsewhere[7]—that in the end the kind of institution that Rothbard believes would arise "on the free market," in order to provide the "necessary services of protection" of individual rights from domestic and foreign threats, is not like the coercive states of these major statist thinkers but closer to Rothbard's "private, 'anarchistic,' voluntary courts."[8] My major caveat is that the kind of competition we witness in free markets would obtain in a very subtle manner between "competing" governments. To wit, they would compete for citizens, somewhat as apartment complexes compete for tenants. In any case, having said something about a point of difference between Professor Rothbard's libertarianism and my own, let me hasten to turn to a more productive endeavor.

I want to address the question, "Why do governments appear to have the right to be coercive?" We are not asking whether governments may use force. Force is not necessarily coercive, only when it violates individual rights. But clearly many think that governments do have the authority to be coercive. What is there in morality that appears to give governments permission to do what private persons may not—e.g., to conscript, tax, license, regulate, inspect us, and so forth?

This question is of interest here because the argument Rothbard sometimes invokes against coercion would appear to be absolutely decisive for anyone who takes issues of morality seriously, the very matter on which most people rest their case for a coercive state. In his defense of Frank S. Meyer as essentially a libertarian rather than a "fusionist" thinker, Rothbard notes that Meyer's "most important contribution to conservatism was his emphasis that to be virtuous in any meaningful sense, a man's actions must be free."[9] Then he adds the categorical statement that "no action *can be* virtuous unless it is freely chosen."[10] In this Rothbard echoes the dramatic statement of Ayn Rand, that "morality ends where a gun begins."[11] If a just society must protect the morally good life, it cannot be one that is systematically (rather than accidentally) coercive.

Yet despite what seems to be an elementary point about the nature of justice, innumerable political thinkers from Plato to George Will and Ronald Dworkin sanction coercion by governments, supposedly in defense of such noble moral ideals as virtue and justice. It won't do to simply dismiss this saying that such people want power and invoke specious arguments to support it. The fact cannot be evaded that many persons with no such designs at all have found these arguments convincing. It behooves us, then, to seek out some understanding of the power behind such statist arguments, ones that essentially sanction state coercion.

America's Politics and the Coercive State

The most widespread coercion by governments is taxation. There are other, more specific forms of coercion, such as military conscription, mandatory licensing of professions, and government regulation of business. Anyone aware of current socio-political life knows about this and most of us have personal experience with it. Why do these measures win moral approval?

We should note from the start that most thoughtful people in the United States and indeed in most of Western culture find the coerciveness of the state somewhat lamentable. In short, they find it a necessary evil, and wish it didn't have to be. But there are others who think differently and indeed see it as a virtue of governments to be coercive. Some are quite forthright about their support of "statecraft as soulcraft"[12] and believe that soulcraft requires a good dosage of coercion. Others try to smuggle coercion into our culture by labelling it something else, such as "justice."[13] Still others believe that government coercion is really the use of force on behalf of a certain kind of freedom—they call it positive freedom or respect for welfare rights or the right to equal respect as a person.[14] Here it is difficult to spot the doctrine of coercion because it is obscured by conceptual muddles.

Most people know that the American political tradition rests on ideals which morally prohibit coercion. So in order to make room for it in our moral consciousness, it has to be re-christened, in an Orwellian "newspeak" fashion. Coercive government had been the nemesis of not just the Founding Fathers but especially of John Locke, whose views largely undergird the political thought of the United States of America.[15]

Locke's philosophical ground for opposing coercion of one person by another had been that he regarded individual human beings as by nature morally free, independent, and equal. This means that he regarded us all, in adulthood, as responsible to make our own decisions or choices in life. Thus no adult is inherently subject to the authority of another. This also means that we are all politically equal. That, indeed, is the only egalitarianism inherent in the American political tradition. (It is also clear from this why Murray Rothbard would regard himself a Lockean and what he means by "self-ownership."[16])

From this basic frame of reference a conception of government arose which regards the state as an institution of laws administered by a group of "elected (hired)" persons who are essentially "employed" by those who hire them, the people. The authority to make use of force on the citizens comes, roughly, as does the authority of a referee at a tennis game or on a basketball court—through the consent of the participants. The courts, the police, the legislature, the armed forces, and so forth are seen to be agents of the people. Here, too, the theory of government within the Lockean framework is not different from the theory of a "private, 'anarchistic,' voluntary" system of rights protection Rothbard endorses.

The precise way in which the use of force can be authorized is a complicated matter.[17] In any case, for John Locke and many of the founders of this political society, government should use force only if the citizens consented to having it used on them and only to the extend that the citizens themselves are justified in using it. That is what "due process of law" really means, namely, that government is justified in the use of force only if it adheres to specific standards.

Aggressive use of force, or coercion, is not sanctioned by the political philosophy which supported the American system of government, even if subsequent practice has diverged from it. (Indeed, the U.S. Constitution is itself a compromised document as far as the principles spelled out in the Declaration of Independence are concerned. But there is nothing mysterious about why in a given community the practical arm of the dominant political ideal might embody serious inconsistencies.)

Now, prior to when the revolutionary idea of free and limited government took hold on a large enough population so as to make a political difference, the coercive state had been looked upon with great favor by those who wielded the power of the pen. Locke himself forged his own views against the paternalistic political ideals of Sir Robert Filmer.

Sadly, however, not long after Locke's ideas flourished, once again the coercive state appeared to gain the support of moral philosophy. So the career of the free society, whereby government was to have been restricted to noncoercive use of force, was short lived, not only in practice (where it had never been complete), but also as a respectable idea.

Clearly, the dominant post-Lockean moral and political theory has been supportive of the coercive state. It will be worthwhile to consider then the features of moral theories and systems which so insistently seem to not just sanction or tolerate but eagerly to endorse government coercion, even following a most powerful and earthshaking rejection of this idea in Western history, namely, the birth of the United States. Why does the use of aggressive force appear once again, as in the past, to have the support of morality?

A Few Words on Morality

Why morality?[18] We need to know a bit about this so as to understand why our question is really very important. If one were to regard morality as quite dispensable, then one would not need to be very disturbed if many moral systems give credence to coercion. One could simply reject morality through and through, as indeed have some who take an exclusively social scientific (e.g., economic) view of human life.

Persons, unlike other beings, must choose what they will do and they can choose badly or well. Morality is the most basic code or set of standards by which one can determine whether a choice is a good or a bad one. However much we might wish to dispense with morality, so long as human beings lack innate guidance to their conduct, it will be in vain to try. The economist's attempt to reduce everything to "workability," "usefulness," "practicality," or "efficiency" just won't work, since each of these invite the question, "For what purpose?" Thus something can only be judged workable if we know the purpose it is to serve. When it comes to assessing the merits of goals or purposes, it cannot be sufficient to talk of workability or efficiency. Something else is required, namely, "Is it a good, just, virtuous purpose we are talking about or is it something morally questionable?"

One could embark on lengthy discussions about the reasons for all this. E.g., what is it about human nature, reality in general, that gives choice such a basic role in our lives, how compatible is having to make choices with science, etc? But that would take us too far afield.

What we now need to do is to see something of various moral systems so that we can tell why so many of them give support to coercion. In the end when we concern ourselves with public policy, the most serious issue is whether it meets standards of morality. Much else may be important, especially in a democracy. But in the end any public policy that is morally approved will have a far greater likelihood of success with policy makers than one which goes against the moral grain. For this reason the case against coercion needs to stand for morality. And for this reason, too, the case for it has always appeared to do so.

Morality and Coercion

Most of us know a bit about how much controversy there exists about moral systems. Moral skepticism has indeed done very well, partly because so little firm agreement can be found in this area. I will not try to refute moral skepticism here. I would like to suggest, however, that when we deal with a field in which one's very own quality as a person is at stake, and given the wide variety that exists in the quality of human beings, there should be no wonder about all the controversy. We are all inclined to paint ourselves pretty, morally speaking. It is understandable that sometimes we would even stoop to adjusting morality itself so as to make ourselves, our own chosen goals, etc., seem morally justified. As a last resort we may even deny that there is any moral truth, just so that we escape having its wrath fall upon us.

In any case, what is crucial to note is that within moral systems certain components tend to give rise to coercion. In a nutshell, it is the *value component* of moral systems that gives rise to coercion.

One may find this difficult to understand. Doesn't every moral system have a value component? Then wouldn't every moral system support coercion?

Actually, only those moral systems support coercion which fail to place their value components in the proper human context. Let me explain.

Every moral system requires a theory of the good. Even before we can talk about what human beings ought to do—which is the main concern of any morality—the question has to be answered: "What is our goal? What is the point of conduct in the first place?" A theory of the good provides our answer to this.

If our goal is the collective happiness of humankind, then when we wish to know that we ought to do, we need only to answer the technical or practical question: "Whatever will promote the collective happiness of humankind?" If it's God's will, then again we ought to obey it.

If it is our self-interest, then again we need to know and follow it, and so forth. In short, a moral system presupposes a theory of the good which identifies our proper goal in life and for which morality enables us to reach.

Now, whenever a moral system lays exaggerated emphasis on its theory of the good—forgetting something else, to which I'll turn in a moment—which, of course, is vital to it, it is likely to encourage coercion. In utilitarian morality, for example, extreme stress can be placed on the greatest happiness of the greatest number (with happiness usually understood as well-being or pleasure or wealth). The good is seen as the overall well-being of humanity or members of a society. In most religious moralities various forms of behavior are seen as the manifestation of goodness and the realization of such behavior is then regarded as the goal which moral conduct must pursue.

Let me note here that although Soviet Marxism supposedly gains much of its support from science, in fact a basic theory about values is most crucial to it, as it is to every political outlook. In the Marxist-socialist conception of the state, the most powerful underlying justification relies on a vital evaluative component, namely, the *summum bonum* of labor.

Now, any morality can lay extreme stress on its ultimate goal, at the expense of another crucial feature morality must possess. And this can be transferred to public policy within any human community.

Morality and Coercive Public Policy

If, as far as personal ethics is concerned, a moral system gives primary emphasis to goals, it is also likely to stress goals as far as public policy is concerned. Suppose that the members of a society morally prize helping the poor (or social harmony or economic stability or prosperity or spiritual and military superiority). In each case, public policy will very likely be geared toward the attainment of these ends, regardless of (or at least with little regard for) the means by which this is to be brought about.

A good example is ecological purity. It is prized highly by many, indeed regarded by them to be a supreme moral goal. So all forms of coercion are seen to be justified in its behalf. Because coercion seems such an efficient method for certain limited purposes—after all, *force* is the primary instrument of efficiency in classical mechanics and of much of modern technology—such an emphasis on achieving ends will promote its use.

To summarize my points thus far, first we need to appreciate the vital role morality has in human life and in the justification of public policy; second we need to note that the theory of the good which every moral system presupposes can be emphasized in a way that lays primary stress on the achievement of goals—or, to use Robert Nozick's term, "end-states."[19] This, then, gives support to the instrument of coercion in the attainment of various public purposes.

What we now need to see is why this is all a very serious mistake and why it is indeed a distortion of morality. It is clear that Murray Rothbard was aware of the point, yet it will be useful to explain again that morality, rightly understood, does not support the use of coercion but, on the contrary, requires its abolition.

Freedom of Choice and Morality

As distinct from the theory of the good within every moral system, morality must also be concerned with the specifically human mode of the good. What is this?

To answer, let us remember that there is goodness in connection with all life. Botanists, zoologists, and biologists are all involved in evaluations, judging things to be good or bad. This is because the best theory of the good links goodness to the phenomenon of life. It is the perishable nature of life that gives goodness a role in existence. For things which cannot perish, the idea of the good is inapplicable. But for living things there can be conditions, processes, etc., that are good and ones that are bad. It depends on how they further or thwart life.

But regarding all life other than human life, to the best of our knowledge there can be no concern about *moral* goodness. The reason is that all such life lacks the unique *volitional* element, or the feature which we have come to know by the terms "freedom of the will."

Since the time of Aristotle[20] it should have been understood very clearly that as far as morality is concerned, freedom of choice is essential. Human nature is such that the human good is inseparable from each individual's having to choose what constitutes his or her good conduct. If some goal or purpose is indeed right for us, we are *morally* right pursuing it strictly speaking only if we see the point of its value *and* choose it. Our own moral character, which is our highest good— our very excellence as persons—flourishes if and only if the good behavior we engage in, the good ends we promote, the good states of affairs we bring about, are all a matter of choice.

We can here consider a wonderful mental exercise presented to us by Murray Rothbard:

Suppose, for a moment, that we define a virtuous act as bowing in the direction of Mecca every day at sunset. We attempt to persuade everyone to perform this act. But suppose that instead of relying on voluntary conviction we employ a vast number of police to break into everyone's home and see to it that every day they are pushed down to the floor in the direction of Mecca. No doubt by taking such measures we will increase the number of people bowing toward Mecca. But by forcing them to do so, we are taking them out of the realm of action and into mere motion, and we are depriving all these coerced persons of the very possibility of acting morally. By attempting to compel virtue, we eliminate its possibility. For by compelling everyone to bow to Mecca, we are preventing people from doing so out of freely adopted conviction. To be moral, an act must be free.[21]

Without the element of choice, our type of involvement with values is no different from that of other living things that behave from instinct or innate drives. Dogs, plants, birds, forests, and so forth are not moral agents. How they behave is a matter open for evaluation, but not for moral praise or blame. The reason is that such living things are incapable of choice. It is irrelevant to their goodness or good behavior (flourishing, thriving, health) whether their behavior is chosen. And this is precisely what sets us apart from them, first and foremost.

Accordingly, those moralities which fail to pay sufficient heed to this are not just wrong but fundamentally eskewed. When choice is taken away from a moral system's conception of human goodness, it ceases to be a moral system proper. It can still be a system of values, of course, but not of basic human values.

Conclusion

The basic moral support for the coercive state then is the failure to remember that morality is a system of principles serving a basic human purpose, namely, to enable human individuals to be good as *human* individuals. To even approach being a successful moral theory, this feature of free choice must be included within a moral system. For example, if utilitarianism becomes overly concerned with the general welfare or if any religious ethics sees some rituals or forms of behavior as having a priority over the fact that these rituals and forms of behavior must be chosen for them to give merit to human individuals, then these systems are actually pseudo-moralities or mere value theories, aiming at identifying good things, but not the human good.

The coercive state is not then founded on any *bona fide* moral system but on systems which try but fail to be moral systems. Their failure to embody not just values but also free choice that must be involved in seeking these makes bad candidates for moral systems.

No public policy can live long if it loses its moral standing. The coercive state has lost it from the start.[22]

Notes

1. Murray N. Rothbard, "Frank S. Meyer: The Fusionist as Libertarian Manque," in G. Carey, ed., *Freedom and Virtue, The Conservative/Libertarian Debate* (Lanham, Md.: University Press of America, 1984), p. 106.
2. Ibid., p. 96.
3. Ibid., p. 106.
4. Murray N. Rothbard, "Society Without a State," in Tibor R. Machan, ed., *The Libertarian Reader* (Totowa, N.J.: Rowman and Littlefield, 1982), p. 53.
5. Ibid., p. 55.
6. Ibid.
7. Tibor R. Machan, *Human Rights and Human Liberties* (Chicago: Nelson-Hall Co., 1975); idem., "Dissolving the Problem of Public Goods: Financing Government Without Coercive Measures," in *The Libertarian Reader.*
8. Rothbard, "Society Without a State," p. 58.
9. Rothbard, "Frank S. Meyer," p. 92.
10. Ibid, p. 93.
11. Ayn Rand, *Atlas Shrugged* (New York: Random House, 1957), p. 1023.
12. The phrase comes from the most recent conservative defense of the coercive state, George Will, *Statecraft as Soulcraft* (New York: Simon and Schuster, 1982). Will defends his statism by reference to Aristotle's alleged wholehearted support of statism. There is reason to think, however, that even in this historical reference, let alone in substance, Will has got it wrong. The *polis* is not the same as the state. See, Fred D. Miller, Jr., "The State and Community in Aristotle's *Politics*," *Reason Papers*, 1 (1974). See, also, Tibor R. Machan, "An Aristotelian Foundation for Natural Rights?" *This World*, 11 (Summer 1985).
13. In the end this is what must be said about John Rawls's monumental work, *A Theory of Justice* Cambridge, Mass.: Harvard University Press, 1971).
14. See, e.g., Patricia Werhane, *Persons, Rights & Corporations* (Englewood Cliffs, N.J.: Prentice-Hall, 1985); Allen Gewirth, *Reason and Morality* (Chicago: University of Chicago Press, 1979); Ronald Dworkin, *Taking Rights Seriously* (Cambridge, Mass.: Harvard University Press, 1977). I discuss some attempts to transform the meaning of rights to imply enablement or empowerment by means of coercive redistribution of assets and endowments in my "Wronging Rights," *Policy Review* 17 (Summer 1981): 37-58. See, also, my "Moral Myths and Basic Positive rights," *Tulane Studies in Philosophy* (1985).
15. There is debate about just how much direct influence Locke had on the polity of the United States. I will just stand with those who, quite plausibly at least, argue that the Declaration of Independence contains a great deal of vital substance that is distinctively Lockean—e.g., the doctrine of natural rights, the right of popular revolution.
16. Murray N. Rothbard, "Justice and Property Rights," in Samuel L. Blumenfeld, *Property in a Humane Economy* (LaSalle, Ill.: Open Court, 1974).

17. Tibor R. Machan, "Individualism and the Problem of Political Authority," *The Monist* 66 (1983): 500-16. In this paper I discuss some of the Rothbardian anarchist objections to government.
18. I discuss this issue in considerable detail in my "The Classical Egoist Basis of Capitalism," in T. R. Machan, ed., *The Main Debate: Communism versus Capitalism* (New York: Random House, 1987). My answer draws a good deal from what I have learned from Ayn Rand, "The Objectivist Ethics," in *The Virtue of Selfishness: A New Concept of Egoism* (New York: New American Library, 1964); and from Eric Mack, "How to Derive Ethical Egoism?" *The Personalist* 52 (1971).
19. Robert Nozick, *Anarchy, State, and Utopia* (New York: Basic Books, 1974), passim.
20. Machan, "An Aristotelian Foundation for Natural Rights?" The point is that Aristotle said that "the virtues are modes of choice or involve choice" (*Nicomachean Ethics*, Book II, chap. 5, 1106a4). Now he also said a lot that suggests that he supports "soulcraft," i.e., political means by which to habituate citizens into a virtuos life. Yet even here argument abounds as to whether such legislation would involve forcing citizens to behave in virtuous ways or offering them the opportunity to do so.
21. Rothbard, "Frank S. Meyer," p. 93.
22. My work on this essay was made possible by support from the Reason and the Progress Foundations, for which I wish to express my thanks.

18

Historical Entitlement and the Right to Natural Resources

Jeffrey Paul

O ne of the most vexing problems in political philosophy is how to appropriately distribute non-human objects among a given population of persons. The problem has been addressed in a variety of ingenious ways over the centuries. However, recently it has been argued that only one principle of distributive justice, the historical entitlement principle, is consistent with liberty[1] (Robert Nozick) and provides a coherent assignment of rights[2] (Hillel Steiner). For both theorists, if the normative priority of either liberty or rights is assumed, then the historical entitlement principle follows. This principle holds, in Nozick's words, ". . . that past circumstances or actions of people can create differential entitlements or deserts to things."[3] Both theorists believe themselves to be unequivocal in their endorsement of this principle in determining the rightful distribution of objects which have already been extracted from their virginal condition in nature and assigned to a first owner. According to them, ownership, subsequent to this primordial ownership, ought to be determined by the history of successive transfers of that initial entitlement. The conformity or nonconformity of those transfers to the appropriate historical principle will determine the legitimacy or illegitimacy of any subsequent distribution of goods.

The appropriate historical principle according to Nozick and Steiner is the principle of the voluntary transfer of legitimately held goods. The problem for both is to propose a principle of distribution by which an initial assignment of property titles to unowned goods can be justifiably made. While both are attracted to a historical principle of just entitlement according to which assignments of previously unowned virginal objects will be made strictly according to whether the assignee historically produced the object by his efforts; both have difficulty devising a defense of this exclusively historical basis for initial property assignments. Thus, while both claim that a historical principle of entitlement can be applied unconditionally so as to yield subsequent distributions of owned objects, they deny that such a principle can be so applied in the case of unowned non-human natural resources. This denial is significant in two respects. First, both theorists, but especially Nozick, are viewed as uncompromising defenders of historical entitlement on questions of distributive justice. Second, both imagine that this rejection of historical entitlement at the virginal level is compatible with its adoption at the level of transfer.

In this paper, it will be argued: (1) that while both theorists accept the principle of historical entitlement in regard to the transfer of already owned property, they abandon it in their accounts of how property is legitimately acquired from an unowned state, (2) that this abandonment introduces an inconsistency in their theories, and (3) that this inconsistency is not endemic to historical entitlement of distributive justice. In Part I of the paper I will contend, first, that while Nozick intends to be a historical entitlement theorist on matters of initial acquisition, his introduction of the Lockean proviso constitutes a critical breach of the entitlement principle. Next, I will demonstrate that Steiner, in contrast to Nozick, explicitly argues against the entitlement theory as applied to the original acquisition of natural resources. Part II will be devoted primarily to an analysis of why their reasons for abandoning the historical entitlement thesis in regard to original acquisition are erroneous, and why it is inconsistent of them to accept the principle at the transfer level and, yet, reject it at the stage of initial acquisition. In conclusion, it will be argued that a fully consistent historical entitlement view of distributive justice is defensible.

I

In contrast to what they conceive to be their unqualified commitment to a purely historical criterion in deciding what constitutes the legitimate title to and transfer of an owned object, Nozick[4] and Steiner both at least partially embrace an end-state standard of distributive justice when the problem of how to assign ownership to unowned objects arises. In order to explicate the basis of their asymmetric treatment of these two issues, we will examine separately their respective positions.

A

Nozick favors a historical approach to issues of income and asset distribution primarily because all teleological standards of economic allocation require, in his view, continual interferences with individual liberty. This historical standard of justice in allocation is applied by him in the determination of the distributive shares of owned objects for a given population in two separate cases.

The first case is that of the voluntary transfer of owned objects. Here, he reasons that if individuals have exclusive title to their physical persons by right, and if certain non-human objects are owned by them, then subsequent rights over the latter are to be determined in the following way. A voluntary transfer of title to an object from A to B occurs and is valid just in case A has done something that was permissible, namely given to B that to which he justifiably had title. The justice of the consequent transfer depends upon the legitimacy of the history of what was done, not some end result sought by either the parties to the transfer or anyone else. The past title legitimately acquired justifies the present act of its conveyance to another.

But, how are legitimate titles created according to Nozick? This brings us to his second and more fundamental application of the historical principle. If someone, A, legitimately owns objects O_1 and O_2 and by his labor combines them into some new object, O_3, then he, according to Nozick, must own O_3 as it was created exclusively from the use of things to which he previously had legitimate title, his person, O_1 and O_2. Thus, a legitimate title to some new object, O_3, is created by virtue of the *history* of its creation, not by virtue of some end result realized by the assignment of title. The history of the O_3's creation reveals that all of the elements whose synthesis gave rise to O_3 were legitimately owned by A who, therefore, owns their synthetic product, O_3. To summarize the principle involved, if anything, O_x, is created from objects, $O_1 \ldots O_n$ belonging to someone, A, with A's labor, then O_x belongs to A in virtue of $O_1 \ldots O_n$ and A belonging antecedently to A.

Now we have seen how distributive justice is achieved with respect to two categories of objects, "old" objects already legitimately owned, whose transfer is being presently contemplated, and "new" objects whose production has been achieved through the use of legitimately owned "old" objects. Now, clearly the lacuna exists with respect to a third category of non-human objects, unowned virginal resources. (We have, for purposes of brevity, not questioned Nozick's assumption that all adult persons are self-owned and that therefore, no fourth category emerges.) While the role that the historical principle plays in assigning ownership to previously owned objects or new ones created from such objects is easily discernible, the part that history might play in unambiguously establishing title to natural, unused resources is not so apparent. This lack of perspicuity in resolving history's role in establishing title to previously unowned objects is readily understood when we consider that the "new" object issues from the synthesis of that which is owned by someone, his efforts (i.e., the use by him of his body), with that which is not owned, a natural resource. The resultant synthetic object thus has an ambiguous lineage. One aspect of its heritage is encumbered with the vestiges of ownership, another is not. To whom, then, does the newly created object rightfully belong? Its material component was the contribution of "nature," while the new arrangement or location of that component was the product of someone's self-owned labor. Thus, the historical principle that Nozick employs in order to affix legitimate titles to previously owned objects and objects newly emergent from previously owned ones does not seem to establish title in the case of the unowned natural resources with which one has combined one's labor. For how does the unowned portion get transferred to the "laborer"? *Who* is there to transfer it, given that it is unowned in the first place?

In Locke, of course, this problem does not arise in this form. God, having produced all resources *ex nihilo*, is their initial owner, and so transfers His rightful title to them to mankind. The problem for Locke, then, is how to transmit elements of what is the collectively held property of humanity to the individual members of that collectivity. It is important to distinguish Locke's formulation from Nozick's, as the latter poses far greater difficulties for the construction of a theory of the just acquisition of previously unowned resources. In Locke's account virginal resources are never unencumbered with ownership and, therefore, his problem is amenable to a historical solution strictly analogous to Nozick's principle of justice in transfer. That is, given that everything is initially produced by someone, God, and is therefore owned by Him we have only to trace the history of the voluntary transfer of objects, by their original Divine Owner, to determine whether the present human holders of property are the legitimate owners of it. (God, in Locke's scheme, voluntarily transfers the whole of his creation to mankind collectively, under the proviso that it be apportioned individually by a labor admixture formula qualified by spoilation and fairness constraints.) But, for Nozick, there are no original owners of natural resources because there are no original producers of them and, hence, natural resources that have been transformed by someone are not incontestably that person's or anyone else's. How to make them so is Nozick's problem.

Nozick, first, considers the possibility of developing one type of purely historical basis upon which to assign initial property titles, a possibility which he quickly rejects:

> Why does mixing one's labor with something make one the owner of it? Perhaps because one owns one's labor, and so one comes to own a previously unowned thing that becomes permeated with what one owns. Ownership seeps over into the rest. But why isn't mixing what I own with what I don't a way of losing what I own rather than a way of gaining what I don't?[5]

He considers another historical account which he also finds defective:

> Perhaps the idea . . . is that laboring on something improves it and makes it more valuable; and anyone is entitled to own a thing whose value he has created. . . . Why should one's entitlement extend to the whole object rather than just to the *added value* one's labor has produced?[6]

Since the whole of an object's value is not attributable to individual effort, Nozick reasons that ownership of the whole object cannot be justified on the basis that labor has improved it. He supplements this argument against full ownership of the improved object with another against the unconditional ownership of that object:

> It will be implausible to view improving an object as giving full ownership to it, if the stock of unowned objects that might be improved is limited. For an object's coming under one person's ownership changes the situation of all others. Whereas previously they were at liberty (in Hohfeld's sense) to use the object, they now no longer are.[7]

In view of those considerations he concludes that:

> A process normally giving rise to a permanent bequeathable property right in a previously unowned thing will not do so if the position of others no longer at liberty to use the thing is thereby worsened.[8]

Having rejected a purely historical basis for distributing unowned resources, Nozick adopts a quasi-end-state, quasi-historical principle of justice in acquisition. According to this principle any person, A, can appropriate an object, O, if, and only if, his act of appropriation (1) improves the value of O to A and (2) does not worsen the condition of all (or any?) other persons by depriving them of the liberty of using O.[9] Further, any person, A, can appropriate O subsequent to his improving O even though he thereby worsened the situation of others, provided he compensates them adequately.[10] Thus, Nozick combines in his principle of acquisition two criteria of just ownership, one historical, the other teleological; that is, one referring to what people have done, the other pertaining to their present and/or future welfare. Nozick denies that in introducing this welfare criterion he has thereby abandoned a purely historical treatment of justice in acquisition.[11] He argues that the welfare principle he calls ". . . the Lockean proviso is not an end-state principle; it focuses on a particular way that appropriate actions affect others, and not on the structure of the situation that results."[12] But on Nozick's own account a social end-state is not merely limited to those of a patterned variety and, therefore, is not to be exclusively identified with such patterned end-states. Any present or future goal which takes precedence over the historical record in determining a just distribution of holdings constitutes a non-historical competing principle of distributive justice. Nozick's "Lockean proviso" is just such a principle and so, Nozick's protests notwithstanding, the theory of just acquisition in Nozick represents a departure from the purely historical theory of distributive justice that he believes ought to govern transfers of ownerships. An historical principle may supply a necessary condition of ownership, according to Nozick, but not a sufficient one.

B

While Nozick's theory of justice in acquisition combines elements of history and teleology, Steiner's theory involves, in contrast, a wholesale departure from the exclusively historical principle that he invokes for either the transfer of previously owned objects or the manufacture of new objects from previously owned objects. And this is because Steiner considers any historical definition of appropriative rights to be erroneous in two ways. First, it is inconceivable, as it presupposes gross contradictions and second, it generates what, according to Steiner's criteria, constitutes an incoherent set of rights. Let us consider these indictments in the above order.

Steiner correctly delineates the historical entitlement theory as affixing ownership rights in produced things as a result of their creation by someone from things owned by him. The newly synthesized object, then, is the product of the use made by the producer of entities to which he alone had title. Hence, this synthetic product is his, as well. He *deserves* this synthetic product because its constituent elements were his initially. And how did he become the rightful owner of these elements according to the historical entitlement view? Well, either he was voluntarily given them by their previous rightful owners or he was the owner of their parts and the catalytic agent that combined them into new wholes. Steiner's justification of current manufactured entitlements is always in terms of previous ownership and productive agency. However, this leaves unsettled the process by which entitlements to unowned objects can arise, for such objects are undeserved by anyone since no one had antecedently owned them. This suggests that Steiner at least implicitly endorses a principle of desert founded in prior ownership. Obviously such a principle cannot generate entitlements to unowned natural resources. To suggest that it can is to propose a blatant contradiction.

He does, however, seem to recommend another variant of the desert principle which equates "that which is deserved" with "that which is the exclusive result of one's past actions." But, this interpretation fares no better as a principle generative of appropriative rights, since the natural resources which are the subject of acquisitive interest are not the result (exclusive or otherwise) of anyone's past actions. Hence, no one can obtain, on this basis, initial title to them, and so they cannot be used. To imply that they can be so obtained is to subscribe to the thesis that what is unproduced is the result of production, another contradiction. It would seem, then, that entitlement theory cannot be applied to initial appropriation but extends only to the activities of manufacture and transfer. Thus, Steiner concurs with Nozick's implicit conception of entitlement theory as intrinsically restricted in its unqualified scope to the allocation of previously acquired goods.

Steiner has a second reason for collaborating in this indictment of entitlement theory. It is not related to the previous criticism of entitlement theory's inability to make use of a desert principle to provide the same foundational support to the problem of initial acquisition that Steiner believes it supplies to the question of subsequent ownership. Rather, it derives from the formal criterion of coherence that Steiner believes ought to apply to any theory of natural rights. Any set of natural rights, Steiner claims, must be universal to all beings with a shared human nature.[13] This property according to Steiner, implies another, coherence. Coherence, for Steiner, is exhibited by a set of rights only if the exercise of any individual's rights within that set cannot prevent the exercise of another's rights within that set.[14] That is, the universality characteristic of natural rights requires that any set of purportedly *natural* rights be compossibly and contemporaneously exercisable. An incoherent set is one in which there is the possibility that some individual might be constrained in the exercise of his rights by the exercise of someone else's rights. Such a set, therefore, would not permit the *universal* exercise of rights by persons and would imply, according to Steiner, the non-universality of such rights. Coherence is achievable only when the objects over which rights are assigned are allocated such that no rightful action can employ an object belonging to another. Such an allocation is one in which there is no ambiguity of ownership:

> A rule or set of rules assigning the possession or exclusive use of a particular physical object to a particular individual will, if universally adhered to exclude the possibility of any individual's actions interfering with those of another in respect of that object. A rule or set of rules assigning the possession or exclusive use of each particular physical object to particular individuals will, if universally adhered to, exclude the possibility of any individual's actions interfering with those of another in any respect.[15]

Having already jettisoned any historical grounds, i.e., production or prior ownership, for the determination of appropriative rights,[16] Steiner considers what sort of distributive principle would, at least, conform to the formal constraint of coherence that any set of natural rights must embody. Coherence, as manifested in a set of appropriative rights, would require that no acquisition of some unowned object, OU, by person A, would simultaneously exclude the possible exercise of a similar acquisitive right by some other person, B. When does the exercise of A's right of acquisition constitute a violation of B's equal right according to Steiner? Only when, he argues, A's appropriative activity strips B of the opportunity to acquire a "quantitatively and qualitatively similar bundle of natural objects."[17] And why is B entitled to the opportunity to acquire an equivalent collection of natural materials, according to Steiner? Given Steiner's claim, that no one has manufactured such materials implies that no one deserves them, he believes there is no logically possible standard of assignment that can be universally applied to all human beings other than equal distribution. To deprive persons of equivalent appropriative opportunities (i.e., opportunities to appropriate qualitatively and quantitatively equivalent bundles of goods) would imply a baseless inequality of desert in the determination of the rights to unproduced objects. To prevent some person, A, from access to a bundle of virginal goods equivalent to those to which all other persons B . . . N have access is, according to Steiner, to deny equal appropriative rights to all and, therefore, to advocate a non-universal set of appropriative rights. And, therefore, according to Steiner, the class of such rights would constitute an incoherent set of *natural* or *human* rights because the rights of those with access to more would deny the exercise of equivalent rights by others. Thus, the only set of appropriative rights which conforms to the standard of coherence is one which distributes to each individual "an equal share of the basic non-human means of production."[18] Such a set obviously contravenes the historical conception of distributive justice, and implies an end-state, egalitarian principle. Steiner argues that a historical conception can only be meaningfully realized once an initial distribution embodying this teleological, egalitarian standard has been made. Therefore, he concludes, the Nozickian historical entitlement theory cannot be coherently extrapolated to all spheres of human activity. Only where the issue of initial ownership has been resolved by the application of an egalitarian distributive principle will the subsequent application of historical criteria "preserve the justice" incorporated within that original allocation. For Steiner, historical standards can never coherently determine an initial division of virginal resources.

Thus, both Nozick and Steiner reject the exclusive application of historical principles in the determination of how initial shares of natural resources are to be allocated to a given population. This rejection (which is only partial in Nozick's case), stands in sharp contrast to their enthusiastic adoption of the historical principle of voluntary transfer to identify the present legitimate division of previously allocated objects. In the next part I will analyze the reasons given by each philosopher in defense of his antithetical treatment of these two areas of distributive concern.

II

In contrast to Nozick and Steiner I believe that the conceptual barriers alleged by them to preclude the unqualified extension of historical standards of distribution to the sphere of initial acquisition of natural non-human objects are weak. Consequently, I will maintain that the removal of those barriers suggests that historical principle of distributive justice can, without qualification, be extended to the sphere of appropriative rights. I will *not* argue that the historical entitlement view can be supplied with suitable foundations. I will only maintain that *if* it can, then it may be comprehensively applied to all issues affecting distributive justice.

In order to grasp why the Nozick-Steiner historical view has a more extensive scope than has been claimed for it by its two proponents, the defects in their arguments against its application to the appropriative arena must be delineated.

A

As mentioned, Nozick rejects the use of historical criteria to determine initial ownership for two reasons. The first is that virginal resources are, *ex hypothesi*, no one's and so, the principle of title transfer which is properly employed to determine the legitimate owner of present holdings cannot be applied here. The mere mixture of one's efforts with a virginal resource does not imply that the resultant object is the *exclusive* product of one's labor. Nozick argues that, at best, one has only *added value* to that which already has an intrinsic natural value. Hence, if it is maintained that in matters of initial appropriation one ought to own only that which is the exclusive product of one's labors, then it would follow that one is entitled only to the value added to the formerly virginal resource. The virginal component of the labor-modified-resource cannot, on historical grounds, be assigned to anyone. Labor, then, cannot entitle one to comprehensive property rights in objects.

A second reason for the rejection of a purely historical principle of distributive justice is that the appropriation of previously unowned objects may worsen the condition of others by depriving them of their opportunity to utilize those objects.

Let us examine his first argument. Nozick seems to be saying that either (1) we are entitled to something because a legitimate title to it had been previously transferred to us, or (2) because it was the exclusive product of our efforts, or (3) because it was the exclusive outcome of an admixture of our effort and objects to which we had title. Since labor-modified-formerly-virginal-objects fit none of these categories they either cannot be owned at all—which would imply that there can never be legitimate forms of ownership, as all objects have a virginal component—or ownership in them must be obtained, at least in part, according to some other principle. But, this other principle, identified by Nozick as the Lockean proviso, cannot, once applied, be restricted in its application to virginal resources, for all manufactured objects are in part virginal. All of them are merely modified natural objects. Therefore, all of them are, in part, not the exclusive product of human effort. If title cannot be assigned, in the first instance, only on the basis of "what was done by someone," why should it be assigned in successive instances only on the basis of "what was done by someone"? If the initial application of labor to a natural resource is insufficient to secure title to it, in spite of the "improved" condition of the modified resource, then subsequent inputs of labor to that resource are likewise insufficient to convey ownership. For neither the initial nor subsequent applications of labor to the resource make the resultant product the *exclusive* result of human effort. And so, if history (i.e., labor) must be abandoned as the sole criterion of ownership in the case of appropriation, due to the virginal trace that remains in the extracted resource, then it must be abandoned in all other cases as well because that trace can never be expunged from manufactured objects.

Moreover, if, as Nozick maintains in his second argument, "human welfare" (as defined by Nozick's Lockean proviso) must be added as a supplementary teleological principle of distribution to the historical one of "labor admixture" (in part because of the absence of a "purely produced object" at the level of appropriation), then the same supplementation is warranted at subsequent stages of production and transfer. Nozick's abandonment of history as a sufficient condition for initial acquisition implies that he must reject its sufficiency for the same reason in all matters affecting the subsequent distribution of objects.

Is Nozick, then logically required to reject altogether the historical theory of distributive justice? No. He is left with this unfortunate consequence only if he persists in defending the spurious theory of value (i.e., utility, not price) which underlies his explicit rejection of a purely historical theory at the appropriative level. That theory of value implies that the "value" (i.e., utility or usefulness) of manufactured objects can be bifurcated into natural and created components. The underlying normative principle which Nozick uses to determine initial ownership is one ought to own that, and only that, which one produces. It then follows that one is entitled only to the created value component of the object, not to its whole value. In opposition to Nozick, I would maintain that the *whole* of a good's value or utility (but not its price, or exchange value) is due to the efforts of the producer. For while any fossil fuel, for example, is of use to someone who desires to obtain its benefits once it has been (1) discovered, (2) extracted from the earth, and (3) processed for employment, the same material has no use value whatever so long as it remains undiscovered, unextracted, and unprocessed. While *discovered* resources may be of value to miners and a *mined* resource may be of value to producers of energy and a *refined* resource may be of value to consumers of energy, any resource which lies undiscovered at time *t* has *no* value (is of no use) to anyone at time *t*. Its subsequent utility, its accessibility to miners, derives from its discovery and that discovery is the product of human efforts, not of natural circumstance. Similarly its utility to refiners derives from its having been mined. Only a once virginal object already transformed in some way to meet some human desire has value to the "desirer." Bereft of such a transformation it is, at that time, without any utility. Hence, the transformer has produced the whole of its value by modifying it so that it can fulfill some human purpose. Therefore, we can argue, that, given a set of human wants, only human labor makes an object useful (able to satisfy those wants) and so, invests it with whatever utility it has. Original titles, are, then, in Nozick's own "improvement" criterion, completely and uniquely ascribable to human labor, to what has been done, and can therefore, be assigned according to historical principles. But if initial ownership is legitimized on the basis of productive effort, and only on such a basis, then the legitimacy of subsequent transfers of ownership can be determined only after an examination of the legitimacy of the previous titles extending backward in time to the moment of initial acquisition. Thus, historical entitlement principles are appropriately used without the supplementation of teleological ones to determine the justice of transfers, if and only if, they may be used to analyze the justice of initial acquisitions as indicated by the productive contribution of the acquirer without the supplementation of teleological ones. The historical entitlement principle, then, is both the necessary and sufficient determinant of *all* questions of distributive justice or of none of them. Nozick's attempt to make such principles necessary and sufficient at the level of transfer, but necessary only at the point of original acquisition is manifestly inconsistent.

Nozick could counter-argue that while labor is the only element that makes a thing useful (prepares an object for human use), labor cannot create the virginal material of which it is comprised and hence, while the whole utility of the thing is attributable to labor, its matter is not. But, what sort of conclusion could be drawn from this analysis? He might wish to conclude that the entire value of the manufactured object as well as the manufactured aspect of the object, ought to belong to the producer of it, while the object's virginal matter should be the collective possession of all mankind. However if this virginal component has been produced by no one and if things ought to belong only to those who have produced them, then on what basis should the unproduced aspect of objects be mankind's communal property? Mankind, after all, never produced this virginal component and, therefore, would be as unentitled to this component collectively as it is individually. Moreover, how can the created and uncreated aspects of an object be physically separated so that their separate owners can simultaneously exercise rights of use and disposition over them? The difficulties of physically transporting the Venus de Milo's form without contemporaneously moving her marble matter are obvious. Moreover, similar problems would arise for any attempt to separate the ownership of a thing's utility from the ownership of the thing itself.

B

Steiner's departure from historical principle at the acquisitive level stems from reasons which are similar to Nozick's in some respects but differ in others. Steiner argues that one is not entitled to use an object without prior ownership of it (or without the owner's consent) or without having produced it. In the case of virginal objects these criteria would seem to effectively exclude any initial use whatever and, therefore, to preclude the very possibility of legitimate appropriation. But, this, Steiner implies, is absurd and, therefore, he concludes that the previous ownership and production criteria are applicable only at the level of manufacture and transfer, not at the level or original acquisition. At the initial level another principle which incorporates the coherence requirement embodied in all rights claims must be found. Steiner claims to have discovered it and finds that it is teleological and egalitarian in nature. Thus, he substitutes equality for Nozick's Lockean proviso at the appropriation level.

In this section I will criticize Steiner's threefold argument against a historical basis for determining the initial ownership of unowned objects, that is, against making an historical condition like labor either a necessary or sufficient ground for ownership. First, in subsection (1), I will show that his contention that ownership must precede usage is false. Second, in section (2) I will contest his claim that if an object is not the product of human effort its ownership must not be determined by historical criteria (labor, first possession, etc.), but by the prior application of some distributive rule. I will dispute this claim partially by showing that, in this view, the right of self-ownership cannot be the

self-evident moral axiom that Steiner believes it to be. Finally, I will oppose Steiner's claim that the rejection of historical grounds for initial
acquisition requires the adoption of an egalitarian distribution of
virginal resources, if that distribution is to result in a coherent assignment of property rights.[19]

1. Of the two grounds, ownership or production, the former is more
fundamental according to Steiner, since an object produced by you is
only yours if the constituents from which it was made were yours. If we
can refute the claim, then, that ownership must precede use, Steiner's
rejection of *historical* entitlement will have been made less plausible. To
refute it we must first explain its basis in Steiner's philosophy.

Steiner derives the "ownership-determines-rights-of-use" criterion
from the formal property of coherence that, he insists, all sets of
human rights must embody. If a set of rights is so constituted that its
members cannot be compossibly and, therefore, contemporaneously
exercised,[20] then that set cannot be universally enjoyed. But a set of
rights which cannot be enjoyed by all persons, is not a set of human
rights. It is rather, a collection of privileges. As rights define classes of
permissible actions and as actions are always uses of objects, then a set
of rights which can be compossibly exercised will consist of assignments of the members of a set of mutually exclusive objects to the constituents of a set of mutually exclusive users of objects. Ambiguities of
ownership might entitle several people to take the same action with
respect to the same object at the same time, an existential impossibility.
The exercise by one of these people of his right will simultaneously
constitute the illegitimate prevention of another's exercise of his rights
within that same set. To avoid such a conflict all human rights must be
compossibly and contemporaneously exercisable and, therefore, must
include mutually exclusive assignments of property titles. Once such
titles have been allocated the coherence or compossibility of the set is
preserved only by observing historical principles in the matters of object modification and title transfer. That is, prior ownership must be
the exclusive determinant of primary rights of use. But, prior ownership cannot be used to determine initial ownership and, therefore,
argues Steiner, it must be abandoned as a distributive principle at the
appropriative level.

This argument ignores a rather important distinction. It is true that
if persons, x, and, y, have an equal right or title to some object O, then
the set, SR, of rights, xRO and yRO, is not what Steiner would call a
logically compossible set. But if neither x nor y nor anyone else have a

right to O, then x's use of O is not a violation of any right of y's, nor is y's use of O a violation of x's right. Now, having the use of an object is distinguishable from having title to it. If anyone may use O and no one, as yet, has title to it, then no one's use of O constitutes an intrusion upon someone else's rights. Therefore, any human being may be permitted the use of any elements within some set of unowned objects, SOU, without giving rise to violations of human or natural rights. This, of course, does not preclude the non-compossibility of the set of use opportunities. That is, the exercise by someone, x, of a use opportunity over objects OU_n at t_i will exclude the *exercise* of an equal opportunity by others over such OU_n at t_i. However, Steiner cannot argue that a set of use opportunities must be compossibly exercisable in the same way that rights must be, because of the following. Opportunities of use do not require an individual entitlement to some thing or bundle of things. That is, while having title requires an exclusivity of use rights over some set of things by someone, the use of a thing does not necessarily require having a title to it (i.e., an unhindered opportunity to use is a necessary condition of entitlement, but entitlement is not—for example, in the case of a usufruct—a necessary condition of use, etc.). Permissible use requires only that no one else have some prior entitlement to it (or that, if the object is owned, the owner has given his consent to its employment by another). Hence, opportunities to use some class of objects do not have to be simultaneously exercisable by all persons as do rights or entitlements to objects. No other person's title to something is violated by the exercise of an opportunity to use it, when that object is unowned. Therefore, while ownership does provide one sort of justification for use opportunities it does not provide the only justification for use, as in the case of unowned entities. While Steiner believes that titles of ownership must be assigned as a precondition of use, we have shown this not to be so. Rather the exercise of use opportunities can form the basis for a subsequent exclusive title to objects. And so, exclusive title can have a historical basis.

2. Steiner's other reason for rejecting a historical foundation for the initial acquisition of that which is unowned is that the justification for the ownership and hence, use of manufactured objects is production. But virginal resources are unproduced and, therefore, unowned. Hence, no one can be entitled to use some set of virginal resources, since all such sets have not been produced by anyone. And so some formula fairly distributing the titles to such objects must be found in order to enable human beings to use them.

Now, this other argument by Steiner proves too much. For if production is a necessary and sufficient normative condition for the initial ownership and, hence, subsequent use of objects, then it follows that nothing at all ought to be owned by anyone including one's own body. And Steiner considers the right to one's own body to be normatively uncontroversial.[21] In the first place, as no one has produced his own body, no one ought to have a title to it. Against this conclusion it may be argued that since your parents produced and so have rightful title to you, they can transfer to you the ownership of yourself. However, two considerations prevail against this counter argument. First, your parents may transfer their title to you only if such title was originally theirs. But, it could be theirs only if the means by which they produced you were originally owned by them, i.e., only if their parents have made them self-owners. And this, in turn, is only possible if their parents were self-owners. Clearly the problem here is infinitely regressive unless a process of legitimate self-ownership has been generated by an unprocreated self-owner like Locke's God. Steiner's own conception of an inalienable right of self-ownership, then, collapses under the weight of the argument that he wields against a production based initial distribution of natural resources.

Moreover, if we apply the conclusion of that argument, according to which those things that are neither legitimately owned nor self-produced ought to be equally divided among persons, then it would follow that entitlement to people and their characteristics ought to be allocated similarly.[22] And as these are not in fact equally distributed, some means must be found of doing so. In the case of persons, if I and all my fellows are to have an equal right to one another, then this must mean that each of us must have title to an equal portion of every other human being, and this implies that each person must secure the consent of all titleholders in order to employ himself in ways preferred by him. However, if the egalitarian distribution is to be made with regard to human characteristics rather than to entire human beings, the means by which those characteristics are to be equally distributed are inscrutable. If I haven't the mean I.Q. of the world's population, it would seem that I should have, *à la* Steiner, a right to employ the intelligence of those who do. But suppose there are not enough average intellects to go around? And what of those persons whose intellects exceed the mean? How are we to divide and distribute their cognitive capacities? Of course, most bodily features cannot be transmitted to another's control and, hence, Steiner's implied personal egalitarianism cannot, even through dismemberment and transplantation, be realized.

3. This brings us to the denouement of Steiner's argument, his egalitarian analysis of appropriative rights to non-human objects. Appropriative rights, Steiner suggests,[23] must conform to the principle of coherence. Now, the principle of coherence states that a set of rights must be compossibly exercisable. This means that the actions that they legitimatize must be compossible, i.e., it must be impossible for a legitimate action A_x to ever contemporaneously interfere with any other legitimate action, A_y. But such a rights set will be coherent, if and only if, the objects which rights-bearers may legitimately employ in any of their acts are not, contemporaneously, the exclusive property of two different persons. Hence, internally coherent rights sets must be comprised of titles representing mutually exclusive linkages of owners and objects. It is this mutual exclusivity which preserves the logical compossibility i.e., the coherence of the set. At the appropriative level this requirement can be preserved by taking the set of all individuals, dividing all natural resources into separate bundles, and giving each person exclusive title to each of these bundles, making certain that no two persons or corporate bodies of persons are given exclusive title to the same object or group of objects. But, Steiner mysteriously insists that the bundles of objects must be qualitatively and quantitatively similar when what we have shown is that coherence is determined not by these two but rather by (1) the distinctness of the bundles and (2) the exclusivity of their ownership, which factors together are necessary and sufficient to achieve compossibility. Contra Steiner, the bundles do not have to be qualitatively or quantitatively similar in order to preserve the coherence of the set of rights thereby generated. Furthermore, it is not even the case that every person has to be granted an entitlement to at least one object or bundle order to maintain the coherence of the set. For it is the mutual exclusivity of ownership which prevents contemporaneous use rights from being assigned over the same object, not universality of property allocation.

The coherence requirement, then, does not by itself imply Steiner's egalitarianism. Rather, the basis for this egalitarianism is merely a Lockean vestige. But the theistic justification for its introduction in the *Second Treatise* in the form of Locke's "enough and as good" criterion is wholly missing in Steiner's account and, therefore, Steiner has no independent basis for its advocacy. Moreover, if the coherency requirement did entail an egalitarianism of goods at the level of initial appropriation then subsequent rights of ownership should also have to conform to the egalitarian principle in order to be coherently exercised. Egalitarianism could not be restricted to initial acquisition but would have to extend to successive transfers of ownership. Thus, Steiner would have to abandon the historical entitlement theory altogether.

If the unequal distribution of natural resources is consistent with Steiner's coherency standard for rights and if a general opportunity to use unowned objects does not have to embody the compossibility requirement, then a historically based appropriative principle can be utilized to establish initial titles to virginal resources. X's original productive use of unowned object OU_1 prevents no other person, y, from using either unowned objects OU_n or objects, O_n, to which y had previously acquired legitimate title.

Conclusion

Nozick and Steiner have both suggested that while the historical entitlement principle of distributive justice can appropriately govern the allocation of owned goods, there are conceptual impediments to its application to the realm of unowned natural resources. We have responded to this allegation first by showing that those impediments are illusory and second, by pointing out that if historical bases of distributive justice are inapplicable to the allocation of previously unowned objects, they fail as well to provide sufficient criteria for the distribution of owned objects.

Finally, if, as I have suggested, historical principles can be extended to the arena of appropriative activity the historical-entitlement thesis is comprehensively applicable to matters of distributive justice in a way not envisioned by either of its contemporary proponents. Whether this thesis can be justified as a principle of distributive justice by its spokesmen so as to exclude its teleological competitors is another matter altogether, a matter, one senses, the difficulties of which are far greater than the "second-order" issues analyzed in this paper.

Notes

1. Robert Nozick, *Anarchy, State, and Utopia* (New York: Basic Books, 1975).
2. Hillel Steiner, "The Natural Right to the Means of Production," *Philosophical Quarterly* 27 (1977): pp. 41-49; idem, "The Structure of a Set of Compossible Rights" 74 (1977): 767-75.
3. Nozick, *Anarchy, State, and Utopia*, p. 155.
4. Nozick's commitment to a purely historical theory of justice in transfer, is not quite as undiluted as Steiner's. Nozick, as will be explained, holds that if the appropriation of previously unowned, natural objects should worsen the condition of others some compensation is due the adversely affected parties from the appropriator. Hence, if such *natural* (i.e., uncreated) objects are so amassed by transfer as to

worsen the condition of others, that transfer can only be effected if compensation is paid to those others. But this dilution of a purely historical principle of justice in transfer with a competing "welfare" criterion is limited to cases where in the welfare of others is worsened by a diminution of their potential liberty in the use of objects. Nozick denies that his "proviso" represents a departure from a consistently historical treatment of distributive justice, ibid. pp. 177, 181, 345. However, his defense of this seems rather thin, ibid., 174-82.

5. Ibid., pp. 174-75.
6. Ibid., p. 175.
7. Ibid., p. 175.
8. Ibid., p. 178.
9. Ibid., pp. 175-78.
10. Ibid., p. 178.
11. Ibid., pp. 177, 181, 345.
12. Ibid., p. 181.
13. Steiner, "The Natural Right to the Means of Production," p. 42.
14. Ibid.
15. Ibid.
16. Ibid., p. 44.
17. Ibid., p. 43.
18. Ibid., p. 49.
19. I will not pursue Steiner's subsequent modification of his egalitarianism in "Liberty and Equality," *Political Studies* 29 (1981). For an excellent discussion of Steiner's subsequent "contractarianism" see Eric Mack, "Distributive Justice and the Tensions of Lockeanism" in *Social Philosophy and Policy* 1 (1983).
20. See Steiner, "The Structure of a Set of Compossible Rights," pp. 767-75.
21. Ibid., p. 44.
22. A similar point is made by Fred D. Miller, Jr., in "The Natural Right to Private Property," in *The Libertarian Reader*, Tibor R. Machan, ed. (Totowa, N.J.: Rowman & Littlefield), pp. 284-85.
23. Steiner, "The Structure of a Set of Compossible Rights," p. 47.

Part 3

Political Science

19

The Role of Government

Randall G. Holcombe

The scholarship of Murray Rothbard has traversed amazing breadth, but he is surely best known for his defense of individual liberty against violation by the government. Most readers of this volume will be familiar with Rothbard's position that in an ideal world governments would not exist. His arguments that we should not have governments are persuasive, and he has supported his views from a number of different angles. This essay will use Rothbard's ideas as a springboard to examine the role of government within a society.

The view that governments should not exist can be defended on several grounds, and indeed Rothbard has done so. One might argue that governments are inefficient and that our well-being would be enhanced without them, but one might also argue that the activities of governments are unethical. Rothbard has eloquently defended both views. Rothbard's work also lends insight into the question of why governments exist. His discussion of government has been so extensive that it provides a fertile foundation for further analysis.

This essay considers several questions about the existence of governments. First is the question about why governments actually do exist, but then are the questions about why and whether governments should exist. As already noted, Rothbard has argued against the existence of government for both ethical and efficiency reasons. Should government really be eliminated? The essay considers this question in closing, with a defense of the defenses of anarchy.

Why Government?

The question that heads this section could be interpreted in many ways. It might ask why governments do exist, or it might ask why governments should exist. As a subset of why governments should exist, one might look for ethical reasons as well as efficiency reasons. This section will discuss why governments do exist, and the two following sections will consider both equity and efficiency rationales for government.

The question of why governments do exist is essentially a historical one, and some insight on the question can be gained by considering Murray Rothbard's discussion about history from his introduction to his four volume treatise on American history, *Conceived in Liberty.* Rothbard states,

> I see history as centrally a race and conflict between "social power"—the productive consequence of voluntary interactions among men—and state power. In those eras in history when liberty—social power—has managed to race ahead of state power and control, the country and even mankind have flourished. In those eras when state power has managed to catch up with or surpass social power, mankind suffers and declines.
>
> For decades, American historians have quarreled about "conflict" or "consensus" as the guiding *leitmotif* of the American past. Clearly, I belong to the "conflict" rather than the "consensus" camp, with the proviso that I see the central conflict as not between classes (social or economic), or between ideologies, but between Power and Liberty, State and Society.[1]

Nobody familiar with Rothbard's work will be surprised at the conflict that Rothbard sees between individual liberty and the existence of the state. It is interesting, however, to see that Rothbard views this as the central theme of history in general. Using this notion as a starting point, one might want to probe the nature of this conflict a bit further.

One can refer to the state in the abstract, but the power that Rothbard refers to as the state is actually a group of individuals, of necessity a minority, that run the government. Rothbard notes,

> [S]ince a majority cannot live parasitically off a minority without the economy and the social system breaking down very quickly, and since the majority can never act permanently by itself but must always be led by an oligarchy, every state will subsist by plundering the majority in behalf of a ruling minority. A further reason for the inevitability of minority rule is the pervasive fact of the division of labor: the majority of the public must spend most of its time going about the business of making a living. Hence the actual rule of the state must be left to full-time professionals who are necessarily a minority of the society.[2]

In the division of labor, most individuals will be engaged in produc-ing goods and services for social consumption, but in an economy productive enough that an individual can produce more than enough for bare sustenance, there will be some surplus above the subsistence level that others could consume. For example, those producing goods and services could provide some of that surplus to those in government in exchange for governance.

This gets slightly ahead of the story, however, for what if there were no government? Hobbes conjectured that life would be nasty, brutish, and short, as the more powerful individuals could rob the less powerful of any surplus they produced, and perhaps more, which would ulti-mately cost them their lives. Seen in this light, a role for government naturally emerges. The government protects the rights of individuals in exchange for payment.

Throughout history this has been the actual role of government. In feudal times, most obviously, the feudal lord would protect peasants in exchange for a share of their production. There was not even the pre-tense that payment was to cover the costs of production of government. Rather, a simple economic exchange was made: tribute in exchange for protection. While this exchange is more obvious in the case of dictator-ships and kingdoms, it is the essence of all government. Citizens pay the government, and in exchange their rights are protected.

This idea is closely in line with Nozick's idea of the minimal state that serves the role of protecting individual rights.[3] But the argument here is not an abstract one about why governments might exist; in-stead, it is descriptive of governments in reality. Governments exist because most people, trying to make a living, cannot devote much time to protecting their rights. It is more efficient to pay tribute to a power-ful individual or group in exchange for protection. In reality, govern-ments do exactly that.

This makes governments appear as institutions imposed on individ-uals from the outside, rather than being institutions chosen by the governed. Often this is the case, but there may be instances where individuals would choose to form governments to further their own in-terests. Rothbard has argued something along these lines about the formation of the government of the United State. Rothbard states,

> [T]he revolution was genuinely and enthusiastically supported by the great majority of the American population. It was a true people's war . . . American rebels certainly could not have con-cluded the first successful war of national libertarian in history . . . unless they had commanded the support of the American people.[4]

Thus, while Rothbard portrays the American revolution as a revolution against the British government, it was also a revolution in support of the independent government of the United States, and a revolution supported by the great majority of Americans.

The point here is that not all governments are foisted on unwilling citizens by some powerful ruling group. Governments might be chosen and desired by their citizens. But even the popularly chosen government of the United States is at its foundation an institution that exchanges protection for tribute. The government of the United States was formed to protect the colonists from the British, emphasizing the exchange of protection for tribute as the key feature in the origin of governments. Rothbard points out that of necessity there will be some ruling minority that will control every government. Even in a government that has a strong element of voluntary choice like that in the United States, the challenge is to design institutions so that the ruling minority has as limited an ability as possible to exploit the majority.[5]

The initial objective of this section was to explain why governments exist. Specific governments may exist because the governed desired them, as in the American case, or because some more powerful individuals conquered less powerful individuals and subjected the conquered to governance by the conquerors. Historically, the latter case is more common, but even this obscures the actual reason why governments of both types exist. Historically, governments have emerged to exchange tribute for protection.

Note the incentives on both sides of this government transaction. Citizens have the incentive to pay the government in order to have their rights protected, but governments too have the incentive to protect the rights of their citizens. Without this protection, the productive capacity of the government's citizens would be greatly diminished, which would also diminish the capacity of the government to collect its revenues. Governments may do many other things than protect rights, of course, such as redistribute income, produce goods and services, and even violate the rights of its citizens, but the actual origin of government is the exchange of protection for tribute.

The Ethics of Government

This essay has, up to this point, considered why in fact governments exist. The next question to consider is whether governments should exist. The present section will consider the issue from an ethical standpoint, considering the morality of government. The following section considers the question from an efficiency standpoint, asking whether a society actually is better off having a government.

It is interesting to note that libertarians have a wide range of opinions on the ethics of government. Ayn Rand and Robert Nozick both see roles for a limited government that protects the rights of individuals. This corresponds with the argument just made that real governments have actually emerged as protectors of rights in exchange for tribute. However, in Rand's view of limited government, the ideal government has a monopoly over the use of force, but is financed voluntarily.[6] James Buchanan, in a contractarian framework, sees the appropriate role of government to be whatever its citizens agree upon.[7]

Rothbard, in contrast, is a complete anarchist. The activities of government are simply unethical, as far are he is concerned. Rothbard argues,

> Taxation is theft, purely and simply, even though it is theft on a grand and colossal scale which no acknowledged criminals could hope to match. It is a compulsory seizure of the property of the State's inhabitants, or subjects.
>
> It would be an instructive exercise for the skeptical reader to try to frame a definition of taxation which does not *also* include theft. . . . If, then, taxation is compulsory, and is therefore indistinguishable from theft, it follows that the state, which subsists on taxation, is a vast criminal organization, far more formidable and successful than any "private" mafia in history. Furthermore, it should be considered criminal not only according to the theory of crime and property rights as set forth in this book, but *even* according to the common apprehension of mankind, which always considers theft to be a crime. [original emphasis][8]

One might add that institutions such as the military draft make government activities include slavery as well as theft. And some might even argue that government income redistribution, by forcing some to work for the benefit of others, is slavery.[9]

One might speculate in a hypothetical framework about an ideal government in the Randian sense that collected payments voluntarily, but in the real world one would be hard-pressed to cite an example of a government funded by voluntary contributions. Such speculation would lead too far afield for the present essay; the point here is that Rothbard views the financing activities of government to be immoral.

Rothbard's critique of the ethics of government is not limited to government's methods of finance, however. He also objects to the government's acquisition of monopoly power by force. He cites instances of enforced monopoly over police protection, the judiciary, money creation, postal services, and more.[10] Clearly, Rothbard, unlike Nozick and Rand, sees any exercise of what is normally thought of as government power to be unethical. From an ethical standpoint, complete anarchy is what Rothbard views as the ideal role of the state.

Rather than evaluate Rothbard's ethical arguments in detail, this essay will consider the question whether Rothbard's ethically ideal state of anarchy would be practically feasible. In other words, what are the implications for economic efficiency in a world of anarchy? Hobbes envisioned life under anarchy as nasty, brutish, and short, but Rothbard has eloquently argued otherwise.

Economic Efficiency and the Role of Government

One of Rothbard's many significant contributions to libertarian thought is his persuasive argument that in the absence of government the market would be able to provide all of the goods and services presently provided by government, and would be able to do so more efficiently. In response to those who argue that government production of some goods and services is necessary if they are to be produced at all, Rothbard has consistently answered that "every single one of the services supplied by government has been, in the past, successfully furnished by private enterprise."[11] Rothbard's most complete argument along these lines is found in his 1973 book, *For a New Liberty*.[12]

Rothbard's *For a New Liberty* and *The Ethics of Liberty* are complementary works. While *The Ethics of Liberty* sets out a libertarian ethical framework and argues against the activities of government from an ethical base, *For a New Liberty* argues more from a practical standpoint, that the activities of government would be better performed in the private sector anyway. Combining the two lines of argument, one should oppose the activities of government because they are unethical, and one should oppose the activities of government because they would be more efficiently performed in the private sector. There are both ethical and efficiency reasons for abolishing government.

Some alternatives to government are more easily pictured than others. For example, it is relatively easy to picture the private sector producing roads than national defense. After all, toll roads and toll bridges are in use today, although typically they are produced by the government. It requires little imagination to see that were it not for such a large amount of competition from freely accessed government roads, there would be a great incentive for private firms to produce bridges and turnpikes.

What about local travel where it is more difficult to charge tolls? Even today, builders of subdivisions build their own roads to provide access to homes in the subdivisions. Typically, they are then deeded over to the local government at no charge because the government will then maintain them using tax revenues. It is not hard to see, though, that if the government did not undertake this activity, the subdivision residents themselves would have an incentive to maintain the roads that provide access to their property. Likewise, today owners of shopping centers provide access roads and free parking for patrons (as opposed to metered parking that is often provided by governments). It is relatively easy to envision the private sector taking over the provision of roads.

What about police protection? Even today, most police services are provided by private services who protect stores, manufacturing facilities, and other commercial establishments. Often wealthy neighborhoods will hire their own police patrols in addition to the government provided protection. Again, it is easy to see that individuals could contract with a private policy organization in the absence of governmental provision, if only because it is frequently done today.

What about courts? Rothbard convincingly argues that private courts would be a superior replacement for the government's current legal system. Rothbard argues that most law is derived from common law, which would be the essence of a private legal system. Private arbitration would replace state courts, and Rothbard argues that not only would it be possible in concept, but that there are historical cases that show the feasibility and superiority of a legal system unencumbered by government. The interested reader should read Rothbard's discussion in its entirety.[13] His arguments are persuasive.

What about national defense? Rothbard seems to become more creative and persuasive the more difficult the issue, and he makes a convincing argument that the nation would be better defended without a government at all.[14] It is easy to see that if the entire world had no governments there would be no reason for national defense, because there would be no countries to attack each other. Rothbard is also realistic enough to see that if a subset of the United States decided to abolish all government authority within its borders, the U.S. government would quickly assert its authority. But what if a large area—say, the United States—decided just to do away with all governments? How would this governmentless area protect itself against foreign aggressors?

Rothbard first questions whether foreign countries would want to attack such an area. What quarrel could foreign countries possibly have with such a governmentless area? But even if some foreign country wanted to take over the governmentless area, Rothbard argues that it would be more difficult to take over the area without a government than if a government were in place.

With a government one needs only to take over the government's leaders and force them to surrender in the name of all of the government's citizens. But with no government to surrender, a foreign aggressor would have to force every individual to surrender, which would be a far more formidable task than simply overpowering the existing government. Rothbard's argument is persuasive, for it is difficult to imagine how one would take over a country if nobody were empowered to surrender in the name of the group. Rothbard's original argument is worth reading.

Rothbard's *For a New Liberty* is interesting reading because it makes complete anarchy sound so reasonable as a way of improving the quality of life. Still, one must be skeptical of the arguments, because while one could imagine a better life in a world without government, one could also imagine the Soviets, bent on conquest, visiting the shores of a society the day after it abolished its government. It is one thing to argue that Rothbard's ideas are interesting, challenging, and persuasive. It is yet another to argue that the world should be patterned along the anarchistic lines envisioned by Rothbard. Yet there is good reason for using Rothbard's vision of the world, not as an immediate replacement for the present one, but as a model to move toward. Rothbard argues that the world would be a better place without government. The next section defends Rothbard's defense of anarchy.

In Defense of Defenses of Anarchy

As noted earlier, libertarians are not in agreement on the appropriate role of government in a society. Rothbard is an anarchist, but others, such as Rand and Nozick, see a role for a limited government to protect individual rights. Some libertarians see such a role for government that they have gone so far as to form a libertarian political party.[15] Should Rothbard's extreme anarchy be accepted? Is it even feasible? Or is it more reasonable to accept the inevitability and even desirability of a limited government to protect the rights of individuals? This section will defend Rothbard's position of extreme anarchy as a reasonable goal, regardless of whether it is attainable. This defense will be laid out in several steps.

The Government is Too Big

The first step, which would have been a controversial proposition in the 1960s, is hardly controversial in the 1980s. The government is too big, and the nation's citizens would be better off with less of it. This is popularly expressed in the differences in political philosophy behind the Reagan government in the 1980s versus the Kennedy-Johnson government of the 1960s, and is finding its way more and more into the academic literature and in economics as well.

Buchanan has noted that economists are more committed to analyzing resources allocation problems in the public sector than was the case in the 1950s and 1960s.[16] Armen Alchian has questioned the property rights system implied in government ownership,[17] Harold Demsetz has questioned the regulation of natural monopolies,[18] and the Chicago school of regulation, led by George Stigler,[19] has argued that regulation in general is controlled by special interests and should not be expected to further the general public interest. These are but a few of many examples that could be cited of academic research arguing that the role of government in the economy should be reduced.

Rothbard's *For a New Liberty* might be compared with Milton Friedman's *Capitalism and Freedom*,[20] but whereas Friedman argues that the scope of government should be reduced, Rothbard argues that it should be abolished altogether. Both agree about the desirable direction of change, but Friedman, while often viewed as an extremist, looks moderate in comparison to Rothbard's more extreme views. The point here is that there is a widespread belief in popular, political and academic circles, that the role of government should be reduced. But there is the question about whether the more moderate stance of Friedman is more reasonable than Rothbard's extreme views.

What is Possible?

The next step in the argument is to note that while there is a widespread belief that less government would be desirable, one can only speculate on the likely results of any intended reform. There is still debate on the likely effects of Friedman's proposed voucher system more than two decades after it was originally proposed. Rothbard argues that the nation would be better off relying exclusively on private education, and the same goes for roads, courts, police, and everything else. How these institutions would work in practice in the modern world must be a matter of speculation, since they do not currently exist as Rothbard envisions them.

Are Rothbard's anarchistic ideas feasible, or are they just too im-practical? To consider this question, imagine a person who has no knowl-edge of the way in which a market economy works, and then imagine trying to propose to that person that a market economy be established to replace whatever economic institutions the person is familiar with. One would argue that individuals try to sell the resources at their com-mand for as much as they can get for them and try to buy the most val-uable resources possible at the lowest possible price. Exchange is facil-itated by organized markets and a medium of exchange, and the result is that each individual, when pursuing his own self-interest, is led as if by an invisible hand to pursue the best interest of the whole society.

Considering all of the complications of the real world, such a story sounds farfetched. It sounds so farfetched, in fact, that even though everyone can see market economies in operation in the modern world, many nations have nevertheless made the collective choice to move away from market allocation toward some more rational form of na-tional economic planning, and intellectuals often argue the theoretical superiority of centrally planned economies. The results of such moves away from the market allocation and the pitfalls of central planning are evident from real world cases, still there are people who seem to shut out the evidence to argue that the market system is simply not a feasible way to allocate resources in the complex world of the twentieth century.

Most readers of this volume will be sympathetic to the idea that the market does allocate resources efficiently, even though the abstract idea of market allocation sounds so simple as to appear simplistic and unrealistic to many. Now return to the question about the feasibility of abolishing government altogether. Rothbard's proposals are so simple that they may also appear simplistic and unrealistic, but really he is ar-guing nothing more than that the market should be allowed to allocate all resources. And while nothing is perfect, including the market, one would be hard-pressed to point out an actual real world case where when things are done both by the market and the government, the government turns out to be more efficient. In the real world, govern-ments have often responded to potential problems that have been fore-seen. But it is difficult to think of examples where the government has intervened to solve an existing problem, and where the solution imposed by government was superior to the original problem. In contrast, there are numerous instances where government allocation of resources has been shown to be inferior to the market.[21]

Perhaps Rothbard's ideas of orderly anarchy are feasible after all. There is certainly no direct evidence that they are not, and for every imagined problem with this type of orderly anarchy there is an imagined solution. Yes, the real world is complex, but this complexity seems to be the environment where the market organizes best. Perhaps the market system taken to its logical extreme where government is eliminated altogether really is feasible and desirable. Rothbard's critics have not proven otherwise. If this is the case, how should one choose between Rothbard's ideal work, Friedman's ideal world, or some other alternative? As is next argued, this is not the nature of the choice facing society.

Marginal Adjustment

Marginal analysis is the economist's stock in trade. Marginal changes are also, in reality, the way the world adjusts. If government as it stands is too big, then its size should be reduced, but in reality it would not even be possible to change overnight from the status quo to some individual's ideal world. Rather, change would necessarily have to be by degrees. Is the optimal government a minimal one like Friedman and Rand discuss, or is it a nonexistent one like Rothbard advocates? For practical purposes, the ideal end state is not as significant as the optimal direction of change.

In the 1960s people saw increased government involvement as the solution to many of the world's problems. Government grew over time. With hindsight, even some of the proponents of larger government saw that government did not solve the world's problems as well as its proponents had imagined. Now the solution is to move toward a smaller government. How much smaller? The change will necessarily be slow, and as long as the change brings about an improvement in the nation's well-being, the change is in the right direction. When the change is no longer an improvement, it has gone far enough. Because the changed final state of affairs must be at this point a hypothetical state of affairs, it is not really possible to say what ultimate outcome will prove to be most desirable.

This abstracts from the ethical arguments about government and considers only the pragmatic issues. But in reality, a reduction in government will come by degrees if it comes at all, and as long as the changes are beneficial, reduction should continue. When changes cease to be beneficial, they should stop. From a practical standpoint, it is not now relevant whether the process stops at Rothbard's ideal state, Friedman's ideal state, or at some other point. In reality, marginal changes will have to be made to seek the optimal state of affairs.

Anarchy: The Ultimate Solution to Smaller Government

The defense of anarchy up to this point has been that government is generally recognized as too large, so should be reduce. It is not really possible to identify ahead of time the ideal state of affairs, but it is not really necessary either, because adjustment to the ideal will be a marginal adjustment. At this point, Rothbard's proposals of orderly anarchy have much to recommend them because Rothbard's brand of anarchy is the ultimate solution to smaller government. Rothbard eloquently explains how it would be possible to do away with all governments, thus providing the logical end to the reduction of government, whether or not that end is practically attainable.

But as just noted, the practicality of the end is not an issue. By illustrating how it is possible, at least in principle, to replace all of the government's activities by market activities, Rothbard points reformers in the direction of less government. Regardless of whether such a world will ever exist in practice, the imaginative and persuasive arguments of anarchists such as Rothbard provide a valuable service by providing an intellectual foundation for the movement toward less government. There is nothing logically inconsistent with a free and wealthy society and the absence of government. This factor alone makes the work of anarchists such as Rothbard a valuable intellectual contribution.

Conclusion

This essay has covered much territory, but all within the general subject matter of the role of government in a society. The essay began by arguing that the fundamental transactions made by governments is the exchange of protection for tribute, and the government has the incentive to provide such protection so that its citizens can continue to be productive and therefore can continue to provide tribute. In reality, this is why governments exist. The next question addressed in the essay is why (and whether) governments should exist.

Rothbard advocates the elimination of government on two grounds. First, he argues that the activities of government are unethical. Second, he argues that all of the goods and services currently provided by governments could be more effectively provided by voluntary private organizations. Rothbard's arguments are interesting and at the same time compelling and persuasive. One always tends to view arguments advocating great change with skepticism, but Rothbard delivers his arguments with such clarity that even his most extreme ideas have an aura of reasonableness.

What in fact is the appropriate role of government in a society? Even libertarians are not in complete agreement, as some see a role for a limited government while others argue that governments should be eliminated altogether. But there is a consensus emerging among the general population in the 1980s that there is too much government involvement in the society.

In order to control government power, its foundations must be understood, and the beginning of this essay which argued that the most important transaction of government is the exchange of protection for tribute was an attempt to further that understanding. The essay went on to examine both ethical and efficiency reasons against government involvement in a society. Ideas such as these are always subject to discussion and debate, but even where there is disagreement one would hope that the ideas provide some food for thought, and ultimately, some motivation for constructive action.

The author gratefully acknowledges helpful comments from Don Boudreaux and Roger Garrison. Any shortcomings remain the responsibility of the author.

Notes

1. Murray N. Rothbard, Conceived in Liberty, vol. 1 (New Rochelle, N.Y.: Arlington House, 1975), p. 10.
2. Rothbard, Conceived in Liberty, vol. 3 (New Rochelle, N.Y.: Arlington House, 1976), p. 351.
3. Robert Nozick, Anarchy, State, and Utopia (New York: Basic Books, 1974).
4. Conceived in Liberty, vol. 3, p. 350.
5. For a model of this process as might be applicable to the U.S. case, see Randall G. Holcombe, "A Contractarian Model of the Decline in Classical Liberalism," Public Choice 35, no. 3 (1980): 260-74.
6. Ayn Rand, "The Nature of Government," in The Virtue of Selfishness (New York: Signet Books, 1964); idem, "Government Financing in a Free Society," in The Virtue of Selfishness (New York: Signet Books, 1964).
7. See James M. Buchanan, The Limits of Liberty (Chicago: University of Chicago Press, 1975).
8. Murray N. Rothbard, The Ethics of Liberty (Atlantic Highlands, N.J.: Humanities Press, 1982), pp. 162-63, 166.
9. In a well-written (if technical) critique of income redistribution, Martin Ricketts, "Tax Theory and Tax Policy," in Alan Peacock and Francesco Forte, eds., The Political Economy of Taxation (New York: St. Martin's Press, 1981), pp. 29-46, draws a parallel between government redistribution and taxation that will delight the critics of the so-called optimal tax literature in the economics journals.
10. The Ethics of Liberty, p. 162.
11. Murray N. Rothbard, "The Fallacy of the Public Sector," in Egalitarianism as a Revolt Against Nature and Other Essays (Washington, D.C.: Libertarian Review Press, 1974), p. 87.

12. Murray N. Rothbard, *For a New Liberty* (New York: Macmillan, 1973).

13. See *For a New Liberty*, pp. 234-47.

14. *For a New Liberty*, pp. 247-52.

15. Note, though, that this may be consistent with the ultimate goal of anarchy, if working within the political system to eliminate government is viewed as a legitimate activity. Rothbard, apparently, would agree, for while he has argued in *The Ethics of Liberty* that the government is unethical and in *For A New Liberty* that the government is inefficient, he has praised the formation of the American government in the American revolution in *Conceived in Liberty* as a vehicle for eliminating the oppressive rule of the British government.

16. James M. Buchanan, "Public Finance and Public Choice," *National Tax Journal* 28 (December 1975): 383-94.

17. Armen A. Alchian, "Some Economics of Property Rights," *IL Politico* 30, no. 4 (1965): 816-29.

18. Harold Demsetz, "Why Regulate Utilities?" *Journal of Law and Economics* 11 (1968): 55-65.

19. George J. Stigler, "The Theory of Economic Regulation," *Bell Journal of Economics and Management Science* 2 (Spring 1971): 1-10.

20. Milton Friedman, *Capitalism and Freedom* (Chicago: University of Chicago Press, 1962).

21. A small listing of economic studies along these lines would include Cotton M. Lindsay, "A Theory of Government Enterprise," *Journal of Political Economy* 84 (October 1976): 1061-77; David G. Davies, "The Efficiency of Public versus Private Firms: The Case of Australia's Two Airlines," *Journal of Law and Economics* 14 (April 1971): 149-65; W. Mark Crain and Asghar Zardkoohi, "A Test of the Property-Right Theory of the Firm: Water Utilities in the United States," *Journal of Law and Economics* 21 (October 1978): 395-408; and Roger Ahlbrandt, "Efficiency in the Provision of Fire Services," *Public Choice* 16 (Fall 1973): 1-15.

20

Caste and Class: The Rothbardian View of Governments and Markets

David Osterfeld

This paper will examine Professor Murray Rothbard's definitions of freedom and power. These definitions will be used to construct a formal model with which to analyze the operations of governments and markets. It will be shown that the model leads to the conclusion that markets result in classes while governments tend to produce castes. The paper will conclude by arguing that this model is a powerful explanatory and predictive device; that what one would expect to find if the model is correct is, in fact, what one tends to find.

Part I:
The Rothbardian Definitions of Power and Freedom

Professor Rothbard is a prolific writer. Practically all of his writing centers around, directly or indirectly, the concepts of power and freedom. In order to understand and assess the Rothbardian viewpoint, it is first necessary to examine what he means by these two terms. "Power" and "freedom" are defined in terms of *violent activities*. "Violence," according to Rothbard, is the direct physical interference, or the threat of such interference, against the person (assault) or property (theft) of another, including the appropriation of another's property under false pretenses (fraud).[1] Terms like "power" and "sovereignty," Rothbard makes clear, "are appropriate only to the *political* realm."[2] And "political-power terminology," he says, "should be applied only to those employing violence."[3] Conversely, "freedom" is defined as "a condition in which one's ownership rights in his own body and his legitimate material property are not invaded, are not aggressed against."[4] Freedom, he says, is the ability "to control what one owns."[5] It refers to the

283

"absence of molestation by other persons."[6] Crime, which is a particular subset of power, is seen as an "invasion by the use of violence, against a man's property and therefore against his liberty."[7] In brief, for Rothbard, "power" is defined solely in terms of the presence of violent activity; "freedom" is defined solely in terms of its absence.

Power

Professor Rothbard argues that since the free or unhampered market is nothing more than the nexus of voluntary exchanges, a market-grounded society would be one characterized by the absence of "coercion" or "political power," i.e., a society in which "the power of man over man" has been "eradicated."[8] Since Rothbard defines both "power" and "freedom" solely in terms of the presence or absence of violent activities, and the threat of such activities, he has been criticized by some for disposing of the question of power relations by means of a semantic sleight-of-hand. Warren J. Samuels's rather truculent critique of Rothbard is a good example of this line of thought.

While a society based on Rothbardian principles would be a "system without a state," Samuels says[9] it would not be a system without power relationships. For, he says, "power, coercion, and externalities . . . are ubiquitous." They exist in all social systems. "The anarchist ideal, contemplated in terms of strict or absolute autonomy, is impossible."[10] Thus, one can "solve" the problem of power in society only by arbitrarily defining it in terms of certain types of coercion but not others. It is only through such "selective perception of mutual coercion," Samuels maintains, "that the anarchist ideal is sensible—and that selectivity begs the critical issues."[11]

Rothbard's definition of power and freedom in terms of physical violence comes in for especially caustic criticism. "Concentration upon physical violence and obedience is an undue narrowing of the focus upon the full range of mutual coercion," he charges. Rothbard's "non-aggression axiom," the prohibition of any violence against the person or property of another, is "misleading and selective with regard to 'invasions.'" He "can only pretend to abolish invasions by selectively admitting them, i.e., [he] abolishes only certain invasions and coercion." And what invasions would Rothbard's axiom abolish? Since his conception of voluntarism and freedom are "specified only in terms of market exchange," they are "incomplete and selective." Thus, "Rothbard's system," says Samuels, "would permit the operation of mutual coercion in the market, but he does not see it as pejoratively and analytically coercion. In other words he would abolish only the coercion he is willing to acknowledge."[12] Given his arbitrarily narrow view of power, Samuels continues, Rothbard cannot see—or won't admit—that the market is itself coercive and that it "gives effect to whatever structure of private power operates through it." Thus, the "stateless-ness" of a Rothbardian society is a mere "pretense"; it is a "play with words" that "only functions to mislead." Consequently, not only would there be the functional equivalent of the state, but it would be a state "skewed in favor of a propertied elite." Rothbard's "anarchism" "is not anarchism but a cleverly designed and worded surrogate for elitist or aristocratic conservatism." It would result in a plutocracy in the truest sense of the word, and "it cannot claim attention as a work of serious scholarship." In brief, "there is more to coercion, to volun-tarism, and to freedom than Rothbard's system admits," and it is only by his "spurious" and, Samuels strongly implies, conscious, "sleight-of-hand of narrowly contemplating externalities and invasions" that he is able to solve the specter of power in his society.[13]

This is a stinging criticism that, despite its polemical tone, does raise an important question: is the Rothbardian—and more generally libertarian—resolution of the power problem simply a product of (con-scious) abuse of the language; of a semantic sleight-of-hand?

While there is, admittedly, very little agreement either in ordinary language or even among political scientists regarding the meaning of the term "power," what little consensus there is follows, I believe, the path taken by such political scientists as Robert Dahl, Harold Lasswell and Morton Kaplan. Since their's is a respected approach to the ques-tion of power it will, perhaps, be worthwhile to examine Rothbard's definition in terms of the Dahl-Lasswell-Kaplan approach.[14]

What is interesting about their analyses is the distinction they make between power and influence. For them, influence is a generic term that includes an entire family of more specific concepts such as power, authority, coercion, persuasion, force, etc. Power, on the other hand, says Dahl[15] is "defined as a special case of influence involving *severe losses* for noncompliance." Similarly, Lasswell and Kaplan[16] note that "it is the threat of sanctions that distinguishes power from influence in general. Power is a special case of the exercise of influence: it is the process of affecting policies of others with the help of (actual or threat-ened) severe deprivations for non-conformity with the policies intended."

A problem with Samuels's critique is immediately apparent. For Samuels power is ubiquitous, but only because he (implicitly) defines it as synonymous with influence. But if the Dahl-Lasswell-Kaplan ap-proach is followed power is clearly not ubiquitous. It is only one specific

type—that involving severe deprivations or losses—of the far more in-
clusive concept of influence. Rothbard never denied that influence
may be ubiquitous, but power certainly is not. If there is any abuse of
the language it lies with Samuels, not Rothbard.

But even if one follows this approach the issue is far from being
resolved. For is there, or can there be, market influence strong enough
to constitute severe deprivation, i.e., can there be "economic power"?

There are two standard ways of proceeding: that of classification
and that of comparison. The method—or perhaps more accurately,
technique—of classification establishes two or more mutually exclusive
and exhaustive categories or classes and then assigns the phenomena
to one or the other of the classes. The comparative technique proceeds
by establishing a continuum based on a particular concept or criterion
(say "influence") and then ranks the phenomenon along the continuum according to the degree to which the unit possesses the
criterion. Thus, classification deals with the question of "either/or"
while comparison concerns itself with the question of "more or less."[17]

The approach taken by Dahl is that of comparison. He envisions
taking a particular aspect of influence, such as scope, domain, cost of
compliance, probability of compliance, etc., and ranking individuals
or actions along a continuum ranging from low to high. Any individual ranked higher on the continuum than another would be considered to have "more" influence. Rankings above a designated point
would be termed "power"; rankings below it would be denoted by
some other term, say "persuasion." The problem with this approach,
as Dahl readily admits, is that the choice of a cut-off point between the
degree of influence to be termed severe deprivation or power and that
called minor deprivation or persuasion is "somewhat arbitrary." Even
more importantly, it leads inevitably into a morass of subjectivism.
"No doubt," Dahl, acknowledges,[18] "what a person regards as severe
varies a good deal with his experiences, culture, bodily conditions, and
so on." What may be considered as severe deprivation by one individual may be of little or no consequence to another.

The problem of using the comparative approach in this particular
case is that its subjectivism robs it of any empirical import. It is not, in
other words, "operational."[19] To be useful one would have to ascertain
the degree of deprivation or pain suffered by any one individual in any
particular situation. But given the subjectivity of feelings, it is obviously impossible for any one individual to determine precisely the
degree of pain felt by another. But if one cannot do this then one cannot accurately, i.e., meaningfully, determine the degree of deprivation

felt by another. And if one cannot do this then one certainly is unable to make *interpersonal* comparisons of deprivation. While one would be inclined to say that the degree of deprivation associated with the loss of a dollar would be greater for an indigent than a millionaire, how can we be sure? The indigent might be St. Francis of Assisi, who took a vow of poverty and for whom money was of no use, while the millionaire might be Howard Hughes or, even worse, Jack Benny, for whom every cent is infinitely precious. Regardless of the individuals involved, there is simply no meaningful way to ascertain with certainty and then compare the subjective feelings of one individual with another. Is the degree of pain that Jack Benny regards as severe of the same intensity as that which Helen Keller, the Marquis de Sade, or Joe Smith regard as severe? And even if it is, how can we ever tell? In short, the application of the comparison technique to the concepts of power and influence robs these terms of any empirical import.

What of the classification technique? This approach, as we have seen, does not compare things according to "more/less" but establishes criteria to construct mutually exclusive and exhaustive categories and then applies the criteria to assign the phenomena to one of the categories. This is the approach adopted by Rothbard. While it tends to be less discriminating than the comparative technique, it does have the inestimable value in this case of giving the concept of power something that the comparative technique could not: empirical import.

Rothbard doesn't deny the ubiquity of influence. But rather than trying to determine the *degree* of influence one person exercises over another, he looks to the *means* one uses to obtain influence. Those attempts to influence others by violent means, defined in Lockean-fashion as physical force, or its threat or equivalent (fraud), against the person or property of another, is termed power. All non-violent, or what may be termed persuasive, means of influencing others are designated as voluntary. What of "economic power"? Since the only "economic power" anyone can exercise is the ability to refuse to agree to a proffered exchange, and since this is nonviolent according to Rothbard's definition, it is not considered power at all. Thus, the market, according to this definition, is a system of social coordination in which power is *completely* absent.[20]

A possible objection is that power would not be absent from the market because, according to the Rothbardian paradigm, anyone would be permitted to either enter the business of providing protection to clients for a fee or purchasing the services of a defense company or police company. But this conclusion is incorrect. Defense agencies would, of course, be empowered to exercise force to protect the rights of their clients. But this would occur *subsequent* to a prior market exchange or agreement between an agency and its clients. Thus, even an exchange empowering a defense agency to use force to protect the rights of a client is a purely voluntary exchange characterized by the absence of power relationships.

Two caveats should be borne in mind. First, Rothbard looks at the means to influence rather than the degree of influence actually exercised. His taxonomy says nothing about the effectiveness of any particular influence-attempt in any particular situation. It is certainly consistent with his taxonomy for non-violent methods of influence to be more effective in a particular case or with a particular individual than violent ones. To use Jack Benny again, it is conceivable that "economic sanctions" such as the refusal to make an exchange profitable to Jack would be a more effective method of influencing his behavior than to threaten him with bodily harm.

Second, since one can define a concept in any way one desires, it is technically meaningless to speak of the "correctness" of a definition. But to be understandable a definition must bear some congruence to the way the term is commonly used. It would be ridiculous to define power in terms of, say, the length of one's shoe strings. But within this limit the ambiguity surrounding the term provides one with fairly wide discretion to stipulate a particular definition. Rothbard's definition of power in terms of physical violence certainly falls within the limits of common usage. For, as Dahl notes[22] after acknowledging the ambiguity of the term, "probably among *all peoples*" physical violence such as "exile, imprisonment and death would be considered as severe punishment." Dahl does not limit power to acts of physical violence as Rothbard does. But his statement, if correct, does indicate that the acts Rothbard denotes as violent are the ones that *everyone* can agree as being powerful. One can disagree with this definition of power and, given the stipulative aspect of definitions, it would be pointless to argue that Rothbard's definition is the "only correct one." But it must certainly be admitted to be *a* correct and plausible use of the term. It is therefore highly unfair to argue, as does Samuels, that Rothbard's definition of power is an abuse of the language and a (consciously) misleading sleight-of-hand. On the contrary, H. E. Frech,[23] who is otherwise critical of Rothbard, applauds him for "excellently sharpening the language," precisely in the ambiguous area of power relationships.

We are now in a position to flesh out the remaining elements of what may be termed the Rothbardian influence-attempt taxonomy.

While power has been defined as the use of violence, we have not distinguished between its legitimate and illegitimate uses. Yet Rothbard does make this distinction. For him, the initiated use of power is illegitimate while its defensive use is legitimate. This fits perfectly with the Dahl-Lasswell-Kaplan approach, which also distinguishes between the legitimate and illegitimate uses of power. Power that "is said to be legitimate,"—however that term is defined—notes Dahl, is "generally called authority," while that which is said to be illegitimate is referred to as "coercion."

The Rothbardian influence taxonomy can now be summarized as follows:

Influence-Attempts

Persuasion
voluntary influence-attempts

Economic Persuasion
includes:
    market exchanges
    negotiated agreements
    advertising

Social Persuasion
includes:
    speech
    gifts
    bribes
    ostracism
    discrimination

Power
violent influence-attempts

Authority
legitimate power:
defensive violence

Coercion
illegitimate power:
initiated violence
    individual, private coercion
    institutional, public coercion

The concept of "coercion" is perhaps the most interesting aspect of this taxonomy. Government does act to combat such individual, private acts of coercion as murder, theft, rape and the like. In that sense, government does exercise authority or legitimate violence. However, in order to exercise such authority it must first obtain operating revenues. Since government has, by definition, (1) claimed a monopoly in this area and (2) provides its defensive services to all (more or less) equally and regardless of payment, it has rendered the provision of defensive services a collective good. In order to eliminate "free riding" inherent in this manner of providing such goods and services, it is forced to use coercion, viz., taxation, in order to acquire its revenues. This means that governmental coercion is logically antecedent to governmental authority. That is, before it can use authority against *individual, private coercion* it must first engage in what may be termed *institutional, public coercion*. This presents an extremely interesting dilemma for the statist. For if, as is clearly implied in the term itself, the "illegitimate use of power" is immoral, and if governments must, of necessity, engage in such use of power, this means that government is an *innately immoral institution.*

In the purely voluntary, free market society advocated by Rothbard, power and even coercion would still be present. What is significant, however, is that since no one would have the right to initiate the use of power, institutionalized, public coercion would be completely absent. Individuals would have the responsibility of defending themselves, either directly or, more likely, through the purchase of the services of a police company or defense agency. Interestingly, since these services would (1) be provided competitively rather than monopolistically, and (2) on a selective rather than an equal access basis, the collective character of the service would be eliminated and with it the "free rider" problem. Those wanting protection could purchase the quantity and quality desired, the same as for any other good or service. Those preferring to fend for themselves would not be *forced* to purchase the services of any defense agency. While the defense agencies or police companies would use force, its legal use would be restricted solely to its defensive use, i.e., the exercise of authority. No agency would be empowered to initiate the use of force, i.e., to act coercively. This means that while individual, private coercion would be present in a Rothbardian society, institutionalized, public coercion, i.e., crime would be entirely absent.

There is one additional point. Rothbard's goal is to minimize coercion. "The libertarian doctrine," he writes,[24] advocates the "elimination of the *power of man over man*." But isn't it conceivable that although there would be no "public sector" and therefore no public coercion in a Rothbardian society, the *total amount* of coercion in a statist society, viz., public plus private, would be less than the total amount of private coercion in a stateless society? While this is a logical possibility, it is certainly unlikely. As even Rothbard's critics readily admit,[25] the market is far more efficient than government. Hence, if the market were permitted to expand into areas now controlled by government there is every reason to believe that such a problem as the provision of police protection and security would be handled much more effectively. If so, one would expect the amount of coercion in a Rothbardian society to be *considerably* less than that in a statist society. It is noteworthy that what limited empirical evidence exists clearly supports the Rothbardian position.[26]

Ramifications of the Rothbardian Influence Taxonomy

A few illustrations will help to clarify what is meant by such terms as "voluntarism," "violence," "coercion," and "power." A fairly common argument is that such things as a closed shop agreement, where some workers are "frozen out" of particular employment opportunities, or private discrimination, where some individuals are socially ostracized because of their color, nationality, religion, or on the basis of some other criterion, are inherently coercive, or at least powerful acts, which places Rothbard in a dilemma: either he must permit such acts, in which case he is opening the door to private coercion, or he must set up a state to combat them, in which case he is abandoning his anarchism.

Rothbard is on strong grounds in arguing that the dilemma is only apparent and results from the failure to adhere consistently to the definitions of power and coercion specified above. Power and influence were defined not in terms of the *degree* of influence exercised by A over B but by the *means* A chooses to influence B. Thus, a closed shop agreement or an act of discrimination may or may not be coercive. This depends not on, say, the number of people adversely affected or even the magnitude of the adversity, but on the way the agreement was consummated or the private act was undertaken.

If government, or some other uninvited third party, orders a closed or even an open shop, then it is coercive; not because it is either closed or open but because the parties were threatened with initiated violence if they did not comply. However, if (1) the employees agree to ban together and present a united front to their employer, and if (2) the employer agrees that he will not hire anyone who does not belong to the union, a closed shop will have been voluntarily agreed upon. Coercion, i.e., the initiation of the use of violence, was, in this case entirely absent. True, if someone wants to work for that particular employer he must join the union. But this is hardly coercion for, as the Italian legal theorist, Bruno Leoni[27] has commented, "You do not 'constrain' someone if you merely refrain from doing on his behalf something you have not agreed to do." The only thing the members of the union did was to agree among themselves not to work for the employer unless he agreed to hire only union members and the employer, in return, agreed to the demand. It makes no more sense to say that non-union members are being coerced in this situation than to say that one is coercing Gimbles by buying socks from Macy's. But if the employer were told by the union that unless he agreed to their conditions his factory would be burned or by the government that he would be fined or imprisoned, the closed shop agreement would be coercive *in this case*, since it was obtained through the threat of violence. The same would be true if the employer hired strike-breakers to crush the union or if Macy's hired agents to harass Gimbles's shoppers.

The situation is identical for acts of private discrimination. In a libertarian world all property would be privately owned and any individual would have the right to use his property in any non-violent way he desired. "It might be charged that all this will allow freedom 'to discriminate' in housing or the use of streets," Rothbard notes.[28] And, he acknowledges, "there is no question about that. Fundamental to the libertarian creed is every man's right to choose who shall enter or use his own property, provided of course that the other person is willing." Clearly, if private discrimination is simply the right of an owner to determine who shall use his property then, regardless of how morally reprehensible it may be, it is, according to the libertarian definition, non-coercive. It is a method of exercising voluntary influence over another. What would be coercive, however, would be an order by an uninvited third party, which included the threat of physical sanctions for noncompliance, for either discriminatory or nondiscriminatory behavior on the part of any individual. As with the case of the closed shop, neither discriminatory nor nondiscriminatory behavior is in itself coercive but may be depending on how they were undertaken.

While voluntary private discrimination would be permitted, Rothbard believes that the market would tend to *minimize* such behavior by placing a cost on the shoulders of the discriminating property owner. Suppose, says Rothbard, that a landlord of an apartment building

> is a great admirer of six-foot Swedish-Americans, and decides to rent his apartments only to families of such a group. In the free society it would be fully in his right to do so, but he would clearly suffer a large monetary loss as a result. For this means that he would have to turn away tenant after tenant in an endless quest for very tall Swedish-Americans. While this may be considered an extreme example, the effect is exactly the same, though differing in degree, for any sort of personal discrimination in the

marketplace. If, for example, the landlord dislikes redheads and determines not to rent his apartments to them, he will suffer losses, although not as severely as in the first example.[29]

In short, individuals seldom are aware of whether a good they are purchasing was made by a caucasian or a black, a man or a woman, a Christian or a Jew. It is this ignorance or, if you will, this "impersonality of the marketplace" that prevents consumers from discriminating against others for reasons that have nothing to do with economic productivity and, consequently, imposes an economic sanction on those employers who do discriminate. The available empirical evidence provides considerable support for this proposition.[30]

Freedom

Freedom, as defined by Rothbard, is a "condition in which a person's ownership rights in his own body and his legitimate property are *not* invaded, not aggressed against. A man who steals another man's property is invading and restricting the victim's freedom, as does the man who beats another over the head."[31] For Rothbard, it is clear, freedom is a social concept, i.e., a condition characterized by the absence of *interpersonal* violence. In this sense it is not only "negative" but, as Hayek points out,[32] it "refers solely to a relation of men to other men, and the infringement on it is coercion by other men." Defining freedom in this fashion means that in a libertarian society everyone would have an equal amount of freedom, e.g., the right to engage in any non-violent activity they desired. But it is important to realize that this does not mean that everyone would have an equal ability to use that freedom. While the poor would have the same amount of freedom as the wealthy, the range of options is undoubtedly more limited for the poor than the wealthy. Unlike the wealthy, the prospect of an ocean cruise on the Caribbean or a vacation on the French Riveria would not be within the range of effective choice for most poor. The cognition that the ability to use one's freedom is partly a function of one's economic position is probably what Harold Laski meant by his remark that "liberty in a laissez faire society is attainable only by those who have the wealth or opportunity to attain it."[33]

Not only Harold Laski, but "progressives" such as J. R. Commons and John Dewey and "idealists" such as T. H. Green also define freedom as the *"effective power* to do specific things," thereby viewing it in terms of the number of options open to a person. Libertarians, however, maintain a strict distinction between the *absence of coercion and the power or ability* to engage in specific things, and reserve the term "freedom" for the former. While acknowledging that the range of options open to an individual is an important question, it is, argues Hayek irrelevant to freedom:

> The rock climber on a difficult pitch who sees only one way out to save his life is unquestionably free, though we would hardly say he has any choice. Also most people will still have enough feeling for the original use of the word "free" to see that if the same climber were to fall into a crevasse and were unable to get out of it, he could only figuratively be called "unfree," and that being "held captive" is to use these terms in a sense different from that in which they apply in social relations.[34]

Since, in a libertarian society, no one would have the right to initiate violence, such a society would, according to Rothbard, be "totally free."[35] That is, since freedom is automatically restricted by any coercive act, the governmental transfer of several million dollars from a millionaire to a group of indigents would restrict freedom even though it might increase the options open to the indigents without perceptibily limiting the options of the millionaire. It is *conceivable*, therefore that freedom could be restricted at the same time that the number of alternatives open to particular individuals or groups might increase.

This raises the significant question of how important such freedom actually is. It is to this issue that we now turn.

Part II:
The Rothbardian View of Market and Government

The Nature of the Free Market

One of Rothbard's central contentions is that the free market invariably increases "social utility." His reasoning is as follows. Since any voluntary exchange will take place only when each participant expects to benefit, "the very fact that an exchange takes place demonstrates that both parties benefit (or more strictly *expect* to benefit) from the exchange." Thus, since the free market is nothing more than "the array of all voluntary exchange that takes place in the world," and since "every exchange demonstrates an unanimity of benefit for both parties concerned, we must conclude" that, provided all major externalities have been internalized, as they would be in a Rothbardian world of universal private property, *the free market benefits all its participants.* . . . We are led inexorably, then, to the conclusion that the processes of the free market always lead to a gain in social utility. And we can say this with absolute validity as economists, without engaging in ethical judgments."[36]

This statement demands careful consideration in order to understand precisely what is and is not being claimed. It is well known that one can demonstrate an increase in "social utility" only when (1) at least *one* individual benefits and (2) *no one* is left worse off because of any exchange. But in the real world (1) peoples' expectations about the future are often mistaken and, hence, businesses suffer losses or go bankrupt and anticipated profits from investments often do not materialize. Further (2) individuals are often disappointed because their *proffered exchanges* are rejected. Aren't both of these examples of where the market renders at least one individual worse off and thus refute Rothbard's statement that the market *always* increases social utility?

Future Expectations. It is certainly true that businesses sometimes go bankrupt and the expected profits from investments do not materialize. And Rothbard is certainly aware of this as his writings about profits *and losses* make abundantly clear.[37]

Rothbard only claimed that individuals maximize their utility *ex ante*. This is certainly consistent with bankruptcy, unprofitable investments, the purchase of (losing) lottery tickets, etc. This can be easily demonstrated. Assume for simplicity that one has a .5 chance of having an investment yield a profit and a .5 chance of suffering a loss. If the individual believed that a profit would increase his *future* utility more than a loss would reduce it, the discounted *present* value of that investment would be positive. This means that, *regardless of the actual outcome*, the decision to invest would increase one's present utility, while the decision not to would reduce it. Thus, the decision to invest would increase one's utility *ex ante*, even if it proved to be a mistaken choice and thus reduced his utility *ex post*.

The significant point is that it is not the market, itself, that was responsible for reducing one's utility but the uncertainty of the future. And this uncertainty, it must be emphasized, is an ineradicable element of nature and is therefore *independent* of any particular economic system.

In fact, since there are gains from trade to be made on the market by enabling others to reduce the risks they face, the market actually works to minimize uncertainty by enabling individuals to purchase insurance against practically any risk imaginable.[38]

In short, reduced utility resulting from mistaken expectations about the future is not inconsistent with the Rothbardian position regarding decisions *ex ante*. Further, such mistakes are due to the uncertainty of the future. This uncertainty is not the result of the market but is inherent in nature. Finally, it is actually the market process that operates to minimize this uncertainty.

Rejected Offers. But what of the second category of action? Would it not be correct to say that one who had his offer of an exchange rejected had his utility reduced?

Assume for the sake of simplicity that two job applicants, Abbott and Costello, have equal ability. If Abbott offers to work for, say, $5.00 per hour while Costello makes an offer of $4.75 per hour, the employer will hire Costello. But if Abbott makes a counter offer of $4.50 per hour the employer would then hire Abbott. Costello must now decide whether he will offer less than $4.50 per hour. Suppose he decides against this. Abbott would then be hired at $4.50. Clearly, both participants, the employer and Abbott, gain. But what of Costello? Didn't he lose? Wasn't his utility reduced? The answer is no. First, Costello had the option of underbidding Abbott. The fact that he did not do so indicates that for him no job was a better option than a job at less than $4.50 per hour. Thus, Costello chose the better of the two options that actually faced him. That option was to make no exchange. That is, if Costello were coerced, either by a gun-wielding employer or the government, into working for less than $4.50 per hour, his utility would be *lower* than it would be in the absence of coercion. Thus, Costello made the choice which *maximized his utility given the options facing him at the time of that choice*.

But Costello desired a job at $4.75 per hour. His hopes were dashed when Abbott offered $4.50 per hour. Wasn't his utility reduced by having his hopes for the job at $4.75 dashed? Costello's failure to get the job does not mean that he is any worse off than he was *before* he made his offer. He did not have the job before he made the offer; he does not have the job after his offer was rejected. Thus, his *realized* or *real world* utility plane is *unchanged*. What has happened is that his hoped for increase in utility did not materialize; that is, his *realized utility plane* is lower than his hoped for or *fancied utility plane*, i.e., the utility resulting from an alternative that either could not occur or could occur only through the use of violence. Of course, there *must* always be a discrepancy between ones' actual and desired abilities, between one's realized and fancied utility planes. If this were not the case, if everyone's desires were *fully* satisfied, all action would cease for any action would, by definition, entail a reduction in utility.

Put differently, the free market operates to increase every individual's *realized* utility plane. To complain of a discrepancy between realized and fancied utility planes is simply to complain that one's desires have not been fully satisfied. But this complaint reduces itself to the mundane observation that more is better than less, that abundance is better than scarcity. But scarcity, like uncertainty, is an ineradicable element of nature which is independent of any particular economic system. In fact, while scarcity cannot be eliminated, one can point out that the market is the most efficient institution for production yet discovered and is therefore a powerful engine for *reducing scarcities*. This can be briefly demonstrated.

Since consumers only buy what they intend to use, one can make a profit only by producing what consumers desire. This, of course, means that it is the consumers who ultimately direct production by their buying and abstention from buying. To produce their goods the entrepreneurs must bid for the needed resources. They therefore stand in the same relation to the sellers of factors as the consumers do to the sellers of final goods. Thus, the price for the factors of production tend to reflect the demand for them by the entrepreneurs. Since what the entrepreneur can bid is limited by his expected yield from the final sale of his product, factors are channeled into production of those goods most intensely demanded by consumers. If returns are not high enough to cover the cost of a particular operation this means that there is, in the eyes of the consumers, a more important use for the factors of production elsewhere. The market, therefore, allocates resources to their most productive point relative to the priority system that the consumers have established.

This can be demonstrated by the following. Assume that the market is in equilibrium. Also assume that a new technological breakthrough has enabled the production of a new commodity that is highly valued by consumers. The production of the commodity, however, requires the use of factor A. Those entrepreneurs who perceive this new profit opportunity will begin to bid for the factor. This increased competition for the available supply of A will cause its price to rise, forcing some of the users of A to curtail their purchases. But who will be the ones forced to curtail their purchases? Clearly, it will be those employers of A who are receiving the least renumeration for their product from the consumers, i.e., those who are employing A in its least product point. In this way the use of A is channeled from uses that the consumers value less highly into uses they value more highly. But further, the rise in the price of A will encourage other entrepreneurs, also anxious to make profits, to expand the production of A. In this way the free market works to employ "every possible factor of production for the best possible satisfaction of the most urgent needs of the consumer."[39]

The important point is that if market prices are interfered with, they become distorted and no longer reflect the demands of "society." Resources are misallocated and production impeded. Since these inefficiencies reduce the size of the economic product relative to what it would have been on the unhampered market, intervention can only serve to increase the discrepancy between realized and fancied utility.

The Nature of Government

Government is that agency which exercises a monopoly on the legal use of coercion in society. Government is not a productive institution. It has no resources which it has not first taken from others. This means that in order for it to *defend* individuals from aggression by others it must *first* exercise *prior* aggression viz., taxation, in order to obtain operating revenues. Thus, violence is inherent in every act of government.

In order to analyze government it is necessary to distinguish between the actual or *real world situation*, i.e., the existing state of affairs, and what may be termed the *counterfactual situation*, i.e., the state of affairs that *would have occurred* had its emergence not been coercively prevented. Since on the free market all individuals must either remain on the same utility plane or move to a higher one, the market, provided major externalities have been internalized, would increase "social utility." And because coercion, either present or prior, is inherent in government, any government action *must* reduce at least one individual's actual or realized utility relative to his counter-factual utility, i.e., to what it would have been on the unhampered market. The logical conclusion, as Professor Rothbard points out, is that "no act of government whatever can increase social utility." Hence, he continues, "a free and voluntary market 'maximizes' social utility" provided, he quickly adds, terms such as "maximize" and "increase" are interpreted in an ordinal rather than a cardinal sense.[40]

Currently in excess of 50% of the budgets of practically all governments in the world are devoted to transfer payments. This makes wealth transfers, at least quantitatively, the most important function of government. The official justification for these activities is that they increase "social utility." Since transferring wealth from some individuals to others reduces choice sets of the former while expanding them for the latter, this means that some are forced to choose between options that provide them with less utility than those they would have chosen on the market while others are able to choose from options that would not be open to them on the market. Since the utility of some is reduced while that of others is increased, any claim that "social utility" has been increased implies the ability to compare, if not measure, the utilities of different individuals. Thus, the *justification* for wealth transfers clearly implies the use of utility in its cardinal sense, defined here as the ability to measure and/or compare the utilities of different individuals.[41] Those who maintain that wealth transfers can and do increase "social utility" should be able to support this claim with adequate evidence. The claim will be examined using two different standards (a) what may be termed absolute *or apodictic certainty* and (b) the more relaxed standard of *reasonable certainty*.

What can be said with *absolute certainty* about the effect of government wealth transfers on utility in a cardinal sense? Since no one has been able to show that direct interpersonal comparisons of utility are possible,[42] *nothing* can be said with absolute certainty about "social utility" when there are both gainers and losers. It is possible that the beneficiaries benefit more than the losers are harmed, thereby increasing "social utility." The reverse is also possible. This means that it is impossible to ascertain whether a given government action increased, or decreased "net social utility" or left it unchanged. As Professor Rothbard has put it, "[a]s economists we can say nothing about social utility in this case since some individuals have demonstrably gained, and some have demonstrably lost in utility, from the government action."[43] But there is *one* possibility from which it is possible to draw conclusions which are absolutely certain even when coercion is present. If a coercive act (a) makes no one better off but (b) leaves at least one person worse off, it follows that "social utility" is reduced.

The results of the foregoing are interesting. One may say with certainty that the market *always* increases "social utility." On the other hand, one can *never* state with certainty that any act of government ever increases "social utility," and the only conclusion one could ever make with absolute certainty is that a given act of government *reduced* "social utility." And this, as we shall see, is not as unlikely as might be thought.

This is as far as one can go while remaining in the realm of *absolute certainty*. However, by relaxing the standards from absolute to *reasonable certainty*, one can say much more.[44] There are two ways to examine this issue: (1) indirect, interpersonal utility comparisons within a given time-slice, and (2) intrapersonal utility comparisons over time. The question is, even using the relaxed standard of "reasonable certainty" do these approaches provide any convincing evidence that coercive wealth transfers may increase "social utility"?

Indirect, Interpersonal Utility Comparisons. In ordinary speech we make interpersonal comparisons of mental states. We often hear or make statements to the effect that A is happier, sadder, more in love or in greater pain than B. Granted that such loose talk can hardly qualify as scientific assessment, nevertheless, it would be rash to dismiss it as meaningless.

There is, obviously, wide variation in *what* makes different individuals happy or sad, and some variation in *how* individuals express these mental states. But that there is a great deal of "sameness" or "commonality," especially in the outward expressions of our mental states, cannot be denied. For example, laughter denotes happiness; a grimace, pain. One can state with conviction, even of a stranger, that he had a happy expression, a friendly face, was the picture of health, did not look well, was in pain, etc.

In a similar vein, peoples' tastes are in a large part a product of their past personal histories, the quality and quantity of their education, their culture, etc. It is therefore reasonable to suppose that there is a great deal of variety, especially cross-culturally, in what affects our utilities. Observation appears to confirm this. But, again, this should not be interpreted as meaning that there are not equally significant similarities. Observation bears this our as well. Whenever and wherever people in socialist countries have been permitted to express their preferences, such as in post-Mao China, and to a lesser extent in the countries of Eastern Europe and the Soviet Union, during the past two decades or so, they have opted for higher standards of living. And probably the major reason socialist politicians have been so successful in the Third World is that they have been able to convince large numbers of people that "redistribution" from the rich to the poor will being them abundance with little or no effort. It seems clear that such politicians would receive very little support if they promised oppression and poverty. Indeed, the uniformity of the desire for material wealth, even cross-culturally, is remarkable, with Japan being only the most striking example. It is not too much to say that the life style of the "materialistic West" is the envy of the world. Indeed, the lure of the "American Way of Life" sparked the largest migration in the history of the world.[45]

This is not to say that all individual preferences are identical. This is obviously not the case. It is only to say that there is probably enough similarity to enable us to make *rough comparisons with reasonable certainty.*

This conclusion is strengthened by the "Law of Marginal Utility" which informs us that *all* individuals *always* act to satisfy their most urgent (satisfiable) desire first, their second most urgent desire second, their third, third, etc. This, of course, deals solely with the intraper-sonal rankings of preferences and therefore does not, in itself, permit interpersonal comparisons, much less measurement, of utility. But while this law says nothing about either the content or degree of par-ticular individuals' utility, it does show that all individuals act accord-ing to the same *process* or *principle*, viz., the maximization of their util-ity, broadly conceived.

Put differently, the fact that all of us are members of the same species, homo sapiens, not only means that we must, by definition, possess cer-tain essential traits in common, it also means that *introspection* is an in-valuable tool in understanding the members or units of that class. "Whenever we discuss intelligible behavior," Hayek, has observed:

> we discuss actions which we can interpret in terms of our own mind. . . . If we can understand only what is similar to our own mind, it necessarily follows that we must be able to find all that we can understand in our own mind. . . .
>
> I am able to fit into a scheme of actions which 'make sense' just because I have come to regard it not as a thing with certain physical properties but as the kind of thing which fits into the pattern of my own purposive action.
>
> If what we do when we speak about understanding a person's action is to fit what we actually observe into patterns we find ready in our own mind, it follows, of course, that we can under-stand less and less as we turn to beings more and more different from ourselves. But it also follows that it is not only impossible to recognize, but meaningless to speak of, a mind different from our own. What we mean when we speak of another mind is that we can connect what we observe because the things we observe fit into the way of our thinking.[46]

If Hayek is correct, then such universal principles of human action as the law of marginal utility combined with the observed similarities in such things as individual preferences and the outward manifestation of mental states permits us, after making due allowance for the ob-served variation in individual preferences, *not* to measure utilities but, rather, to make *reasonably certain rough comparisons of utility.*

If one insists on conceiving of utility in cardinal rather than ordinal terms, it follows that one must view it, just like any other phenomenon amenable to measurement, in terms of a continuum rather than a dichotomy. But since one cannot make *exact* measurements but, at best, only rough comparisons, the result would resemble a black/white color spectrum. One can distinguish black from white but as one moves down the spectrum one cannot tell where black ends and white begins. There is a massive "gray area" in between which is neither black nor white. Similarly, one can distinguish a child from an adult. One can even chart the evolution of the child into an adult, marking not just the years but the months, days, hours and even seconds. Yet, despite the precision of the measuring instrument one is still unable to point to an exact time that the child becomes an adult. The same is true of the "utility continuum." Given (a) the differences in individual preferences and (b) the indeterminacy of interpersonal utility comparisons, assessments of differences in interpersonal utility planes are possible with even reasonable certainty *only at polar extremes.* To expect any more than this would be like trying to thread a needle with a jack hammer.

What, then, can be said with reasonable certainty of interpersonal utility comparisons? Compare, for example, the position of multimillionaire Robert Baron, III, with that of an indigent, Herb, living at or near starvation. An extra dollar would enable Robert to satisfy a preference that is ranked, say, one millionth on his utility scale while that same dollar would enable Herb to satisfy a preference that is ranked fifth on his. It is *reasonable* to suppose that the satisfaction of Robert's one millionth preference would not provide as much utility to Robert as the satisfaction of Herb's fifth preference would provide to him. It is, of course, *conceivable* that the reverse is the case. But for a dollar to provide Robert with "more" satisfaction than the indigent would so deviate from what observation, experience and introspection tell us is typical for human beings as to be characterized as abnormal. And since an abnormality is, by definition, a departure from the norm, the burden of proof is on those who assert an abnormality to demonstrate its existence rather than on others to disprove the assertion. In the absence of some fairly convincing demonstration of why and how either Robert's or Herb's sensibilities differ so markedly from those of ordinary human beings, the claim can be treated with a large degree of skepticism, if not contempt.

Doesn't this lead to the conclusion that a massive redistribution of wealth would increase "social welfare." I think not.

Wealth transfers can be divided into three types: (1) upward wealth transfers, where wealth is transferred from poorer to wealthier individuals or groups, (2) intra-group wealth transfers, where wealth is transferred from one poor individual or group to another poor individual or group, or from one middle-class individual or group to another, etc., and (3) downward wealth transfers, where wealth is transferred from wealthier individuals or groups to poorer ones.

Upward transfers of wealth would reduce the choice set among those whose choice set is already relatively small and expand the choice set among those whose choice set is already relatively large. The result is clear: it would reduce preference satisfaction among those who were already in the position of satisfying the fewest of their preferences. And it would increase satisfaction among those already in the position of satisfying the largest number of their preferences. Since such transfers move us in the position of polar extremes one can be reasonably certain that upward transfers of wealth reduce "social utility" and therefore could not be justified on the basis of welfare criteria.

Since polar extremes are not present in intra-group transfers, it is reasonable to suppose that the benefits of the recipients are roughly offset by the costs to the payers. It is not possible, therefore, with any degree of certainty to show that transfers either did or did not increase "social utility." Given this uncertainty such transfers in and of themselves could not be justified on the basis of welfare considerations.

Downward transfers present the most interesting case. We have already seen that it is reasonable to assume that an additional dollar for Herb would increase Herb's utility more than the loss of a dollar by Robert would reduce his utility. Hence, downward transfers would appear to increase "social utility." But appearances can be deceiving. For transfers, especially if they are either downward or intra-group, initiate a process the outcome of which makes even the initial beneficiaries of the transfers worse off than they would have been even without the transfer. In order to understand this process we need to turn to the second approach, the intrapersonal comparison of utility over time.

Intrapersonal Utility Comparisons Over Time

The second approach differs from the first in that it does not attempt to compare the utilities of different individuals but to compare the utilities of the same individual at different times.

Wealth can be obtained through two fundamentally different means: (1) voluntarily, i.e., through production, exchange or as a gift, or (2) coercively, i.e., by taking, seizing, it from others.

Assume that Robert's wealth was obtained coercively. The transfer of all or a large part of Robert's wealth would reduce his utility. But there are additional results. Since he could no longer benefit from his coercive activities, the transfer would act as a deterrent or disincentive to coercion. And if Robert were permitted to retain noncoercively obtained wealth, the transfer would operate as an incentive for him to divert his energies from coercion to production. The result would not only be an increase in Robert's utility from what it was after the transfer but his production would increase "social output" and therefore "social utility." Moreover, if the transfer went to those who had originally earned the wealth, not only would it increase their utilities immediately, but keeping the rewards or gains from their production would, it is likely to assume, stimulate producers to expand their outputs, thereby increasing not only the utilities of the producers but "social utility" as well.

If we assume that Robert obtained his fortune voluntarily, the incentives created by wealth transfers are exactly reversed. The immediate effect of the government transfer from Robert to Herb would be, as shown in Figures 1 and 2, to reduce Robert's utility while increasing Herb's. But this is only the beginning of the process. How would Robert react to the continued appropriation of his earned income (the area $ABCD$ in Figure 1)? Put differently, how would he react to policies that prevented him from raising his income beyond a certain level, say A in Figure 1?

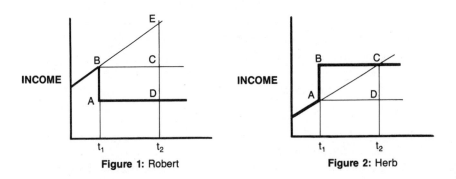

Figure 1: Robert   **Figure 2: Herb**

If Robert has obtained the highest utility plane possible under the circumstances, he would of course, cease trying to increase his utility and rest content with simply maintaining it at the current level. This means that the transfer activities would, at time t_2, result in a discrepancy between Robert's realized income D, and his counterfactual income, E. Moreover, it means that "society" as a whole would be impoverished by the loss of Robert's production equal to the area BCE.

The wealth transfer is likely to have an equally significant impact on Herb's behavior. Since the transfer brings about an immediate increase in Herb's income from A to B (in Figure 2), and since Herb knows that the government will not permit his income to drop below that level, it is obvious that it would reduce, perhaps even eliminate, his incentive to produce. So long as Herb's earned income falls below B his work is simply wasted effort on his part. That is, since work is a disutility any work yielding an income at or below line BC would reduce Herb's utility since he could obtain the same or greater wealth without work. Thus, the transfer means that Herb would be better off by reducing the hours he works or by not working at all. If, for simplicity, we assume that Herb reacts to the transfer, like Robert, by maintaining his earned income at his current level (A in Figure 2), the transfer, represented by the area $ABCD$, increases Herb's income at point t_1. At time t_2 his total income, earned plus transferred, is C. But this is the *same* income he *would be enjoying* had he not received any transfers in the first place. Hence, other things being equal, Herb is no better off at t_2 with transfers than he would have been in their absence; and "society" is poorer to the extent of Herb's lost production, i.e., the area ACD in Figure 2.

The result is interesting. The government transfer hurt Robert. On the other hand it did not benefit Herb, at least in the *long run*. Since no one was benefitted and at least one person was hurt, the transfer "benefits" actually *reduced* "social utility" in this case.

One possible counterargument is that both Robert and Herb simply exchanged more leisure and a smaller income for a larger income with more work, and since leisure is a valuable good which contributes to one's utility, neither have had their utility levels reduced. Leisure is a valuable good and we are constantly making incremental adjustments between leisure and wealth. But it is important to recognize that if one's preferred option is additional wealth and if this option is coercively barred, then even if additional leisure is the best of the remaining options it still represents a decline in utility. If there is a reduction in the overall economic growth rate in a particular country and if that reduction can be traced to government policies it is clear that most if not all of that government's citizens would have preferred the additional wealth. This, of course, would be especially true if the slowdown resulted from declining productivity and therefore produced little if any additional leisure. Recent empirical studies provide some indication that this, in fact, is the case.[47]

Similarly, if economic output increases following a reduction in government regulation, one can conclude that all or most members of the society preferred additional income to leisure and that enforced leisure, provided there was some, meant that the members' realized utility was below their counterfactual utility. The dramatic increase in agricultural output in those Third World countries that have recently reduced government interference in the agricultural sector compared to the continued low or even declining outputs of those countries with prohibitive taxes on and extensive government involvement with agriculture indicates that low economic output does not represent a preference for leisure over wealth.[48]

One can also argue that there is no reason that long run interests should take precedence over short run interests. But it is a serious mistake to phrase the issue in this way. Individuals maximize their utility by making trade-offs "at the margins." They choose to consume X units of goods A, $X+1$ units of good B, and $X-2$ units of good C, etc. In similar fashion individuals maximize their utility by choosing to satisfy some desires in the present, others at $t+1$ and still others at $t+n$. One may choose to eat a hamburger now, buy an automobile next year and go to college in 10 years. We live in *both* the present *and* the future. We are constantly making trade-offs between satisfying certain desires now and satisfying other desires at various times in the future. The important point is that if one is to choose his optimal mix of present and future satisfactions the "rules of the game" should not be rigged so as to encourage or even induce individuals to behave in the short run in ways which produce long run results which even the actors themselves would disapprove of. For example, a 100% tax on all production would, it is fair to assume, eliminate all productive behavior. This would be the result even though the consequences would be (a) easy to foresee and (b) those which everyone would disapprove of. In short, the tax would induce or *trap* people into behaving in the short run in ways which would produce in the long run results which they not only could predict but would regard, *even at the time of their choices*, as undesirable or "irrational." Whether or not a choice is "rational" depends on both the goals and values of the individual making the choice and the context within which the choice is made. It is possible that *within a given context*, the most rational choice open to an individual has consequences which even he would regard as irrational, i.e., counter to his own preference rankings. There is increasing evidence that government tax policies, transfer payments and the like place individuals within decision making contexts of this type.

There is, for example, substantial evidence that the Great Society and War on Poverty programs of the 1960s not only failed to eliminate poverty in the United States but actually led to an increase not only in the number but in the percentage of poor. In trying to explain this phenomenon, Charles Murray pointed out that "A government's social policy helps set the rules of the game—the stakes, the risks, the payoffs, the tradeoffs, and the strategies for making a living, raising a family, having fun, defining what 'winning' and 'success' mean. . . . The most compelling explanation for the marked shift in the fortunes of the poor,"[49] from the mid-1960s on, says Murray,

> is that they continued to respond, as they always had, to the world as they found it, but that we . . . had changed the rules of their world. . . . The first effect of the new rules was to make it profitable for the poor to behave in the short term in ways which were destructive in the long term. Their second effect was to mask these long term losses—to subsidize irretrievable mistakes. We tried to provide more for the poor and produced more poor instead. We tried to remove barriers to escape from poverty, and inadvertently built a trap.[50]

Numerous other studies, both of the United States[51] and of foreign nations[52] reached much the same conclusions: government transfer programs, tax policies and the like make it rational for the poor to choose options which will retard or even reverse their economic development. That is, it induces individuals to make choices which are counter to their *own* preferences.

There is one remaining but vitally important question: how long would it take for natural economic growth to put someone like Herb on a higher utility plane than he was after the receipt of the income transfer? This cannot be stated with certainty. It depends on many factors such as the size of the benefits received by Herb, the overall disincentive impact of income transfers, etc.

Nevertheless, some rough assessments can be made. Norman Macrae has shown that between the year 1 A.D. and 1776, the date of publication of Adam Smith's *Wealth of Nations*, average per capita income remained fairly constant at about $250 (in 1975 dollars). The percentage of mankind living below the poverty level was 99%. Today, the percentage is less than 65%. Since world population has increased sixfold during this time, this represents an eightyfold increase in world output between 1776 and 1975.[53]

If one uses more current data, Landau has shown that the annual growth rate of per capita GDP for the 16 most developed market economies averaged 6.3% for the 1955-73 period. The average share of government was 27% in 1955 but rose to 43% by 1979. Interestingly, the average economic growth rate for the 16 countries dropped to a mere 2% during the 1973-79 period.[54] Landau's rather cautious conclusion is that "the growth of government consumption and investment expenditure has helped 'cause' the slowdown in economic growth."[55]

If, then, one assumes that 6.3% is the *normal* growth rate for a free market economy, per capita output would double every 11 years. This means that if transfers increased Herb's income by, say, 33%, his realized income, even with transfers, would fall *below*, his counterfactual income in about five years. If growth rates were faster, which seems likely since the 6.3% growth rate occurred while government was consuming 27% of the GDP, the time frame would be even shorter.

Thus, there is good reason to believe that government actually reduces intrapersonal income over even relatively short periods of time. And since the evidence also shows that the vast majority of people prefer more to less wealth, it is reasonable to conclude that government transfers from rich to poor reduce the intrapersonal utility of all involved including recipients.

Conclusion

The market process, provided it operates within a legal framework which internalizes externalities, operates so as to perpetually increase the utilities of all participants. In contrast, the very existence of government reduces "social utility." This can be demonstrated with *certainty* when utility is interpreted in ordinal terms. Although nothing can be said with certainty when utility is interpreted in cardinal terms we have found no *convincing evidence* that government transfers *ever* increase "social utility," but considerable evidence that they *reduce* it. In short, the best available evidence indicates that government transfers inevitably reduce "social utility" regardless of whether that concept is interpreted in ordinal or cardinal terms.

It may be objected that only government transfer policies have been considered and that other government policies may have very different effects. But the fact is that there are no "other" policies. *All* government policies transfer wealth either explicitly or implicitly. Minimum wage rates, for example, "represent an implicit transfer *within the least advantaged classes,* from the most unskilled workers (who can no longer get any sort of job) to the best unskilled (who are integrated relatively more easily into the labor market). In the last analysis it is a regressive social measure,"[56] i.e., it is an upward transfer of wealth.

But if (1) *all* government policies transfer wealth, and if (2) all the available evidence shows that transfers *reduce* "social utility" regardless of whether that term is interpreted in ordinal or cardinal terms, then the inescapable conclusion is that, *based on welfare criteria*, government is an unjustifiable institution.

Part III:
Caste and Class

If government reduces "social utility" the obvious question is: Why the state? Why did the state emerge and why does it persist? This is both a legitimate and important question.

The Rothbardian View of the Origin
and Persistence of the State

Rothbard was heavily influenced by the early twentieth century German sociologist, Franz Oppenheimer. It was Oppenheimer who introduced the distinction between the "political" and the "economic means," a distinction which has assumed a central position in the Rothbardian analysis. Oppenheimer's fundamental insight was that man can satisfy his desires through two mutually exclusive means. One is work; the other robbery. Work, by which he means one's labor as well as what one receives in exchange for one's labor, he designated as "the economic means."[57]

Robbery, the "unrequited appropriation of the labor of others," is termed the "political means." While these two *means* are mutually exclusive, their *purpose* is identical: the acquisition of wealth. Oppenheimer therefore views "all world history, from primitive times up to our own civilization" simply as "a contest . . . between the economic and the political means."[58]

There are two ramification of this conceptual framework which Oppenheimer is quick to point out: (a) the state is the institutionalized embodiment of the political means, and (b) since production necessarily precedes robbery, society, by use of the economic means, must have obtained a certain level of economic development before the emergence of the state was possible.

This latter point, Oppenheimer feels, explains why no state ever existed among such groups as the primitive peasants (grubbers) or the primitive huntsmen.

The grubbers, for example, are attached to the land and live in both abject poverty and relative isolation. Such a situation provides no foundation for the rise of a state, for the primitive peasants are too impoverished to support one and too scattered from one another, physically, to organize even for their own defense. It is much different, however, with the herdsmen. Accidents of nature (luck) as well as the cleverness and diligence of the breeder produce distinctions in fortune and, consequently, distinctions of class. But since luck cannot be controlled and such traits as cleverness are not hereditary, economic equality soon begins to re-emerge. It is quite natural for the existing wealthy to block this trend by recourse to violence. This utilization of the political means is of the utmost significance, says Oppenheimer, because with it economic and social equality is "destroyed permanently," and the foundation of the state is laid.

Theft is easier and more exciting than the tedious and disciplined routine of production. Thus the political means tends to breed on its own success. Its successful use in one case encourages its use in others. Consequently, the herdsmen began to turn more and more to the political means. The weaker herdsmen are able to flee before their onslaught, but the peasant cannot. His livelihood being tied to the land, he yields to subjection, and pays tribute to his conqueror; *that is the genesis of the land states in the old world.*" The state therefore emerges, according to Oppenheimer, when the developing economic means of the peasantry are subordinated, by the use of the political means, to the direction of the herdsmen.

Rothbard's answer to the question: Why the state? is clear. Although the state inevitably reduces "social utility" it can be, *and is,* used by the group that is able to control it to provide benefits to itself at the expense of everyone else in society. This group has a vested interest in the creation and perpetuation of government. Moreover, it has the entire panoply of government resources, from use of tax revenues to purchase the allegiance of important groups, to political indoctrination through the "public" school system, to the use of force to quash any threat to its existence, at its disposal. In short, the group in control of the reigns of government is able to use the government's monopoly on force to render both its own position and the government, itself, virtually unassailable.

Clearly, this line of reasoning points to the existence of a ruling elite, and Rothbard does not shy away from drawing this conclusion. "Those who succeed in any occupation will inevitably tend to be those who are best at it," he says. And,

those who succeed in the political struggle will be those most
adept at employing coercion and winning favors from wielders
of coercion. Generally, different people will be adept at different
tasks . . . and hence the shackling of one set of people will be
done for the benefit of another set.[59]

The state, he writes elsewhere "constitutes, and is the source of the
'ruling class.'. . ."[60]

The next question is: Who constitutes this dominant group? Who is
the "ruling elite"? In primitive times it was easy to spot. One group,
employing the political means, would subject another to its will and
begin to extract tribute from them. Gradually, as this arrangement per-
sisted, it came to be accepted and the extraction of tribute became sys-
tematized in the periodic payment of taxes to the "government." As
Walter Grinder, an economist influenced by Rothbard, summarizes,
"[i]t is to this more powerful group that the wealth, plundered by the
political means, accrues. In time this group becomes entrenched both
politically and economically, through its plundered wealth."[61]

But this relatively straight-forward process becomes much more
complicated in today's world. Now, all areas are ruled by governments.
Hence, one cannot simply organize a military band, impose one's will
on a stateless society, call oneself a government, and begin to collect
taxes. Further, since the government is the most powerful institution
in society, a direct assault is usually doomed to fail. While in primitive
societies the ruling elite was able to set up its own government, today
this is no longer, or only rarely, possible. The ruling elite of today is
that group which, working through the existing power structure, is
able to obtain control of the government and use it for its own purposes. This means that the vast bulk of the government bureaucracy
are not really members of the elite except in the broadest sense of the
term, but rather conscious or unconscious servants of that group. It
also means that, and this is perhaps more important, the essence of the
state has remained unchanged from primitive times. It is still the insti-
tutionalization of the political means for the purpose of the transfer of
wealth from the producing group to the exploiting or ruling group.

Though it might at first seem paradoxical, Rothbard believes that
the ruling group of today is composed of the upper echelons of the capitalist class, or what Grinder refers to as the "corporate-financial super-
rich," although certainly not everyone who is rich is part of this elite.
He reasons as follows. The position of the entrepreneur on the market
is always insecure. Just as the market provides opportunities for the ac-

quisition of wealth, it also presents the possibility of loss. This means that the entrepreneur could never relax. No sooner would he triumph over one competitor than he would be met by others intent upon cutting into "his" share of the market. No sooner would he uncover a lucrative area for returns on investment than other entrepreneurs would follow suit, the increasing production forcing the profit rate down. And as soon as he would fail to take advantage of the latest investment opportunities or adopt the latest methods of production he would risk losing his investment to those who did. And behind all of this there is, of course, the ever present possibility of entrepreneurial error. Since the first concern of the capitalist is to realize a profit, and since the rigors of the market mean that this is a difficult and perpetual struggle for an ever elusive object, the capitalist has no concern for the market, as such. Hence it was only natural for him to turn, whenever possible, to the state which, with its monopoly on the use of force, could institutionalize profits by implementing various statist measures such as tariffs, subsidies, licensing restrictions, etc., in order to keep out competition, raise prices and keep wage rates low. As Rothbard has put it, "all the various measures of federal regulation and welfare statism . . . are not only now backed by Big Business, but were originated by it for the very purpose of shifting from a free market to a cartelized economy that would benefit it."[62]

In other words, Rothbard believes that there is a natural affinity between wealth and power. Those who have political power can use it to obtain wealth. On the other hand, the wealthy are able to use their wealth to obtain political power. Once in control of the state, they are in a position to use the political means to perpetuate and even enhance their own positions in the socio-economic hierarchy. As Rothbard sees it, this creates a vicious circle: wealth can be used to acquire political power which in turn can be used to acquire more wealth. While the circle is not completely closed, its opening is certainly quite small. The "rise to the top" by those from the lower economic strata is not ruled out completely. However, its occurrence which would be difficult under any circumstances is made even more so by the *artificial obstacles* imposed by the elite. Such, in brief, is the individualist anarchist theory of the state as an instrument of elite rule.

Evaluation of the Rothbardian Viewpoint

Before evaluating this argument, two points need to be clarified. First, although Rothbard usually uses the term "class analysis," "caste analysis" would be more appropriate.[63] The key distinction between "class" and "caste" is that the former is characterized by fluidity; the latter by rigidity. Individuals may move into and out of a class; such movement is precisely what is missing in a caste.

The distinction is crucial for grasping the Rothbardian position. It is a characteristic of the market process that wealth is dispersed unevenly. But if the market is free there are no external impediments preventing an individual or group from rising from a lower to a higher economic position. For example, such racial groups as the Jews and the Overland Chinese have generally abstained from politics. Yet without exception they have achieved economic success wherever they have migrated. In fact, this success was often achieved in the face of governmentally mandated discrimination.[64] Similarly, the vast majority of immigrants to America were penniless upon their arrival. This was a strictly *temporary* phase. After adjusting to American life, which usually meant adjusting to the shock of moving from a rural to an urban environment, these invididuals, and in fact entire ethnic groups, began to ascend the economic ladder, their places at the bottom being taken by succeeding generations of immigrants. Thus, while there is a permanent "bottom twenty percent" the individual occupants of that category were constantly changing. In brief, *markets produce classes.*[65]

In contrast, a caste is characterized by its rigidity: one born into a caste remains in it for life. If the individualist anarchist is correct and the wealthy are able to use government to institutionalize their position one can refer to this as the *transformation of a class into a caste.* What is important for the anarchist position is that it is only through government that a socio-economic position can be institutionalized. As shown in Figure 3, this means that while the market results in classes, governments produce castes. These concepts are pure types. The question is not: which is present, class or caste? Elements of both

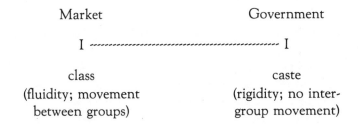

Market   Government

I --- I

class   caste
(fluidity; movement   (rigidity; no inter-
between groups)   group movement)

Figure 3. Class and Caste Distinctions

can be found in all societies. The key question is the *cause* of the relative mix of class and caste. If Rothbard's analysis is correct, one would expect to find relatively fewer castelike features, i.e., more fluidity, in more market oriented societies than in the more government dominated ones.

The second point needing clarification is the notion of conspiracy. The anarchist's caste analysis should *not* be interpreted as a conspiracy theory. Analyses of the distribution of power in society are usually divided into two broad descriptive *categories*: pluralism and elitism. Pluralism insists that power is widely diffused; elitism maintains that it is highly concentrated. The anarchist analysis, of course, is in the elitist tradition. Now it should be evident that the real question is not: is power diffused or concentrated? Rather, it is: to what *degree* is power diffused (or concentrated)? Posing the question in this way enables us to see that rather than viewing elitism and pluralism as mutually exclusive categories, they are relative positions on a spectrum running from total concentration at one pole to infinite diffusion at the other. This is shown in Figure 4.

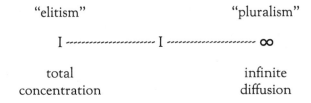

Figure 4. Degree of Power Concentration (Diffusion)

The extremes of total concentration and infinite diffusion are, of course, pure types. While they are useful for analytical purposes there are few if any "elitists" who believe that power is concentrated in the hands of a single person or even a few individuals; similarly, there are few if any "pluralists" who claim that power is infinitely diffused throughout society. One can, as was done in Figure 4, divide the spectrum in half and label those on one side "elitists" and those on the other "pluralists." This is a convenient way of dealing with the differences and there is nothing wrong with this procedure provided one realizes that the real difference is a matter of degree; that one position shades into another and any line of demarcation is arbitrary. All that one can say is that those who are termed "elitists" believe that power is relatively more concentrated than those labelled "pluralists."

When viewed in this light, it is clear that in its most extreme version elitism is *compatible* with the notion of a small, unseen conspiratorial elite, ensconced behind closed doors, busily pulling strings, bribing politicians and manipulating the key institutions throughout society. But nothing so sinister is *required* and neither the elitists in general nor Rothbard in particular subscribe to such a position. Rather, the validity of elitism hinges upon the presence of two things:

(a) a set of social institutions which regularly operates to the advantage of a relatively small group, i.e., *the group benefits*; and

(b) this group is primarily responsible for establishing and/or preserving those social institutions, i.e., *the group rules*.

It should be pointed out that neither of these propositions *requires* (1) that the elite is either omnipotent or omniscient; (2) that the elite always wins; (3) that the elite is a completely cohesive group; (4) that the elite is completely unresponsive to the needs and demands of the other groups in society; (5) that the presence of a ruling elite means that the other groups in society are made worse off in any absolute sense; (6) or that there is no mobility between the rulers and the ruled. This is because, it must again be pointed out, the difference between elitism and pluralism is one of degree, not kind. For example, the degree of "responsiveness" or "upward mobility" required of a particular theory would depend on the point at which the theory would place itself on the spectrum. The closer a theory is to the pole of "infinite diffusion" the greater the degree of responsiveness demanded of it. Similarly, such things as "elite omnipotence" or the complete absence of intergroup mobility is required only of those extremist theories falling on or near the poll of "total concentration." The further one moves from this pole, the more mobility permitted by a theory. Having cleared away the underbrush the caste analysis can now be evaluated.

"In all societies, from societies that are very meagerly developed . . . down to the most advanced and powerful societies," wrote Italian political sociologist Gaetano Mosca,

two classes of people appear, a class that rules and a class that is ruled. The first class, always the less numerous, performs all political functions, monopolizes power and enjoys the advantages that power brings, whereas the second, the more numerous class, is directed and controlled by the first.[66]

This is a succinct statement of the elitist position. Is it congruent with the evidence?

One must admit that it is an accurate description of dictatorship. In the Soviet Union the Communist Party monopolizes control of the government and through it the entire society. It is the sole political party; no others are permitted to exist. Admission to the party is rigidly controlled, party membership kept to about 5% of the general population. Within the party power is concentrated in the hands of a very small group known as the Politburo. Since the Politburo determines its own membership, it is a self-perpetuating oligarchy. It is clear that party members, and in particular party officials, monopolize power. Not surprisingly, this group also "enjoys the benefits that power brings." Officially, wealth is distributed fairly evenly. But this is quite misleading because of the huge economic and social benefits that accrue to party membership. Because of these benefits, there is a waiting list for admission to the party.[67]

Dictatorships such as the Soviet Union fit the Rothbardian caste analysis: a small, distinct ruling group monopolizes power and uses that power for its own benefit. But what of democracies such as the United States? Isn't it precisely because democracy introduces competition and thus the ever-present possibility of removal from office, that the rulers neither (1) constitute a ruling caste nor (2) are able to use their power to their own advantage?

Is there a ruling caste in the United States? Although space precludes a full-scale historical investigation, the evidence is at least very suggestive.

While more open than in the Soviet Union, acquiring elite positions in the United States can hardly be said to be equally accessible to all. Political scientists Kenneth Prewitt and Alan Stone among others have concluded that the wealthiest 20% of the families in this country supply about 90% of the ruling elite. Of the remaining 10% about 9% is drawn from families in the second 20% with the remaining 1% scattered among the bottom 60%.[68] This is shown in Figure 5.

Family Ranking Based on Wealth	Percent of Elite Supplied
top 20%	90
second 20%	9
bottom 60%	1

Figure 5. Income Groups and Elite Recruitment

In itself, this merely demonstrates the existence of a ruling class, not a caste. It is conceivable that there is a rapid turnover in the top 20%. But this does not appear to be the case. The ruling elite is composed of white, well-educated, wealthy, native-born, Protestant, middle-aged, males, the same traits, Dye and Zeigler have noted, that were required for elite status in 1789.[69] This evidence suggests that while individuals of exceptional intelligence, drive and/or luck can and do attain elite status, the elite is a relatively small, homogeneous, permanent and largely closed group.

This does not imply either that the elite is a conspiratorial group or that elite status is solely a matter of birth. "Achievement is the final arbiter of elite recruitment." But there is a high correlation between birth and achievement. A Harvard graduate from a wealthy family with good connections is certainly much more likely to enter the elite than a son of a Midwestern garage mechanic. The simple fact is that opportunities are not distributed equally.

But it is not achievement in the abstract that is important, but a specific type of achievement. To cite Prewitt and Stone:

> Persons who reach elite positions will have demonstrated ability to manage, direct and command. . . . This again suggests why the better-off contribute so disproportional to the elite groups. The wealthy or well-born have the initial advantages that provide the education and contacts necessary to gain positions in which talent and ability can be demonstrated on a grand scale. The used car salesman may be as skilled . . . and as hard-working as the president of General Motors, but he was born into the working class, not the upper classes . . . his friends also sell used cars, rather than direct corporations that sell them. . . . When the list is compiled of possible appointees to the Cabinet or possible candidates for the ambassadorship, it seems never to include the skilled, personable, hard-working used car salesman.[70]

A final consideration is that individuals tend to associate with others of the same social status. It is quite natural, then, that the ruling elite would recruit most heavily from those with upper class backgrounds similar to their own, just as those with upper class backgrounds naturally gravitate toward elite positions. For the same reason those from lower classes tend to enter less esteemed positions. The son of the president of General Motors is far more likely to become a corporate executive than a mechanic; the son of a garage mechanic is much more likely to become a mechanic than a corporate executive.

In brief, the evidence does suggest that there is a ruling elite, that this elite is largely closed and tends to perpetuate itself, that elite recruitment is based on achievement but that there is a close affinity between achievement and birth. Moreover, none of this, it was argued, implies a conspiracy. On the contrary, the method of recruitment and self-perpetuation is quite natural. Although it may be too strong to refer to the ruling elite as a caste, it does exhibit a caste-like quality. The question that now must be addressed is: does this elite use its position to benefit itself?

Even granting the existence of a ruling elite, doesn't competition for votes insure that the rulers will be responsive to the demands of the ruled? According to Anthony Downs this is precisely the case.[71]

The goal of a political party, according to the Downsian model, is to win elections. As such it can be compared to the firm in the business world. Just as in a competitive situation the firm will maximize profits by maximizing sales, so a party will win elections by maximizing votes. And just as the profit motive insures that the entrepreneur will respond to the demands of the consumer, the vote motive, assuming that the voters are well informed, constrains the political entrepreneurs to respond to the demands of the electorate. The moment the entrepreneur, in either case, fails to serve his clients the clients will turn to alternative suppliers.

Given the assumptions of *vote maximization* on the part of parties and *perfect information* on the part of voters, the conclusion that the parties will respond to the demands of the electorate must necessarily follow. This is a most comforting theory indeed. While consistent with the existence of a ruling elite this model assures us that the elite will be constrained from abusing its power by the ever-present possibility of displacement from office in the next election. Is this an accurate description of the democratic process?

Donald Wittman has challenged both of Downs's assumptions.[72] The real goal of a party, he says, is not to win elections but to maximize its *utility*. This is done by adopting policies in accord with the preferences of its *members*. Winning elections is a necessary means to this goal but should not be confused with the goal itself. A party will maximize its utility by adopting a platform which will maximize the party's chances of winning the election while still retaining as many benefits for itself as possible.

Both the information level of the voters and the number of existing parties are key factors in the choice of a party's strategy. With totally uninformed voters voting would be a random process. Since each party would then have an equal chance of winning regardless of its stand on issues, the rational party would adopt that platform which would provide itself with 100% of the benefits. Presumably, the more informed the voters the larger the share of benefits each party would be forced to offer the voters. At this point, the Downs and Wittman models are in agreement. Other things being equal party responsiveness is a function of the information level of the voters. Their difference here is that for analytical purposes Downs assumes perfect information while Whitman assumes a totally uninformed electorate. These positions are seen in Figure 6. The Downsian position is *D,D'*; Wittman's is *W,W'*. But this agreement is more apparent than real. The relationship between

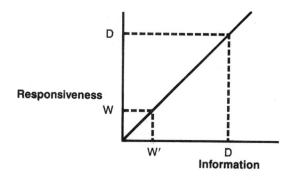

Fig. 6: Responsiveness as a Function of Information

information and responsiveness is never questioned by Downs. Given the assumption that parties are interested solely in winning elections, it is obvious that the relationship must hold, since winning is a zero-sum game. However, argues Wittman, if parties are interested in maximizing utility, and if the number of parties is sufficiently small, collusion rather than competition may be the optimal strategy. In fact, what is more interesting is that the better informed the electorate, the greater the incentive for collusion. As shown above, the better informed the electorate the more benefits the competitive party would have to provide the voters. This, of course, is precisely Downs's point. But this also means the fewer the benefits retained by the party. Thus, party competition with informed voters would all but eliminate the benefits to party members. In such a situation instead of competing against one another to serve the voters, it becomes rational for parties to collude with one another against the voters. Major issues are then avoided, the competition is limited to "advertising and product differentiation," and the voters are denied a choice on fundamental policy issues.

Collusion prevents the benefits from flowing to the voters. They are retained by the parties for internal distribution. Thus, either way, according to Wittman, the voters lose. If voters are completely uninformed the parties might compete but they will adopt policies that will provide themselves with all of the benefits. With two parties, each party would have a 50% chance of winning 100% of the benefits. If voters are informed parties will collude, in which case each party will have a 100% chance of receiving 50% of the benefits. This is shown in Figure 7.

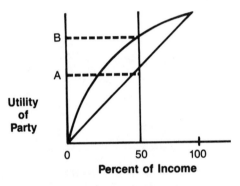

A = Expected Utility with 50% chance of 100% of the income and 50% chance of 0% of the income (competition).

B = Expected Utility with 100% chance of 50% of the income (collusion).

Fig. 7: Party Utility Under Competition and Collusion

In brief, in contrast to the Downsian model in which parties are viewed as sales-maximizing firms, Wittman depicts them as profit-maximizing oligolopists:

> Just as oligolopists often collude against the consumers, the parties may collude against the voters. In such cases the distinction between multiparty systems and one party systems may not be very great.[73]

For our purposes it is not necessary to prove collusion, although several examples come immediately to mind: the 1940 agreement between Roosevelt and Wilkie to avoid the issue of the war in Europe;

the apparently tacit agreement between the parties to avoid such issues as civil rights in the 1950s and the war in Vietnam in the 1960s. Since Downs's model hinges on the correlation between responsiveness and information, we need only examine this relationship. Public opinion studies consistently indicate an appalling lack of political knowledge on the part of the average citizen. Only about 50% even know that each state has two Senators; fewer still can name their Congressman or know the length of his term, much less what party he belongs to or how he voted.[74] Given this dearth of information, most voters would be much closer to W,W' than D,D'. That is to say, information levels are too low to insure much in the way of responsiveness.

Interestingly, while Downs assumes perfect information, he nevertheless comments that since the preservation of the democratic process is a public good, voting and the acquisition of political information are irrational. Put differently, while the Downsian model works only when the voters are well informed, Downs himself says that given the marginal costs and benefits of political information it is rational to be politically ignorant. This admission deprives the model of its previously comforting conclusions as Downs appears to be saying one shouldn't really expect the democratic process to be very responsive after all. But this was precisely Wittman's contention all along. Ultimately, their only major difference, then, is whether parties will compete for all of the benefits or collude for a share of the benefits.

Although political parties might not insure a responsive system, some commentators have argued that the interest group does. This is the position taken by the pluralists.[75] Individuals who perceive a problem will naturally gravitate toward one another and form a group. Often this group will then make demands on government. These groups are so numerous that no single group can ever reach a position of dominance. If it ever appeared that a group was beginning to become too powerful other groups would join forces to counter this. Government is seen as an umpire mediating between the demands of these groups. Decisions are reached through compromise and bargaining in which every group gets some of what it desires, but no group gets all of what it wants. This too is a comforting theory. Government is responsive to the public, this time not as expressed through political parties but through interest groups.

Although far more sophisticated than this, the foregoing is the gist of the pluralist position. There is no doubt an element of truth in pluralism, but the picture is far less rosy than the pluralists would have it. To operate effectively in the interest group system three things are required: time, money and expertise. Both time and money are required to put together an effective interest group; money is also required to hire the services of lobbyists; and some expertise is needed to know how to manipulate the political system. The simple fact is that these traits are not distributed randomly but are clustered at the top end of the politico-economic ladder. As one commentator has put it, the interest group system is "skewed, loaded, and unbalanced in favor of a [wealthy] minority." And, he adds, probably "about 90 percent of the people cannot get into the pressure system."[76] This means that in so far as the government responds to the demands of interest groups, and those demands are more or less restricted to a wealthy minority, government policies will reflect the interests of this minority. Politicians, writes Alfred Cuzan "have no incentive to redistribute income and wealth from 'the rich' to 'the poor.' A politician gains nothing taxing well-organized, well-informed, high-income groups and spending the money among a larger number of unorganized low-income people who might not even realize the benefits of the action. On the contrary, the organized, high-income groups will oppose him while the unorganized poor will do nothing." "Political profit is made," Cuzan continues, "by taxing the uninformed and the unorganized and spending on the informed and organized." The former tend to be the poor; the latter the rich. Cuzan terms this the "iron law of political redistribution."[77]

Far from representing the interest of the public at large, as claimed by the pluralists, the interest group system is, in fact, almost ideally suited to the interests of a wealthy elite. Thus, neither political parties nor interest groups prevent the emergence of a ruling elite. Nor, it would seem, do they prevent that elite from using its position to benefit itself.

From the foregoing one would expect that government would make class lines more rather than less fluid. A full scale test of this hypothesis would take us too far afield. But a cursory review of the data does lend support for it.

The standard interpretation of the Progressive Period of the late nineteenth and early twentieth centuries holds that many businesses had achieved monopolistic positions which they were using to gouge the public. Responding to public pressure government intervened to subject business to regulatory control. Recent historical and economic scholarship has largely discredited this view by showing that the business elite actually favored government regulation. Why? Far from tending toward monopolism markets in practically every area were becoming increasingly competitive. To cite a single example, in 1894

AT&T was the only company in its field. By 1907 AT&T found itself in competition with over 22,000 companies. Similar trends, if less dramatic, existed in such fields as oil, steel, meat packing and automobile production to name but a few. Big business desired government regulation as a means to rescue itself from the increasing competition. And such regulation did serve to institutionalize its economic position. As one historian phrased it,

> political power in our society after the Civil War responded to power and influence in the hands of businessmen, who have often had more leverage over political . . . then over business affairs—and they were quick to use it to solve business problems"[78]

The New Deal is another period in which government is usually viewed as responding to popular pressures to shackle big business. Yet, as historian James Martin notes, "contrary to the brave talk of the 'reformers' financial concentration steadily piled upon between 1933 and 1941."[79] Similar findings were reported by Prewit and Stone,[80] and Radosh and Rothbard[81].

Finally, analyses of current income transfers do not indicate any transfer from the rich to the poor. Although the federal income tax appears to be progressive, much of the progressivity is eliminated by loopholes. And when this is combined with the regressive nature of social security and most state and local taxes, the overall effect is that the tax burden is "essentially proportional for the vast majority of families."[82]

When one considers the direct effect of such government programs as subsidies to businesses such as Lockheed and the Chrysler Corporation, and the indirect effect of such policies as licensing restrictions and tariffs, which cost consumers in excess of $130 billion a year, the overall effect of government policies appears to be a slight transfer of wealth from the less well off to the better off. Two examples serve to illustrate this point. A study of the Shaw-Cardozo ghetto in Washington, D.C. revealed that in 1967 the federal government spent $45.7 million to fight poverty. However, it took out of that same area $50 million in taxes.[83] And economist Walter Williams has determined that $250 billion dollars is spent annually at all levels of government in the name of "fighting poverty."[84] Now, if all of this were simply divided equally among those families with reported incomes below the poverty line, each family would receive a yearly stripend of $34,000. Of course very little of this ever reaches the poor. Most of it gets eaten up in bureaucratic overhead or siphoned off by private contractors.[85]

We can now conclude. According to the Rothbardian caste analysis the upper classes are able to use their wealth to capture control of government. They are then able to use the coercive arm of government to institutionalize their positions. In this process economic and social mobility becomes more restricted as the economic class congeals into a political caste. This holds true *regardless of the type of government.*

Although dictatorships tend to be more castelike than democracies, the evidence does indicate support for the anarchist position. Neither political parties nor interest groups have prevented a ruling elite from emerging. While this elite is not completely closed, it does appear to be relatively permanent enough to be termed castelike, if not actually a caste. And finally, evidence was adduced which indicates that this elite does "enjoy the advantages that power brings."

Conclusion

The Rothbardian paradigm has been presented in some detail, from its logical origins in the distinction between "freedom" and "power" to its analysis of markets and governments. It was shown that the market maximizes "social utility" when that term is used in its ordinal sense. Moreover, even when "social utility" is interpreted in a cardinal sense there is no convincing evidence that any act of government ever increases "social utility" relative to the market. It was also shown that the logical corollary of the Rothbardian analysis is that markets produce classes while governments transform those classes into castes. Finally, an overview of the empirical evidence indicates that the model has very strong explanatory power.

In short, the Rothbardian paradigm is a potent analytical tool which enables us to accurately survey the complicated politico-economic landscape.

Notes

1. Murray N. Rothbard, *Power and Market* (Menlo Park, Calif.: Institute for Humane Studies, 1970), pp. 179-80.
2. Murray N. Rothbard, *Man, Economy, and State* (Los Angeles: Nash, 1970), pp. 179-80.
3. Ibid., p. 561.
4. Murray N. Rothbard, *For A New Liberty* (New York: Macmillan, 1973), p. 43.
5. Rothbard, *Power and Market*, p. 179.
6. Ibid., p. 164.
7. Rothbard, *For A New Liberty*, p. 43.
8. Rothbard, *Power and Market*, p. 172.

9. Warren J. Samuels, "Anarchism and the Theory of Power," in *Further Reflections In the Theory of Anarchy*, Gordon Tullock, ed. (Blacksburg, Va.: University Publishing, 1974), p. 48.

10. Ibid., p. 40.

11. Ibid., p. 40.

12. Ibid., p. 51.

13. Ibid., p. 49-46.

14. Robert Dahl, *Modern Political Analysis* (Englewood Cliffs, N.J.: Prentice-Hall, 1970), p. 14-34; idem "Power," *International Encyclopedia of the Social Sciences*, vol. 12 (New York: Macmillan, 1968), pp. 405-15; Harold Lasswell and Abraham Kaplan, *Power and Society* (New Haven: Yale University Press, 1950).

15. Dahl, *Modern Political Analysis*, p. 32.

16. Lasswell and Kaplan, *Power and Society*, pp. 74-76.

17. Arthur Kalleburg, "The Logic of Comparison: A Methodological Note on the Comparative Study of Political Systems," *World Politics* (October 1986): 69-82.

18. Dahl, *Modern Political Analysis*, p. 32.

19. Not everyone, however, regards the lack of "operationalizability" as a liability. See, for example, Giovanni Sartori:

   > Now, we are surely required to reduce ambiguity by cutting down the range of meanings of concepts. But the operational criterion of reducing ambiguity entails drastic losses in conceptual richness and in explanatory power. Take, for instance, the suggestion that 'social class' should be dismissed and re-placed by a set of operational statements relating to income, occupation, education level, etc. If the suggestions were adopted wholesale, the loss of conceptual substance would be not only considerable, but unjustified. The same applies, to cite another example, to 'power.' To be concerned with the measurement of power does not imply that the meaning of the concept should be reduced to what can be measured about power—the latter view would make human behavior in whatever collective sphere almost inexplicable" (Giovanni Sartori, "Concept Misinformation in Comparative Politics," *The American Political Science Review* [December 1970]: 1045).

   Two things are worthy of note. First, the use of imprecise concepts may well be worth-while, even needed, at the level of research. But this can hardly be the case at the level of application, i.e., as used by decision makers. And it is the level of application that Rothbard is concerned with. Second, even at the level of research, "conceptual richness" may well prove to be merely a euphemism for "conceptual confusion."

20. In this context it is worth noting that in his review of Rothbard's *Power and Market*, Milton Shapiro has aptly noted that perhaps a better title would have been *Power or Market*; Milton Shapiro, "Power OR Market: Government and the Economy: a Review," *Libertarian Analysis*, vol. 1, no. 4 (1971): 22-29. Regardless of the title, *Power and Market* is probably the most sustained and intellectually brilliant critique of government *ever* written.

21. Rothbard, *For a New Liberty*, p. 219-52; idem, "Society Without a State," *Libertarian Forum* (January 1975): 3-7.

22. Dahl, *Modern Political Analysis*, pp. 32-33.

23. H. E. Frech, III, "The Public Choice Theory of Murray N. Rothbard: A Modern American Anarchists," *Public Choice* 14 (1973): 249-50.

24. Rothbard, *Power and Market*, p. 172.

25. Robert Nozick, *Anarchy, State, and Utopia* (New York: Basic Books, 1974); John Hospers, *Libertarianism* (Santa Barbara, Calif.: Reason Press, 1971); idem, "Will

Rothbard's Free Market Justice Suffice? No," *Reason* (May 1973); James Buchanan, "Social Choice, Democracy, and Free Markets," *Journal of Political Economy* (April 1954); and Gordon Tullock, *Private Wants, Public Means* (New York: Basic Books, 1970), p. 170.

26. William Wooldridge, *Uncle Sam the Monopoly Man* (New Rochelle, N.Y.: Arlington House, 1970), pp. 116-17; David Osterfeld, *Freedom, Society and the State* (San Francisco: Cobden Press, 1986), pp. 350-63.

27. Bruno Leoni, *Freedom and the Law* (Princeton: Van Nostrand, 1972), p. 55.

28. Rothbard, *For A New Liberty*, p. 208.

29. Ibid., p. 209.

30. See Thomas Sowell, *Race and Economics* (New York: Longman, 1975); idem, *Ethnic America* (New York: Basic, 1981); idem, *The Economics and Politics of Race* (New York: William Morrow, 1983); and Walter Williams, "Commentary," *Newsweek* (24 September 1979); idem, *The State Against Blacks* (New York: McGraw-Hill, 1982).

31. Rothbard, *For A New Liberty*, p. 43.

32. F. A. Hayek, *The Constitution of Liberty* (Chicago: Henry Regnery, 1972), p. 12.

33. Harold Laski, "Liberty," *Encyclopedia of the Social Sciences*, vol. 9 (New York: Macmillan, 1946), p. 443.

34. Hayek, *The Constitution of Liberty*, pp. 12-13.

35. Rothbard, *Power and Market*, p. 160.

36. Murray N. Rothbard, "Toward a Reconstruction of Utility and Welfare Economics," in *On Freedom and Free Enterprise*, Mary Sennholz, ed. (Princeton: Van Nostrand, 1956), p. 250.

37. Rothbard, *Man, Economy, and State*, pp. 463-69.

38. Ibid., pp. 498-501; idem, *Power and Market*, p. 161.

39. Ludwig von Mises, *Human Action* (Chicago: Henry Regnery, 1966), p. 744.

40. Rothbard, "Towards a Reconstruction," p. 252-53.

41. Julian Simon, "Interpersonal Welfare Comparisons Can Be Made—And Used for Redistribution Decisions," *Kyklos* 27 (1972): 63-98.

42. Simon argues that "it is scientifically wrong to say that *in principle* individuals' welfare cannot be compared." "In principle, the definition (and measurement) of 'utility' is no more difficult than the definition (and measurement) of 'chair' or 'money.' One simply describes a set of operations that seem to fit one's common or intuitive associations of the word 'chair,' 'money,' or 'utility.' Of course no operational definition is perfect." But "If *no* operational definition of a word makes any sense, we may take this as a sign that the word we seek to define is metaphysical or nonsensical or non-scientific." Simon proposes to use such things as "suicide rates," "murder rates," "surveys of verbal reports about well being," etc. I must admit that I do not find any of these very convincing. Now Simon maintains that if one does not believe that these, or other measurable rates, are reasonably accurate proxies for utility then the term utility is "nonsensical." But I simply do not see that because a concept is not measurable it logically follows that it is "nonsensical." I simply do not see why it is illogical to maintain that (a) utility does exist; that it does have an ontological status, but (b) it is not measurable. Simon's position, it seems to me is based, on the *non sequitur* that if it cannot be measured it doesn't exist, ibid., pp. 64-67.

43. Rothbard, "Towards a Reconstruction," p. 252.

44. Whether one wishes to admit as evidence conclusions based on such relaxed or weak assumptions is another question altogether.

45. Sowell, *Ethnic America*, p. 3.

46. F. A. Hayek, *Individualism and Economic Order* (Chicago: Gateway, 1972), pp. 66-68. Adam Smith reaches much the same conclusion:

As we have no immediate experience of what other men feel, we can form no idea of the manner in which they are affected, but by conceiving what we ourselves should feel in the like situation. Though our brother is upon the rack, as long as we ourselves are at our ease, our senses will never inform us of what are his sensations. . . . By our imagination we place ourselves in his situation, we conceive ourselves enduring all the same torments, we enter as it were into his body, and become in some measure the same person with him, and thence form some idea of his sensations, and even feel something which, though weaker in degree, is not altogether unlike them. . . . Whatever is the passion which arises from any object in the person principally concerned, and analogous emotion springs up, at the thought of his situation, in the breast of every attentive spectator" (Adam Smith, *The Theory of Moral Sentiments* [New Rochelle, N.Y.: Arlington House, 1969], pp. 3-5).

47. See D. L. Landau, "Government Expenditure and Economic Growth in the Developed Countries: 1952-76," *Public Choice* 47, no. 3 (1985): 459-78; Mancur Olson, *The Rise and Decline of Nations* (New Haven: Yale University Press, 1982); and Melvyn Krauss, *Development Without Aid* (New York: McGraw-Hill, 1983), especially pp. 157-60.

48. "In Praise of Peasants," *The Economist* (2 February 1985): 86-87; David Osterfeld, "Famine in Africa," *The Journal of Social, Political and Economic Studies*" (Fall 1985): 259-74; "China: Capitalism in the Making," *Time* (30 April 1984): 26-34; David R. Francis, "China's Economy Picks Up Speed," *Christian Science Monitor* (7 March 1985).

49. Charles Murray, *Losing Ground* (New York: Basic Books, 1984), p. 9.

50. Ibid., p. 9.

51. See James Gwartney and Thomas McCaleb, "Have Antipoverty Programs Increased Poverty?" *The Cato Journal* (Spring/Summer 1985): 1-16; Dwight Lee, "The Politics of Poverty and the Poverty of Politics," *The Cato Journal* (Spring/Summer 1985): 17-36; and David Osterfeld, "The Government, the Market and the Poor," *The Freeman* (November 1980): 643-59.

52. Lee, "The Politics of Poverty"; Krauss, *Development Without Aid*; Peter Bauer, *Reality and Rhetoric* (Cambridge, Mass.: Harvard University Press, 1984); Peter Bauer and Basil Yamey, "Foreign Aid: What Is at Stake?" in *The Third World*, W. Scott Thompson, ed. (San Francisco: Institute for Contemporary Studies, 1983), pp. 115-35; Thomas Sowell, "Second Thoughts About the Third World," *Harpers* (November 1983): 34-42; David Osterfeld, "Assessing the New International Order: Prospects for Third World Development," *The Journal of Social, Political and Economic Studies* (Spring/Summer 1982): 3-26; idem, "Famine in Africa"; idem, "Resources, People, and the Neomalthusian Fallacy," *The Cato Journal* (Spring/Summer 1985): 67-102.

53. James Schall, "The Bishops' Pastoral on Economics and Social Justice," *The Intercollegiate Review* (Fall 1975): 7-15.

54. Landau, "Government Expenditure and Economic Growth," p. 460.

55. Ibid., p. 473.

56. Henry Lepage, *Tomorrow, Capitalism* (LaSalle, Ill.; Open Court, 1982), p. 122.

57. Franz Oppenheimer, *The State* (New York: Free Life Editions, 1975), pp. 1-41.

58. Ibid.

59. Rothbard, *Power and Market*, p. 127.

60. Murray N. Rothbard, "The Anatomy of the State," in *The Libertarian Alternative*, Tibor R. Machan, ed. (Chicago: Nelson Hall, 1974), pp. 69-93.

61. Walter Grinder, "Introduction" to Albert Jay Nock, *Our Enemy, the State* (New York: Free Life, 1973), pp. xviii-xix.

62. Murray N. Rothbard, "Confessions of a Right-Wing Liberal," *Ramparts* (15 June 1968): 51.

63. Rothbard has, on rare occasions, used the term "caste." But this has been either relegated to footnotes (*Power and Market*, p. 198, 5n) or placed in parentheses ("The Anatomy of the State," p. 82).

64. Sowell, *The Economics and Politics of Race*.

65. Sowell, *Ethnic America*.

66. Gaetano Mosca, *The Ruling Class*, (New York: McGraw-Hill, 1939), p. 50.

67. Konstantin Simis, *USSR: The Corrupt Society* (New York: Simon and Schuster, 1982), pp. 535-64; Hedrick Smith, *The Russians* (New York: Balantine, 1984), pp. 30-64.

68. Kenneth Prewitt and Alan Stone, *The Ruling Elites* (New York: Harper and Row, 1973), pp. 136-37.

69. Thomas Dye and Harmon Zeigler, *The Irony of Democracy* (Monterey, Calif.: Duxbury, 1981), pp. 19-107.

70. Prewitt and Stone, *The Ruling Elites*, pp. 143-44.

71. Anthony Downs, *An Economic Theory of Democracy* (New York: Harper and Row, 1957).

72. Donald Wittman, "Parties as Utility Maximizers," *American Political Science Review* (June 1973): 490-98.

73. Ibid.

74. Dye and Zeigler, *The Irony of Democracy*, p. 191.

75. See David Truman, *The Governmental Process* (New York: Alfred Knopf, 1951); Robert Dahl, *Who Governs?* (New Haven, Conn.: Yale University Press, 1962); Earl Lathan, *The Group Basis of Politics* (New York: Octagon Books, 1965).

76. E. E. Schattschneider, *The Semisovereign People* (Hillsdale, Ill.: Dryden Press, 1975), pp. 34-35.

77. Alfred Cuzan, "Political Profits: Taxing and Spending in the Hierarchical State," *American Journal of Economics and Sociology* (July 1981): 165-71.

78. Gabriel Kolko, "Power and Capitalism in 20th Century America," *Liberation* (December 1970): 21-26. Also see, idem, *The Triumph of Conservatism* (Chicago: Quadrangle Books, 1967); D. T. Armentano, *The Myths of Antitrust* (New Rochelle, N.Y.: Arlington House, 1972); A. S. Dewing, "A Statistical Test of the Success of Consolidations," *Quarterly Journal of Economics* (1921): 84-101; Roy Childs, "Big Business and the Rise of American Statism," in *The Libertarian Alternative*, Tibor R. Machan, ed. (Chicago: Nelson-Hall, 1974), pp. 502-524; Yale Brozen, "Is Government the Source of Monopoly?" in *The Libertarian Alternative*, Tibor R. Machan, ed. (Chicago: Nelson-Hall, 1974), pp. 149-68.

79. James Martin, "Business and the New Deal," *Reason* (December 1975): 20-26.

80. Prewitt and Stone, *The Ruling Elites*, pp. 44-50.

81. Ronald Radosh and Murray Rothbard, eds., *A New History of Leviathan* (New York: E. P. Dutton, 1972), pp. 111-87.

82. Joseph Pechman and Benjamin Okner, *Who Bears the Tax Burden?* (Washington, D.C., Brookings Institution, 1974), p. 10.

83. Rothbard, *For A New Liberty*, p. 190.

84. Williams, "Commentary," p. 57-59.

85. See George J. Stigler, "Director's Law of Public Income Redistribution," *The Journal of Law and Economics* (April 1970): 1-10; and Gordon Tullock, "The Charity of the Uncharitable," *Western Economic Journal* (December 1971): 379-92.

21

The Political Importance of Murray N. Rothbard

Murray N. Rothbard

O 322

Ron Paul

I t would be difficult to exaggerate Professor Murray N. Rothbard's influence on the movement for freedom and free markets. He is the living giant of Austrian economics, and he has led the now-formidable movement ever since the death of his great teacher, Ludwig von Mises, in 1971. We are all indebted to him for the living link he has provided to Mises, upon whose work he has built and expanded.

But many are less aware of Rothbard's political influence. Some would say that while he is undoubtedly an excellent economist, his political efforts have been less than successful.

I would deny this. Rothbard is the founder of the modern libertarian movement, and of the Libertarian Party which is its political incarnation, and he thus has built the necessary foundation for liberty by inspiring the most important third-party movement ever. And in my own political work, I have been profoundly influenced by the lucid and brilliant works of Rothbard.

In his first correspondence with me after I was elected to office, Rothbard expressed surprise and delight to find a real Congressman who wrote that "taxation is theft," and approvingly quoted his article, "Gold vs. Fluctuating Exchange Rates." I, of course, was thrilled to hear from someone whose works I had studied and admired for so many years.

The aura that has traditionally surrounded American politics in this century has turned to suspicion during the past decade. The scandals of Watergate (and, let us hope, Iran-Contragate as well) convinced the public, for a time, that it is naive to trust any mainstream politician. Rothbard was delighted with the whole event, saying in 1979 that, "it is Watergate that gives us the greatest single hope for the short-run victory of liberty in America. For Watergate, as politicians

329

have been warning us ever since, destroyed the public's 'faith in government'—and it was high time, too."

Rothbard rejoices, saying, "government itself has been largely desanctified in America. No one trusts politicians or government anymore; all government is viewed with abiding hostility, thus returning us to that State of healthy distrust of government that marked the American public and the American revolutionaries of the eighteenth century." For the sake of liberty, let us hope this hostility isn't just a passing phase.

Most understand that what a politician says during his campaign is rarely compatible with his performance. Still, this broad—and healthy—cynicism does not translate into clear public understanding of the lies of the average politician.

It is incredible how a politician can maintain an image while the facts clearly point in the opposite direction. Many still see President Reagan as a budget-cutter while he has proposed the largest budgets and deficits in our history.

While it is perhaps understandable that the public remains naive about the realities of politics, given the Establishment-media conspiracy to hide the truth, but the tendency of scholars to gloss over facts and misrepresent realities is absolutely inexcusable. Academics tend to cling to old interpretations, or worse, old Statist ideals which blur their view of reality. And when prevailing historical orthodoxy is challenged, those who have an interest in maintaining myths attempt to silence their opponents.

Just one example from his works is the case of Murray Rothbard's revisionist analysis of Herbert Hoover's pre-Depression years. When Rothbard set out to tell the story of Hoover, consider what he was up against. Republicans, who for the most part opposed Roosevelt's New Deal, blame the enormous growth of government that occurred during those years on the Democrats. Conversely, the Democrats, who are proud of the New Deal, take credit for it. Thus Republicans are taught that "Hoover's only problem was that he did not have a Republican Congress," and Democrats are taught that government should solve any crisis that "socially Darwinian free markets inevitably cause," just as Roosevelt did. And intellectuals are notoriously stubborn about accepting new historical interpretations, especially if the revision favors free markets over government planning.

It is a tough job to change historical interpretations—no matter how false—which have been solidified for generations in the minds of State-protecting partisans. Nevertheless Rothbard announced in 1963: "Herbert Clark Hoover must be considered the founder of the New

Deal in America." And in fact "Franklin D. Roosevelt, in large part, merely elaborated the policies laid down by his predecessor."

Rothbard's analysis is stunning and exhaustive. He set out to prove his proposition and did so without question. Hoover was an interventionist. He was philosophically committed to using the coercive machinery of government to bring about full employment, insure the survival and influence of labor unions, manipulate the price level for farmers' benefit, maintain wage levels and deport immigrants, prevent bankruptcies, and above all to inflate the money supply. Hoover did this in spite of the "bitter-end liquidationists" who thought the Depression represented a necessary correction in the malinvestment of the previous decade.

And indeed, against all odds, Rothbard has made inroads to changing the way history treats Hoover. The eminent British historian Paul Johnson, who became the darling of the conservative movement with his massive study on the history of Christianity and his history of the world during the twentieth century, *Modern Times*, was directly influenced by Rothbard's reconstruction of Hoover. In *Modern Times*, Johnson calls Hoover's fiscal and monetary policies "vulgar Keynesianism," a point upon which Rothbard had previously elaborated.

Idols for Destruction, a scholarly work by Herbert Schlossberg now causing much talk in conservative and evangelical circles, enthusiastically echoes Rothbard's historical revision of Hoover. "Herbert Hoover, amazingly referred to even by historians as a partisan of laissez-faire, energetically supported . . . a powerful central State that would coordinate the efforts of business."[1]

The New Deal was not new after all. It has hatched in the decade prior to Roosevelt's ascension to power. Rothbard's analysis, directly and indirectly, has led many to be more objective when evaluating partisan politics, both now and in the past.

Years before I ever thought of running for Congress, I came across Rothbard's *America's Great Depression*. Before reading it, my thinking was clouded by the temptation to divide these issues and ideas in partisan terms. Rothbard fixed that.

America's Great Depression was a key book in my conversion to pure free-market, libertarian thinking. The confidence I gained with ammunition supplied by Rothbard encouraged my entry into politics, since I needed the reassurance that my intuitive allegiance to liberty was shared by great thinkers. Rothbard taught me to always keep the distinction between peaceful market activity and State coercion in my mind. It served as a constant guide once I was in office.

I wanted to see the brilliant writings of theoreticians such as Rothbard translated into practical political action. To my surprise there was a strong constituency for these views, and I was elected to four terms.

Even a person familiar with only a small part of the vast work Rothbard has produced during his career knows his attitude towards politics. Like Mises, he labels the State as the "social apparatus of violent oppression."

How do we minimize the role of the State? To bring about radical and permanent change in any society, our primary focus must be on the conversion of minds through eduction. This is a task to which Rothbard has dedicated his life. That's why he was such a willing participant on so many occasions in the educational functions I held for interns, staffers, and Members of Congress. After speaking at a seminar I held, he expressed delight at the large turn-out, saying it "shows the extent to which our ideas have permeated politics and public opinion, far more than I had hoped or believed."

But because Rothbard sees education as the primary vehicle for change, that does not mean, of course, that he is opposed to getting directly involved in political action towards a libertarian society. As he had said, "since the State will not gracefully convert itself out of power, other means than education, means of pressure, will have to be used."

That's why I asked his help when I was appointed to the U.S. Gold Commission, and Rothbard produced brilliant material on American monetary history in the nineteenth century, especially as related to gold and the evils of central banking. These are issues that Rothbard has refused to compromise on, despite enormous pressure from inside and outside the movement. To this day, he remains the most persuasive monetary theorist and consistent critic of inflation and fiat paper money. When gold is once again restored to a central place in our monetary system, we will owe a gigantic debt to the work of Rothbard.

In fact, Rothbard's work with the Gold Commission helped us get on the road to a gold coin standard, because out of the Gold Commission came support for my legislation to mint the American Eagle Gold Coin. And his encouragement and support helped me make up my mind to run for the Presidency of the United States on the Libertarian Party ticket.

In a multitude of ways, Rothbard's work has given not only me but all of us the ammunition we need to fight for the American dream of liberty and prosperity for all mankind.

Notes

1. Although he is cited in the footnotes, Rothbard—economics' "hot-potato"—is not mentioned directly in the text of either book.

Part 4

History

22

A Utopia for Liberty: Individual Freedom in Austin Tappan Wright's *Islandia*

Arthur A. Ekirch, Jr.

Islandia is that rarity among literary Utopias—a novel that does not rest on the hope of establishing a socialist society. Instead Austin Tappan Wright's ingenious book describes a country dedicated to an individualist, humanist philosophy. Although *Islandia* has never received the wide attention that it deserves, it has not been completely ignored or forgotten. Now, more than forty years since its original publication in 1942, the book's message remains gentle but clear. Like all Utopias, it offers criticism as well as commentary.

The story of how *Islandia* came to be written is in itself both interesting and tragic. During the 1920s its author was a law professor, first at Berkeley and then at the University of Pennsylvania. Suddenly, in 1931, an unfortunate fatal accident at the age of 48 cut short a distinguished professional career. It was only later, when his widow showed his manuscripts to a former colleague, that Wright's amazing other life came to light. Like many before him, he had dreamed of a new and different kind of world—a unique Utopia. Youthful visions gradually became a literary reality as he sketched out in enormous detail the history, laws, and customs of his imaginary Karain continent which he located in the South Pacific. On the southern tip of this continent, behind a mountain barrier, was the country of Islandia with its three million people. From reams of factual material, which he had already set down in his notes, Wright distilled his novel. Later, a decade after his death, his daughter reduced *Islandia* to publishable size, being careful, however, to preserve the framework of Wright's manuscript and its striking contrast between the Islandian and American ways of life.

Contemporary reviews of *Islandia*, with a few exceptions, were favorable. Harold Strauss in the *New York Times* called it a "superb novel . . . a unique, brilliantly conceived and brilliantly executed book." Norman Cousins in the *Saturday Review of Literature* noted that "Austin Wright wanted Islandia to sound real and convincing; and this book is a monument to the success of that ambition." For the *New Yorker*, Clifton Fadiman wrote: "The book is assuredly one of the most remarkable examples of ingenuity in the history of literary invention. The detail is fabulous yet logical. . . ." Vernon Louis Parrington, Jr., from his study of American Utopias, concluded that "*Islandia* is the most carefully written and literary. . . . Had it been published at the end of World War II rather than at the beginning," he suggested, "the sale might have been far greater." Although briefly on the best seller lists, *Islandia* seemed out of step. Hostile to industrialism and technology, and isolationist in the foreign policy which it urged for Islandia, the book offered an image which the wartime New Deal era found difficult to accept.

Despite *Islandia's* size, some one thousand pages, the plan of the book is relatively simple. John Lang, Wright's hero or protagonist, goes to Islandia as its first American consul. This is possible only because the Islandians decide to open their country for a limited time to foreign visitors and possible trade. Lang, through a prior acquaintance at Harvard with Dorn, a visiting student from Islandia, is well qualified for the appointment to his unusual mission. Once arrived, after a long ocean voyage of three weeks, Lang with Dorn's help becomes familiar with Islandia's way of life. He also is able to win the confidence of its leading families. In this he is aided by his personal heroism in an Islandian military crisis, and by his love affairs with several rather stilted young Islandian women. Lang in his own emotions seems extraordinarily reserved. His restraint, however, may be in part a result of his equivocal role in a country hostile to any foreign intrusion. Although in the end he comes home to marry an American girl, they return to Islandia to live. Lang meanwhile has been singularly honored by the grant of Islandian citizenship which allows him to buy property and have a family in his adopted nation.

Unlike so many Utopian novels, *Islandia* is not dull. Lang's adventures give pace to the narrative, while Wright in his descriptive passages makes the Islandian environment realistic and appealing to his readers. But it is, of course, the interplay of the two cultures which gives the book its major interest and significance. Through Lang's conversations with his hosts, one comes to understand the Islandians' isolationist foreign policy and to appreciate their suspicion of Western progress and technology. Reverence for the land, as well as a free and sensible code of personal morality, are among the exemplary qualities of the Islandian people. Islandia seems, indeed, a model humanist society.

While they are at Harvard, in the beginning of the tale, Lang learns from Dorn that Islandia throughout its history "had been menaced and occasionally overrun by the peoples of the north." Primitive and savage, this vast Negro population was mixed with Arabic settlers who inhabited the immediate border area close to the mountains which isolate and protect Islandia. Recently trouble had been created by English, French, and German influence, seeking to organize the native population and penetrate Islandia's isolation. "Islandia's policy had been one of defensive self-protection. At times her borders had been extended beyond the natural lines, but afterwards she had always withdrawn behind her rampart of mountains. That she should remain there was Dorn's view."

But the Mora family, political opponents of Dorn's family, succeed in persuading the Islandian parliament to wage an aggressive war against its northern enemies. In this conflict, Lord Mora's governing faction is achieving success and, at the same time, proposing to open Islandia to European trade and commerce. "I am not afraid of war," young Dorn tells Lang, "but I am afraid that Mora and his followers will change us from what we now are, and that we cannot help it because of all the political contracts."

John Lang as a part of his consul's duties is an interested observer and reporter of the domestic struggle between the Lord Dorn and Lord Mora parties. And he also becomes involved in the border warfare to the north as he accompanies his friend Dorn on a dangerous intelligence mission across the mountains. Drawn more and more into the Dorn social and familial circle, Lang finds himself in growing sympathy with its anti-foreign political position. This, of course, conflicts with his responsibility as the American consul to seek out opportunities for trade and investment. At first he tries to defend industrial civilization. As the two friends travel north some ninety miles on horseback from the coast to the mountains through "scenery unsurpassed," Dorn tells Lang that a railroad route has been surveyed.

"It would save time," Lang observes.

"Speed, is that progress?" Dorn asks. "Anyway, why progress? Why not enjoy what one has? Men have never exhausted present pleasures. . . . Decide on an indispensable minimum. See that everyone has it, don't let anyone have any more."

"Dorn, you sounds like a socialist," Lang replies.

"Oh no," Dorn rejoins, "not with us. We grew that way, because we enjoyed so much what we had that we never really wanted more. It is individualism—that is, the individual enjoys so much what he has that he does not crave other things from the community."

Although Lang suffers some private social humiliation, he is able to persuade the Islandian girls to dance with him. But to them the American waltz is embarrassing. In the Islandian hedonistic culture it is a strange custom indeed "that makes a man and woman embrace without feeling anything!"

As Lang later tells his American fiancée, in Islandia *ania*, or romantic love, and *alia*, or friendship, are interlocking emotions, closely tied to "family feeling."

"They have no word for 'wife,' " he explains, "except one which literally means: *alia*-sharing lover."

But there is another conception: "*apia*, desire for a woman or man not as an *alia* sharer."

Although he enjoys the unfruitfulness of *apia* relationships with several Islandian young women, Lang dreams of *ania*, or the American conception of marriage, only with Dorn's sister, Dorna. In their rather intellectual courtship, sailing blissfully together along the coast on the *March Duck*, he tells Dorna of his reasons for coming to Islandia, and of the United States's hope of developing trade. American agricultural machinery, he explains, will save time and money. "There would be greater power to enjoy life."

"Do you think so?" she asks seriously. "There is no lack in that power now, John Lang. But I don't want to seem prejudiced. You said these machines would save time. That's worthwhile. If ever your countrymen try to sell us agricultural implements let them sell those that save time."

But Lang overstates his case when he argues the advantages of specialization from mass production. "You can accomplish more doing one thing. You become more skillful."

"But you touch life in fewer ways," Dorna says, as she defends the quiet, yet varied, Islandian hedonistic, agrarian, non-industrial way of life:

If we go on here as we have been, and are let alone, life hundreds of years from now will be as it is now; and life now, with growing things all about us and changing weather and lovely places kept beautiful and new people growing up, is too rich for

us already, too rich to endure sometimes. We haven't half exhausted it, and we cannot—we cannot so long as young people
are born and grown up and learn new things and have new
ideas. All that is to us the vital thing, John, and the changes foreigners propose—railroads to carry us about, new machines to
till the soil, electric lights, and all that—are just superficial
things, and not worth the price we have to pay for them in
changing our whole way of living, in threatening our children
with the chance of ruin!

Despite their great attraction for each other, Dorna must reject
Lang because she has been selected by Tor, the young Islandian King,
to be his bride. Lang also knows that a victory for Lord Dorn and his
party in the coming parliamentary debate and elections will result in
Islandia's resumption of its traditional isolationism, and in his own enforced return to the United States. To help resolve the dilemma of his
growing attachment to Islandia, Lang resigns his job as consul.

"Suppose a man remained in your country a long time and lived exactly the same sort of life you live?" he asks Dorn, who explains:

That would be only the beginning. He would have to do more
. . . He must enjoy our way of life for its own sake. . . . And he
would have to be stirred to the depths of his nature by something that was Islandian through and through.

"You are like Dorna," Dorn tells Lang. "You believe in mere feelings. They are untrustworthy things when they can't be expressed."
Americans, however, are Puritans who are afraid to express their
feelings, and who ignore realities. The real Islandian philosophy has
not yet been expounded for the rest of the world by a trained philosopher, but to Dorn it is "hedonism with a kind heart." Perhaps, he ventures, Lang will be the man to explain Islandia and its culture to
Europe and America. Meanwhile Dorn complains:

It is not true that the world is interested in Islandia. A group of
businessmen is interested, and their governments, who are
behind them, send these foreign diplomats. Their demands are
not the demands of the world upon Islandia. The voice of foreign government is not the voice of its people, for the people are
too diverse in their lives and aims to have a single voice. "Government" abroad is merely a mask with a terrible face put on by
different groups at different times.

In parliament Lord Dorn overcomes the adversary party under Lord Mora who had negotiated the temporary break in Islandia's historic isolationism. "The majority of the people of Islandia wish the situation to be what it was before Lord Mora made his treaty," Lord Dorn announces.

All foreign diplomats are given three months to arrange their affairs and depart. Lang alone enjoys an exception; he has been granted citizenship by King Tor and Queen Dorna. From Lord Dorn's extensive holdings, he purchases a farm to which he brings Gladys, his American bride. In Islandia, he explains to her, their children

will succeed us at the farm. They will know it better than we ever can, and it will therefore be for them a larger and richer world in itself. It will give them shelter, food, and it will be their greatest pleasure. It will lie back of all their dreams. . . . The farm will lie beneath these hopes and wishes of theirs, a reality they know. Their ambitions will be just as broad and deep and all-absorbing as ambitions can be in the United States, but because of the farm they will be solid and such as can be realized. They won't have fretting ambitions as the result of discontent and a wish to escape confusion. And what we must be careful to do is not to infect them with the restlessness that is our heritage and which we have brought from our former homes.

Thus, Austin Tappan Wright's *Islandia* stands strong as a Utopia for liberty and individual freedom.

23

John Prince Smith and the German Free-Trade Movement

Ralph Raico

Germany
~~4210~~   4220
0443   0322

J ohn Prince Smith was the creator of the German free trade movement and its leader form the 1840s until his death in 1874.[1] He was born in London in 1809, and, after leaving Eton prematurely, on account of the death of his father, began working at the age of thirteen for a London commercial firm, later turning to journalism. His journalistic activity brought him to Germany, where in 1831 he took a position as a teacher of English and French at the Gymnasium in Elbing, in East Prussia. It was in these years that he acquired fluency in the German language, to the point where he was later able to earn a living as a writer on economics and politics.

It appears likely that Prince Smith's acquaintance with economic literature, while still a young man in England, was not extensive and that he taught himself the elements of the discipline after he had settled in Germany.[2] He claimed that Bentham's utilitarianism exerted a strong influence on his thinking.[3] As we shall see, however, his commitment to laissez faire was considerably more "doctrinaire" (or consistent) than Bentham's. Prince Smith's interest in economic questions may also have been stimulated through personal acquaintance with some of the leaders of the anti-corn law agitation which was occurring in England at the time and which he followed closely.

While still a teacher at the Elbing Gymnasium, Prince Smith contributed articles to the local paper, including one, in 1835, on the question of how wages are determined. In this piece he presented an "optimistic" view, that is, suggesting a steady, long-range improvement in living standards for working people in a free market economy. That he was already in some wider sense a liberal by the mid-1830s is shown by his attitude towards the "Göttingen Seven," the professors at the Uni-

341

versity of Göttingen who in 1837 protested the revocation of the Hanoverian constitution and were accordingly dismissed.[4] Prince Smith attempted to stir up a protest in Elbing, eliciting a stinging reprimand from the office of the Prussian minister of the interior. Further difficulties with the educational administration (stemming in part from his lack of any talent for teaching twelve and thirteen year olds) led to his leaving his post in 1840. He turned to free-lance journalism full-time.

His first production was a series of articles entitled, "Apology for Industrial Freedom," in which he dealt, among other subjects, with the source of pauperism. This he attributed mainly to the costs of a bloated military establishment.[5] Prince Smith's anti-militarist and anti-war attitudes remained constant, at least until the last years of his life, when the heady Prussian triumphs over Austria and France seem to have affected him as they did so many other liberals. Twenty years after this early work, in 1863, he wrote in his essay, "The Market":

> The great evil for the workers lies in this, that the profit on capital and capital accumulation are to such a great extent diminished by state expenditures on unproductive purposes—the capitalists would be able to give to the people who work for them much more to consume, if they did not have to support so many peacetime soldiers besides, whose consumption is not reimbursed through labor. If the Swiss militia system were introduced in all European states, in a short time capital would so increase, wages would so rise, that there would be no more question of want in the working class. Here lies the solution of the worker-question.[6]

It may be remarked that the proposal to replace the Prussian standing army with a citizens' militia would tend to cast Prince Smith as a much more *politically* radical thinker than has usually been supposed. For one thing, the consequences for the Prussian authoritarian (*obrigkeitlich*) monarchy would have been incalculable and perhaps fatal.

In 1843 Prince Smith published a pamphlet, in Königsberg, "On Hostility to Trade," a major event in the history of the free trade movement in Germany. Here he placed the cause of free trade in a historical and sociological context more reminiscent of the industrialist school of French thinkers of the early nineteenth century than of Bentham. He already had to submit to attacks as "the Englishman,"[7] although by this time he had become in spirit and legal fact a Prussian. An Address to Robert Peel which Prince Smith composed and which he and several of his associates sent in 1846 congratulated the British Prime Minister on his work in connection with the income tax, the bank act, and, above all, repeal of the Corn Law. Peel replied, which created something of a *cause célèbre* and thereby fostered public discussion of the free trade question. Later that year, Prince Smith moved to Berlin.

By now a crusading free trader,[8] his aim was to establish a movement on the model of the Anti-Corn Law League, and lead it to victory. In December 1846 he gathered a number of business leaders and scholars together to consider the formation of a German Free Trade Union (*Deutscher Freihandelsverein*). Despite some harassment from the police, the organizing meeting took place the next March in the Hall of the Berlin Stock Exchange, where about 200 people, the great majority of them businessmen, were present (among them a Mendelssohn).[9] Some of those attending objected to Prince Smith's concept of an association devoted to propagating free trade ideas, preferring one that would *discuss* the question of free trade versus protectionism. In deference to this group, the name "Scientific Union for Trade and Industry" (*Wissenschaftlicher Verein für Handel und Gewerbe*) was adopted; very soon, however, the organization came to be referred to simply as the Free Trade Union (*Freihandelsverein*). Branches were set up in Hamburg, Stettin, and other German towns.

Prince Smith led the German delegation to the famous Free Trade Congress that met in Brussels on September 16, 1847, at the invitation of the Belgian Free Trade Union. His biographer, Otto Wolff, characterized the banquet that concluded the conference as "the high point of that first period of the European free trade movement, which had celebrated its greatest triumph in the reform of the English tariff and which doubtless would even then have led to practical free trade reforms in a great part of the continent, if the revolution of 1848 and its consequences had not intervened."[10]

Prince Smith seems to have remained comparatively unaffected by the great movement for liberal constitutional reform and national unification of 1848; his efforts were, and continued to be, focused instead on economic reform in a free trade direction. He addressed a petition to the National Assembly in Frankfurt on "Protection Against the Limitation of Trade," outlining his views on the current state of affairs.[11] The European situation, in his view, was one of "armed peace," characterized by the maintenance of standing armies, excessive governmental power, "monstrous" taxes, mass impoverishment, and threats to the social order. The cause he identified as the ambitions of the political power, which has become an end in itself. Free trade and maximum economic freedom were the remedies.

The petition, however, attracted little interest or support from the liberals at the Paulskirche, who were concentrating their efforts precisely on the issues Prince Smith considered secondary. By now he had married Auguste Sommerbrod, the daughter of an affluent Berlin banker and settled in quarters on Unter den Linden; after the revolutionary turmoil died down, he turned to renewed activity on behalf of his cause.

His chief goal was to establish a free trade association that would cover all of Germany, and, probably with the experience of the Anti-Corn Law League in mind, he was very conscious of the need for substantial amounts of money to achieve this end. Money was needed to publish brochures and books, to arrange to have articles sent to the newspapers, and to train talented journalists in the principles of political economy. An organization was formed, the Central Union for Freedom of Trade (*Zentralbund für Handelsfreiheit*), which did not, however, succeed in attracting any considerable support. It was chiefly helpful in funneling contributions from free trade circles in seacoast cities like Hamburg and Stettin to Prince Smith for use in propaganda. The plan to train journalists fell through for lack of suitable candidates. (In the 1860s and early 70s, free trade views came to dominate the German press.) Prince Smith was active, however, in disseminating good translations of the works of Frederic Bastiat and in gathering about him a circle of like-minded enthusiasts.[12]

A good deal of his activity in this period consisted in persuading the German *political* liberals of the desirability of free trade. Many of the leading liberals of southern and western Germany, such as Robert von Mohl, were protectionists. As Becker notes: "At that time liberal and free-trader were indeed so little identical that the south-German liberals were the most interested representatives of the protective tariff system, while conversely the conservative farmers of the north and east figured as the chief supporters of the free trade party . . . as a consequence of later political constellations, the appearance has emerged that political liberalism was always Manchesterite and that Manchesterism was always liberal-democratic. Nothing is as false as this view."[13]

In order to influence liberal and radical opinion, Prince Smith, along with his friend and fellow free-trader Julius Faucher, collaborated on the Berlin newspaper, the *Demokratische Zeitung* (later the *Abendpost*). It would seem that it was in this period that the polarization of liberal and free trader on the one side and socialist and collectivist on the other began to form.[14] When the *Abendpost* was closed down by the censors, Prince Smith wrote:

The purpose of my collaboration on the *Abendpost* has to a great extent been achieved. I have brought respect for the free trade doctrine to the most extreme left. Free trade and bureaucracy, or competition and exploitation no longer count as identical with the party whose absurd conception of property made it dangerous. I have demonstrated that the doctrine of economic freedom is much more progressive [*freisinnig*] than all the projects and teachings of ordinances on property and earnings that are arbitrary and realizable only through barbaric force and that, moreover, could not in the long run be implemented by any conceivable force.[15]

The extension of the Zollverein, or German customs union, was proceeding apace at this time, and Prince Smith, who was acquainted with a number of the Prussian leaders, including the chief minister, Manteuffel, probably influenced them in the free trade direction. At any rate, his preference was always for working to persuade those in power, rather than adopting an oppositional stance. Continuing his agitation, he composed a declaration on behalf of commercial and landed associations in West and East Prussia that were calling for occupational freedom (*Gewerbefreiheit*) and free trade. This declaration is of political interest, since it shows the strong support for free trade principles in the regions of Prussia most "backward" from the point of view of political liberalism. Its theoretical interest stems from the fact that in it he associated "protectionism" with "systematic socialism," a linkage that was standard in the writings of Bastiat.[16]

In 1858, the *Kongress deutscher Volkswirte* (Congress of German Economists) was founded, assembling the chief believers in the cause, many of whom had been led to it by Prince Smith during his previous twenty years of labors. Now there were many others to join him in his propagandistic and agitational work. Although Prince Smith did not assume the presidency of the Congress (evidently for various reasons), he participated in the yearly meetings, submitting papers such as the one at the 1860 gathering in Cologne against the legal limitation on interest rates. At the 1863 meeting in Dresden he spoke against patents, and the next year, in Hanover, he attacked "unredeemable paper money with so-called compulsory exchange-rate."[17] He also kept closely involved with the Congress's various activities, which continued to promote laissez faire until the end. (Its last meeting was held in 1885.) Those members who grew increasingly disenchanted with the Congress's position on the "social question" left and, with others, founded the *Verein für Socialpolitik*, in 1872, in Eisenach. In his opening address at this conference, Gustav Schmoller testified to the influence of the movement that Prince Smith had created when he referred to "the economic doctrines which unconditionally dominate the day's market, those which have found expression in the Congress.[18]

From 1860 until his death Prince Smith was the head of the Economic Society (*Volkswirtschaftliche Gesellschaft*), the successor to the Free Trade Union. His home in Berlin became a meeting place for Prussian politicians, some of whom went onto form the Progressive Party (*Fortschrittspartei*) soon after.[19] In 1863, the *Vierteljahrschrift für Volkswirtschaft, Politik, und Kulturgeschichte* (*Quarterly Journal for Economy, Politics, and Cultural History*) began to appear in Berlin, under the editorship of Julius Faucher, perhaps Prince Smith's closest collaborator. The chief theoretical organ of classical liberalism in Germany, this periodical continued to be published for the next thirty years. Prince Smith was an important contributor to the *Vierteljahrschrift*, and a number of his most important essays were first printed there.

The quarterly journal, the Berlin society, the congress of economists, and the informal influencing of politicians and officials were all elements of the same movement, facets of the same activism, and all fired by the spirit of John Prince Smith. This was the case also with the *Handwörterbuch der Volkswirtschaftslehre* (*Concise Dictionary of Economics*), edited by H. Rentzsch, published in 1866.[20] This work is similar in many respects to the one edited by Coquelin and Guillaumin in France. For the *Handwörterbuch*, it was Prince Smith who was selected to write the article on "Freedom of Trade-Free Traders."

The article presents his characteristic views on economics and politics. "Liberalism," he writes, "only recognizes one task which the State can perform, namely, the production of security."[21] Gide and Rist, perhaps relying too heavily on anti-liberal German sources, comment that "Liberalism had nowhere assumed such extravagant proportions as it had in Germany. Prince Smith, who is the best-known representative of Liberalism after Dunoyer [sic], was convinced that the State had nothing to do beyond guaranteeing security, and denied that there was any element of solidarity between economic agents save such as results from the existence of a common market."[22] At any rate, Prince Smith's "minimalist" view of the functions of the state goes considerably beyond Bentham's "agenda."[23]

From 1862 to 1866, Prince Smith represented Stettin in the Prussian House of Deputies, where he was not an outstanding figure, addressing the House only seldom and then mainly on economic questions. This was the period of the bitter—and ultimately decisive—constitutional struggles between Bismarck and the German liberals, whose vanguard had formed the Progressive Party in 1861. Prince Smith's *political* views had always been "moderate," and as the liberals became radicalized in the face of what they viewed as the government's arbitrary and unconstitutional actions, he distanced himself from them increasingly. In 1866, he declined to stand for reelection.

With Königgrätz and the crushing Prussian victory over Austria, Bismarck scored a victory over the recalcitrant liberals as well, one that some believe sealed the fate of German liberalism before Reich was even formed.[24]

Prince Smith was elected to the German Reichstag from Anhalt-Zerbst, but failing health prevented him from taking any but a negligible part in the proceedings, except for addressing the body on two occasions, in November 1871, on the question of currency reform.

He died in 1874, his patriotism and economic liberalism both gratified by the reality of a Germany united and committed to free trade. In Becker's words:

He had the luck, which is granted to few men in public life, to die at a moment when the definitive victory of the ideas he represented seemed to be a question of only a short time, and when the few contrary signs still, by a long way, gave no hint of how quickly the whole splendor would collapse.[25]

This is not, however, entirely correct. In his history of German economic thought (published in the same year as Prince Smith's death), Wilhelm Roscher, after mentioning some of the practical achievements of the German free trade school, was moved to write: "But also *theoretically* I must warn as much against the underestimation of this school, which now is frequent, as against that overestimation which permitted it at an earlier time to be mistaken for economics altogether."[26]

There is little doubt that in historical retrospect Prince Smith—as well as German liberalism as a whole—has suffered from the rout of the system he fought for. The eclipse of liberalism by national-social and imperialist currents and by Marxist (later pseudo-Marxist) socialism has tended to relegate the *entschieden* liberals[27] of nineteenth century Germany to the class of historical curiosities, even of creatures absurdly out of their natural element. Yet, the thinking of John Prince Smith deserves consideration, from a number of points of view.

For example, Prince Smith's famous essay, "On the So-Called Worker-Question,"[28] was for decades after its first publication, in 1864, the target of harsh attacks,[29] for which its contentious title probably bears some responsibility. Yet there can be little doubt that the essay is motivated by a genuine good will toward workers and a desire to aid in the improvement of their living standards; furthermore, it is at least arguable that it is informed with an intelligent appreciation of how that improvement is most likely to be effected.

The reference to "so-called" worker-question should not be taken to indicate any "heartlessness" on the part of Price-Smith to what he well knew to be the stringent conditions of the laboring class. The cause of the sarcasm (if that is what it is) stems form his belief that: "By 'worker-question' one understands namely the question: 'How can the economic situation of workers be suddenly improved, independently of the general rise of the economy, which one does not wish to wait for?'"[30] Prince Smith held that:

> For a scarcity in the means of satisfying wants there is obviously no other remedy than increased production. And evidently more can only be produced by increasing knowledge, skill, industriousness, and above all capital.[31]

To the "iron law of wages" proclaimed by Lassalle, Prince Smith opposed a "golden law," which affirmed the steady, long-range improvement in living standards of working people.[32] As for the poor:

> The ones really in want are those whose labor power lacks nearly any support through capital and therefore produces correspondingly little, those who have remained on a pre-economic level, and for whose integration into genuine economic enterprise the available capital is still insufficient. Yet all the capital sufficient for full employment can easily and even quickly be created with full freedom of economic action—as long as the state does not devour too much of what is created.[33]

A field in which greater originality has been claimed for Prince Smith is historical sociology. In the view of Georg Mayer, Prince Smith's early essay, "On the Political Progress of Prussia" (1843), shows a surprising resemblance to historical materialism; for Prince Smith, "it is exclusively changes in the economic structure that are considered as the ultimate motives of events." Because of economic developments,

Prussia is entering the stage in which the feudal element must necessarily dwindle internally and peaceful commercial relations become the rule in foreign affairs.[34]

Although Mayer emphasizes the "Marxist" overtones of this essay,[35] it appears that Prince Smith's thinking here bears a much greater resemblance to the ideas of the French Industrialist school and of the Benjamin Constant of *De l'esprit de conquéte*. (It is likely that by the 1920s, when Mayer was writing, these writers had been completely lost sight of in Germany.) There would perhaps be a place for a study on Prince Smith and his historical sociology, which would serve also to draw attention to the French writers mentioned above. At the same time it would help correct commonly accepted legend of Marxism's monopoly on the idea of the "priority of the economic over the political."

Notes

1. Julius Becker, *Das Deutsche Manchestertum* (Karlsruhe: G. Braun, 1907), p. 26. Wilhelm Roscher refers to Prince Smith as "the leader of the whole [free trade] tendency"; Roscher, *Geschichte der National-Oekonomik in Deutschland* (Munich: R. Oldenbourg, 1874), p. 1015. W. O. Henderson terms him the rival of Friedrich List: see his "Prince Smith and Free Trade in Germany," *The Economic History Review*, Second Series, II, no. 3, (1950): 295-302. The standard biography is by Otto Wolff, *John Prince-Smith: Eine Lebensskizze*, in John Prince Smith, *Gesammelte Schriften III*, Karl Braun, ed. (Berlin: Herbig, 1880), pp. 209-398. See also Donald G. Rohr, *The Origins of Social Liberalism in Germany* (Chicago and London: University of Chicago Press, 1963), pp. 85-91.

2. Wolff, *John Prince Smith: Eine Lebensskizze*, p. 215.

3. Ibid.

4. Ibid., pp. 226-27. Göttingen University had been a main center for the spread of the free trade ideas of Adam Smith throughout Germany in the last decades of the eighteenth century; see, Wilhelm Treue, "Adam Smith in Deutschland: Zum Problem der 'Politischen Professors' zwischen 1776 und 1810," in Johannes U. Ruth Muhle, ed., *Deutscheland und Europa: Historische Studien zur Völker-und Staatenordnung des Abendlandes* (Dusseldorf: Droste, 1951), p. 102.

5. Wolff, *John Prince Smith: Eine Lebensskizze*, pp. 234-35.

6. John Prince Smith, *Gesemmelte Schriften*, I, Otto Michaelis, ed. (Berlin: Herbig, 1877), p. 20.

7. Later his protectionist enemies spread the story that he was in the pay of English interests. Georg Mayer, *Die Freihandelslehre in Deutschland: Ein Beitrag zur Gesellschaftslehre des wirtschaftlichen Liberalismus* (Jena: Gustav Fischer, 1927), p. 53.

8. Prince Smith used the term "free trade" in a wide sense, as in his assertion in Rentzsch's *Handwörterbuch der Volkswirtschaftslehre* that "To the state free trade assigns no other task than just this: *the production of security.*" Cited in Becker, *Das Deutsche Manchestertum*, p. 103 (emphasis added). It may be of importance that Prince Smith makes use of the term popularized by Charles Dunoyer and other of the French school of liberal economists.

9. Wolff, *John Prince Smith*, pp. 267-68.

10. Ibid., p. 273.

11. Ibid., p. 286.

12. Ibid., pp. 296-97, 309-11.

13. Becker, *Das Deutsche Manchestertum*, pp. 33-34.

14. Prince Smith was aware of the danger socialism posed for his cherished social system as early as 1850, and wrote to a friend on how crucial the need to "conquer the masses" for free trade. Wolff, *John Prince Smith*, p. 315.

15. Ibid., pp. 315-16.

16. It would be desirable to know more about Prince Smith's connections with the French liberals of his time. He was perfectly fluent in French and contributed to the *Journal des Économistes*. Ibid., p. 335.

17. Ibid., pp. 337, 346-47.

18. Becker, *Das Deutsche Manchestertum*, p. 100.

19. Wolff, *John Prince Smith*, p. 339.

20. Becker, *Das Deutsche Manchestertum*, p. 100. According to Becker, Rentzsch later gave up free trade. Ibid., p. 108.

21. Quoted in Charles Gide and Charles Rist, *A History of Economic Doctrines from the Time of the Physiocrats to the Present Day*, trans. R. Richards (Boston/New York/Chicago: D. C. Heath, n.d.), p. 439n.

22. Ibid., p. 439.

23. On Bentham, see Lionel Robbins, *The Theory of Economic Policy in English Classical Political Economy* (London: Macmillan, 1953), pp. 38-43.

24. Ludwig von Mises, *Omnipotent Government* (New Haven: Yale University Press, 1944), pp. 27-28.

25. Becker, *Das Deutsche Manchestertum*, p. 41.

26. Roscher, *Geschichte der National-Oekonomik in Deutschland*, p. 1017.

27. The term is standard; see, e.g., Ina Susanne Lorenz, *Eugen Richter: Der entschiedene Liberalismus in wilhelminischer Zelt 1871 bis 1906* (Husum: Matthiesen, 1981). *Entschieden* means "determined" or "firm."

28. John Prince Smith, G. S., I, pp. 26-42.

29. Besides Becker, *Das Deutsche Manchestertum*, pp. 81-86; see Heinrich Herkner, *Die Arbeiterfrage: Eine Einführung* (Berlin: J. Guttentag, 1908), pp. 512-17; Werner Sombart, *Sozialismus und Soziale Bewegung* (Jena: Gustav Fisher, 1908), p. 192, where Prince Smith's essay is dismissed as "pitiable"; and Hans Gehrig, *Die sozialpolitischen Anschauungen der deutschen Freihandelsschule* (Jena: Gustav Fisher, 1909), pp. 19-21. Gehrig at least concedes what many critics have not, that there was an ethical basis to Manchesterism and Prince Smith's position: "Because we are ourselves responsible, therefore we must be free: so runs the argumentation of a teaching that has often enough been reproached with materialism, and in characterizing which only the negative sides, as the 'theory of the nightwatchman state,' have been emphasized." Ibid., p. 24. Contrast with Becker, *Das Deutsche Manchestertum*, pp. 106-07, who asks whether Ferdinand Lassalle was not "completely correct" when he wrote of the "Manchester men": "Those modern barbarians who hate the state, not this or that state, not this or that state-form, but the state altogether. And who, as they now and again clearly have admitted, would most prefer to abolish the state, auction off justice and police to the cheapest suppliers, and have war run by joint-stock companies, so that there should nowhere in all of creation still be an ethical point from which resistance could be offered to their capital-armed mania for exploitation."

30. John Prince Smith, G.S., p. 29.

31. Ibid., p. 27. The unsupported assumption of most of his critics in this area seems to be that the "social question" in the mid-nineteenth century could have been "solved" by trade-unionism and the redistribution of wealth from capitalists to workers.

32. Ibid., pp. 21, 32-33.
33. "Der Markt," in ibid., pp. 21-22. A curious feature of the essay on the working class is Prince Smith's discussion of the *underclass* of modern society, "an old and entrenched hereditary derelict culture," from which "most of the criminals proceed." "As ineradicable lichen and fungi coat every lightless, damp surface, so these demoralized ones nestle and multiply in all the unclean recesses of human dwelling places. . . . Against proliferating demoralization there is only one remedy: it must be exterminated, as dry-rot is exterminated, by letting in the air and light of civilization down to the deepest and most hidden spaces of the social edifice, and where possible snatch the children from their moldy birthplaces." Ibid., p. 37.
34. Georg Mayer, *Die Freihandelslehre in Deutschland*, pp. 56-57.
35. The dependence of both political evolution and the structure of ideas on economic change in Prince Smith's thought is also emphasized by Julius Paul Köhler, *Staat und Gesellschaft in der deutschen Theorie des auswärtigen Wirtschaftspolitik und des internationalen Handels von Schlettwein bis auf Fr. List und Prince Smith* (Stuttgart: W. Kohlhammer, 1926), pp. 118-23. Köhler, however, does not link this to the thought of Marx, stating simply that it "reflects contemporary sociologies," p. 123.

24

Commentator on our Times:
A Quest for the Historical Rothbard

Sheldon L. Richman

M urray Rothbard was once asked for his opinion of a book titled *Shirtsleeve Economics: A Commonsense Survey* by William A. Paton.[1] He wrote that while a good high-school-level economics text was needed, *Shirtsleeve Economics* alas was not it. He found it badly written, too dependent on quotations, and poor in content. He asked some penetrating questions about Paton's case for government: "Why should those citizens who prefer to defend themselves by private bodyguards be forced to subscribe to another defense agency against their will? Isn't this extortion on a large scale?"

He also complained that Paton's sole concern was economic efficiency. For example, Paton wrote that "we might all support such a program" to fund government by soaking the rich *if* it would not "impair our productive powers." Rothbard, paraphrasing the sage Sam Goldwyn, commented, "Kindly include this observer 'out' in this 'we might all' category."

Finally, Rothbard flashed that famous wit. Paton wrote that the business cycle was inherent in the market, but embraced it nonetheless on grounds that man "wouldn't know what to do with himself if thrust into an environment where everything was sweetness and light, and there was no anxiety, no struggle."

Quipped Rothbard, "Somehow, I would be willing to take my chances."

What is noteworthy about this is that the review was written June 26, 1952, when Rothbard was a 26-year-old doctoral student at Columbia University.[2] The review, written for the internal use of the William Volker Fund, was apparently the first of a few hundred book reviews commissioned of him by the Volker Fund between 1952 and about

1962.[3] Rothbard was one of several people regularly asked to comment on books. His colleagues in this activity were Rose Wilder Lane, Frank S. Meyer, Leonard P. Liggio, Henry Hazlitt, Roscoe Pound, and a few others. Rothbard, Lane, and Meyer reviewed the most books, with Rothbard leading the league. His reviews, ranging from less than one page to 15 single-spaced pages and consuming 3 to 15 hours of work, were thorough and written as though they were to be published.

Rothbard later used some of them in the *National Review* and his old journal *Left and Right*. Part of the material turned up in other forms, for example, in his book the *Ethics of Liberty*. But most of the material has never been published.

The Volker Fund originally asked for the reviews to keep tabs on who was doing worthy scholarship within the broad classical liberal tradition. According to Kenneth Templeton, a Volker principal, the National Book Foundation (NBF) was later established because as long as the information was being gathered it might as well be put to better use.[4] The NFB was established initially to place books sympathetic to individual liberty into libraries around the country. Templeton said that a common right-wing complaint in the late 1950s was that libraries were not stocking non-leftist books. Volker surveyed libraries and found the charge untrue. Nevertheless, it wanted to help them get the books and also help the publishers. So it went ahead with the NBF. Later, NBF focused on professors, enabling them to get 10 copies of a book without charge.[5]

The task of the NFB reviewers was to advise whether a book was suitable for distribution. The Volker Fund was interested in many disciplines. This gave Rothbard the chance to review books on a broad spectrum of subjects, including economics, history, philosophy, political theory, psychology, psychiatry, public policy, agriculture, water, ecology, and more. What is interesting about these reviews is not so much whether Rothbard liked a given book or not, but what his reviews reveal of his own beliefs, values, and ideals. Those who know the present Rothbard either personally or through his writing will find the Rothbard of 1952-1962 thoroughly familiar. Looking back through the telescope of 34 years, one is impressed at how steady he is in so many ways, a Rock of Gibraltar—intellectually, philosophically, even stylistically.

This is not to say that his views have not changed at all. In some cases they have, as we shall see. But on matters of bedrock principle, methodology, scholarly commitment, and above all human liberty, he is admirably—refreshingly—steady and uncompromising.

Another thing revealed in these reviews is the breadth and depth of Rothbard's knowledge. In commenting on books, he routinely showed how authors ignored or neglected important research. He often contrasted a book with others on the same subject. As one would expect, he could do this in economics, but, remarkably, he did it with nearly any subject he wrote about.

It is worth pausing on this point. Here is a man who at an early age had both a broad overview as well as a detailed knowledge of the "humane sciences." (He had written *Man, Economy, and State* before he was 34.) Some might have worried back then that he would spread himself too thin and suffer burn-out. By now I presume it is safe to say that this isn't likely to happen. Undoubtedly, Rothbard pursued such a large scholarly agenda because he loved (and loves) knowledge and liberty, in the service of which his knowledge has always been put.[6] But he may have had other reasons. After all, in the 1950s there were not enough libertarians and classical liberals to support a finely drawn division of scholarly labor. Someone as dedicated to liberty as Rothbard would almost inevitably be tempted to do everything. Today, of course, things are different, due in no small part to Murray Rothbard. The freedom movement is fortunate that he had the energy and talent along with the dedication.

Mercifully, he didn't expect the same versatility of other scholars. When commenting on an economist's essay about Cordell Hull and the Trade Agreements Program, Rothbard wrote that it omitted "any discussion of the political issues in the Reciprocal Trade program, i.e. the strengthening of arbitrary Federal Executive power as against Congress, which abdicates responsibility, but *it is probably too much to expect an economist to discuss such matters*."[7] The irony, of course, is that Rothbard, an economist, was discussing such matters.

The values he reveals in these reviews would come as no surprise to any Rothbard watcher. His standards include logic, theoretical soundness, historical accuracy, methodological integrity, forthrightness, solid scholarship, clarity, good writing, and love of liberty. Each of these is important for Rothbard. He often threw roses to an author who scores high in one, despite shortcomings in others. But his final evaluation took all these factors into consideration.

Another noteworthy trait of Rothbard is his ability to stand outside the fashions of the day. Positivism, psychoanalysis, and other shiny theoretical costume jewelry could never lure Rothbard from the straight path he strode.

He was impatient with bad writers. He bemoaned the prevailing "style" forced on Ph.D. dissertation writers and rejoiced when he found one that broke the rules. He was unmerciful when it came to dullness. In his review of *Economics and Social Reform* by Abram L. Harris,[8] Rothbard wrote, "There is one word, I think, that best describes [this book] and that is: pedestrian. Professor Harris performs the quite remarkable feat of writing about some of the most exciting, influential, and mischievous social theorists of the last hundred years, and making the whole thing seem dull as dishwater. . . . This book is, I am afraid, a sheer waste of print."

He likewise despised vagueness. ". . . [T]he book is almost incomprehensible," he wrote of John R. Commons's *The Legal Foundations of Capitalism.*[9]

> The style is abominable, often almost pure gibberish, and what is worse, it becomes apparent that the style is not *sui generis* but is a reflection of the inherent garble of the idea-content. Take, for example, Page 1 of the book; I defy anyone to make sense out of a single sentence of the page, much less the page as a whole.

He confronted "middle of the roadism," or wishy-washiness, in a similar way. On O. H. Taylor and his *Economics and Liberalism*, Rothbard wrote, "If a man is a vacillating lightweight, that is his privilege, but why oh why does such a man become a political economist and political philosopher, and why is he selected to be a full professor at one of our most eminent universities [Harvard], and why are his writings collected in one embarrassing volume?"[10]

In this connection, Rothbard had a theory that could be called the Rule of Extremism. As he wrote in 1960, "The clear and logical thinker will always be an 'extremist,' and will therefore always be interesting; his pitfall is to go wildly into error. But, on the other hand, while the orthodox 'middle-of-the-road' thinker will never get that far wrong, neither will he ever contribute anything either, aside from being generally deadly dull."[11] In one book he found "another illustration of the rule that, often, only 'extremists' make sense, while eclectics and moderates are entangled in contradictions."[12]

Rothbard had a strong sense of what we can call scholarly manners. Not that he avoided bluntness—on the contrary. Rather, he objected to personal criticism and ridicule. Writing on Alexander Gray's *The Socialist Tradition*, he chided Gray

> for his use of personal ridicule against the socialist and anarchist thinkers discussed. Ridicule against a nonsensical argument is

one thing; ridicule against the person, and then intertwined with criticism of the argument, is much different, and most unfortunate. The personal sneers, to which Gray, a man of obvious wit, is addicted, detract, in a scholarly audience, more from the author than the recipient, and properly so.[13]

These are his "procedural" values. They are the hallmarks of a disciplined and inquiring mind, striving for reason and clarity and expecting it in others. His substantive beliefs also come to light in the course of his comments on the books. These can be grouped into several themes.

The State

Rothbard, it should go without saying, was a solid libertarian in those days, having come to this philosophy much earlier in life. His opposition to the state is often eloquently expressed in the book reviews. He never missed an opportunity to expose an author as a state worshipper and he was most impatient when an author camouflaged his state-worship. In his review of Yves Simon's *Philosophy of Democratic Government*, Rothbard debunks the claim that the individual should submerge himself in collective, that is, state, activities. He takes a scalpel to the activities Simon exalts:

> Military parades, where music—one of man's highest cultural achievements—is put to use to glorify butchery and the deliberate degradation of the dignity of the individual; inaugurations, where everyone is asked to solemnly revere the new Supreme Tyrant upon his accession to state rule; national funerals, where we are all asked to pay tearful homage to the Supreme Tyrant (or one of his top lackeys) who has just passed away at last; and the raising of the flag, where innocent children, dragooned by bayonet into government's "educational" barracks, are forced to stand in awe while the bloody battle flag and standard of their captors is being raised on high.[14]

Economics

Most of the books on economics were assigned to Rothbard, unsurprisingly. In reviewing these books, Rothbard rigorously applied the analytical tools of Austrian economics. He exposed the fallacies of statist economists while holding high the ideals of laissez faire, sound money, free banking, free trade, free bargaining between employee and employer, free competition unburdened by antitrust laws, and so on.

As he is today, Rothbard was a passionate advocate of Misesian praxeology, leading him to criticize trenchantly Milton Friedman's methodological writings. In reviewing Friedman's famous *Essays in Positive Economics*, Rothbard wrote that "it can be flatly stated that his position is *the* most important, and most pernicious (in light of current trends), methodological fallacy in economic thought today."[15] When he read Melvin Greenhut's *Full Employment, Inflation & Common Stock*, he commented, "The Greenhut volume has only one conceivable merit: Greenhut being a member of the 'Chicago school,' this book is the quickest way of convincing many 'conservatives' of just how thoroughly Keynesian the Chicago School position is."[16]

Despite disagreement with Friedman ("an apostle of totally managed, fiat money"), Rothbard expressed his respect for him as a thinker. He called *A Program for Monetary Stability* "the product of a brilliant, clear, and logical mind, and it is, therefore, always provocative and stimulating, even though fundamentally and basically mistaken and wrongheaded."[17]

On the other hand, Rothbard was overjoyed with Lionel Robbins's book *The Great Depression*.[18] Robbins was an early follower of Ludwig von Mises, and his book set forth Mises's theory of the business cycle. Calling the book "one of the great economic works of our time," Rothbard, who would soon write his own history of the depression,[19] applauded Robbins's "application of the best economic thought to the explanation of the cataclysmic phenomena of the Great Depression." Robbins was one of several prominent Misesians who renounced Austrian economics in the wake of the Keynesian revolution. He repudiated *The Great Depression*.

Rothbard wrote of both praxeology and entrepreneurship when he reviewed W. Paul Strassmann's *Risk and Technological Innovation*.[20] In this passage, he faults Strassmann for bad methodology, which leads him to misunderstand the risk of the marketplace. Strassmann begins, as so many scholars do, with an epistemological error: "he tries to use history to test empirically what is really a problem of praxeology. In short, he tries to measure risk, and concludes by saying that it was negligible, largely by recording the fact that most innovations were successful, and that the rate of failure among innovating firms . . . was low. It is of course not surprising that when one 'reads the tape backward,' past innovations look remarkably easy; since most innovations succeeded, and it seems to *us* evident that they would succeed, the risks incurred at the time are conveniently forgotten. Furthermore, on the market those who are best at innovating, and at entrepreneurship in general, will be those who will gravitate to business and stay with it, so it is not surprising that the rate of business success is high among those who remain. But Strassmann illegitimately uses his rate of success to try to prove that risk didn't really exist."

Rothbard was always eager to learn something new from his reading and when this happened he did the written equivalent of jumping for joy. An example is his review of Lawrence Abbott's "masterpiece," *Quality and Competition*.[21] He found Abbott's definition of quality competition "completely original." "Before this, economists, including myself, have thought that *theory* need not account specially for quality because a different quality good for the same price is equivalent to a different price for the same good. A different quality would, further, be simply treated as a different good for most purposes, as the same good for others. Up till now, no one has been able to distinguish theoretically between a different quality and a different good. Abbott furnishes an excellent distinction based upon the thesis that the same good satisfies the same *want*, so that there can be quality variations within the same want. This is consonant with the Austrian tradition and is an innovation within it."

He seems to temper his enthusiasm later in the review when he adds, "I am not prepared to say how fruitful Abbott's distinction will turn out to be, particularly in the development of economic theory, where my hunch is that current Austrianism will do well enough without tacking on Abbott's 'quality models' to the price models of current theory."

Rothbard has been a spirited participant in recent epistemological debates within the Austrian school. But this is not new for him. He addressed the same issues in a review of G. L. S. Shackle's *Time in Economics*.[22] He applauded Shackle's criticism of economic orthodoxy, but added, "[u]nfortunately, these good points are counterbalanced by the obvious fact that Shackle has never familiarized himself with praxeology and the praxeologic tradition."

> As a result, Shackle's proffered positive theories are almost uniformly erroneous. So far does he go in the direction of subjectivism that he unfortunately splits up people's actions into noncomparable single moments, with all things taking place within the individual actor's mind for each moment—as a result, he fallaciously denies even the *individual himself* the right to sum up after the event and say that his actions were erroneous.

Rothbard noted that Shackle mistakenly rejected Böhm-Bawerk's time-preference theory of interest in favor of an uncertainty theory. He also wrote that Shackle, though critical of the "quasi-mathematical Walrasian approach," felt it was necessary to maintain it to reveal the interconnectedness of all economic phenomena. Characteristically, Rothbard responded that Shackle should have known that Austrian theory "*supplies* the view of general interconnectedness which is badly needed in economics, *without* distorting reality."

Finally, Rothbard expressed hard-hitting critical opinions about the newly developed Public Choice school when he reviewed *The Calculus of Consent* by James M. Buchanan and Gordon Tullock.[23] Public Choice has grown in influence tremendously in the 27 years since, and Buchanan, of course, won the Nobel Prize for Economics in 1986.

It is not that Rothbard found nothing of value in the book. On the contrary, he appreciated its searching for methodological individualism in political science, emphasis on unanimity rather than majority rule, and "a harking back to the constitutional system of 1900 as better than the situation today." But this was not enough to satisfy him: "But these merits are, I believe, more *ad hoc* than integral to the main body of the work. In considering the work as a whole, they are far overshadowed by the numerous flaws and fallacies."

First, he argued that Buchanan and Tullock's use of the "unanimity" rule works more to "put a stamp of approval" on existing government actions rather than as an ideal at which we should aim. How?

> The basic way is to set up a dichotomy between "constitutional decisions" and concrete decisions of government policy. B and T [Buchanan and Tullock] admit that concrete decisions might represent a conflict: A and B winning out over and even at the expense of C. But "constitutionally," which is a term that they use quite vaguely but which apparently mean [sic] the rules for government decision-making, they assume that these rules are somehow "unanimously" agreed to, and therefore that, in a sense, the concrete political decisions are also unanimous. Thus, the unanimity rule, seemingly libertarian, actually turns out to be more of a fallacious support for the *status quo*—whatever the status quo happens to be—than a plea for libertarian principle.

Rothbard faulted Buchanan and Tullock for attempting to find unanimous consent for constitutional decisions, and particularly for their "veil of ignorance" reasoning, according to which no one knows what his interests are when he consents to constitutional rules, so everyone consents to rules that are genuinely in the public interest. He also took them to task for watering down "unanimity" to mean" relative unanimity" or "80% unanimity." "In short, when the chips are down, they are willing to waive unanimity in order that the 'costs of decision' for the group or society can be minimized," Rothbard wrote.

He criticized Buchanan and Tullock's defense of income insurance as a rationalization of the status quo. According to Rothbard, Buchanan and Tullock assert that the wealthy consent to their being taxed to provide income insurance because it will be available to them if they become poor. "And in another place," wrote Rothbard, "they [Buchanan and Tullock] say that people really want to be coerced so long as they are *all* coerced, so that everybody is really *not* being coerced."

> Not only do I consider all this nonsense, but it is dangerous nonsense as well, because it provides new support for the idea that anything that the State does, no matter how blatantly coercive, is "really" backed by everyone.

A fundamental objection of Rothbard to Buchanan and Tullock's approach to political economy was their treating the state as more or less just another service agency in society. He wrote:

> The State is assimilated into the rubric of just another voluntary agency (albeit with complications), and each individual therefore decides on his value scale how much to allocate to private agencies and how much to government. This, I say, is the nub of the entire analysis of the book and I think it is utterly and absolutely wrong. . . . Buchanan and Tullock would obliterate the most vital distinction between State and market activity.

Rothbard also scored Buchanan and Tullock for their notion of social costs with regard to government activity. "[B]ut how can 'social costs' be even discussed when some people are gaining *at the expense* of others? . . . The upshot is, that despite much talk by B and T of their staunch individualism, especially methodological individualism, that they are not consistent individualists at all," he wrote. "They smuggle in, through the back door, societarian and organicist conceptions, viz. in their discussions of social costs."

History

One of Rothbard's great loves is history. In these reviews, he expounded on historiography, as well as his interpretations of the American Revolution, the Constitution, Jacksonian period, World War II, and the Cold War. He was, as he is today, a devotee of revisionism, but this is not to say that he embraced everything to which that misunderstood label was attached.

He wrote of the method of writing history in his review of James C. Malin's *On the Nature of History*.[24] Rothbard approves of Malin's methodology, commenting, "Probably most important is his vigorous rejection of determinism, his belief in free will," which leads to a rejection of laws of history and inevitability.

Rothbard on the objectivist/subjectivist debate among historians:

> . . . [An] historian *must* select his material, and if he does, then immediately there arises the question: on what basis, on what principles, do I make the selection? This does not mean that all truth is "subjective"; but it does mean that selection of facts must be based on some sort of rational and valid principles. Furthermore, I fail to see anything wrong with "presentism" and "functional history," *provided* that this means *not* that history is deliberately distorted to fit propaganda myths of the moment, but that present interests determine what aspects of history the historian will write about. . . . The historian fails in a major part of his task if he just photographs or chronicles, and fails to interpret and explain events on the basis of knowledge established in other sciences, such as economics.

Elsewhere, Rothbard declared, "[T]he historian's science is an art, it is one where the historian's judgment must, in the final analysis, be brought to bear. History is *not* an exact science, for history deals with individual persons exercising their free will. The historian never knows, with *exact proof*, the motives of his subjects; but he can use his best judgment from the evidence. This is his methodology."[25] Rothbard often attributed his views on writing history to Mises.

His review of Donald L. Kemmerer and C. Clyde Jones's *American Economic History* gave him a chance to write on another methodological issue.[26] "It is increasingly clear that an historian, unless he is completely possessed of ultra-Marxist bias (and few are these days), is apt to fall prey to one besetting bias: of assuming that 'whatever was, was right.'

Whatever happens, whatever transpired, was somehow the mark of destiny and deserves the rubber-stamp of historiographical approval."

He then elaborated:

> In American economic history, a 'whatever was, was right' attitude means that whatever branch of economic history one is treating, the 'onward and upward' theme must be ever dominant. And so it is with K and J [Kemmerer and Jones]. If K and J are in a chapter on manufacturing, then we find a fairly sound treatment, dealing with the progress of manufacturing development, the carving out of new economic frontiers by businessmen, etc. But let K and J shift to a chapter on labor, then, curiously enough, we find the heroic and forward struggles of the 'labor movement'. . . against the exploiting bosses. . . .
>
> . . . Not only is each act of government regulation welcomed in turn, but K and J, true to their implicit code as celebrants of all aspects of the American past, welcome them *only* as they come in the temporal order. In short, if a certain regulation was imposed on business in 1892, then 1892 was, providentially, just about the time when this regulation was 'needed,' when the legislature 'came to realize,' etc.

"How blissful a country," Rothbard gushed, "where statesmen were almost never too early or too late!"

Rothbard's overview of history focuses on the struggle between Liberty and Power. It comes up again and again. He invoked it when he challenged what he regarded as spurious class-analysis. Though an advocate of a particular class (caste) analysis, he wrote tirelessly in opposition to "garbled and twisted variants." In reviewing *The Antifederalists* by Jackson Turner Main[27] Rothbard rejected the Beard-Jensen quasi-Marxist class-struggle interpretation of the Constitution that he saw Main trying to salvage. This analysis held that the contending sides in the fight over the Constitution were the rich, land-holding urban elitists against the poor agrarian, egalitarian democrats. Here Rothbard set out his view of classes and the salient historical struggle.

> Naturally, in every country and every age, there are well-born, poor, and people in between. And if one wants to separate them into "classes," one can spend one's time doing so, though fruitlessly. But so are there an infinite number of other "classes" in society: occupational groups, religious groups, chess players and non-chess players, etc.

Rothbard faults Main for insisting that classes are *inherently* in conflict, that farmers are invariably against merchants, creditors against debtors, small property owners against large property owners. Rothbard, though, finds a "small nub of truth" in this class-struggle thesis. But the nub had been twisted beyond recognition by the Marxists and neo-Marxist historians, "indeed by Marx himself."

> Marx acquired his class theory from Saint-Simon, who, in turn, garbled and twisted it from its *original* thesis, which was, in contrast, highly libertarian. This thesis—which Mises would call as *caste* conflict theory—and which anticipated its modern formulation by Albert Jay Nock, was developed by Charles Dunoyer and Charles Comte in the Restoration period in France. This postulated *two* essential "classes" or castes: the *State*, and its subsidized favorites; and the *public*, who are exploited by the state. *This* was the original "class" analysis and exploitation analysis; the State, and its subsidies, *exploited* the producing public. The producers included everyone on the free market, from manufacturers to laborers. Saint-Simon, Marx, etc. twisted this around to *add* the "capitalists" to the list of exploiters, and to dub the "producers" as only the proletariat.

Rothbard took up the inadequacy of standard class analysis again when he commented on the article "The Massachusetts Land Bankers of 1740" by George Athan Billias.[28] He praises Billias for showing that "the leading advocates [of an inflationary land bank scheme], *as well as the opponents*, were wealthy Boston merchants, real estate men, etc." (Emphasis added.) He then generalized,

> The essence of modern revisionism . . . is to have learned . . . that, lo and behold!, the inflationists were not poor agrarians at all, but wealthy urban merchants and real estate speculators, who, while they may well have been debtors, were hardly "poor" in the sense generally used. Inflation *and* sound money were led by the respectable, sophisticated, urban merchants and intellectuals.

Clearly, Rothbard's position in this controversy is rich and complex. He is not against the economic method in history, that is, tracing people's economic interests in everything from a tariff bill to the Constitution. But he is against economic determinism, Marxist or Beardian. In a devastating review of Lee Benson's *Turner and Beard*,[29] he defends

Forrest McDonald against Benson's charges of economic determinism. Not true, wrote Rothbard, because McDonald's very act of "atomizing" Beard's class categories—the nub of McDonald's great contribution to historiography—was to shift the emphasis from Marxist class struggle to "the actual realistic categories of *individual* economic interest. This is, indeed, a shift from fallacious Marxian historiography to realistic, individualistic, even 'libertarian,' historiography."

I should mention that Rothbard's opinion of Jackson Turner Main changed several years later. Where he earlier said Main's book was a desperate attempt to save the Beard analysis, in 1974 he called Main's "neo-Beardian *The Antifederalists* . . . a brilliant work that provides . . . by far the best explanation of the forces battling for and against the Constitution. . . ." He said Main shows that the Constitution was a conspiracy by the ruling elite, wealthy public creditors, protectionists, and others who wanted a strong central government.[30]

As noted, Rothbard believed that tracing economic interests was a valid and important part of the historian's task. J. Fred Rippy's *Globe and Hemisphere* excited Rothbard by its courage to do this. He commented:

> For some reason, almost all other "right-wing" historians, economists, or observers of the current scene have considered it somehow "Marxist" or anti-capitalist or perhaps just plain impolite and bad-mannered, to point out the probably true motivations for government actions and for pressures for those actions. Now, this, I have maintained for a long time, abdicates the responsibility of the historian to weigh and estimate, as best he can, the motivations for different actions. But because of this abdication, the field for this realistic investigation has been left to the distortions of the Marxists. As a result, the common charge against sound, free-enterprise economists that they are "apologists for business interests" is invested with a good deal of truth. . . . The great thing about J. Fred Rippy . . . is that he is not afraid to dig for the camouflaged economic motive.[31]

Rothbard combined his interest in class analysis with his interest in the Jacksonian period and launched a virtual one-man crusade to promote what he saw as the correct interpretation of that era. Rothbard had written his thesis on *The Panic of 1819* and so was well versed in the monetary and political events that led up to the rise of the Jacksonians. Nothing disturbed him more than an author's recitation of the standard view that the Jacksonians were early welfare-statists trying to tame aggressive capitalists. So he was delighted when he read *The Concept of Jacksonian Democracy* by Lee Benson almost a year after his salvo against Benson's book on Turner and Beard.[32] Benson, Rothbard wrote,

> squarely and candidly refutes the "Jacksonian Democracy" thesis. . . . Benson squarely recognizes that the Democrats were the Libertarian party, and the Whigs the Statist party, and therefore, properly, concludes that the "precursors of the New Deal" in this period were not the Jacksonians but the Whigs.

But though he praised Benson for this realization, he faults him for discounting the importance of the Liberty vs. Power dichotomy.

In a related issue, Rothbard welcomed a biography of one of his heroes, Martin Van Buren. In his review of Robert V. Remini's *Martin Van Buren and the Making of the Democratic Party*,[33] he writes in a postscript, "I have perhaps written too long a review of this work, but it deals with a subject in which I am particularly interested." He notes that Remini's book "sets out to right the historiographic balance for a critical period in Van's life, and does a good job of it. . . . Remini also shows, in excellent fashion, that Van Buren's main aim, at which he succeeded brilliantly, was *ideological*."

Rothbard's interest in the revisionist history of America's wars is also prominent in the Volker reviews. He thrilled to A. J. P. Taylor's classic and controversial *Origins of The Second World War*, which showed that the war did not result from any grand plan of conquest by Hitler, but rather from ubiquitous diplomatic bungling and intrigue.[34] A "scintillating book," he called it in his 14-page-plus, single-spaced letter.

In reviewing Taylor, Rothbard set out his own view of foreign affairs. He discussed what he calls the "Fu Manchu myth": the view that a foreign leader or country is not just bad but irredeemably evil and malicious, and will conquer the world unless faced down by the Good Guys. This assumption, invariably used by national leaders for propaganda, leads to warmongering. Writes Rothbard, "This is the almost idiotic Morality Play in which Americans and Britons have cast international relations for half a century now, and this is why we are in the mess we are today."

The fallacy that Rothbard identifies is that the Bad Guy himself may fear that he will be attacked or that, evil as he is, his particular complaint may be legitimate (as with the Treaty of Versailles), or that he can't afford to back down from a show of force by the Good Guys. "And so to war," writes Rothbard.

Like Taylor, Rothbard favors the Munich settlement because it was a belated, if aborted, attempt to revise the Versailles Treaty.[35] He blasts the allies for setting up artificial states in Eastern Europe after World War I and preparing the stage for World War II. Historians and diplomats have long wondered what to do about Eastern Europe. Rothbard added his own view, a combination of realism and libertarian idealism.

> The reality of Eastern Europe is that it is always fated to be dominated by either Germany or Russia or both. . . . [I]f there is to be peace in Eastern Europe, both Germany and Russia must be friends.
>
> Now don't misunderstand me; I have not abandoned moral principle for cynicism. My heart yearns for ethnic justice, for national self-determination for all peoples. . . . But, to paraphrase Sydney Smith's famous letter to Lady Grey, please let them work this out for themselves! Let us abandon the criminal immorality and folly of continual coercive meddling by *non*-Eastern European powers (e.g. Britain, France, and now the U.S.) in the affairs of East Europe. Let us hope that one day Germany and Russia, at peace, will willingly grant justice to the peoples of East Europe, but let us not bring about perpetual wars to try to achieve this artificially.

Rothbard, of course, meant his words on the Fu Manchu myth and Eastern Europe to be applicable to the Soviet Union and the Cold War. In this connection, he praised the revisionist *Perpetual War for Perpetual Peace*, edited by Harry Elmer Barnes, as an "excellent work.[36]

The Cold War was the major issue (though not the only one) that divided libertarians and conservatives after World War II. Rothbard was a major figure insisting that the issue of war and peace was central and that free-market advocates who favored an American global anticommunist crusade were tragically—dangerously—inconsistent. The central flaw he found in the anticommunists was their belief that the communists were uniquely evil and "Luciferian." He discusses this matter in his review of Frank S. Meyer's *The Molding of Communists*.[37] Meyer was a former top-level American communist, who later renounced communism and became part of the *National Review* "new right." He was more libertarian than most of that crowd and he was a close friend of Rothbard's.[38] Nevertheless, Meyer proposed an aggressive foreign policy designed to defeat the Soviet Union.

In his 18-page, single-spaced letter, Rothbard distinguishes between anticommunists and antisocialists. Antisocialists are concerned with ends, ideas, and ideology; they oppose, ideologically, all movements that aim to subject individuals to state power. Anticommunists, in contrast, concentrate on means and people. To them the communists are unique because their methods are unique. ". . . it must be clear that there is no hope of 'reconciling' the anti-Communist and the anti-Socialist positions as I have described them," Rothbard wrote. "The emphasis, the outlook, the conclusions, are totally incompatible."

Meyer held two fallacies, according to Rothbard. The first was his belief that only communists engage in the bad practices cited; the second was his condemnation of practices that are actually admirable. Meyer wrote, for instance, that the communist parties totally control their members and expect loyalty. Rothbard responded that so do many other organizations and movements, including mainstream ones.

> My own observation of the Randian movement (followers of Ayn Rand) is that an absolute dictation is imposed on the total life of each member that makes the life of the cadre Communist seem like a bed of roses. For while the Communist party, sensibly, does not interfere with any activities of the members which are not "anti-Party," the Randians insist on total control—in the name of reason and even individualism—of all aspects of a member's life.

He found curious Meyer's belief that only communists choose their friends from among their ideological comrades or spend a good part of their time talking and thinking about ideology. Further, he criticized Meyer for attacking the Marxists' interest in building a grand interdisciplinary system.

> To carve out an architectonic, a system which enables one to hold a consistent and integrated view of all the disciplines of man is a great and noble aim, and I believe that a rationalist individualist philosophy can accomplish this goal. . . . This aim of the Marxists is simply the old Greek rationalist aim to make philosophy once more the queen of the sciences and the intellectual disciplines.[39]

Rothbard's ultimate explanation for Meyer's and other anticommunists' attitude is that they are Converts; they invested years advocating a ridiculous doctrine, and now they ameliorate their guilt by positing a diabolical, hard-to-resist force. Rothbard closes his review with a sober comment about Meyer's identifying the American people with the government. "It is disquieting, but perhaps not astonishing," he wrote,

> that Frank Meyer should reveal a deep-rooted and fundamental Statism in his political philosophy; it is almost impossible to agitate for the *State* to kill Communists throughout the world without adopting statism at the root of one's social philosophy.

The break between the libertarians and the Buckley right is a fascinating episode. Even more than today the libertarians were regarded as part of conservatism. In a passing comment,[40] Rothbard referred to a book on conservatism by historian Clinton Rossiter, presumably *Conservatism in America: The Thankless Persuasion*. He was amused to see that "all our friends are listed." He then adds this tidbit:

> The whole theme is vicious, of course, but I was interested to see that Rossiter caught the fact that there is a distinction between the general right-wing intellectuals and the more 'anarchistic' Chodorov-Rand-Nock group. Good thing in one particular sense: when they talk about intellectual Rightists of today, since there are very few around, the very fact of discussing them weights the importance of us purists very heavily. In other words, the very writing of such a book gives an undue weight to the influence of the purists, precisely because the proportion of purists to general Rightists may be very small, but it is quite large in proportion to the total of *intellectual* Rightists. This tends to give purist views more publicity than they would otherwise receive, induces college and graduate students to read purists, etc. Good for the cause.

To close this history section, it is interesting to note that Rothbard rejected vogue revisionism when it clashed with his knowledge of history. He did this emphatically in his view of the history of American foreign and domestic policy. In his review of Richard W. Van Alstyne's *The Rising American Empire*,[41] he rebutted the school of thought that denied America's isolationist past and held that it was imperialist even before the Spanish-American War in 1898. "Now this guiding thesis I believe to be nonsense," he wrote.

> . . . While it is true that America and American agents did many aggressive and imperialist things throughout the 19th cen-

tury, they can hardly be comparable in extent with the brazen acquisitions of the Spanish-American War. American expansion throughout the world *since* 1898 can also hardly be called mere consolidation of previously-won Empire;[42] *it* is the real shift from Republic to Empire.

Similarly, Rothbard disputed the school of thought that argued that America had no age of laissez faire. In his review of Carter Goodrich's *Government Promotion of American Canals and Railroads, 1800-1890*[43] he identified Goodrich as the "eminence grise" of the movement dedicated to the proposition that "the existence of *laissez faire* in 19th century America was largely a myth" and that there was no "revulsion" against government's internal "improvements."

Now this general picture, with qualifications only hastily admitted, is, I believe, a distorted one; from Goodrich's pages alone, it becomes clear that there *was* a "revulsion" movement of very considerable proportions. . . .

True, there was not complete laissez faire, especially in transportation, "where, historically, the State has always, along with other such 'command posts' of the economy as money, postal service, the army and police, etc., reached out to take over *first*. However, it is still true that America approached *laissez faire* more closely then, and more than other countries. It developed as well as it did, because of its free-market elements, and in spite of the governmental elements, the latter disrupting matters as such as it [sic] could."

Philosophy

Next to history, Rothbard's reviews dealt most with philosophical issues. In general, his concern was to uphold reason and its ability to discover the truth about all matters, including ethics. He was a foe of positivism, relativism, and skepticism. He was an unabashed champion of natural law and natural rights.

He was also a champion of John Locke, whom in the course of these reviews he defended from malignment and misinterpretation. In his review of Willmoor Kendall's *John Locke and the Doctrine of Majority Rule*,[44] Rothbard wrote, "The usual interpretation of John Locke is that he was the father of individualist, natural rights theory. From my own reading of Locke, I believe that this 'orthodox' interpretation is the correct one. Willmore Kendall . . . challenges this view to assert that Locke was, fundamentally, the father of all-out majority rule theory. . . . [T]his book propounds what I consider to be a totally wrong interpretation of Locke, and is an unjustified attempt to deprive the history of libertarian thought of one of its most important figures."

Later he returned to Locke in a review of Richard H. Cox's *Locke on War and Peace*:[45]

> [Cox] continues in the current tradition, spearheaded by Leo Strauss, of regarding John Locke as not a libertarian at all, but rather a statist follower of Hobbes. In my opinion, this is a serious misinterpretation of Locke, who should rather be regarded as a confused, inconsistent libertarian rather than as a convinced statist. . . . It is certainly equally, if not more, plausible to think of Locke as a secret pure libertarian than as a secret Hobbesian.

Rothbard pinned the misinterpretation of Locke on Leo Strauss. He had more to say about Strauss—good and bad—in three reviews of his books. In his review of Strauss's *Natural Right and History*,[46] Rothbard praises him for his brilliant rehabilitation of the concept of natural rights, showing that "it is the answer of reason as opposed to the nihilists and the conventionists, who take their morality from convention alone." Rothbard goes on,

> Strauss makes a very interesting distinction between the "classic" natural right theories of the classical Greek philosophers and Aquinas, and the modern natural right theories of Hobbes and Locke. Strauss prefers the former group, while I prefer the latter which contains the essential elements of a libertarian political philosophy, although with overlardings of other material, and omission of the economic argument. However, his book is useful in making the distinctions. A judicious combination of Hobbes and Locke would make an excellent libertarian framework; it is unfortunate that Strauss's rejection of the "modern" natural rights school leads him away from a staunchly liberal position, in the direction of vagueness.

Rothbard continued this line of criticism when he reviewed Strauss's *On Tyranny*.[47] "Strauss is at his best," wrote Rothbard, "on only one fundamental point: when he is criticizing ethical relativism and advocating a grounding of ethics on natural law. . . . Any more specific topic, however, either in detailed *content* of the natural law, or in historical discussions of political philosophers, shows Strauss to be a fallacious political philosopher, and a worse historian."

He goes in for the kill in his review of Strauss's *What is Political Philosophy?*[48] "The great defect," Rothbard wrote, "is that Strauss, while favoring what he considers to be the classical and Christian concepts of natural law, is bitterly opposed to the seventeenth and eighteenth century conceptions of Locke and the rationalists, particularly their 'abstract,' 'deductive' championing of the natural rights of the individual: liberty, property, etc. Strauss, in fact," Rothbard continued,

> has been the leading champion, along with Russell Kirk and the Catholic scholars in America, of a recent trend in Locke, etc. historiography to sunder completely the "bad", individualistic natural-rights type of natural law of the 17th and 18th Centuries, from the "good" classical-Christian type—good, presumably because it was so vague and so "prudential" that it offered very little chance to defend individual liberty against the state. In this reading, Hobbes and Locke are the great villains in the alleged perversion of natural law. To my mind, this "perversion" was a healthy sharpening and development of the concept. My quarrel with Strauss, Kirk, *et al.*, therefore, is not only valuational: that they are anti-natural rights and liberty and I am for them; but also factual and historical: for they think that the Lockians had an entirely different concept of natural law, whereas I think that the difference—while clearly there—was a sharpening development, rather than a perversion or a diametric opposite. The Strauss-Kirkians overlook for example, that while true that Aristotle and Plato were statists in their approach to natural law, the Stoics were fine individualists.[49]

What are these natural rights that Rothbard defends so vigorously against those who would deny or ignore them? Rothbard sums them up in a single phrase: property rights. He elaborated on the centrality of property rights in two reviews. In William Zelermyer's *Invasion of Privacy*[50] Rothbard finds "an instructive object lesson of the Pandora's box of evils that will unfold when one establishes or advocates any 'right' which is not subsumable under natural-law, property right." Zelermyer wants to establish a right to privacy without grounding it in this type of property right. For Rothbard the attempt fails. "Even a seemingly plausible 'enlargement' of such rights of the individual results in invasion of property right. . . . Such is the case with the so-called 'right of privacy,' which was invented by Louis Brandeis and Samuel Warren in a famous legal article in 1890. The perniciousness of the seemingly plausible 'right of privacy' is that it goes beyond the right of property (or the right of contract, explicit and implicit, subsumable under the right of property)."

Then Rothbard launches into his fundamental views on the nature of rights.

> The more I study the fascinating discipline of jurisprudence, the more I am convinced that the key to the whole problem is the absolute inviolability of property right; . . . all legitimate 'human' rights are subsumable under property right. On the other hand, any 'human right' *not* subsumable under property right is *itself* an invasion of the right of property, and hence should be outlawed.

Rothbard found a way to resolve the so-called privacy problem in which someone's picture is used in an endorsement of a product without permission. To him such use is a "fraudulent invasion of the buyer of the product" who is misled about who endorses the product, and it is "virtual *forgery*, and therefore a theft-misappropriation of the name of someone else."

His rejection of a right to privacy *per se* leads him to an interesting position on government wiretapping, which Zelermyer and other (welfare state) liberals usually opposed. He thought the issue was complex, despite "one's first libertarian instinct" to oppose it. Rothbard wrote, "[g]ranted that wiretapping is an invasion of property right, a *criminal* deserves to be invaded in such a way, because a criminal has lost his property right to a large extent." Evidence of *real* crime that is gathered by wiretap should be admissible. But government agents should be stiffly punished, even jailed for wiretapping innocent people. "In short," he wrote, "I would neither outlaw wiretap entirely, *nor* would I permit wiretap on the basis of . . . 'reasonable expectation' by the official that the man might be a criminal."

Rothbard returned to the basis of rights when he reviewed Milton R. Konvitz's *Fundamental Liberties of a Free People*.[51] The book, he said, "presents an instructive example of what happens when a political theorist tries to uphold the absoluteness of various 'human rights' of liberty, without considering, or caring about, property rights." He continued:

Property rights are not only essential, they are also the true basis, and provide the only intelligible criterion, for all other "human rights" and their demarcation. . . . All the problems which Konvitz wrestles with unsuccessfully: the limits of religious freedom, speech, etc. would have been precisely solved if he had rigorously applied property right throughout.

Just as he defended Locke from his misinterpreters, so he defended natural rights from those who misunderstand or distorted them. He took exception with Joseph Dorfman[52] and Rexford Guy Tugwell who objected to natural property rights in a discussion of Francis Leiber in their book *Early American Policy: Six Columbia Contributors*.[53] In this review Rothbard stated "the essence of natural property right theory":

[T]he theory, while couched in historical form, is a *logical*, universal-form theory (akin to praxeology) and is not really history. In short, the insight that property right of an individual *precedes* society and the State is a logical insight to the nature of man; it is not an historical assertion at all. And this insight *establishes* the natural law ethic that property *should* be defended. But modern positivists, empiricists, etc. can never understand what they consider an illegitimate fusion of fact and value, and mistake a logical inquiry into man's nature, or the nature of the State, as solely historical.

Rothbard made a similar point earlier when he reviewed Karl Popper's *The Logic of Scientific Discovery*.[54] "Popper," he wrote, "can best be described as a moderate positivist, and he attacks the extreme positivists who wished to bury all of philosophy as being 'metaphysical.' In essence, however, Popper is a positivist; his famous criterion of 'falsifiability' is certainly not very different from the orthodox positivist criterion of 'verifiability,' and his 'degree of corroboration' about the same as the positivists' substitution of 'probability' for absolute truth. At bottom, neither Popper nor the other varieties of positivists understand the doctrine of natural law, which concept resolves the famous 'problem of induction,' and resolves it in a rational, scientific manner not dependent—as most everyone believes nowadays—on Catholic theology."

Rothbard could not understand the modern claim that the seeking, not finding, of truth is the important thing. His charming retort is, Why bother to look for something if you know you can't find it anyway? He repeatedly chides authors for being anti-absolutist. When he reviewed Frank H. Knight's *Intelligence and Democratic Action*,[55] he noted, "The absolute is Knight's bugbear, and he combats it at every turn. . . . Knight champions the modern, secular, humanist, relativist, 'spirit of free inquiry,' which he associates with the last few centuries."

> For Knight, freedom is almost indissolubly tied to change, open-mindedness, relativity of truth, etc. . . . Knight's aversion to the absolute permeates all of this thought, weakening its rigor and sharpness, rendering his overall adherence to liberty and the free market more a *mood* or a tendency than a sharply consistent architectonic.

He made similar points in his review of Leon Bramson's *The Political Context of Sociology*.[56] Rothbard liked Bramson's attack on sociology and his linking of the modern left with nineteenth century conservatism. But he criticized Bramson's ethical and epistemological relativism. "It is *not* true," Rothbard wrote, that social science and its conclusions rest on value-judgments; much of it does not."

> Only political or ethical *conclusions*, and judgments, rest on value-judgments. The demonstration that price control causes shortages, for example, rests on no value-premises whatever; but the *conclusion* that price control *should not* be imposed is a policy judgment which *rests on* ethical theories as well as on the economic law just mentioned. (E.g. the ethical principle: that it is bad to cause shortages in this way.) And it is not *true*, as Bramson believes, that all value-judgments and ultimate ideological positions are as good as any other, and that the choice is purely an arbitrary one. Some ethical doctrines or ideological positions are objectively and rationally good and some are bad.

Rothbard was an ever-ready defender of the mind, of thought, of free will. He found much to defend them from in psychiatry. Reviewing Nathan Masor's *The New Psychiatry*,[57] he praised the attack on Freudianism and expressed approval of thyroid-vitamin injections as a treatment. But he challenged Masor's rejection of mind and values. "I am afraid that Masor," Rothbard wrote, "is basically a biochemical determinist, who leaves out the essential primacy and importance of the mind, of free will, of the ideas—the value-systems that the mind adopts, as a cause of neuroses, psychoses, etc."

Thomas Szasz's *The Myth of Mental Illness* came under similar criticism:[58] "Szasz's fundamental philosophic error, perhaps, is his deliberate overthrowing of thinking in terms of 'entities' and 'substances,' i.e. eighteenth century, natural-law, Aristotelian thinking, and his replacement of them by the modern fashions, especially 'thinking in terms of processes,' and therefore games, roles, etc."

Miscellaneous

In reviewing such a broad variety of subjects Rothbard had the opportunity to comment briefly on many issues. For example, his review of Charles L. Black's *The People and the Court*,[59] which favors judicial review as a means of expanding government power, stated, "The book emphasizes for me . . . that the Constitution, regarded as an attempt to limit government, was one of the most noble attempts at limiting government, at curbing the State, in human history but that it has failed, and failed almost ignominiously. One reason for such a failure, as [John C.] Calhoun predicted, is the monopoly Supreme Court. At any rate, this failure points up the necessity of other new, more stringent means of limiting and curbing government power."[60]

On secession: "Not only am I pro-secession on strict-constructionist grounds, but also because some bright fellow will eventually get the idea: well, if the South can secede from the Union, and Georgia can secede from the South, and X County from the State of Georgia, and Y village from the county, etc., etc. why can't I secede?"[61]

On ecology: "I am not an expert in this field, but I am inclined to believe that the organic farming people, basing their case on ecological laws of nature, make a pretty eloquent case, and one that is too often represented as being 'crack-pot' by our official organs of opinion and the mass media."[62] Also, "[Walter] Firey[63] is typical of conservationists, then, in admiring a coerced, fixed, stagnant, static system, unblemished by free men instituting changes in the patterns of nature."

On modern literature's portrayal of man: "When a modern novelist writes of criminals or rapists, they are considered guiltless, tragic victims of society or their environment, or 'happy bums'; when Dostoevsky wrote of them he *took sides*; he showed that criminals had tragically chosen, of free will and error, their own guilty path."[64]

On Marx: "Let it be said here and now: Marxism is, to be sure, a monumental system, but a monumental system which was totally fallacious at every single step of the way. . . . Indeed, of all of Marx's economic, social, and philosophic system, only his theory of classes has interest, not because of Marx's 'contribution,' which we have seen was total confusion, but because it was derived from the Saint-Simonians and Thierry, who, in turn, had created a tragically garbled and distorted version of what Saint-Simon had originally picked up from his former mentors Charles Dunoyer and Charles Comte."[65] And: "Marx made almost no blueprints for the operation of the socialist society, and the Soviet system is Marxism applied in action."[66]

On TV teaching: "It is true that, at least *per se*, teaching by TV would permit an enormous drop in the number of teachers needed per pupil. . . . And yet . . . yet, quality is as important as economy, and here is one case where I must agree with the educationists, albeit for very different reasons. Perhaps I am prejudiced by my antipathy to all TV, but I cannot favor subjecting children to more TV-pap than they are already getting. Simply watching TV induces an enormous passivity among children, a mindless emphasis on 'fun' and being entertained, that would probably rob them of what little education they are now getting. And what a tragedy to deprive children of that highly inspiring—and highly educational—personal and active contact with teachers: including the opportunity to ask questions and discuss, that would not be present in canned TV-education."[67]

On Gandhi: ". . . it became increasingly evident that Gandhi's stature as a systematic political thinker is extremely low. . . . it develops that the concept of non-violence in politics is *not* the essence of Gandhian *satyagraha*. For *satyagraha* encompasses not only non-violence, but also an extreme variant of 'love thine enemy,' as well as an extreme doctrine of 'self-suffering.'. . .Along with his anarchistic strain there is a theme of belief in a kind of communalistic syndicalism, as well as State welfare measures. . . . It is obvious, then, that Gandhi's numerous confusions have little to offer us in political philosophy. . . ."[68]

On nonviolence: ". . . the concept of non-violence, of mass action against governmental tyranny through civil disobedience rather than violent revolt, has a great deal to recommend it. It is far less likely to lead to undesirable consequences, and is far more effective in keeping revolutionaries to their original anti-tyrannical views. Power corrupts, and non-violent revolutionaries would not be in a position to be corrupted. But, apart from that, non-violence might be the only *practical* way to revolt against a totalitarian government."[69]

Rothbard truly is a commentator on our times. But more than that, he is a dedicated philosopher, historian, and teacher of liberty.

I would like to thank the Institute for Humane Studies at George Mason University, custodian of the Volker Fund files, for permitting me to use those files to write this paper. Leonard P. Liggio, Walter E. Grinder, John Blundell, and Emilio Pacheco offered helpful suggestions. Of course, any errors of fact or interpretation are mine.

Notes

1. William A. Paton, *Shirtsleeve Economics: A Commonsense Survey* (New York: Appleton-Century-Crofts, 1952).

2. He got his Ph.D. in economics in 1956.

3. The Volker Fund was an early source of support for libertarian and classical liberal scholars. A Volker grant supported Rothbard's writing of *Man, Economy, and State*. As David Gordon put it, "Few groups have done so much as that foundation did in a few short years to advance the cause of classical liberalism" (*Murray N. Rothbard: A Scholar in Defense of Freedom* [Auburn, Ala.: Ludwig von Mises Institute, 1986], p. 9).

   For the record, Rothbard was already a published author. His review of H. L. Mencken's *A Mencken Chrestomathy* appeared in the August 1949 issue of *Analysis*, edited by Frank Chodorov.

4. Personal interview.

5. When the Volker Fund's endowment expired in 1961 it effectively went out of existence, but its cause was pursued by the new Institute for Humane Studies, founded by F. A. "Baldy" Harper, who had worked for the Volker Fund. One can see in the Volker activities the beginning of the academic networking that became a major activity of IHS.

6. For a discussion of how a passionate libertarian can also be a cool, objective scholar, see David Gordon's essay cited above.

7. Emphasis added. From review of *Isolation and Security*, edited by Alexander DeConde. Date of review unknown.

8. Abram L. Harris, *Economics and Social Reform* (New York: Harper & Bros., 1958); reviewed February 1, 1959.

9. John R. Commons, *The Legal Foundations of Capitalism* (Madison, Wis.: University of Wisconsin Press, 1957); reviewed June 16, 1959.

10. O. H. Taylor, *Economics and Liberalism* (Cambridge, Mass.: Harvard University Press, 1955); review dated June 11, 1959.

11. Milton Friedman, *A Program for Monetary Stability* (New York: Fordham University Press, 1959); review October 31, 1960.

12. William Zelermyer's *Invasion of Privacy* (Syracuse, N.Y.: Syracuse University Press, 1959); reviewed October 6, 1960.

13. Alexander Gray, *The Socialist Tradition* (New York: Longmans, Green, 1947); reviewed August 24, 1961.

14. Yves Simon, *Philosophy of Democratic Government* (Chicago: University of Chicago Press, 1951); reviewed February 24, 1960.

15. From Rothbard's review of Milton Friedman, *Essays in Positive Economics* (Chicago: University of Chicago Press, 1953); reviewed October 4, 1961.

16. Melvin Greenhut, *Full Employment, Inflation & Common Stock* (Public Affairs Press, 1961); reviewed November 26, 1961.

17. See note 11, Friedman, *A Program for Monetary Stability.*

18. Lionel Robbins, *The Great Depression* (New York: Macmillan, 1934); reviewed November 14, 1959. The book was written in 1934.

19. Murray N. Rothbard, *America's Great Depression* (Kansas City, Kans.: Sheed and Ward, 1963).

20. W. Paul Strassmann, *Risk and Technological Innovation* (Ithaca, N.Y.: Cornell University Press, 1959); reviewed July 19, 1960.

21. Lawrence Abbott, *Quality and Competition* (New York: Columbia University Press, 1955); reviewed July 21, 1958.

22. G. L. S. Shackle, *Time in Economics* (Amsterdam: North Holland, 1958); reviewed August 16, 1961.

23. James M. Buchanan and Gordon Tullock, *The Calculus of Consent* (Ann Arbor, Mich.: University of Michigan Press, 1962); reviewed August 17, 1962.

24. James C. Malin, *On the Nature of History* (Lawrence, Kans.: James C. Malin, 1954); reviewed April 1, 1955.

25. Lee Benson *Turner and Beard* (Glencoe, Ill.: Free Press, 1960); reviewed September 27, 1960.

26. Donald L. Kemmerer, *American Economic History* (New York: McGraw-Hill, 1959); reviewed May 30, 1961.

27. Jackson Turner Main, *The Antifederalists* (Chapel Hill, N.C.: University of North Carolina Press, 1961); reviewed April 23, 1962.

28. George Athan Billias, "The Massachusetts Land Bankers of 1740," *University of Maine Bulletin* (April 1959); reviewed January 25, 1962.

29. Lee Benson, *Turner and Beard.*

30. "The American Revolutionary Heritage," *Laissez Faire Review* (May/June, 1979): 1.

31. J. Fred Rippy, *Globe and Hemisphere* (Chicago: Regnery, 1958); reviewed February 21, 1959.

32. Lee Benson, *The Concept of Jacksonian Democracy* (Princeton: Princeton University Press, 1961); reviewed November 11, 1961.

33. Robert V. Remini, *Martin Van Buren and the Making of the Democratic Party* (New York: Columbia University Press, 1959); reviewed March 8, 1961.

34. J. P. Taylor, *Origins of the Second World War* (New York: Athenaeum, 1962); reviewed April 18, 1962.

35. For a criticism of Munich from a noninterventionist perspective, see Earl C. Ravenal, *Never Again* (Philadelphia: Temple University Press, 1978).

36. Harry Elmer Barnes, *Perpetual War for Perpetual Peace* (Caldwell, Id.: Caxton Press, 1953); reviewed March 26, 1962.

37. Frank S. Meyer, *The Molding of Communists*, reviewed October 29, 1961. It was later published as "The Communist Bogey-Man" in *Left and Right*, 3, no. 2 (Spring/Summer 1967): 22-42; also *Supra* (General, N. 61) 1967.

38. Meyer called his mixture of libertarianism and conservativism "fusionism." Critical as Rothbard was of Meyer's foreign policy, Rothbard denied the fusionist category and put Meyer's fundamental beliefs squarely in the libertarian camp. See "Frank S. Meyer: The Fusionist as Libertarian," in George W. Carey, ed., *Freedom and Virtue: The Conservative/Libertarian Debate* (Lanham, Md.: University Press of America, 1984), pp. 91-111.

39. "Incidentally," writes David Gordon, "it is, in the Trotskyist phrase, 'no accident' that one of Rothbard's favorite words is 'architectonic.' He is one of the great classifiers and systematizers." *Scholar in Defense of Freedom*, p. 8.

40. Clinton Rossiter, *Conservatism in America: The Thankless Persuasion* (New York: Alfred Knopf, 1955); contained in his April 1, 1955, letter.

41. Richard W. Alstyne, *The Rising American Empire* (New York: Oxford University Press, 1960); reviewed March 18, 1962.

42. As Van Alstyne maintained.

43. Carter Goodrich, *Government Promotion of American Canals and Railroads, 1800-1890* (New York: Columbia University Press, 1960); reviewed June 25, 1961.

44. Willmoor Kendall, *John Locke and the Doctrine of Majority Rule* (Urbana, Ill.: University of Illinois Press, [1941], 1959); reviewed May 16, 1961.

45. Richard H. Cox, *Locke on War and Peace* (Oxford: Clarendon Press, 1960); reviewed July 22, 1962.

46. Leo Strauss, *Natural Right and History* (Chicago: University Chicago Press, 1953); reviewed May 4, 1954.

47. Leo Strauss, *On Tyranny* (Political Science Classics, 1948); reviewed July 4, 1960.

48. Leo Strauss, *What is Political Philosophy* (Glencoe, Ill.: Free Press, 1959); reviewed January 23, 1960.

49. Rothbard was not finished with Strauss. His review of *Thoughts on Machiavelli* (Glencoe, Ill.: Free Press, 1958); February 9, 1960) brims with insights and scores Strauss for his "crackpot" scholarship. "The more I read Strauss's attack," Rothbard wrote, "The more I concluded that Machiavelli had more good points in his philosophy than I had imagined."

50. William Zelermyer, *Invasion of Privacy*.

51. Milton R. Konvitz's, *Fundamental Liberties of a Free People* (Ithaca, N.Y.: Cornell University Press, 1957); reviewed March 22, 1961.

52. Rothbard's mentor at Columbia under whom he wrote his dissertation on the *Panic of 1819* (New York: Columbia University Press, 1962).

53. Francis Leiber, *Early American Policy: Six Columbia Contributors* (New York: Columbia University Press, 1960); reviewed April 19, 1962.

54. Karl Popper, *The Logic of Scientific Discovery* (New York: Basic Books, 1959); reviewed December 22, 1959.

55. Frank H. Knight, *Intelligence and Democratic Action* (Cambridge, Mass.: Harvard University Press, 1960); reviewed October 1, 1960.

56. Leon Bramson *The Political Context of Sociology* (Princeton: Princeton University Press, 1961): reviewed June 20, 1962.

57. Nathan Masor, *The New Psychiatry* (New York: Philosophical Library, 1959); reviewed October 14, 1960.

58. Thomas Szasz, *The Myth of Mental Illness* (New York: Hoeber-Harper, 1961); reviewed May 25, 1962.

59. Charles L. Black, *The People and the Courts* (New York: Macmillan, 1960); reviewed March 24, 1961.

60. Contrast with his later review stated above.

61. James C. Malin, *On the Nature of History*.

62. Geoffrey Dobbs, *On Planning the Earth* (Liverpool: KRP Publications, 1951); reviewed January 28, 1961.

63. Walter Firey, *Man, Mind and Land* (Glencoe, Ill.: Free Press, 1960); reviewed July 2, 1962.

64. Edmund Fuller, *Man in Modern Fiction* (Vintage Books, 1958); June 22, 1962.

65. Fred M. Gottheil, *The Economic Predictions of Karl Marx* (Ph.D. Dissertation; Duke University, 1959); reviewed October 10, 1961.

66. Harry Heckman, *The Economics of American Living* (Chicago: Rand McNally, 1959); reviewed April 12, 1962.

67. Roger A. Freeman, *School Needs in the Decade Ahead* (Washington, D.C.: Institute for Social Science Research, 1958); reviewed December 29, 1958.

68. Joan Bondurant, *Conquest of Violence: The Gandhian Philosophy of Conflict* (Princeton: Princeton University Press, 1958); March 17, 1961.

69. *Ibid.*

Part 5

Personal

25

A Funny Thing Happened on the Way to the Forum or the Reviews of "Mr. First Nighter"

Justus D. Doenecke

Though Murray Rothbard has been the subject of countless articles and book chapters, there has been little, if anything, written on Rothbard as "cultural critic." Yet Rothbard does not simply write profusely on economics and public policy. He offers many comments on American culture in general and brings to this a verve seldom seen since H. L. Mencken or Dwight Macdonald. He is unequivocally on the side of what he calls the "Old Culture," something symbolized by the likes of Noel Coward performances ("elegant wit and romance"), classic jazz ("an exciting blend of European melody and harmony with African rhythm"), and *The Maltese Falcon* ("that superb movie"). Particularly this is true in the case of cinema, a topic to which Rothbard devoted much space in his own monthly, *The Libertarian Forum*.

Rothbard cannot help but compare modern comedy with its counterpart of the 1930s, an era graced by "the scintillating wit, the high style, the sophisticated intelligence of hero and heroine." His models were the films of Cary Grant and Carole Lombard. Oscar Wilde's spoof, *The Importance of Being Earnest* (1952), Rothbard said in 1973, was perhaps the greatest film ever made. The fifties too, he claimed, had fine comedy, and here his models were such Spencer Tracy and Katherine Hepburn films as *Pat and Mike* and *Adam's Rib*.

In commenting on the newer genres, Rothbard praised such spoofs of Jewish culture as *Bye, Bye Braverman* (1968) and *The Heartbreak Kid* (1972). He found *A Touch of Class* (1973) uneven, claiming that George Segal was out of his depth in attempting classic comedy. As far as efforts to recreate the "madcap" comedies of the thirties goes, Rothbard gave high marks to *The Hot Rock* (1972) and *SOB* (1981), lower ones to

Arthur (1981) and *Continental Divide* (1981). Rothbard enjoys the con-man film, as seen by his endorsements of *The Sting* (1973) and *Bad News Bears* (1976). Also heralded were the Pink Panther series. Peter Sellers's Inspector Clouseau, Rothbard wrote in 1977, "has now taken on an almost mythical status." But Rothbard is not afraid to pan what most critics acclaim. *Tootsie* (1982), which featured Dustin Hoffman impersonating a female, was simply "a one-joke movie carried on too long."

If Rothbard has a contemporary comic hero, one as outstanding in his particular acting style as Carole Lombard and W. C. Fields were in theirs, it is Woody Allen. In 1974, Rothbard called Allen the outstanding film comic of our time. In *Sleeper* (1973), the story of a man who suddenly woke up in the year 2173, Allen was hearkening back to the great days of the silent film comedians of the 1920s, Harold Lloyd and Buster Keaton. *Annie Hall* (1977), Rothbard said, was a superb satire on phony Hollywood values, rock music, the fashionable snorting of cocaine, and excessive reliance on the automobile. The bittersweet *Manhattan* (1979) spoofed art criticism, avant-guarde movies, and the new, swinging, "humanist" therapists. However, Allen's *Midsummer Night's Sex Comedy* (1982) was "one of the worst movies ever made," the results of his "*serioso* and pretentious flirtations with the Bergmans and the Fellinis."

Rothbard usually enjoys Mel Brooks films. Except for the genre made popular by the Marx Brothers and W. C. Fields, Brooks's are the funniest pictures yet filmed. In 1974, Rothbard called *Blazing Saddles*, a spoof on Westerns, unquestionably the most humorous movie of the past several years. Before that, it was *The Producers* (1968). This mockery of Broadway hucksters Rothbard found the most hilarious movie of the previous two decades. Also recommended was *Young Frankenstein* (1974), "a sweet, affectionate tribute to the horror film"; *Silent Movie* (1976), a spoof on the old "silents"; and *High Anxiety* (1977), a mockery of psychiatry and of Alfred Hitchcock films as well. However, when Brooks came out with *History of the World: Part I* (1981), Rothbard assailed him for his obsession with scatology, that is human excrement. Brooks only redeemed himself by producing *My Favorite Year*, a comedy set in the fifties and one that Rothbard called the best picture of 1982.

Rothbard takes pride in attending, reviewing, and sometimes even praising what high-brows avoid. In doing so, he sees himself as the voice of an intelligent middle-class public that refuses to be cowed by lofty and arrogant critics. As far as musicals are concerned, Rothbard lauded *Gigi!* (1958), found *Mary Poppins* (1964) banal, and—while enjoying *My Fair Lady* (1964)—preferred the old Wendy Hiller-Leslie Howard version of *Pygmalion* (1938). Turning to disaster films, he claimed that *The Poseidon Adventure* (1972) was gripping, though marred by "phony philosophy" and "even more phony theology." *Jaws* (1975) was better than *The Towering Inferno* (1974) and *Earthquake* (1974), a "turkey," as *Jaws* avoided their "phony moralism." However, he saw the acting poor and the ending idiotic.

When it comes to Westerns, Rothbard is an unabashed fan of the Duke. "There is no such thing as a bad John Wayne picture," he wrote in 1974. He called *The Wild Bunch* (1969) "one of the great Westerns of all time." Directed by Sam Peckinpah, whom Rothbard greatly admires, it dealt with a rather violent outlaw band, circa 1913, who undertook one last fling by working for a Mexican general. Yet another Peckinpah film, *The Getaway* (1972), was full of disastrous acting, with Ali McGraw performing particularly abysmally. Rothbard was upset when Clint Eastwood, another Rothbard favorite, directed and starred in *High Plains Drifter* (1973), a film he found far too pretentious.

Then there is science fiction. Rothbard called the much-touted *Star Wars* "such a silly, cartoony, comic-strip movie that no one can possibly take it seriously. . . . No one, that is, over the age of 8." A "pretentious, mystical, boring, plotless piece of claptrap," it could not be compared with such "science fiction greats" as *The Thing* (1951), *It Came from Outer Space* (1953), *The Night of the Living Dead* (1968), and "the incomparable" *Invasion of the Body Snatchers* (1956).

Occasionally Rothbard will endorse a horror film, provided that is it is done in the classic tradition. Nostalgic for a vanishing breed of movies, he plugged *Theatre of Blood* (1973), a Vincent Price film in which a hammy Shakespearean actor killed each of his critics in a most gory manner.

Rothbard also praises what few critics do, the "blaxploitation" film, movies where black private eyes and white gunmen chase each other in ruthless pursuit. Here he grants kudos to *Shaft* (1971), *Cotton Comes to Harlem* (1970), and *Trouble Man* (1972). While panning *Shaft in Harlem* (1972), he praised *Shaft in Africa* (1973) for "adding an international espionage flavor to the Harlem dude." These were all "fun pictures," where "the audience identifies with the characters, shouts at the screen, applauds and hisses." Only "insufferably *serioso* left-critics" opposed them, preferring—in a most patronizing manner—to depriving black Americans of real entertainment while promoting such depressing and boring pictures as *Sounder* (1972). However, sagas of black sharecroppers can never substitute for "street-private eye-police" culture.

Rothbard continually shows his love of "rough action" films. He praises what he calls "the defender-of-justice theme, in which a tough, smart, decisive, laconic hero defends right and justice against villainy and evil." This kind of detective, invented by Dashiell Hammett in the late 1920s, became corrupted, wrote Rothbard in 1984, by "the cynicism and implicit psychobabble of Raymond Chandler and his numerous followers, including Ross McDonald and his California variant (the Lew Archer series)."

Yet Rothbard rejoices that the "tough cop" still lives, as proven by *McQ* (1974), *Death Wish* (1974), and *Death Wish II*, the latter two Charles Bronson features. He found *The French Connection* (1971) both brilliantly directed and suspenseful, far better than its sequel *Badge 373* (1973). In praising *Shamus* (1973), in which Burt Reynolds is beaten to a pulp, Rothbard wrote, "It is true that the plot tends to be incoherent at times, but in a movie like this, who cares?"

Almost anything starring Clint Eastwood gets Rothbard's commendation, for as he wrote in 1974, "Eastwood is the polar opposite of the whining modern anti-hero beloved by the *avant-guarde*." Particularly lauded are *Dirty Harry* (1971), *Magnum Force* (1974,) and *The Enforcer* (1976). One exception was *Thunderbolt and Lightfoot* (1974), an action-suspense movie marred by witless horseplay, interspersed with much moping and "tragedy."

The Godfather (1972) was definitely Rothbard's kind of picture. He wrote, "It is gloriously *arriere-garde*. . . . It is a picture with heroes and villains, good guys and bad guys; there is not a trace of the recently fashionable concern with the 'alienation' of schnooks and cretins searching endlessly for a purpose in life." Though *The Godfather-Part II* (1974) lacked "the tightly wrought magnificence" of Part I, it was good enough to deserve an Academy Award. "On to Part III," wrote Rothbard in 1975.

Commenting on the critics' attitude towards violence, Rothbard noted that critics loved *A Clockwork Orange* (1971), with its random and meaningless violence, but deplored films where violence was used as an instrument of justice and defense against crime. "In short," wrote in 1973, "they hate *Dirty Harry* or such great John Wayne films as *Chisum* or *Rio Bravo*, and they have the gall to denounce such Sam Peckinpah masterpieces as *The Wild Bunch*."

It would hardly be surprising to find Rothbard an ardent adventure-spy fan. He loves what he calls "the pre-World War II originals," John Buchan and Eric Ambler, the faster paced post-war Helen MacInnes, and the modern tough-guy genre, as revealed through Ian Fleming,

Donald Hamilton, and Robert Ludlum. If there are negative models, they lie in Graham Greene and John LeCarre, who take an "all-sides-are-bad" attitude. Writes Rothbard, "The main problem with the Greene-LeCarre works is that they become deadly boring, since if the spies on all sides are bored time-servers and *they* don't care about the outcome of the lot, why in hell should we care?" (Rothbard did make an exception for the BBC series *Tinker, Tailor, Soldier, Spy*).

High on Rothbard's list were *The Guns of Navarone* (1961), an Allied commando adventure; *Frenzy* (1972), the story of a London strangler; *Fear is the Key* (1972), an Alistair McLean yarn about international drug trafficking; *Puppet on a Chain* (1970), another McLean thriller; and *The Day of the Jackal* (973), which centered on an attempt to assassinate President de Gaulle. As far as more orthodox "mystery" goes, Rothbard endorsed *Masters* (1972), a gentle detective drama; *Sleuth* (1972), a lighthearted tour de force of changing identities; and *Family Plot* (1976), a Hitchcock effort at a tongue-in-cheek thriller. In lauding *The Tamarind Seed* (1974), an espionage-romance film, he noted that it flouted current convention to such an extent that Julie Andrews and Omar Sharif did not "hop into bed at the first opportunity." Surprisingly, Rothbard panned *Murder on the Orient Express* (1974). An Alfred Hitchcock could have built suspense out of small details; director Sidney Lumet dragged the movie pointlessly.

Among Rothbard's favorites are the James Bond series, the "quintessence of the Old Culture: marvelous plot, exciting action, hero vs. villains, spy plots, crisp dialogue and the frank enjoyment of bourgeois luxury and fascinating technological gadgets." He called *From Russia With Love* (1963) a great film classic. *Live and Let Die* (1973), despite the substitution of the "too slight and debonair" Roger Moore for Sean Connery, is one of the best of the series. The fact that all the villains wore black and that the film was unabashedly sexist, with Bond converting the female villains to the path of righteousness by sheer macho virility, caused Rothbard to praise the film for its fidelity to the novel and for bringing back "the delightful old clichés of the action pictures of the 1930s and 1940s."

In the *Forum*, Rothbard continually expresses his nostalgia for the "Old" or "Movie-Movie," marked by a strong plot and central characters with whom the audience could identify. The plot emerged logically and step-by-step from purposive action, and from the conflicts that this action engineered. Rothbard's criteria for good cinema lies in the thirties and forties, an era he calls a golden age. "It was then," he writes, "that we could delight in *Gone With the Wind*, in *Snow White*, and *The Lady Vanishes.*" The *Thin Man* series were the most delightful films ever made, he claimed at one point.

Rothbard makes no secret of his dislike for what he called the "non-linear" movie, that is a production in which "very little of the film makes any sense at all, either in philosophy, plot, continuity, or camera work." The New Movie assumes that individuals have no aim. Rather they respond mechanically and haphazardly to equally random events.

But if there is no purpose, there can be no plot. Moreover, as Rothbard noted in 1976, "it is impossible for the audience to identify with them or give a damn what happens to them. Who cares about random response mechanisms?" As Rothbard commented in 1973, "The Enemy on the movie front is not the California porn king; our war to the metaphorical knife is not with the maker of *Deep Throat* but with the Bergmans, the Bunuels, the Antonionis, the Fellinis, the Godards. The truly obscene is not the happy, fun-loving *School Girl*, but such monstrosities as *Juliet of the Spirits* and *Last Year at Marienbad.*"

Little wonder Rothbard is quick at discovering pretentiousness. In dealing with *Deliverance* (1972), the film based on James Dickey's novel of the same title, Rothbard accused director John Boorman of adopting "the oldest trick in the business: if you want a movie to seem Profound when you have nothing much to say, then draw out the action, make the camera dwell endlessly on each scene, and focus on the face of each actor as he struggles painfully to emit some inarticulate banality. In other words, if you make the film dull enough, it will trail clouds of Profundity for our gullible moviegoers—especially the gullible critics." The fact that none of the four intrepid canoeists described in the film ever charted a dangerous river in advance caused Rothbard to ask, "What sort of *schlemiels* are these?"

An Unmarried Woman (1978) was another such disaster. It was a feminist film centering on one Erica, who must "cope" when her husband moves out on her. Wrote Rothbard, "Ye gods, there were hundreds of films of the Old Culture that portrayed women who were ten times as independent and a hundred times as intelligent as the drip Erica, portrayed by Jill Clayburgh. Think of all the movies with Katharine Hepburn, Bette Davis, Claudette Colbert, Joan Crawford, Susan Hayward, etc!"

Other New Movies received the same debunking. Rothbard saw *Morgan* (1966), which dealt with a jilted husband and his eccentric escapades, and *The Ruling Class* (1972), a comedy about a British heir who confuses himself with Jesus, as examples of this mindlessness. *The Paper Chase* (1973), a film about the pressure of Harvard Law School, suffered from "diffusion, meandering, lack of organization." *Daisy Miler* (1974) was simply typical of Henry James's "endless, quibbling, and plotless stories." The epitome of this genre was *Nashville* (1975), a plotless attack on the right-wing ideology and country music that permeates much of the American heartland.

The sexual revolution made little impact on Mr. First Nighter. *Shampoo* (1975), far from being a "profound" statement about our time, lacked even the wit of a Restoration play by Molière. The movie was a muddy satire of southern California, centering on a restless hair-dresser, played by Warren Beatty, and his demanding female customers. Rothbard found Julie Christie mindlessly bellowing four-letter words on film in a dialogue that "generally gravitates between the banal and the inchoate." In his review of *Rich and Famous* (1981), Rothbard saw the story of two "sexually liberated" women a vapid one, the dialogue non-existent. "At least a lesbian scene would have relieved a bit of the monotony," he wrote.

Rothbard usually does not like message movies. *The Way We Were* (1973) was a throwback to the left-wing films of the 1940s. In this romance between Jewish political activist Barbra Streisand and her waspish Joe College boyfriend Robert Redford, the Communist Party was shown as "basically right as rain, though perhaps a wee bit strident."

Rothbard also panned *The Front* (1976), doing so on basically the same grounds. Though it featured the comedian he admired most, Woody Allen, Rothbard found it "tendentious, crude, hokey, over-simplified, pretentious and sententious to the point where it must be, for any sensible observer, counterproductive." Communists were portrayed so favorably that "God forgive that the Communists were ever out of power."

Julia (1977), the story of playwright Lillian Hellman's resistance activities in Europe in the mid-30s, drew some of Rothbard's most scathing comments. "Strip away the current Hellman cult, strip away the fuzzy leftism and the fact that Hellman was a Stalinist when it counted, and *Julia* would have never left the studio."

Rothbard is no narrow ideologue, for he will endorse a left-wing picture if he finds it cinematically sound. He conceded that *Citizen Kane* (1941) was "a left-liberal message picture," but one "done with brilliance and with power, with highly charged and purposeful, conflicting characters on a grand scale." Similarly, *Z* (1969) and *The Battle of Algiers* (1966) show that being left wing does not disqualify a movie from being a superior picture.

Of course, Rothbard does cheer films with libertarian themes. He called *Sometimes a Great Notion* (1941) "a rugged, heroic, explicitly individualist piece," for it featured Henry Fonda tackling union goon squads. Also hailed was *Walking Tall* (1973), which dealt with "an authentic hero," the citizen-farmer-turned-sheriff Buford Pusser, who battled moonshiners and crooked gamblers in rural Tennessee. He found *The Man Who Would Be King* (1975) the best movie John Huston had directed in years. More important, it had a libertarian moral to it: the conqueror of Kafiristan was ruined by the hubris of power.

Of course, Rothbard loved films with overt anti-state themes. He praised *All the President's Men* (1976), the exposé of Watergate, as it identified "the prime evil as resting in government" and did so with "excitement and panache." So too did *The Omen* (1976), showing how a family unwittingly adopted a baby anti-Christ. Rothbard loved the confirmation of the theological prediction that the anti-Christ would in some way stem from government, something he saw fulfilled when "evil kid" wound up in the bosom of a Kennedyesque president of the United States.

The eighties saw more libertarian films. *Absence of Malice* (1981) was a "rough, trenchant movie" that was "outspokenly pro-civil libertarian, anti-FBI, anti-muckraking press, and at least mildly pro-Mafia." *The Verdict* (1982) too struck a responsive chord, for it dealt with a lawyer who fights "the legal flimflam and technicalities which the Establishment habitually uses to betray the interests of truth and justice." Rothbard found libertarian themes in *Red Dawn* (1984), a movie dealing with a Communist invasion of the central United States. The movie was "an enjoyable teen-age saga," glorifying not interstate strife but "guerilla conflict that the great radical libertarian military analyst, General Charles Lee, labelled 'people's war' two centuries before Mao and Che."

But to Rothbard, heavy-handed message films were inevitably flawed. The strength of *True Confessions* (1981), the story of two Irish-Catholic brothers caught in a web of general and church corruption, lay in the fact that it lacked overt polemicism. Just plain good in Rothbard's eyes was *Chariots of Fire* (1981), the story of two British Olympic runners, though he could not help but note that it celebrated the such traditional values as dedication and individual integrity against a bigoted Establishment and the British state.

As far as acting is concerned, Rothbard is sparse in his praise. Among the few he admires are Diana Rigg ("who always projects a fascinating blend of beauty and high competence"), Gary Cooper, and Sylvester Stallone, who in *Rocky* (1976) played a "hero with a touching vulnerability and sensitivity."

But Rothbard's comments on actors can be damning. In 1972, he called Peter O'Toole "one of the most overrated actors in the last two decades." "Given anything like his head," wrote Rothbard, "he will twitch, shake, and generally chew any and all of the available scenery. . . . Even in that superb film, *Lawrence of Arabia*, that twitching and quivering augured badly for the future." Steve McQueen "has always been one of our poorest actors: his expression ranges from surly-and-quizzical to surly-and-quizzical." Sir Lawrence Olivier "always tends to overact and chew the scenery, especially in productions that he obviously feels are beneath him."

The same holds true for certain actresses. Wrote Rothbard in 1973 of Ali McGraw, "Miss McGraw has never been able to act." And in 1975 of Goldie Hawn, "Miss Hawn comes over as a nitwit even when she is not trying." (Rothbard did praise her performance in *Swing Shift* (1984), the story of two women workers on the home front in World War II. He called the film itself "the picture of the year—a lovely valentine to a lost world.") Judy Garland was "one of Hollywood's all-time worst singers and actresses"; her daughter, Liza Minelli, "impossibly awkward and pseudo-elfin."

Rothbard's strength lies in his irreverence. He refuses to suffer fools gladly. He does not obtrusively make a pitch for libertarianism, his political philosophy, but uses aesthetic criteria to appraise most of the films he watches. There are few forms of writing in which Rothbard's superb humor is more revealed. Indeed, as far as style is concerned, one can find some of his best writing in these reviews.

One is only sorry Mr. First Nighter did not comment more often, and one yearns for a renewal of a monthly *Libertarian Forum*. Would his love of adventure have extended to *Raiders of the Lost Ark* (1981)? Would his aversion to leftist films have extended to *Reds* (1981), *Ragtime* (1981), and *Daniel* (1983)? What would he have said about Meryl Streep's performance in *The French Lieutenant's Woman* (1981), or in *Sophie's Choice* (1982)? Would his anti-war attitudes have created empathy with *Gallipoli* (1981), *Breaker Morant* (1981), and *Gandhi* (1982)? Would he share the same opinion of the sequels to *Star Wars* and *Rocky* that he thought of the originals? How about the new James Bond films? Would he have seen *Being There* (1979) as Peter Sellers's most brilliant film?

In his film reviews, Rothbard shows himself to be one of America's most perceptive—and humorous—social commentators. The world of cinema needs far more of his criticism.

26

Himself, at Sixty
With Apologies to Ogden Nash

Robert Kephart and Dyanne Petersen

Silent Cal's in the White House, and Babe Ruth's in his prime,
Long before Keynesian Voodoo made a buck worth a dime,
Ma and Pa Rothbard had met at an anarchist ball,
And soon *Conceived In Liberty* a child to be called
Murray N. Rothbard, our honored guest at this session,
He grew up on the West Side, during *America's Great Depression*.
Prohibition was in, moonshine and bordellos,
Here in the Manhattan playground of that runt, Fiorello.
He survived adolescence, as the war reached a halt,
And grew into manhood, a handsome young Galt.
Then on to Columbia after the second war ended,
He was the campus right-winger, but rarely commended
For singing the praises of Lindbergh and Taft,
Those Columbia pinkos thought him slightly daft.
Now hardened for battle our hero debates,
The most likely tactic for smashing the state.
Forget armed revolution, that would bring no improvement,
But wait—we could start—a Libertarian Movement.
A movement for liberty throughout the land,
Murray suggests the idea to—Ayn Rand.
"A is A," she responds, and then starts to holler,
"My economists heroes they have to be—taller."
"Rothbard, you're a hooligan, like all of the rest,"
"Nixon and Greenspan, I like them the best."
He wasn't discouraged by Ayn's rude rebuff,
But objectively speaking, he'd had quite enough.
So the movement matures, and the years tick away,

Strange people pass through, and some of them stay.
Now the Libertarian Party spurs Murray to action,
He loves all 500 members, and all 5,000 factions.
Words are his weapon, ideas are the ammo,
He becomes for the movement, a scholarly Rambo,
Our hero offends some, but he never does bore 'em,
When he milks sacred cows in *Libertarian Forum*.
In the "movement" you're no one, and no issue is burning,
Unless the *Libertarian Forum*'s knife is in the jugular turning.
"Mr. First Nighter" is brutal to films he dislikes,
The same goes for books, plays and music despite
His love for the arts, Fats Waller, Big Bands,
And Chuck Bronson's "Death Wish," of course, is just grand.
From the Curmudgeon's pet causes, we learn much of his id,
The gold standard, The Party, and Short People's Lib.
But you'll never see Murray give the Gipper a break,
He exposes his rhetoric and hair color as fake.
His revisionist history has a good many fans,
But none are in Israel, though a few in Falklands.
And conspiracy theory, he thinks right in the main,
And offers as proof, Koch, Cato and Crane.
The Kochtopus Monster makes him rant and rave.
Also Bella Abzug, Bill Buckley and the Kondratieff Wave.
But don't think the Curmudgeon is unreasonably tough,
I'm here to tell you that he's just a cream puff.
When the movement's history is written, they're sure to acknowledge,
The hot air, and that vote in the electoral college.
But history can't ignore, try it ever so hard,
The brilliant corpus of work of Murray Rothbard.
His lifelong companion is Joey, his wife,
An exceptional woman who shares Murray's life.
When Murray proposed, Joey agreed they should try it,
And she has enriched both his life and his diet.
He's our joyful, witty, optimistic sage,
Three score by the calendar, but he acts half his age.
He returned from the West Coast, and it set me a'reeling,
When he offered to share both his space and his feelings.
But California corruption, the laid back revival,
Won't wash in New York, where the word is survival.
So I end with two questions, and he's not worth his salt
Unless he tells us tonight: "Who *is* John Galt?"

And one final question, try to answer this, Smarty,
What *is* an anarchist doing in the Libertarian Party?

Delivered at the Ludwig von Mises Institute's birthday party celebration, New York, March 1, 1986, in honor of Murray N. Rothbard on the occasion of his sixtieth birthday.

27

Rothbard as Cultural Conservative

Neil McCaffrey

M urray Rothbard and I make an odd couple. More exactly, the
Rothbards and the McCaffreys make an odd quartet, since
Murray's wife Joey and my wife Joan are both essential to our gatherings.

We met in the late fifties, under the auspices of *National Review*.
Frank Meyer, everybody's friend, was running the back of the book,
and Murray was one of his pet reviewers on economics. I was working
at Doubleday but moonlighting *NR*'s circulation promotion. When we
finally got to shake hands I had already read a lot of Murray, learning
as I read. Differences between conservatives and libertarians existed
even then, and always had; but they were muted. The old, perhaps
adventitious alliance that had blossomed during the New Deal was still
alive and well.

So we became friends—just in time, as it turned out. Because by the
middle sixties, the old ideological alliance was fraying; Vietnam was
the catalyst. Many libertarians, led by Murray, moved to a more
radical position. Many conservatives, Joan and I among them, grew
more conservative (if that is possible). Murray and Joey drifted away
from the conservative scene as Murray emerged as the fountainhead of
radical libertarianism. In the normal ebb and flow of friendships, the
Rothbards and the McCaffreys might easily have become former
friends. But music intervened to rescue us.

Somewhere along the way, Murray and I discovered that we shared
a Dirty Little Secret. We were both devoted to jazz and popular music
of the classic periods; not to modern jazz, we each learned to our relief.
And, God save us, certainly not to rock. In fact, as the rock plague
swept across the once civilized world, Murray and I found in each
other a refuge. Nothing knits like a common hatred. Now when the
Rothbards and the McCaffreys gather, usually to hear a good traditional band or to dust off the old records, the music is favored with im-

precations heaped on the despoilers of good music. Some feelings run deeper than ideology.

For some reason I haven't been able to divine, I seem to have given the music more time than Murray has. That casts me into the role of senior partner. Yet if I know more of the history and the trivia, I don't think that has given me a keener ear than Murray's. He turns to good music instinctively, without the effort and the mistakes that are the usual lot of the beginner. In the Swing Era, your typical buff might have started by finding himself dazzled by the virtuosity and drive of Harry James (most often by his less interesting work). He might then discover more authority and inventiveness in the playing of Roy Eldridge or Billy Butterfield or Bunny Berigan. Only if he followed these giants of the second generation back to the sources did he come to appreciate the seminal genius of Louis Armstrong and Bix Beiderbecke.

Murray goes right to the source—sometimes without realizing it. In so doing he will miss some of the pleasant tributaries, only to discover them later with the zest that marks everything he embraces. What is the heart of his instinctive good taste?

Murray has a rare ear for melody. Growing up in the Golden Age of popular music, his instinct could be both challenged and satisfied by our premier songwriters: Porter, Berlin, Rodgers and Hart, the Gershwins; not to mention the dozens of composers and lyricists of the second rank whose work bears comparison with the giants: Carmichael, Arlen, Mercer, Kern, Gordon and Revel, Ellington (here considered as a songwriter; his jazz originals, much the larger body of his work, put him on another plane), Warren, Whiting, McHugh, Waller, Coslow, some two score more.

But to hear these songwriters of genius, one must hear their works *played*. Enter jazz—and enter the quasi-jazz of the superior dance bands and singers. People with pedestrian ears don't much care how a song is played. Most of them will even settle for elevator music. But someone like Murray soon gets beyond the song itself. (He *learns* a song, and most of the lyrics, on one hearing!) He must hear the song *performed* with grace and imagination. It is but a step from good popular songs to good jazz, and Murray took the step back in his teens and early twenties.

That ear for melody also explains why he has no patience with modern jazz. Contrary to myth, the jazz of the classic periods is not simply black music, but a happy marriage of European and black music. No matter how hot a band played in the Golden Age, the melody—rooted in European music, was always there, stated or implicit. And if Tin Pan Alley fertilized jazz, jazz repaid the songsmiths. One can't call Porter or

Berlin or even Gershwin a jazz composer and let it go at that (as naive critics did in the days of *Rhapsody in Blue*). But equally, the great song-writers would sound more like Victor Herbert without the influence of jazz. Whereas modern jazz moved ever farther from mere melody, aping the antiphonal abstractions of avant-garde concert music. Murray likes to recognize the tune.

In movies as in music, Murray prefers the Golden Age. "Movie movies" are his pets, as every devotee of Mr. First Nighter in *Libertarian Forum* will attest. The Rothbardian scorn for pretension is at work here. "Movie movies" tell a story about believable people (or at least believable figures of fantasy). Like the classic stories from every age, they are as accessible to children of average intelligence as to deep thinkers. Most of all, "movie movies" don't take themselves all that seriously. Does that lower the esthetic content? I think Will Shakespeare would feel more comfortable with Louis B. Mayer than with an auteur theorist from the Left Bank.

Thus the paradox: Rothbard the theorist and pal of radical libertarianism, and Rothbard the cultural conservative. The paradox extends beyond movies and music to architecture as well. I won't pretend that I can resolve this apparent contradiction. But it is not unique to Murray. T. S. Eliot, radical in his poetry, was profoundly conservative in his worldview. Many of the more original and individualistic among us defy the easy categories.

Speaking of which, I've portrayed Murray as a lover of good popular music and jazz—but instinctively. He can sing along with zest, and carry a tune as well as many a professional. But he is above all a fan, and makes no claim to be an expert. When John Wilson retires as jazz critic of the *New York Times*, Murray won't make the list of candidates to replace him. That being so, you may find it hard to believe that Murray has left to jazz, and the world, a legacy. I rejoice to pass it on because it deserves immortality.

One night in the late seventies, the Rothbards and the McCaffreys were enjoying an evening at the Red Blazer Too (correct spelling; trust me). The Blazer features on Tuesdays a band called Vince Giordano's Nighthawks. What's in a name? In the case of the Nighthawks, a conscious policy of harkening back to the music of the twenties and early thirties, and to bands like the Coon-Sanders Kansas City Nighthawks. As the band was blowing the years away, Murray paused in his humming to express his afflatus. "Life-affirming music!" he pronounced. Nobody has ever said it better. Nobody ever will.

28

My View of Murray Rothbard

JoAnn Rothbard

When Murray was in school, he always went out for the class play, because, as anyone who is acquainted with him knows, he is a great ham. One year he discovered that the two male leads were the Handsome Young Prince and the Fat Old King. He also found out that he was expected to play the part of the Fat Old King. Now, this annoyed him, and he began a campaign to get the part of the Handsome Young Prince. There were two reasons for this. First, the assumption that he would be the Fat Old King, rather than the Handsome Young Prince, rankled. And secondly, the Handsome Young Price at one point in the play, kissed the hand of the Beautiful Young Princess, and the part of the Beautiful Young Princess was being played by a girl whom he had a crush on. He was determined to get to kiss her hand. Such a fuss did he make that finally he was awarded the part of the Handsome Young Prince. Then began rehearsals, and the devastating directions, "You take her hand in your palm, raise her hand, bow over it, and kiss *your own thumb*."

And so life bumbled along for a boy, whose parents thought they were giving him a Scottish moniker when they named him Murray. But now he has made sixty, and he may have had to kiss his own thumb that time, but he has always been the handsome young prince to me.

He has always been enormously enthusiastic about his interests—jazz of the 20s and 30s, German baroque churches, and liberty.

But long before I knew about the jazz, or liberty, and before even he knew about German baroque churches, I was attracted by his intelligence, and especially his sense of humor. He was and is always ready to laugh. Thirty-five years ago, we were chastised for laughing in the Columbia University library. And recently, I found him in a dark movie theater, by following his familiar laughter.

His enthusiasms lead him all over the map—from the Marx brothers to the pietists versus the liturgicals, and, of course, the Ludwig von Mises Institute. One never knows where his interest will land next. Recently, I woke up in the middle of the night, and Murray was delighted to have someone to tell his newest discovery to. "That bastard Eli Whitney didn't invent the cotton gin after all."

So, I hope he'll have plenty more time to indulge in laughter and enthusiasm, and that at sixty, he's only at the mid-point of his life, or as his grandmother would have said, "bis ein hundert und zwanzig."

Delivered at the Ludwig von Mises Institute's birthday party celebration, New York, March 1, 1986, in honor of Murray N. Rothbard on the occasion of his sixtieth birthday.

29

Testimonial

Margit von Mises

Thank you for giving me this opportunity to say *Happy Birthday* to my dear friend, Murray Rothbard, and to congratulate him on the great work he has done and is still doing to return the world to freedom.

I cannot say this without—at the same time—praising the warm friendship and thoughtfulness of Murray's devoted wife, Joey Rothbard. It gives me great pleasure, Joey, to thank you tonight and to tell this gathering what a wonderful friend you have been to me all these years since my husband died.

Tonight, I have only one regret, and that is that Ludwig von Mises cannot be here to see and hear the out-pouring of admiration and love for his pupil Murray Rothbard, another great scholar in the Austrian tradition.

Surely all of you must know that Murray Rothbard was one of my husband's most devoted pupils and loyal followers. No one—with exception of Professor Kirzner—can claim to having done more to advance my husband's ideas than has Murray Rothbard. And no one could have described my husband's work more effectively than did Murray Rothbard in his short but elegant essay, *The Essential von Mises.*

To state that Murray Rothbard admired my husband, hardly does him justice:—He *loved* my husband, I would say, as a devoted son loves a father. Yet Murray did not slavishly parrot every one of my husband's ideas without reasoning things out on his own and developing his own ideas.

And sometimes his daring led him to conclusions with which my husband did not agree. Specifically, if I remember well, they differed in their views about Russia. Yet that did not diminish their mutual affection and respect.

An even greater difference in their convictions, however, involved their beliefs on government. Although my husband, in all his books constantly criticized the interventions of government into the market, and the tendency of governments to control people and their lives, he still believed government to be a necessity for society. Professor Rothbard, on the other hand, as you probably all know, thinks that we will never have a peaceful society until—to take a phrase from the title of one of his own books—we replace *POWER OVER MARKET* with *MARKET OVER POWER*. In other words, until we replace all of the functionaries of government by the mechanism of the market.

There were other, smaller, differences between them, involving not government but economic theory. Not about the fundamentals of Austrian economics, mind you, only some very fine points concerned with monopoly theory.

Those of you who have read my book, *My Years with Ludwig von Mises* will remember that my husband had great respect for Murray's abilities and opinions, even when he did not agree completely with them.

In that book I described an incident that took place at a Mont Pelerin Society meeting in Stresa, Italy. Dr. Joaquin Reig, a lawyer from Madrid, approached my husband and asked him to comment on the fact that his pupil, Professor Rothbard, did not agree with him on monopoly theory. My husband's answer came immediately. He replied: "Whatever Rothbard has written in this work is of the greatest importance."

And I shall take the liberty of extending my husband's remark to say: "Whatever Murray Rothbard writes in *any* book is of the greatest importance."

My dear friend Murray, I toast your birthday and your past accomplishments, and I wish you continued success in bringing the message of the free market to more and more people in the coming years. Do carry on your good work.

Thank you.

Delivered at the Ludwig von Mises Institute's birthday party celebration, New York, March 1, 1986, in honor of Murray N. Rothbard on the occasion of his sixtieth birthday.

Selected Bibliography of
Murray N. Rothbard

Books

America's Great Depression. Kansas City, Kans.: Sheed and Ward, 1963. Reprint. Los Angeles: Nash Publishing, 1972; 2nd rev. ed. New York: New York University Press, 1975. Reprint. New York: Richardson and Snyder, 1983.

Conceived in Liberty. Vol. 1, *A New Land, A New People: The American Colonies in the Seventeenth Century.* New Rochelle, N.Y.: Arlington House, 1975. Reprint. San Francisco: Cobden Press, 1987.

Conceived in Liberty. Vol. 2, *Salutary Neglect: The American Colonies in the First Half of the Eighteenth Century.* New Rochelle, N.Y.: Arlington House, 1975. Reprint. San Francisco: Cobden Press, 1987.

Conceived in Liberty. Vol. 3, *Advance to Revolution: 1760-1784.* New Rochelle, N.Y.: Arlington House, 1976. Reprint. San Francisco: Cobden Press, 1987.

Conceived in Liberty. Vol. 4, *The Revolutionary War: 1775-1784.* New Rochelle, N.Y.: Arlington House, 1979. Reprint. San Francisco: Cobden Press, 1987.

Economic Depressions: Causes and Cures. Lansing, Mich.: Constitutional Alliance, Inc., 1969, title page reads: "Depressions: Their Causes and Cure." Constitutes part of the *National Issues Series of Politics,* Vol. IV, No. 8. Reprinted in Richard Ebeling (ed.), *The Austrian Theory of the Trade Cycle and Other Essays.* New York: The Center for Libertarian Studies (Occasional Paper Series #8), 1978. Also republished by the Ludwig von Mises Institute, Washington, D.C., 1983.

Education, Free and Compulsory: The Individual's Education. Wichita, Kans.: Center for Independent Education, 1972.

Egalitarianism As a Revolt Against Nature and Other Essays. Washington, D.C.: Libertarian Review Press, 1974.

For a New Liberty: the Libertarian Manifesto. New York: Macmillan, 1973. Revised edition with preface and a new Chapter 1, *The Libertarian Heritage*. New York: Collier Books, 1978.

Individualism and the Philosophy of the Social Sciences. San Francisco: Cato Institute (Cato Paper No. 4), 1979.

Left and Right: Selected Essays 1954-1965. New York: Arno Press, 1972.

Ludwig von Mises: Scholar, Creator, Hero. Auburn, Ala.: Ludwig von Mises Institute, 1988.

Man, Economy, and State: A Treatise on Economic Principles. 2 Vols. Princeton, N.J.: Van Nostrand, 1962. Reissued. Los Angeles: Nash Publishing, 1970; New York: New York University Press, 1979. Chapter X was translated into book form as *Monopolio y Competencia*, Buenos Aires: Centro de Estudios Sobre la Libertad, 1965.

Power and Market. Menlo Park, Calif.: Institute for Humane Studies, 1970. Reissued. New York: New York University Press, 1977.

Protectionism and the Destruction of Prosperity. Auburn, Ala.: Ludwig von Mises Institute (Occasional Paper), 1987.

The Essential Ludwig von Mises. Lansing, Mich.: Bramble Minibooks, 1973. Reprinted in Ludwig von Mises, *Planning for Freedom*, South Holland, Ill.: Libertarian Press, 1980; and Washington, D.C.: Ludwig von Mises Institute, 1983. Translated into Norwegian by Arild Emil Presthus as Ludwig von Mises, *Hans Liv Og Laere*. Printed in 4 parts in *Ideer om Freihet* (July 1981; Winter 1982; Spring 1982; and Winter 1983). Translated into Spanish by J. Reig as *Lo Esencial De Mises*. Madrid, Spain: Union Editorial, 1974. Portuguese translation forthcoming by Instituto Liberal, Rio de Janeiro, Brazil.

The Ethics of Liberty. Atlantic Highlands, N.J.: Humanities Press, 1982.

The Mystery of Banking. New York: Richardson and Snyder, 1983. Reprint. Fort Worth, Texas: American Bureau of Economic Research, 1988.

The Panic of 1819: Reactions and Policies. New York: Columbia University Press, 1962.

What Has Government Done to Our Money? Larkspur, Colo.: Pine Tree Press, 1964. Published as *Moneda, Libre y Controlada*. Buenos Aires: Centro de Estu Dios Sobre la Libertad, 1962. Appears in *What is Money*. New York: Arno Press, 1972.

Articles

"A Note on Burke's Vindication of Natural Society." *Journal of the History of Ideas* (January 1958): 114-18.

"Breaking Out of the Walrasian Box: The Cases of Schumpeter and Hansen." *Review of Austrian Economics* 1 (1986): 97-108.

"Consistent Libertarian." *Menckeniana* (Fall 1963): 4-5.

"Deflation Reconsidered." *The Wall Street Review of Books* 4, No. 2 (Special Issue, June 1976): 35-41. Reprinted in *Geographical Aspects of Inflationary Processes, Part One.* Edited by Peter Corbin and Murray Sabrin. Pleasantville, N.Y.: Redgrave Publishing, 1976.

"Epistemological Problems of Economics: Comment." *Southern Economic Journal* (April 1962): 385-87.

"F. A. Hayek and the Concept of Coercion." Vol. 31. *Ordo, Jahrbuch Fur Dier Ordnung von Wirtschaft und Gesellschaft* (1980): 43-50.

"Huntington on Conservatism: A Comment." *American Political Science Review* (September 1957): 784-87.

"In Defense of 'Extreme Apriorism.' " *Southern Economic Journal* (January 1957): 314-20.

"Is Their Life After Reagonomics?" *Money World* 2 (August 1988).

"King on Punishment: A Comment." *Journal of Libertarian Studies* (Spring 1980): 167-72.

"Law, Property Rights, and Air Pollution." *Cato Journal* (Spring 1982): 55-99.

"Ludwig von Mises and Natural Law: A Comment on Professor Gonce." *Journal of Libertarian Studies* (Summer 1980): 289-97.

"Mises, 'Human Action': Comment." *American Economic Review* (March 1951): 181-85. Followed by a rejoinder by George Schuller.

"Praxeology as the Method of Economics," Vol. 2. *Phenomenology and the Social Sciences* (June 1973): 311-39. Reprinted as "Praxeology as the Method of the Social Sciences," in *Individualism and the Philosophy of the Social Sciences.* Washington, D.C.: Cato Institute, 1980.

"Praxeology: Reply to Mr. Schuller." *American Economic Review* (December 1951): 943-46.

"Robert Nozick and the Immaculate Conception of the State." *Journal of Liberation Studies* (Winter 1977): 45-77.

"Foreign Policy of the Old Right." *Journal of Libertarian Studies* (Winter 1978): 85-96.

"The Frankfort Resolutions and the Panic of 1819." *Register of the Kentucky Historical Society* (July 1963): 214-19.

"The Hermeneutical Invasion of Philosophy and Economics." *Review of Austrian Economics*, 3 (Fall 1988).

"The Laissez-Faire Radical: A Quest for the Historical Mises." *Journal of Libertarian Studies* (Summer 1981): 237-53.

"The Logic and Semantics of Government." *Pacific Philosophy Forum* (December 1963): 95-100.

"The Myth of Neutral Taxation." *Cato Journal* (Fall 1981): 519-64.

"The Politics of Political Economists: Comment." *Quarterly Journal of Economics* (February 1960): 659-65.

"The Sociology of the Ayn Rand Cult." Townsend, Wash.: Liberty Publishing, 1987.

"Theory and History." *Austrian Economics Newsletter* (Fall 1984): 1-4.

"Timberlake on the Austrian Theory of Money: A Comment." *Review of Austrian Economics* 2 (1987): 179-87.

"Value Implications of Economic Theory." *American Economist* (Spring 1973): 35-39.

Chapters in Books

"Austrian Definitions of the Supply of Money." In *New Directions in Austrian Economics*, edited by Louis Spadaro. Kansas City, Kans.: Sheed Andrews and McMeel, 1978.

"Biography of Ludwig von Mises." In *International Encyclopedia of Social Sciences*, XVI, 1968.

"Capitalism versus Statism." In *Outside Looking in: Critiques of American Policies and Institutions, Left and Right*. New York: Harper and Row, 1972.

"Catallactics." In *New Palgrave: A Dictionary of Economics* Vol. 1, edited by John Eatwell, Murray Milgate, and Peter Newman. London: Macmillan, 1987.

"Economic Thought: A Comment." In *The Growth of the Seaport Cities: 1790-1825*, edited by D. T. Gilchrist. Charlottesville, Va.: University Press of Virginia, 1967.

"Frank A. Fetter, 1863-1949." In *New Palgrave: A Dictionary of Economics* Vol. 2, edited by John Eatwell, Murray Milgate, and Peter Newman. London: Macmillan, 1987.

"Freedom, Inequality, Primitivism and the Division of Labor." In *The Politicalization of Society*, edited by Kenneth Templeton. Indianapolis, Ind.: Liberty Press, 1978. Originally appeared in *Modern Age* (Summer 1971).

"Gold vs. Fluctuating Fiat Exchange Rates." In *Gold is Money*, edited by Hans F. Sennholz. Westport, Conn.: Greenwood Press, 1975.

"Harry Elmer Barnes as Revisionist of the Cold War." In *Harry Elmer Barnes, Learned Crusader: The New History in Action*, edited by A. Goddard. Colorado Springs, Colo.: Ralph Myles, 1968.

"Herbert Hoover and the Myth of Laissez Faire." In *A New History of Leviathan*, edited by R. Radosh and M. Rothbard. New York: E. P. Dutton, 1972.

"Historical Origins." In *The Twelve Year Sentence*, edited by William F. Rickenbacker. LaSalle, Ill.: Open Court Publishing, 1974.

"Imputation." In *New Palgrave: A Dictionary of Economics* Vol. 2, edited by John Eatwell, Murray Milgate, and Peter Newman. London: Macmillan, 1987.

"Interventionism: Comment on Lavoie." In *Method, Process, and Austrian Economics*, edited by Israel Kirzner. Lexington, Mass.: Lexington Books, 1982.

"Justice and Property Rights." In *Property in a Humane Economy*, edited by Samuel Blumenfeld. LaSalle, Ill.: Open Court Publishing, 1974.

"Lange, Mises, and Praxeology: The Retreat from Marxism." In *Towards Liberty*, Vol. II. Menlo Park, Calif.: Institute for Humane Studies, 1971.

"Ludwig Edler von Mises, 1881-1973." In *New Palgrave: A Dictionary of Economics* Vol. 3, edited by John Eatwell, Murray Milgate, and Peter Newman. London: Macmillan, 1987.

"New Light on the Prehistory of the Austrian School." In *The Foundations of Modern Austrian Economics*, edited by Edwin G. Dolan. Kansas City, Kans.: Sheed and Ward, 1976.

"Praxeology, Value Judgments, and Public Policy." In *The Foundations of Modern Austrian Economics*, edited by Edwin G. Dolan. Kansas City, Kans.: Sheed and Ward, 1976.

"Punishment and Proportionality." In *Assessing the Criminal: Restitution, Retribution, and the Legal Process*, edited by Randy E. Barnett and John Hagel, III. Cambridge, Mass.: Ballinger, 1977.

"Society Without a State." In *Anarchism (Nomos XIX)*, edited by J. Pennock and J. Chapman. New York: New York University Press, 1978.

"The Austrian Theory of Money." In *The Foundations of Modern Austrian Economics*, edited by Edwin G. Dolan. Kansas City, Kans.: Sheed and Ward, 1976.

"The Case for a Genuine Gold Dollar." In *The Gold Standard: An Austrian Perspective*, edited by Llewellyn H. Rockwell, Jr. Lexington, Mass.: Lexington Books, 1985.

"The Case for a 100 Percent Gold Dollar." In *In Search of a Monetary Constitution*, edited by Leland B. Yeager. Cambridge, Mass.: Harvard University Press, 1962.

"The Federal Reserve as a Cartelization Device." In *Money in Crisis*, edited by Barry Siegel. San Francisco: Pacific Institute for Public Policy Research, 1984.

"The Great Society: A Libertarian Critique." In *The Great Society Reader: The Failure of American Liberalism*, edited by M. Gettlemen and D. Mermelsteing. New York: Random House, 1967. Also appears in 2nd edition, 1971; and in *Views on Capitalism*, edited by R. Ramano and M. Leiman. Beverly Hills: Glencoe Press, 1970; and *Government in the American Economy*, edited by Robert Carson, Jerry Ingles, Douglas McLaud. Lexington, Mass.: D. C. Heath, 1973.

"The Hoover Myth." In *For a New America: Essays in History and Politics From Studies on the Left, 1959-1967*, edited by J. Weinstein and D. Eakins. New York: Random House, 1970.

"The Mantle of Science." In *Scientism and Values*, edited by Schoeck and Wiggins. Princeton, N.J.: Van Nostrand, 1960. Reprinted in *Individualism and the Philosophy of the Social Sciences*. San Francisco: Cato Institute (Cato Paper No. 4), 1979.

"The Myth of Efficiency." In *Time, Uncertainty, and Disequilibrium*, edited by Mario J. Rizzo. Lexington, Mass.: Lexington Books, 1979.

"The New Deal and the International Monetary System." In *Watershed of Empire: Essays on New Deal Foreign Policy*, edited by Leonard Liggio and James Martin. Colorado Springs, Colo.: Ralph Myles, 1976. Reprinted in *The Great Depression and New Deal Monetary Policy*. San Francisco: Cato Institute (Cato Paper No. 13), 1980.

"The Origins of the Federal Reserve." In *Central Banking and the Federal Reserve*, edited by Llewellyn H. Rockwell, Jr. Auburn, Ala.: Ludwig von Mises Institute, forthcoming.

"The World at the Brink: Pushing for a Return to Gold." In *In the Escalation of Debt, Disinflation, and Marketmania: Prelude to Financial Crash*. Toronto: Bank Credit Analyst, 1988.

"Time Preference." In *New Palgrave: A Dictionary of Economics* Vol. 4, edited by John Eatwell, Murray Milgate, and Peter Newman. London: Macmillan, 1987.

"Total Reform: Nothing Less." In *Nonpublic School Aid*, edited by E. G. West. Lexington, Mass.: Lexington Books, 1975.

"Toward a Reconstruction of Utility and Welfare Economics." In *On Freedom and Free Enterprise*, edited by Mary Sennholz. Princeton: Van Nostrand, 1956. Published in Spanish as "Hacia Una Reconstructcia de la Utilidad y de la Economia del Bienestar." In *Libertas* 4 (May 1987).

"War Collectivism in World War I." In *A New History of Leviathan*, R. Radosh and M. Rothbard. New York: E. P. Dutton, 1972.

"Why Inflation Must Lead to Recession or Depression." In *Everything You Need to Know about Gold and Silver*, edited by Louis E. Carabini. New Rochelle, N.Y.: Arlington House, 1974.

Name Index

Abbott, Lawrence, 358
Abraham, Larry, 152
Ackley, Gardner, 98
Aden, Mary Anne, 167
Aden, Pamela, 167
Alchian, Armen A., 277
Allen, William R., 93
Aquinas, Thomas, 129, 370
Aristotle, 101, 195-97, 200, 202, 204-05, 209, 211, 230, 234, 236, 243, 371
Axelrod, Robert, 19, 23
Band, Richard, 151
Barnes, Harry Elmer, 366
Baruch, Bernard, 157
Bastiat, Frederic, 344, 345
Baumol, William J., 184-85
Bentham, Jeremy, 341, 342
Berlin, Isaiah, xii
Billias, George Athan, 363
Black, Charles L., 375
Blanchard, James U. III, 151, 163-64, 168
Böhm-Bawerk, Eugen von, ix, xv, xvi, 49, 54, 141, 145, 359
Bork, Robert, xv, 5
Bramson, Leon, 374
Brandeis, Louis, 372
Bronfenbrenner, Martin, 96
Browne, Harry, 151, 152, 161-62, 168
Brozen, Yale, xv, 5
Buckley, William F. Jr., 368, 393
Buchanan, James McGill, xiii, xiv, 16, 17, 120, 188, 210, 273, 277, 359-60
Burns, Arthur, 141-45, 171
Calhoun, John C., 375
Casey, Douglas R., 151, 152, 168
Cassel, Gustav, xv, 49, 50, 54
Carter, James E., 100, 165, 170
Chase, Salmon Portland, 34

Chodorov, Frank, 368
Clark, John Bates, 49, 54
Coase, Ronald H., 16
Commons, John R., 293, 355
Comte, Charles, 363, 376
Cournot, Augustin, 96
Cox, Richard H., 370
Coxon, Terry, 168
Crane, Edward H., III, 393
Cuzan, Alfred, 322
Dahl, Robert, 285-88
Darwin, Charles, 94, 101, 108
Debreu, Gerald, 89
Demsetz, Harold, 5, 277
Dewey, Donald, 54
Dewey, John, 293
Dines, James, 151, 163, 168
Dohmen-Ramirez, Bert, 166, 167
Downs, Anthony, 318-21
Dworkin, Ronald, 238
Eastwood, Clint, 385-86
Einstein, Albert, 95
Exter, John, 164
Faucher, Julius, 344, 346
Fertig, Lawrence, 141
Fetter, Frank A., 54
Filmer, Sir Robert, 240
Fisher, Irving, 45, 52-55, 156
Franklin, Benjamin, 94
Friedman, Milton, 45, 97-98, 152-53, 158, 277, 279, 357
Gandhi, 376
Galbraith, John Kenneth, 93-94, 100,
Gauthier, David, xiv, 176-77
Goodrich, Carter, 369
Goodspeed, Bennett W., 157, 158
Granville, Joe, 163
Gray, Alexander, 355

411

Green, T. H., 293
Greenspan, Alan, 392
Gresham, Sir Thomas, 160
Grotius, 215, 219, 220, 223
Groseclose, Elgin, 151, 161
Grune, Joy Ann, 126
Harris, Abram L., 355
Harrod, Roy Forbes, 105
Harsanyi, John, xiv, 175-90
Harwood, E. C., 151, 163
Hayek, Friedrich August von, xii, 49, 53, 55, 80-85, 95, 103, 114, 118, 151, 154, 169, 186-87, 197-98, 207-09, 293-94, 301
Hazlitt, Henry, xvii, 139-42, 148, 152, 161, 353
  Economics in One Lesson, 139-40, 152
  Failure of the "New Economics," 141
  From Bretton Woods to World Inflation, 141
  selected bibliography for, 148
Hegel, Georg W. F., 98, 224, 237
Heller, Walter, 97-100
Hession, Charles, 158
Hicks, John R., 55
Hitchcock, Alfred, 384, 387
Hobbes, Thomas, 211, 222, 271, 274, 370-01
Hoppe, Donald J., 151, 162, 164, 166
Hoover, Herbert, 145, 330-31
Hughes, Chief Justice Charles Evans, 39, 40
Hull, Cordell, 354
Hume, David, 60, 207-08
Hutt, William H., xvii, 139, 142-44, 148-49
  A Rehabilitation of Say's Law, 142
  Economics of the Colour Bar, 142, 144
  Economists and the Public, 142, 143
  selected bibliography for, 142
  The Strike-Threat System, 142
  The Theory of Idle Resources, 143
  Theory of Collective Bargaining, 142
Johnson, Lyndon B., 98
Johnson, Paul, 102, 331
Jones, C. Clyde, 361-62
Kant, Immanuel, 63, 100, 205, 207
Kaplan, Morton, 285
Kemmerer, Donald L., 361-62

Kendall, Willmoor, 369-70
Kephart, Robert D., xviii, 163
Keynes, John Maynard, xiii, 45, 107, 141, 143, 151-53, 158, 160, 392
  See also Keynesian school of economics
Kirk, Russell, 210, 371
Kirzner, Israel M., xiii, xiv, 7, 49, 55, 117, 400
Knight, Frank H., xv, 45, 46, 49, 55, 96, 374
Koch, Charles G., 393
Kondratieff, Nikolai D., 166, 393
  See also Kondratieff wave theory
Konvitz, Milton R., 372-73
Kuhn, Thomas S., 92
Lachmann, Ludwig M., 102, 105, 154
Lane, Rose Wilder, 353
Laski, Harold, 293
Lassalle, Ferdinand, 348, 350
Lasswell, Harold, 285-87
Leibenstein, Harvey, 112
Leiber, Francis, 373
Liggio, Leonard P., 353
Lindbergh, Charles A., Jr., 392
Locke, John, xv, 65, 134, 214-15, 236, 239-40, 248, 250, 252, 257, 259, 262-63, 369-73
  See also Lockean proviso
Lutz, Friedrich August, 55
Machan, Tibor, 200
Machlup, Fritz, 93
Madison, James, 13
Main, Jackson Tucker, 362-64
Masor, Nathan, 374
Marshall, Alfred, 50, 78, 105
Martin, James, 323
Marx, Karl, 45, 46, 129, 130, 142, 237
  See also Marxism
McDonald, Forrest, 364
McKenzie, Richard, 14-15
McCaffrey, Neil, 161
McKeever, Jim, 166
Mencken, Henry L., 141
Menger, Carl, ix, xvi, 55, 141, 145
Meyer, Frank S., 196-97, 206, 237, 353, 366-68, 395
Mill, John Stuart, 205

Mises, Ludwig von, xi, xiii, xv, xvi, xviii, 7, 8, 49, 53, 55, 56, 60, 61, 62, 93, 95, 100, 105, 139, 141, 145, 152, 156, 159, 162, 329, 322, 363, 400
  Credit Anstalt, 156
  See also Human Action
Mises, Margit von, xviii, 159
  My Years with Ludwig von Mises, 401
"Mr. First Nighter," 383-91
Mohl, Robert von, 344
Montesquieu, 199
Mosca, Gaetano, 315
Murray, Charles, 307
Myers, C. Vern, 164
Nietzsche, 231
Nixon, Richard M., 169, 171, 392
Nock, Albert Jay, 363-68
North, Gary, xiii, 89-109, 151-52, 160
Nozick, Robert, xii, xvi, 133, 134, 243, 247-64, 271, 273-74
Oppenheimer, Franz, 309-10
O'Driscoll, Gerald P. Jr., 55
O'Neil, June, 127, 133
Paris, Alexander P., 164
Paton, William A., 352
Peel, Robert, 342-43
Pigou, Arthur Cecil, 78, 114
Plato, 202, 204-05, 208, 371
Popper, Sir Karl, 373
Posner, Richard A., xv, 4, 16, 22-23
Pound, Roscoe, 353
Prewitt, Kenneth, 316, 323
Prichard, H. A., 233
Pugsley, John, 151, 152, 160, 164
Quesnay, Francois, 46
Rand, Ayn, 195, 208, 234, 238, 273-74, 276, 279, 367-68, 392
Rawls, John, 177-83, 187-88
Reagan, Ronald W., 166, 168, 170, 171, 330
Reig, Joaquin, 401
Remini, Robert V., 365
Ricardo, David, 45
Rippy, J. Fred, 364
Robbins, Lionel, 80, 105, 357
Rockwell, Llewellyn H., Jr., xvii, 162
Röpke, Wilhelm, 152
Roosevelt, Franklin D., 36, 38, 145, 330, 331

Roscher, Wilhelm, 347
Rossiter, Clinton, 368
Rothbard, JoAnne, xviii, 393, 395
Rothbard, Murray N.
  America's Great Depression, ix, 90, 102, 145, 155, 160, 331
  Conceived in Liberty, xi, 147, 270
  The Ethics of Liberty, xii, 11, 60, 61, 75, 147, 274, 353
  The Essential von Mises, 400
  For a New Liberty, xii, 274, 276-77
  Man, Economy, and State, x, 54, 56, 102, 147, 159, 160-61, 401
  The Panic of 1819, ix, 102, 144, 145, 364
  Power and Market, xi, 17-18, 147, 124, 401
  selected bibliography for, 149-50
  Toward a Reconstruction of Utility and Welfare Economics, 146
  What Has Government Done to Our Money?, 160
Rueff, Jacques, 151
Ruff, Howard, 151, 164, 168
Rousseau, Jean-Jacques, xv, 75, 215-26, 237
  See also The Social Contract
Ruttan, Vernon W., 115
Saint-Simon, 363, 375-76
Salerno, Joseph T., 147
Samuels, Warren J., 284
Samuelson, Paul A., 92, 97, 153, 160
Sartori, Giovanni, 325
Schlossberg, Herbert, 331
Schultz, Harry D., 162, 163
Schumpeter, Joseph A., 47, 55
Sen, Amartya, 177, 182
Sennholz, Hans F., 152, 156, 163, 168
Shackle, G. L. S., 102, 105, 358-59
Simon, Yves, 356
Sinclair, James, 169
Skousen, Mark, 169
Smith, Adam, 78, 177, 227
Smith, George H., 234
Smith, Jerome, 151, 153, 163, 164, 165, 168
Smith, John Prince, xvi, 341-51
Snyder, Julian, 151, 166
Sowell, Thomas, 127

Spencer, Herbert, 189
Steiner, Hillel, xvi, 247-64
Stigler, George J., 277
Sterba, James P., 182-83, 185, 189
Stone, Alan, 316, 323
Strauss, Leo, 199, 370, 371
Szasz, Thomas, 374-75
Taft, Robert, Sr., 392
Taylor, A. J. P., 365-66
Taylor, D. H., 355
Tugwell, Rexford Guy, 373
Tullock, Gordon, 14-15, 359-60
Van Alstyne, Richard W., 368
van Buren, Martin, 365
Veatch, Henry, 207

Vieira, Edwin, 41
Viner, Jacob, 96
Volcker, Paul, 169, 171
Walras, Leon, 47, 159, 359
Warren, Samuel, 372
Wayne, John, 385
Whitney, Eli, 399
Wicksteed, Philip, 141
Williams, Walter, 144, 323
Willis, Norman, 127, 128
Wittgenstein, Ludwig, 230
Worcester, Dean A., Jr., 119
Wright, Austin Tappan, xvii, 335-40
Yeager, Leland B., xiii, xiv, xv, 49, 50, 55
Zelermyer, William, 371-72

Subject Index

Action, human; *See* Praxeology

Affirmative action; *See* Quotas

Aggression, 69, 70, 76; *See also* Non-aggression principle

Agricultural Adjustment Act, 36

American Federation of State, County, and Municipal Employees v. State of Washington, 125, 137, 138

American history; *See also* United States of America

American Revolution, xi, 271-72

Civil War, 34

Colonial period, xi

Constitutional Convention of 1787, 33

Ethnic and religious aspects, 399

Spanish-American War 368-69

Anarchism, xiii, xiv, xvi, 13, 32, 210, 236, 280, 312-13, 376, 394, 401

Anti-Corn Law League, 343

Anti-militarism, 342

Anti-trust policy, 3-6, 10, 357

reform movement, 5-7

See also Monopoly

Apartheid, 134, 144

Aprioristic reasoning, xiii, xvi, 62, 63, 66, 72, 90, 92, 102, 157

Architecture, baroque, 398

Argumentation, 62-64, 67, 72, 74

Arlington House, 161, 162

Austrian school of economics, ix, x, xi, 57, 77-78, 79, 83, 88, 139, 147-48, 156, 168

See also Mises, Ludwig von; Menger, Carl; Böhm-Bawerk, Eugen; Rothbard, Murray

Bank of the United States, ix, 34

Banking, xvii, 36

Fractional reserve, xv, 24-31, 36, 332

Free, 42, 102, 357

One-hundred percent reserve, ix, xv, 102, 145

Bayesian Rationality, 176

Boycotts, xii

Bretton Woods, 141-42

Bribery, xii, 104

Business cycle; *See* trade cycle

Calculus, 105

Capital; structure of production, ix, 46, 50, 52

Caste; *See* class analysis

Cato Institute, 393

Central bank, ix, 140, 145, 155, 160

Central planning; *See* Planning

Charity, 199, 202

Chicago school of economics, 97, 147

See also Monetarism

Civil Rights Act of 1964, 125, 132, 137

Class analysis, 312-14, 316, 318, 362, 375

Closed shop, 291-02

Coercion, xi, xiii, 14, 17, 18, 147, 196, 236, 241, 242, 245, 283, 287, 289, 293, 304, 310-11

Private power, 284, 285, 287

Coinage Acts; of 1792, 33

of 1834, 34

Cold War, 366

Collectivism, 200, 202-03, 212, 250

Collusion, 319, 320

Columbia University, ix, 97, 392, 398

Community, 203-06

Communist Party, 367, 389

Comparable worth, xvi, 125-38

Competition, 4, 6

Perfect, xiv, 4, 6, 8, 111, 118, 120

Rivalrous, xiv-xv, 4, 118, 143, 237

Congress of German Economists, 345, 346

Conscription; draft, 101, 273

Conservation, 71

Conservative Book Club, xviii

Conservatism; conservative movement, xvi, 69, 202-03, 206-07, 366, 374

Constitutionalism, in political theory, 32, 359, 362

Consumer sovereignty, xv, 7, 135, 143

Contractarianism, 177, 187
  See also Social contract; Buchanan, James M.

County of Washington v. Gunther, 125, 137, 138

Courts, private, xii, 275

Crime, 284

Criminal justice system, xii

Declaration of Independence, 239, 245

Deflation; See Money

Diminishing marginal utility, theory of, 146, 177, 182
  See also Menger, Carl; Walras, Leon

Discrimination, 130, 132, 133-35, 291-93

Draft; See Conscription

Economic calculation, 103, 107
  See also Socialism; Monopoly

Economic coordination, 81, 83-85, 87-88

Economic determinism, 363

Economic liberty; economic freedom, 120

Economics
  as qualitative, 154
  history of thought, xi
  Supply-Side, 141
  welfare, 77, 114
  See also Methodology; Praxeology

Education, xii, 277, 376
  public schools, 310

Efficiency, 6, 7, 110-24
  marginal, 118, 119
  measurement of, 116-17
  social, 7, 9
  X-efficiency theory, 110, 112, 113

Egalitarianism, 61, 175, 177-78, 180-81, 188, 239, 255, 262-63
  See also Equality

Elitism, 210-11, 314-15
  See also Oligarchy

Entrepreneurship, 104, 117, 118, 119, 311, 357-58

Equal pay, 125

Equal Pay Act of 1963, 125, 126, 132

Equality; of opportunity, 134, 135, 187-88
  of results, 134
  See also Egalitarianism

Equilibrium, 8, 47, 111, 120, 122
  Partial-equilibrium analysis, 50, 510

Essentialism, 289

Ethics; morality, xvi, 59, 60-72, 74, 102, 110, 120, 131, 175, 196, 197-212, 223, 229-34, 237, 238-45, 272
  virtue, 195

Ethical relativism, 370

Evenly rotating economy, 105, 109

Externalities, 73, 115

Fault principle, in law, 128

Federal Reserve Bank, ix, 35, 36, 37, 147, 154-55, 165-66, 168-71

Feminism, xvi, 125-38

Film criticism, xvii-xviii, 383-91, 393, 397, 399

Firm, theory of, 112, 123

Fraud, 28, 372

Free market, x, 8, 140, 284
  nature of 294-98
  See also Laissez-Faire

Free-rider problem, 13, 15, 58
  See also market failures

Freedom; See Liberty

Freedom of speech, xi, 373

Freedom of trade, xvi, 357

Full Employment Act of 1946, 97, 100

Game theory, 12-23

George Mason University, 100

German free trade movement, 341,42

German Free Trade Union, 343

Gold clause cases, 32, 35, 38, 41, 43

Gold confiscation, 35, 40, 41

Gold Reserve Act of 1934, 37-38

Gold standard; See Money

Göttingen, University of, 341-42

Government; See State

Great Society, The, 307

Gresham's Law, 33, 160-62

Guild system, 129

Hard money movement; See Money

Hermeneutics, 102
Historical entitlement, 247-64
  equal distribution, 255
  initial acquisition, 248, 252, 255-56, 258-59
  title transfer, 256
  voluntary transfer, 247, 249, 253
Historicism, 207-08, 346
History, philosophy of, xi, 91
Human Action, 56, 73, 107, 141, 159
Human nature, 61, 62, 229, 234, 240
Imputation 45, 46
  See also Value
Index numbers, 105
Indifference curves 103, 104-05
Individualism, methodological, xiii, xiv, 78-82, 140, 359-60
Industrial Revolution, 142
Inflation; *See* Money
Inflation Survival Letter, 164, 165
Interest, 44-55
  rates of, ix, 46, 47, 50, 51, 52, 140, 154
  time-preference theory of, ix, xv, 45, 44-55, 359
  waiting theory of; abstinence theory of, xv, 49-54
International Monetary Fund (IMF), 141
Intervention
  autistic, xi, 147
  binary, xi, 147
  economic, xi, xiv, xvi, 23, 56, 90, 121, 144, 401
Investment
  malinvestment, ix, 155, 168, 170
Isolationism, 337-39, 340
Is-Ought question, 67
Jazz, xviii, 393, 395-97, 398
Jews, 229-30
Justice, 128, 136, 204
  distributive, 247-48, 258
  redistribution, xvi, 13, 68, 71
Justification, 64, 65, 67
Keynesian school of economics, x, xi, xiii, 96, 97, 99, 100, 107, 141-42, 165, 357, 392
  See also Keynes, John Maynard
Knowledge; information, 111, 117, 118, 122

Kondratieff wave theory, 166, 167
  See also Kondratieff, Nikolai D.
Labor, 46, 130, 249-51, 256-57, 271, 338
Labor unions, 142, 144
  collective bargaining, 142
Laissez faire, xii, xiii, xvi, 56, 60, 144-45, 237, 294-98, 357-69, 341
Land, 46
  redistribution of, xii
Law, 124, 128, 205, 239
Law enforcement, 56, 58, 60, 73, 222, 237, 239, 289
  See also Police; Order
Legal tender cases, 32, 34-35, 42
Leisure, 57, 305-06
Liberalism, classical, 207, 211, 346
libertarianism, xiii, xvi, 61, 62, 68, 69, 72, 197, 199-203, 206-07, 209, 211, 236, 237, 276, 293, 329, 341, 346, 368
Libertarianism; *See* Liberalism, classical
Libertarian Forum, xvii, 383, 393
Libertarian Party, 393, 394
Liberty; freedom, xiii, xvi, 7, 73, 195, 208, 217, 224, 237, 249, 293 94, 398
  Science of, ix, xii, 44-45
  See also Economic liberty; Freedom of speech; Freedom of trade
Lifeboat situations, xii
Local Government Antitrust Act of 1984, 11
Lockean proviso, 250, 252, 256, 257, 259
Marginal analysis, 279
Market failures 4, 5, 16
  market imperfections, 4, 14, 16, 57, 58, 115
Market process, x, xiv, 5, 119, 120
Marxism, 92, 100, 101, 207, 362-64, 367, 375
  See also Marx, Karl; Socialism
Mathematics, use of in economics, xiii, 89, 93-94, 156
Methodology, 90, 124, 357, 361
Militia, citizens', 342
Military expenditures, 108, 342
Minimum wage, xi, 138, 143
Mises Institute, xviii, 399
Mobility, 136
Monetarism, 101, 102, 108, 155
  See also Chicago school of economics

Monetary institutions, 145
Monetary Control Act of 1980, 166
Money, xvii
   debasement of currency, 36
   deflation, 37, 164
   fiat currency, xv, 32-35, 42, 155, 169,
      171, 332
   gold standard, ix, xv, xvi, xvii, 32-43,
      141, 145, 160, 165, 393
   hard-money movement, xvii, 102, 151,
      159-60, 163-64, 169
   history of, xi,
   inflation, 38, 45, 105, 140-41, 154, 160,
      166, 169, 170, 332, 363
   neutral, 107, 155
   quantity theory of, 155
Monopoly, x, xiv-xv, 3-11, 56, 118, 119,
   124, 289, 401
   See also Economic calculation
Mont Pelerin Society, 401
Moral perfection, 197, 204-05, 209
Morality; *See* Ethics
National defense, 275
National Book Foundation (NBF), 353
National Labor Relations Act; Wagner
   Act, 138
National Review, xi, 395
National War Labor Board, 132
Natural law; *See* Rights
Natural resources, xvi, 71
Natural rights; *See* Rights
Neo-classical economics, x, xi, 42, 97, 118
New Deal, xi, 323, 330, 331, 395
Nobel Prize, 89-109
Non-aggression principle, 64, 66, 67, 68
   non-violence, 376
   See also Aggression
Objectivity, scientific; value freedom;
   Wertfreiheit, xiii, 59, 62
Opportunity cost, 113, 116, 117, 121
   See also Subjectivism
Oligarchy, 270, 272, 310-11, 315-17
Organic society, 134
Pareto optimality, 79-81, 82, 83, 175, 87
Parker Doctrine, 10
Parker v. Brown, 10
Paternalism, 13, 68, 135

Pauperism; poor; poverty, xii, 61, 307,
   323, 342, 343, 348, 351
   War on Poverty, 307
Persuasion, 197, 289
Physiocratic school of economics, 46
Planning, central, x, 102, 130, 136, 278
Pluralism, 314, 321
Police; Governmental, 76
   Private, xii, 275, 287, 290
   See also Law enforcement
Political action, xvii, 394
Pollution, xii, 114
Polytechnic Institute of Brooklyn;
   Polytechnic Institute of New York, 100,
   145
Poor; *See* Pauperism
Populism, 210
Poverty; *See* Pauperism
Power; *See* Coercion
Praxeology; human action, science of, x,
   xvii, 74, 90, 96, 117, 103
Preference, demonstrated, x, xiv
Price-fixing; predatory practices, 6, 9
Prices, ix, x, 50
   free market, 8, 57
   marginal cost pricing, 8
   Monopoly, x, 7-10, 56-57
Pricing, competitive, 8
Prisoner's dilemma, 12-23
   See also Game theory
Production; factors of, 45-46, 130, 261
   theory of, 112
Productivity, 52, 53
   marginal value of, 46
Progressive Party, 347
Progressive era, xi, 91, 322
Prussia, 341, 342
Public choice school of economics, 123,
   290, 359
   See also Buchanan, James M.
Public goods, xvi, 15, 17, 23, 56, 58, 59,
   60, 73, 123
Public policy, xvii, 3, 4, 110-21, 242, 245
Psychiatry, 374
Quotas; affirmative action, 132
Rational expectations school of
   economics, 96
Rationalism, 61, 62

Realism, 208, 215
Reason, 206-10
Rent control, xi
Relativism, 374
  See also skepticism
Research, 115, 116, 123
Revisionism, historical, xi, 42, 90, 145, 160, 361, 363, 366
Rights
  children's, xii
  coherence, 253-55, 259, 263, 264
  individual, 202-03, 214, 254, 271
  natural (or law), xvi, xvii, 61, 62, 74, 102, 134, 208, 211, 229-34, 236, 247, 245, 369-71, 373
  of privacy, 372
  property, xi, xvi, 16, 61-72, 75, 76, 215-16, 221, 239, 371-73
  welfare, 238
Risk, 122, 176, 178, 182-83, 357-58
Romantic movement, 214
Roads, private, xii, 275
Ruling elite; *See* Oligarchy
Savings, ix
Scarcity, 75, 297
Search and seizure, 372
Secession, 375
Self-perfection, 197, 204-06, 209, 210
Self-ownership, 64, 72, 239, 283
Skepticism, 205-06, 231, 234, 241
Slavery, 273
Social contract, 15, 17, 219, 239
Social Contract, The; *See* Rousseau, Jean-Jacques
Social cooperation, 189, 239, 241
Social cost, 114, 116, 123, 360
Social philosophy, 236
Social order, 198, 209, 212, 222
Socialism, 71, 347, 376
  economics of, xi
  See also Economic calculation; Marxism
Society, 79, 196, 270, 284
State
  government, xiii, xiv, xvi, 12-23, 32, 56, 58, 59, 60, 73, 90, 91, 197-200, 202, 205, 211, 217, 222-26, 236, 259, 277, 308, 314, 330, 356, 360
  limited, 239
  nature of, 298-308, 373
  failure of, 14, 278

Stoics, 371
Subjectivism, 79, 184, 286, 358
  subjective preference, 176
  subjective utility, xiv, xvi, 9, 21, 56, 102, 105, 111, 113, 117, 120, 122, 123, 129
Supreme Court, 32, 34, 39, 41, 375
  Hepburn v. Griswold (1870), 34
  Julliard v. Greenman (1884), 35
  Knox v. Lee (1871), 34
  Norman v. Baltimore & Ohio Railroad Co. (1935), 39, 41
  Nortz v. United States (1935), 39-40
  Perry v. United States (1935), 39, 40, 41
  Veazie Bank v. Fenno (1869), 34
Surplus value; *See* Value
Tariffs, 104
Taxation, xii, xiii, 13, 15, 56, 71, 73, 91, 104, 116, 124, 188, 238, 273, 290, 310, 343
  income tax, xi
  sales, 104
  tax on site value, 104
Teleological eudaimonistic framework, 195, 209
Tort liability, 16
Trade cycle, ix, xvii, 107, 141, 145, 146, 154, 160, 165, 167, 168, 357
  Great Depression, 35, 160, 166
Transaction costs, 12-23, 111
Uncertainty, 111, 117, 120, 122, 123
Unemployment, theory of, 143
Union of Soviet Socialist Republics, 276, 316, 400
Union for Radical Political Economics, 100
United States of America
  Articles of Confederation, 33
  Bill of Rights, 120
  See also American history
U.S. Constitution, xvi, 32-43, 239, 359, 362-63, 375
  Fifth Amendment, 39
  First Amendment, 120
  Tenth Amendment to, 33
U.S. Gold Commission, 41, 332
U.S. Mint, 32, 161
Universalizability, 63, 68, 69, 74, 207
University of Nevada, 145

University of Vienna, 101
Utilitarianism, 38, 60, 61, 102, 188, 242, 244, 341
Utility, x, xiii, xiv, 9, 103, 146, 175, 177, 179, 180, 183, 295-96, 297, 301, 318
    average, 176-77, 189
    cardinal, xiii, xiv, 9, 185, 299
    interpersonal comparisons, 105, 114, 120, 131, 178, 302-03
    law of marginal, 79, 300-01
Water-Diamond paradox, 129
    measurable, 184, 187, 299
    ordinal, xiii, 298
    public, 223
    social utility, xiv, 4, 9, 17, 18, 61, 103, 105, 109, 124, 198, 294, 295, 298, 299, 303-05, 308-10
    utility and welfare theory, 146
Utopia, 335-340
Value, in economics, 46-47, 52, 69-71, 111
    intrinsic; objective, 129
    labor theory of, 129, 130
    marginal utility theory of, 129, 130
    surplus value, 46-47, 48
    theory of, 257
von Neumann-Morgenstern utility function, 183-85, 189
    See also Marginal value; Subjectivism

Versailles, Treaty of, 365-66
Vietnam war, 395
Virtue, xvi
    Collectivist perspective on, 200, 202
    See also Ethics
Volker Fund, 100, 145, 352-53, 365
Voluntarism, 284, 291
Voucher system, 277
Wages, xvi, 125-138, 341
    discrimination, 126, 127, 133-34
Watergate, 329, 390
Wealth, 78, 312
    redistribution of wealth, 302-03
    transfer, 302, 309
Welfare; consumer, 7, 146
    social, 6, 181, 186, 245, 252, 257, 360
Welfare Economics, x, 77-88, 114, 122, 123, 124, 175
Will
    free, 374
    general, 214-226
Wiretapping, 372
Women, 125-38
World Bank, 141
World Market Perspective, 165
World War I, xi
World War II, 132, 229-30, 366

The Editors

Walter Block is director of the Fraser Institute's Center for the Study of Religion and Economics.

Llewellyn H. Rockwell, Jr., is founder and president of the Ludwig von Mises Institute.

The Contributors

Dominick T. Armentano is professor of economics at the University of Hartford, Hartford, Conneticut.

Roger A. Arnold is professor of economics and economics department head at the University of Nevada, Las Vegas.

Gregory B. Christainsen is associate professor of economics at California State University, Hayward.

Douglas J. Den Uyl is associate professor of philosophy at Bellarmine College, Louisville, Kentucky.

Justus Doenecke is professor of history at the University of South Florida, St. Petersburg.

Arthur A. Ekirch, Jr., is professor of history at the State University of New York, Albany.

Antony Flew is professor emeritus at the University of Reading, England, and distinguished research fellow at the Social Philosophy and Policy Center at Bowling Green University, Bowling Green, Ohio.

Roger W. Garrison is associate professor of economics at Auburn University, Auburn, Alabama.

David Gordon is senior fellow at the Ludwig von Mises Institute.

Randall G. Holcombe is professor of economics at Florida State University, Tallahassee.

Hans-Hermann Hoppe is associate professor of economics at the University of Nevada, Las Vegas.

Robert Kephart is a Florida businessman and founder of Audio-Forum, *Personal Finance* newsletter, and many other investment publications.

Israel M. Kirzner is professor of economics at New York University, New York City.

Tibor R. Machan is professor of philosophy at Auburn University, Auburn, Alabama.

Neil McCaffrey is founder and president of the Conservative Book Club and founder of Arlington House Publishers.

Margit von Mises is author of *My Years with Ludwig von Mises* and chairman of the board of the Ludwig von Mises Institute.

Gary North is president of the American Bureau of Economic Research, Fort Worth, Texas, and publishes the *Remnant Review* newsletter.

David Osterfeld is associate professor of political science at St. Joseph's College, Rensselaer, Indiana.

E. C. Pasour, Jr., is professor of economics at North Carolina State University, Raleigh.

Ellen Frankel Paul is professor of political science and deputy director of the Social Philosophy and Policy Center at Bowling Green State University, Bowling Green, Ohio.

Jeffrey Paul is professor of philosophy and associate director of the Social Philosophy and Policy Center at Bowling Green State University, Bowling Green, Ohio.

Ron Paul is a former U.S. Congressman and author of *The Case for Gold*. He publishes the *Ron Paul Investment Letter*, and is the 1988 presidential candidate of the Libertarian Party.

Ralph Raico is professor of history at the State University College of New York, Buffalo, New York.

Dyanne Petersen is a marketing consultant in California.

Sheldon L. Richman is director of public affairs for the Institute for Humane Studies at George Mason University, Fairfax, Virginia.

JoAnn Rothbard has been described by her husband as "the indispensable framework."

Mark Skousen is adjunct professor of economics at Rollins College in Winter Park, Florida and edits *Forecasts and Strategies* newsletter.

Leland B. Yeager is Ludwig von Mises professor of economics at Auburn University, Auburn, Alabama.